WAR
AND A WOMAN'S LIFE IN LETTERS
1835–1867.

EDITED BY
Ann Fox Chandonnet
AND
Roberta Gibson Pevear.

WILMINGTON, NORTH CAROLINA
Winoca Press

"Write Quick": War and a Woman's Life in Letters, 1835–1867
copyright © 2010 by Ann Fox Chandonnet and Roberta Gibson Pevear

PUBLISHED BY WINOCA PRESS • www.winoca.com
Available direct from the publisher, from your local bookstore, or from the authors at
167 Sherwood Forest, 804 Nottingham Dr., Exeter NH 03833

Printed in the United States of America

14 13 12 11 10   5 4 3 2 1

LIBRARY OF CONGRESS CATALOGING-IN-PUBLICATION DATA

Write quick : war and a woman's life in letters, 1835-1867 / edited by Ann Fox Chandonnet and Roberta Gibson Pevear.

p.   cm.

Includes bibliographical references and index.

ISBN 978-0-9789736-8-1 (cloth) — ISBN 978-0-9789736-9-8 (pbk.)

1. Foster, Eliza Howard Bean, 1835–1867 — Correspondence. 2. Foster, Henry Charles, 1834–1864 — Correspondence. 3. Bean, Andrew Jackson, 1828–1919 — Correspondence. 4. Massachusetts — History — Civil War, 1861–1865 — Personal narratives. 5. United States — History — Civil War, 1861–1865 — Personal narratives. 6. United States — History — Civil War, 1861-1865 — Women. 7. United States. Army. Massachusetts Infantry Regiment, 26th (1861–1865) 8. United States. Army. Maine Infantry Regiment, 5th (1861–1864) 9. Foster family — Correspondence. 10. Bean family — Correspondence. I. Chandonnet, Ann. II. Pevear, Roberta Gibson.

E601.W957 2010

973.7'8 — dc22

2010009046

Book cover and interior designed by Barbara Brannon

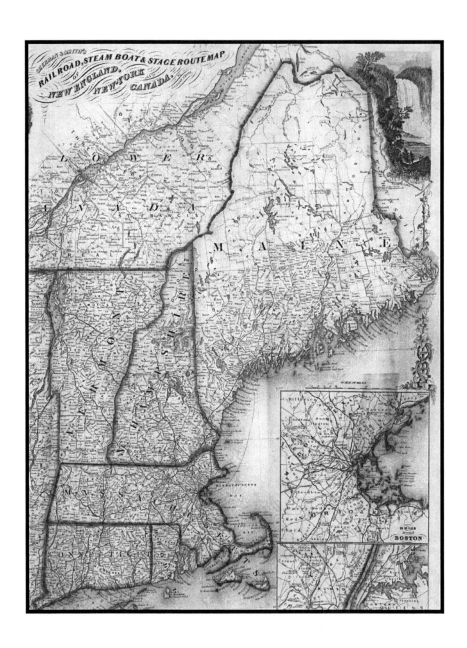

Antebellum New England. Detail from "Sherman & Smith's Railroad, Steam Boat and Stage Coach Map of New England, New York and Canada," J. Calvin Smith, New York, 1850. Courtesy Library of Congress, Geography and Map Division.

Contents.

Contents *continued*

CONTENTS *continued*

ILLUSTRATIONS AND MAPS.

ILLUSTRATIONS *continued*

Bean Family Tree.

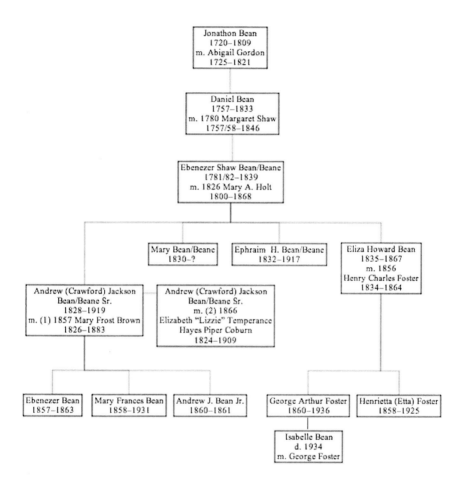

Notes

- Daniel Bean served with a Massachusetts company during the American Revolution, and his name appears on an 1835 pension list.
- Ebenezer married his first wife, Eunice Kendall, in 1804. Eunice died in 1825. Mary Holt was his second wife. By his first wife, Ebenezer sired 10 children, two of whom died shortly after birth. They are not listed here. By Mary, he sired four children.
- Lizzie and Andrew had no issue. In 1867, a year after their marriage, Andrew became guardian of his sister Eliza's two children, Henrietta and George. See Foster Family Tree.
- Mary Frances Bean died unmarried.

FOSTER FAMILY TREE.

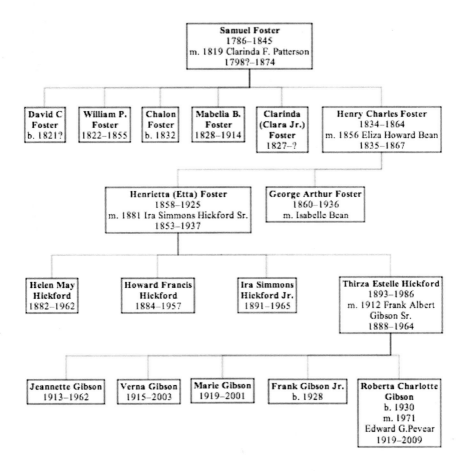

Samuel Foster
1786–1845
m. 1819 Clarinda F. Patterson
1798?–1874

- **David C Foster** b. 1821?
- **William P. Foster** 1822–1855
- **Chalon Foster** b. 1832
- **Mabelia B. Foster** 1828–1914
- **Clarinda (Clara Jr.) Foster** 1827–?
- **Henry Charles Foster** 1834–1864 m. 1856 Eliza Howard Bean 1835–1867

Henrietta (Etta) Foster
1858–1925
m. 1881 Ira Simmons Hickford Sr.
1853–1937

George Arthur Foster
1860–1936
m. Isabelle Bean

- **Helen May Hickford** 1882–1962
- **Howard Francis Hickford** 1884–1957
- **Ira Simmons Hickford Jr.** 1891–1965
- **Thirza Estelle Hickford** 1893–1986 m. 1912 Frank Albert Gibson Sr. 1888–1964

- **Jeannette Gibson** 1913–1962
- **Verna Gibson** 1915–2003
- **Marie Gibson** 1919–2001
- **Frank Gibson Jr.** b. 1928
- **Roberta Charlotte Gibson** b. 1930 m. 1971 Edward G. Pevear 1919–2009

NOTES

- Before 1850, the U.S. Census recorded only the name of the head of household. Samuel Foster's parents have not been identified. Samuel was buried in Plymouth Notch, Vt.
- Clarinda Patterson was the daughter of Chloe Heath Patterson and David Patterson of Castleton, Vt. Clarinda Patterson Foster's second husband was Moses Lynch (1791–1860), father-in-law to her daughter Clara (Jr.). Moses resided in Poultney, Vt.
- For Mabelia's offspring, see Fox Family Tree.
- Ira Simons Hickford, Jr., changed his name to Richard D. Wellington.
- Thirza Estelle Hickford Gibson is buried in Pine Grove Cemetery, Bethel, Maine.

FOX FAMILY TREE.

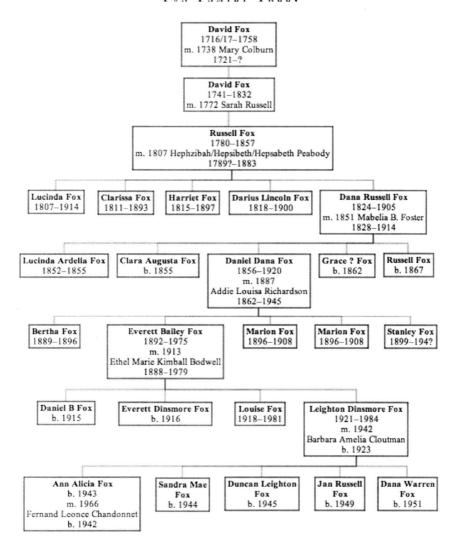

NOTES
- Both of Ethel Marie Kimball's parents were deceased before she was nine years old. She assumed the last name of her foster parents but was never officially adopted by the Bodwells.
- Leighton Dinsmore Fox divorced Barbara Amelia Cloutman in 1957 and married Bobbi Small in 1963. They had no offspring.
- Louise Fox married Robert Atkinson. They had no offspring.

The next generation. Six adults and an infant, Lynn or Lowell, Massachusetts, summer 1913. George Arthur Foster (back row, second from left, with white moustache) is the son of Henry and Eliza Foster; his sister, Henrietta, is seated at front, right.
Middle row: Isabelle Bean Foster, holding Jeannette E. Gibson, born May 19, 1913; Bertha A. Wright Foster; Charles Henry Foster (son of Isabelle and George Foster).
Front row: Ira S. Hickford, Sr., and his wife, Henrietta Foster Hickford. Courtesy Bethel Historical Society.

Dramatis Personae.

MOST OF THE CHARACTERS IN THIS DRAMA are Unknown Americans. Their names are absent from federal census records, city directories, and military rosters. Their obituaries never appeared in newspapers. Other sources are incomplete. For example, genealogist Valerie Dyer Giorgi cites Henrietta Foster but was unaware of Henrietta's younger brother, George.

Basic genealogy of the Beans is featured between the scarlet covers of *The Clan MacBean in North America.* Valerie Giorgi's *William Heath of Roxbury, Massachusetts* presents valuable information concerning Clarinda Patterson Foster Lynch, Henry Charles Foster, Mabelia Foster Fox, Henrietta Foster Hickford, and Thirza Hickford Gibson.

Additional sources included *Early Settlers of Plymouth Vermont* by Blanche Brown Bryant and Gertrude Elaine Baker. An Internet source, the National Park Service's Civil War Soldiers & Sailors System (CWSS), proved useful.

Bobbi Pevear and her husband, Eddie, worked on the genealogy of the Bean, Foster, Fox, Gibson, Hickford, Lynch, Minor, Pevear, and Wood families for twenty years, traveling to battle sites and cemeteries, writing queries to town offices and individuals, photographing buildings and grave markers, and collecting documents. Sadly, Eddie can not enjoy these pages. We mourn his loss.

Extended Family

 **Bean/Beane, Andrew Jackson "Crawford," Sr.** (1828–1919). Son of Ebenezer Shaw Beane and Mary A. Holt. Brother of Eliza Bean Foster and brother-in-law of Henry Foster. Born in Bethel, Maine; died in Lowell, Mass.

Although many documents concerning Andrew use the surname "Bean," the spelling "Beane" appears on his headstone. His first marriage was to Mary Frost Brown, his second to Elizabeth T. Hayes Piper Coburn. He served the Union in the 5th Maine Volunteer Infantry. Following his sister Eliza's death, he became the guardian of her children, George and Henrietta. With his first wife, Andrew Jackson Bean had three children: Ebenezer, Mary Frances, and Andrew Jr. With his second wife, Andrew Sr. resided on Tenth Street in Lowell and assumed guardianship of his niece and nephew. This residence housed the family correspondence and memorabilia now preserved at the Bethel Historical Society.

Bean/Beane, Andrew Jackson Jr., or "Jacky" (b. Aug. 7, 1860, in Albany, Maine; d. Sept. 3, 1861). Son of Andrew Jackson Bean Sr.

Bean/Beane, Ebenezer Shaw (1782–1839). Born in Standish, Maine. A farmer at West Bethel, Maine. His first marriage was to Eunice Kendall in 1804. His second marriage, in 1826, was to Mary A. Holt, by whom he became father of Andrew Jackson, Mary, Ephraim H., Tabitha, Jane, and Eliza H.

Bean/Beane, Elizabeth T. See Elizabeth Temperance Hayes Piper Coburn.

Bean, Ephraim H. (1832–1917). Brother of Eliza, brother-in-law of Henry. Married Mary Ann Johnson (1829–1897). Father of Isabelle, second of his seven children.

Bean, Mary (b. 1830). Sister of Eliza, Ephraim, and Andrew Jackson Bean. She married John Austin Pingree. The couple called their son Suel or "Stubby."

Bean, Mary Frost Brown (1826–1883). First wife of Andrew Jackson Bean. The marriage took place in Lynn, Mass., on Feb. 3, 1857. Judged mentally unstable, she was divorced by Andrew in September 1865, eleven months after his discharge from the Union army. Mary died in the asylum in Augusta, Maine.

Bean, Mary Frances (1858–1931). Daughter of Andrew Jackson Bean, and his only surviving child. Mary later joined Andrew and his second wife in Lowell. She became a teacher.

Bean, Mary A. Holt, or "Mother Bean" (1800–1868). Second wife of Ebenezer Shaw Bean/Beane). Mother of Andrew, Tabitha, Jane, Ephraim, Mary, and Eliza. She wove at home with a hand loom. Her spinning and weaving talents were sought after by neighbors. She moved to Lowell, Mass., some time before Eliza's death in 1867. Mary died less than a year later.

Coburn, Elizabeth Temperance Hayes Piper, or "Lizzie" (1824–1909). Born in Limerick, Maine. Lizzie's first husband was David Piper, who died in Maine in January 1854. Her second was Greenlief Coburn, whom she wed in Dracut, Mass., in October 1855 and who died in June 1865. The twice-widowed Lizzie then became the second wife of Andrew Jackson Bean. The couple married at a church "sociable" in June 1866 at Dracut.

Foster, Amanda Lydia Wood (1826–1897). Widow of William Foster, Henry Foster's brother. Amanda studied homeopathic medicine in New York City in 1858 and 1859. She wed her second husband, Levi Minor (or Minnor), on April 3, 1861.

Foster, Eliza Howard Bean (1835–1867). Youngest daughter of Ebenezer Shaw Bean and Mary A. Holt of Bethel, Maine, and sister of

Tabitha, Mary, Jane, Andrew, and Ephraim. As a teenager, Eliza worked as a mill girl in Maine, and subsequently became an operative with Boott Cotton Mills in Lowell, Mass. She married Henry Charles Foster on December 5, 1856. Mother of Henrietta and George. Widowed in 1864. Succumbed to consumption on Aug. 20, 1867. From the different scripts on her grave marker, it seems that she erected Henry's stone, and that Andrew had Eliza's inscription added later. Eliza is the great-grandmother of Roberta Gibson Pevear.

Foster, George Arthur (1860–1936): Born on High Street in Lowell, Mass., second child of Eliza and Henry Charles Foster. Brother to Henrietta Foster Hickford. George, a carpenter, married his cousin Isabelle Bean. His calling cards read "George A. Foster. Chaplain, Admiral Farragut Camp, No. 78, Lowell, Mass."

Foster, Henrietta, or "Etta" or "Sis" (1858–1925). First offspring of Eliza and Henry Charles Foster. On June 8, 1881, Henrietta married expressman Ira Simmons Hickford. Ira and Henrietta had four children, the youngest of whom was Thirza Estelle Hickford.

Foster, Henry Charles (1834–1864). Youngest son of Samuel Foster and Clarinda F. Patterson (later Lynch). Born in Vermont, later employed  in New York and Massachusetts. Husband of Eliza Howard Bean; father of Henrietta and George. After three years with the Massachusetts Infantry, Henry reenlisted. During this second term of service, he was wounded on Sept. 19, 1864, at the Third Battle of Winchester, Va. He succumbed to his wounds and the consequences of amputation on Sept. 21. He was buried at Winchester, but Eliza later had his body reinterred in Lowell. Also buried in Lot 33, Range 34, of Edson Cemetery are Mary A. Bean, Isabelle Foster, and George A. Foster.

Foster, Samuel (1786–1845). First husband of Clarinda Patterson; married June 10, 1819, in Castleton, Vt. The marriage produced six surviving children: David C. Foster, William Pattison/Patterson Foster, Chalon Foster, Mabelia Foster Fox, Clarinda Foster Lynch, and Henry Charles Foster.

Foster, William Pattison (1822–1855). Henry's older brother. In Plymouth, Vt., in 1847, William married Amanda Lydia Wood (a.k.a. Lydia Amanda Wood).

Fox, Amanda M. (1810–1884). Amanda Malvina Peabody was born in Dracut, Mass., daughter of Amasa Peabody and Lois Runnels. She was married in 1831 to Joseph Varnum Fox, who died at Natick, Mass., in 1843, his thirty-eighth year. Joseph was brother to Dana's father, Russell. The Fox and Peabody families both resided on Marsh Hill Road. Amanda's son George (b. 1841) joined the 6th Massachusetts Regiment, and fell victim to a gunshot wound in Virginia in 1863.

Amanda Fox's first appearance in Lowell records is on the Public Schools page of the 1838 city directory. There she is listed as one of two "female assistants" at the Third Grammar School. She appears as a Boott boarding house keeper in the hand-written 1849 census, and reappears in the same capacity in 1850, 1860, 1866, 1870, and 1880 documents. She is also listed in both the 1853 and 1855 Lowell city directories. A Peabody genealogy confirms her at this address in 1870. The 1884 directory shows her still ruling her Boott roost—a remarkable thirty-five years of service.

Fox, Dana Russell (1824–1905). Born in Plymouth, Vt. Both Dana Russell and his third cousin Gustavus Vasa were descendants of Nathaniel Fox (1683–1765). Dana Russell inherited a hilltop farm in Dracut, Mass. (this was the Amasa Peabody Farm known in the twentieth century as Marsh Hill Farm). Married in 1851 to Mabelia Foster, sister of Henry Foster; they spawned five or six children, of whom three survived: Daniel Dana, Russell, and Grace. Daniel  Dana married Addie L. Richardson (1862–1945). Mabelia wrote to Henry on Jan. 27, 1855, indicating that Dana Russell was working and boarding at Lowell's Boott Corporation.

Fox, Gustavus Vasa, or "Gus" (1821–1883). Gustavus Fox was  born in Saugus, Mass., son of Jesse Fox (a physician) and Olivia Flint Fox, both born in Dracut. He attended Phillips Academy. In 1835, he was appointed a midshipman. During the Mexican-American War, he served in the brig *Washington* in the squadron of Commodore Matthew Perry. His years in the navy gave him considerable firsthand knowledge of waterways that proved crucial in the Anaconda Plan. The 1850 census shows him living with his parents, but he married soon after. After resigning from the navy in 1856, he became an agent for Bay State Mill in Lawrence, Mass., where he specialized in the manufacture of woolen goods. Energetic, honest and efficient, he offered his services to the newly elected Abraham Lincoln. He was sent to aid Major Robert Anderson at Fort Sumter. The position of assistant secretary of the navy was then created by Lincoln for him, and he served in this capacity from August 1, 1861, to May 1866. Before leaving government service, he was dispatched on a special diplomatic mission to Tsar Alexander II. Subsequently he served as agent of the Middlesex Company in Lowell. The 1874 Lowell city directory shows him living at 355 Merrimack Street, a location that no longer exists. Gus is the third cousin, four times removed, of Ann Fox Chandonnet.

Fox, Mabelia B. Foster (1828–1914). Sister of Henry Charles Foster. Born in Vermont. Wed Dana Russell Fox in 1851, and resided in Dracut, Mass. Corresponded with Henry and exchanged visits with sister-in-law Eliza. Mabelia and Eliza proved incompatible; discord in their relationship is documented in Henry's letter of January 26, 1863.

Gibson, Frank Albert Sr. (1888–1964). Born in Yarmouth, Nova Scotia. Gibson earned his living as a woodworker and carpenter. Married Thirza Estelle Hickford. The couple had five children: Jeannette Estelle, Verna Frances, Marie Evelyn, Frank Albert Jr., and Roberta Charlotte.

Hickford, Henrietta Foster. See Henrietta Foster.

Hickford, Ira Simmons (1853–1937). Born in Boston, earned his living as a teamster. Married Henrietta Foster in Lynn, Mass., June 8, 1881. Father of Thirza Estelle (a.k.a. Thirsa Estella) Hickford.

Hickford, Thirsa Coffin. Daughter of Eunice E. Bean and Johnathan Clark Coffin, and wife of George Joseph Hickford.

Hickford, Thirza Estelle (1893–1986) or Thirza  Hickford Gibson. Named for Thirsa Coffin Hickford. Daughter of Ira S. Hickford and Henrietta Foster; granddaughter of Eliza. Married Frank Albert Gibson Sr. in 1912 and bore five children. Lived in Bethel, Maine, for fiftytwo years. She saved the documents on which this book is based. A direct lineal descendant of the founding families of Hampton and Exeter, she was a member of the Daughters of the American Revolution, the Bethel Historical Society, and the Hampton Falls Historical Society. Among Thirza's correspondents was her fifth cousin, Frances Perkins, President Franklin D. Roosevelt's colorful, controversial New Deal secretary of labor from 1933 to 1945. Thirza's youngest daughter is Roberta Charlotte Gibson (later Bobbi Gibson Pevear). "Bobbi," born in Bethel, graduated from Gould Academy at age sixteen, and served five terms in the New Hampshire House of Representatives (1979-88).

Lynch, Chancy/Chauncy/Chauncey (1827–1909). Son of Moses Lynch and his wife Annis. Lived in Lowell for ten years. Farmed 150 acres on Walker Road, three and a half miles out of Poultney, Vt., with his wife Clarinda/Clara Foster. The farm is marked on an 1868 Poultney map as "C. Lynch." Residences of neighbors mentioned in correspondence appear on this map marked with the owners' names: A. French, H. W. French, J. Lewis, A. Buckland, J. Lewis, N. C. Hyde, M. P. Hooker, H. Hesford, and George W. Gibson.

Lynch, Clarinda Patterson Foster (178?–1874). Sometimes  "Clarinda Sr." or "Mother Lynch." Her first marriage was to Samuel Foster in 1819. The couple had five children, the youngest of whom was Henry Charles Foster. Samuel Foster died in 1845. Clarinda's second husband was Moses Lynch, father of Chauncey.

Lynch, Clarinda Foster, or "Clara" or "Clarie" (1827–?). Daughter of Samuel Foster and Clarinda Patterson; sister of Henry; wife of Chauncey Lynch. She often signed her letters with the initials CFL. Lived with her husband on a farm in Poultney, Vt. Clara died before December 1875. Her daughter was "Carrie."

Lynch, Moses (1791–1860). Immigrant from Ireland. Farmer in North Poultney, Vt. With his first wife, Annis, he produced a daughter, Hannah, who did not attain adulthood. Annis died in 1818. With his second wife, née Annie Gerham, Moses produced two sons, Chancy and Sylvester. His third wife was Clarinda Patterson Foster.

Minor Characters

Bean, Lewellyn D. (1839–1892). Son of John Marean Bean (Eliza's older half-brother) and Mary C. Mason. A teacher, skilled carpenter, and cabinetmaker. Kept a diary off and on from late 1862 to 1876. For excerpts, see pp 451–56.

Brice/Brise/Bryce. A man mentioned in letters by J. A. Hobbs, S.A.H., and others.

The Bryce mentioned in letters (Oct. 5, 1863; May 13, 1864) by Clark Edwards is his brother, Bryce McLellan Edwards, who served under him. Bryce enlisted July 28, 1862, with Company I of the 5th Maine Volunteers. Clark Edwards had a second brother serving the Union, James McLellan Edwards, who enlisted in the 14th Maine Volunteers. Bryce's son (Clark's nephew), Sydney Danforth Edwards, enlisted on January 8, 1862, in Co. I of the 5th Maine.

The Brice referred to by Eliza's cousin J. A. Hobbs in a letter dated June 10, 1865, is most probably farmer Brice Edwards Kimball, born Dec. 19, 1842, in Albany. He was the son of Mary McLellan Edwards and Wilder Bowers Kimball, and thus a nephew of Clark Edwards. Brice could have seen Eliza clerking at the store located in the large building next door to the Albany Town House. Brice E. Kimball is listed in the 1860 census and the 1870 census of Oxford County. He married a woman he met during a hunting trip to Nova Scotia. Brice became the grandfather of Howard

G. Inman, a close friend of Bobbi Pevear. Howard was awarded the Purple Heart during World War II.

Hobbs, J. A. Eliza's cousin. Lived in Greenwood, near Bethel, Maine. Wrote to Eliza several times in 1866. Mother of a son about the same age as Eliza's George.

Holt, Sumner G./"Dr. Holt." Cousin of Henry Foster. Assistant surgeon with the 15th Maine, companies F and S. Died March 25, 1863, in Florida.

Kendall, William H. Eliza's cousin. Andrew's letter of Aug. 21, 1859, refers to him. Lived in Greenwood, Maine, in 1865.

McIver, John A. (b. 1836 in Scotland). Carpenter. Friend of Henry Charles Foster. Reenlisted as a veteran volunteer at New Iberia, La., on Jan. 1, 1864. A flirtatious bachelor who sweet-talked Eliza during Henry's furlough.

Pingree, John Austin. Husband of Mary Bean, Andrew Bean's sister. See Mary Bean.

Richardson, Charles Henry, or "Charley." Enlisted in Company A of the 26th Massachusetts Infantry as a corporal and mustered out as a second lieutenant. For extended periods in the field, Charley was Henry's tent mate. Henry wrote of Richardson in his letter of May 22, 1864, "I guess there is no other 2 men stuck together as we in the Co." This may be the same Charles Henry Richardson born to Alfred Rice Richardson and Rebecca W. Gleason in Boston on Jan. 29, 1830, and listed in the 1880 U.S. Census as a Massachusetts resident.

MY CURIOSITY TO SEE A BATTLE IS SATISFIED.
I am quite willing that my demise from earth shall come
ere my eyes behold or my nerves & moral sensibilities be
smitten by another sight so shocking.

REV. FRANCIS SPRINGER
POST CHAPLAIN, FORT SMITH, ARKANSAS.

WHERE WE LOVE IS HOME,
home that our feet may leave, but not our hearts.

OLIVER WENDELL HOLMES.

YOU DEAR OLD HONEY,
how I do want to see you. . . . I look out every night to
see if I can see you coming up the road. Oh, I have faith
to believe I shall put my arms around your neck and give
you a kiss or two pretty soon…you better believe!

HELEN STURTEVANT TO HER HUSBAND, JOSIAH,
WHO SERVED IN THE 17TH MAINE.
from *Josiah Volunteered* by Arnold H. Sturtevant

Three Miniatures.

Andrew Jackson Bean (1828–1919)

Life was catch-as-catch-can for Andrew Jackson Bean. He strove mightily to get ahead, but the nation in which he lived, the world of his namesake, Andrew Jackson, was a chaos of banking collapse, financial panic, and nagging depression. Bean's birth was sandwiched between the Panic of 1819 and the Panic of 1837. During his ninety-one years, he turned his hand to teaching, shoemaking, milling, and landscaping. In Maine, his employment ranged from building barns to performing marriages. After the Civil War, he moved to Massachusetts, where he ran a boarding house and worked as an expressman—a wagon driver who made deliveries.

Andrew was born on October 31, 1828, at West Bethel, Oxford County, Maine, to Ebenezer Shaw Bean and Mary A. Holt Bean. The Beans were some of Bethel's original settlers, while the Holts were among the original land grantees of Albany, the town adjoining Bethel on the south.

Andrew was the second child of Ebenezer's second wife. Birth records show his given middle name as "Crawford." Lapham's 1891 history of

Andrew Jackson Bean in his prime. Courtesy Bethel Historical Society.

Bethel, Maine, listed him as "Andrew Crawford Bean."[1] However, as an adult he assumed the middle name "Jackson"[2]—perhaps in honor of "Old Hickory," the general and seventh president, a champion of western expansion and economic growth. When Andrew Bean enlisted in the Union cause in 1861, this is the form of his name he dictated for the regimental roster. However, he favored it at least a year before, in 1860, when his second son was born, for that son was named Andrew Jackson Bean, Jr.[3]

Andrew's contemporary, William Berry Lapham (1828–1894), sketched the Bethel of his childhood: "I remember the days of lumbering stage-coaches, and mails only once a week, of the hard times for farmers for want of a near market, of the great scarcity of money, and of the enforced economy in household expenditures."[4] Lapham's memories resounded with the spine-tingling howls of wolves and delighted in the rugged beauty of "crystal brooks, the broad intervales, the hills and mountains and all the varied scenery."[5]

An average primary education fitted a youth for reading the Bible and running the farm. Andrew was educated beyond the basics, qualifying for a teacher's certificate. It is possible he attended the Academy at Monmouth during the yeasty reign (1837–1846) of principal Nathaniel True. Dr. True spread before his students an eclectic banquet of interests, from Native Americans to botany, mineralogy, geology, and chemistry—as well as a fervor for maintaining a militia.[6] Or perhaps Andrew attended Bethel's Gould Academy (founded 1836). After acquiring his teacher's certificate, Andrew held teaching positions in the hill country. A photograph shows a dashing, dandified, attractive man.

Andrew sometimes found it necessary to travel beyond Maine's borders to earn a living. At the time of his first marriage in 1857, for example, he resided in Lynn, Massachusetts, employed in the shoe industry.*

America's first tannery was established at Lynn in 1629; the town blossomed into an important regional shoemaking center as early as 1635. Handmade shoes from Lynn shod the Continental Army. After independence, Lynn grew famous for high-end ladies' shoes, with sixty-one firms stitching and hammering in 1832.

In Lynn, on February 3, 1857, Andrew, aged twenty-nine, wed Mary Frost Brown, thirty-one, a native of Albany.** In the nineteenth century, many men married late. However, the average bride's age was twenty-five; Mary would have been considered a bona fide old maid. Like her groom,

---

* How long Andrew lived in Lynn is unknown. The 1856 Lynn City Directory does not list Mary's father, Samuel Brown. It does list two women bearing the name Mary Brown. Andrew could have been residing with his mother, since the directory shows a Mary A. Bean, widow, at "house foot Vine." Andrew and his new bride were back in Albany before the birth of their first child, June 7, 1857.

** At the time of Andrew's birth, Albany was a larger, more prosperous town than Bethel, with its own library, bank and insurance company. However, when the railroad arrived in Bethel, bypassing Albany, the latter began a gradual decline.

Mary was educated. She qualified for a teaching position while Andrew went to war.

Mary may have worked the farm as well. As farmers from Northern and frontier towns marched off to battle, women and girls assumed more responsibilities outside the farm house. A contemporary song described the change from a wife's viewpoint: "Just take your gun and go, for Ruth can drive the oxen, John, and I can use the hoe."[7] As field hands enlisted, farmers began to adopt newly invented labor-saving equipment— horse-drawn planters, cultivators, mowers, rakes, and reapers. A motivated farmer wielding a scythe could cut about an acre a day; a farmer with a horse-drawn mower could cut ten acres.

During the century in which Andrew and Mary were married, as in preceding centuries, couples spent a great deal of their time working the land, scratching out a living, and raising herds of children. Due to death in pregnancy or childbirth, disease, poor medical care, and the losses of men in war or seafaring enterprises, the average marriage lasted only about fifteen years. Village cemeteries were lined with tombstones of husbands flanked by two or three wives and the small markers of infants. Couples needed survival skills and often relied on extended family in the immediate area for emotional support. Andrew and Mary's union produced three offspring: Ebenezer, Mary Frances, and Andrew Jackson Jr. Both boys died as children—while Andrew was absent serving in an infantry regiment (1861–1864).

Most returning soldiers chose to put the memories of close-in combat behind them.[8] Even if he managed to bar that mental door upon his discharge on July 27, 1864, Andrew would have been confronted by reminders of his lost sons in every corner. Perhaps he blamed their deaths on the nearest adult at hand. The ailment known in World War I as shell shock and in the twenty-first century as post-traumatic stress disorder was commonly called "soldier's heart" during the Civil War. If Andrew had suffered from such a condition, his psychological state would have added a sweaty fillip of paranoia to the family's ordinary domestic turmoil. As the saying went, "An unhappy husband will ask you for toasted snow."

The heavy toll of military service is described by Lieutenant Charles Leuschner of the 6th Texas: "I expectat [*sic*] to be happy [now that I am home], and I was for a little while; but it is not so now, my heart has a whegd [wedge] thrown upon it wich cannot so easily be taken off. It pains me. I may forget it a minute or two, but it will come in my mind again."[9]

Rimwracked

Whatever the combination of causes, Andrew was feeling rimwracked, as they say in Maine—worn out, toppling over. He grew to believe that his wife, Mary, was mentally unstable. On September 27, 1865, he divorced her in South Paris, Maine. Mary, declared to be suffering from mania, spent the remaining years of her life in the Maine Insane Hospital in Augusta. Perhaps she suffered from depression as she tried to adjust to having Andrew home again, watching and managing her every move. Perhaps she was unstrung by her sons' deaths or the stress of poverty. We shall never know; the surviving letters to Mary from Andrew show no sign of a rift. The 1880 Maine Census of Defectives lists her as "Mary F. Brown."[10] Did Andrew repossess his surname when he divorced her?

Mary was fortunate that the Insane Hospital, complete with a wing for each sex, existed. Before such institutions were created as the result of a twenty-year campaign by Dorothea Dix and other social activists, hardened criminals, debtors, paupers, and the catatonic were dumped willy-nilly into the same dank, cheerless receptacles: prisons and poorhouses. Dix emphasized the wisdom of separating the mentally ill from criminals and giving them decent living conditions.[11]

After shedding Mary, handsome Andrew bided his time for nine months. Then, in June 1866, he took a second wife—the twice-widowed Elizabeth Temperance Hayes Piper Coburn, of Dracut, a rural Massachusetts town sandwiched between the booming textile hub of Lowell and the forested New Hampshire border. "Lizzie," four years his senior, was born in

Limerick, Maine, on November 24, 1824, the daughter of Sylvanus Hayes (1794–1870) and his wife, Mary Ann Morris (1806–1888).* Limerick, a small town fifty miles due south of Bethel, manufactured blankets for Union troops during the war. Lizzie's grandfather, John, had settled the Limerick homestead in 1810. Sylvanus was a farmer and a mason; he was appointed assessor of Limerick in 1848.[12]

Perhaps Andrew and Lizzie had long been acquainted; surviving papers are mum. At any rate, widows were popular catches in Victorian America—especially if the deceased husband had bequeathed significant wealth. A widow typically received a life estate of a third of her husband's property, and his will might leave her cash or additional property. Should she remarry, her new husband would have the disposal of the income from all her property so long as she lived.[13]

With modern American divorce rates greater than 50 percent, it is jolting to discover just how uncommon divorce was in Andrew's day. In 1860, the divorce rate was just two per 10,000.[14] During the 1860s and 1870s, the divorce rate rose, as it continued to rise a century and a half later among troops serving in the Iraq War. Not surprisingly, a wartime separation of three or four years larded with violent agitations could undermine the bonds of matrimony. On the one hand, the returned serviceman, fed on anticipation and danger, might harbor a restless appetite for adventure. On the other hand, the wife might have modified her role during her husband's absence to become a breadwinner and an independent decision-maker. Mary's teaching during Andrew's infantry service perhaps gave her an independence that quickened her self-sufficiency. At any rate, upon returning home, as one scholar points out, "many husbands chafed at their own inadequacies, and took out their frustrations in liquor, physical abuse, or just plain persistent ill-temper."[15] Marital friction was the result.

---

*Additional information about Elizabeth can be found in Katharine Richmond's *John Hayes of Dover, N.H. A Book of His Family.*

Moose and Hops

Andrew's residences reflect the strong connections between Maine and Massachusetts. Chief among the vital links is that the two political entities had long been one and the same. In 1620, the year the Pilgrims were erecting wattle-and-daub cottages at Plymouth, King James issued the Great Patent of New England covering the land from Philadelphia to the Gulf of Saint Lawrence. This wild territory was governed by a council at Plymouth, England. That same year, a permanent settlement was established on Monhegan Island.

Two years later, land between the Merrimac River of Massachusetts and the Sagadahoc (Kennebec) of Maine was granted to Sir Ferdinando Gorges and Captain John Mason by the Great Council of New England. Maine was named for a region in northwest France. In 1623, the first successful settlement on its rugged mainland was founded at Saco by Richard Vines and other stalwarts. Word spread about the possibilities of colonization, and soon British and French disputed with Native Americans over the vast territory. Plymouth Colony won the day and was granted territorial and trading rights to "all that tracte of lande… [adjoining] the River of Kenebeke."[16]

In 1639, William Gorges was granted a charter by Charles I of England for the region incorporated as "The Province and County of Maine." When Gorges went to his final reward eight years later, Maine's status fell into disarray as a result of "contradictory grants, Indian raids, pirates on [the] coast, and lack of organized government."[17] Massachusetts took advantage of the confusion to claim all of Maine south of latitude 43 degrees 43' 12".

In the 1690 campaign aimed at the French Fortress of Louisbourg in Nova Scotia, soldiers from Sudbury, Massachusetts, marched and fought side by side with British regulars. Subsequently, a settlement named Sudbury Canada was created to reward the Sudbury veterans with homesteads. Movement north gained momentum, and by 1774 settlers of European descent began to displace the Western Abenaki. Colonists sweated and grumbled as they grubbed out stumps for gardens and raised log cabins and outbuildings like meat houses, stables, and corn cribs. It was a time when a ravenous bear fresh from hibernation was likely to carry off plump piglets as easily as if they were kittens. Jeremy Belknap, a New England minister of the late 1700s, estimated that it would take a family "armed with will, courage and patience, along with a good horse and an ox or two" a decade to build a home, clear, fence, and plant crops, and reap the land's bounty.[18]

In 1796, when the town incorporated, "Sudbury Canada" no longer filled the bill. Local clergyman Rev. Eliphaz Chapman suggested a name from the book of Genesis: Bethel[19]—meaning a holy place, a "House of God."[20]

When Maine was admitted to the Union in 1820, statehood was granted as part of the first effort to create a balance between free and slave states. The new state became involved with the Republican Party's birthing in the 1850s, and it elected the nation's first Republican governor. "As Maine goes, so goes the nation" became an aphorism applied to presidential elections.

Between the end of the American Revolution and 1820, Maine grew by nearly two hundred new towns. Many new residents were Revolutionary veterans eager to escape the impoverished farmlands of western Massachusetts and make hay among untouched resources.[21] Fueled by grit, alert to each breaking twig, settlers threaded paths worn by Native Americans or narrow trails marked by blazed trees. Most homesteaders relied on shank's mare, accompanying an oxcart carrying their few possessions.

Farming in Maine required the frontier hardiness of a Daniel Boone. Muscle, grit and encyclopedic skill were needed to fell timber, clear pasture, bag a woodland caribou, build fences, drive oxen, birth and raise livestock as well as repair looms and hammer together rudimentary furnishings.[22] Andrew's chores could have included greasing harness, plowing, hoeing, sheering sheep, splitting wood, and milking cows.

During his impressionable youth, Andrew likely absorbed by the fire-

side exciting tales of the American Revolution told by his maternal grandfather, Jacob Holt, and his paternal grandfather, Daniel Bean (1757–1833).
Both Jacob and Daniel fought at the Battle of Bunker Hill. Daniel Bean Jr.,
Andrew's uncle, a veteran of the War of 1812, might have chimed in with
dramas of his own. The scarred bodies of his forebears breathed vigorous
Revolutionary tradition—the idea that freedom must be earned with sacrifice. After the arduous struggle with Great Britain, it was inconceivable
that the Union would surrender a single star of its thirty-three-star banner.

Daniel Sr. hailed from Chester, New Hampshire. In May 1775, the
sturdy eighteen-year-old patriot enlisted under Capt. Stuart in Col.
Edmund Phinney's 31st Massachusetts Infantry Regiment. After Bunker
Hill, Daniel served in and around Boston and Cambridge, routing cocky
redcoats.[23] Daniel and his wife Margaret had thirteen children, the eldest
of whom was Ebenezer Shaw Bean, Andrew's father. The family walked
north to Sudbury Canada in the fall of 1781, carrying Ebenezer, a tender
babe in arms.

In Bethel, Daniel constructed a large, square house—a demonstration
of his intention to stay put. Windows were flanked with Indian shutters,
and cellars concealed tunnels for hiding women and children. Daniel's im-
posing residence, with its massive central chimney, stood head and shoulders above neighbors' squat log cabins.

The native old-growth timber that went into those cabins—black and
white spruce, red and jack pine, aromatic balsam fir—proved the keystone
of Maine's early prosperity. In the 1850s, eastern white pine was hand-
cut and hauled south by oxcart, to take its place in structures in Boston
and New York.[24] The demand for long timbers was such that Maine's
first railroads were chartered as early as 1832–33. The Portland, Saco &
Portsmouth Railroad ran track from Portland to South Berwick in 1842,
and extended service to Maine's border the following year. The PS&P was
bought out by Boston & Maine in 1887. The Boston & Maine greased
the cogs of transportation for New England's principal mill towns, which
gobbled resources like olive oil (applied to tame raw wool before it was

spun), sperm whale oil (for lamps), coal, and timber.[25]

The surname Bean or Beane seems to have originally been "Bane," with roots in Scotland and the north of England.[26] The bough from which Andrew Jackson Bean descended stemmed from an earlier Daniel (b. 1663) of Exeter, New Hampshire. The northern New England Beans were a fecund tribe: historian Eva M. Bean (1895–1969) counts 202 individual Beans in *East Bethel Road*.

Western Maine was the traditional homeland of the Abenaki, an Algonquian people including Amascoggins and Pequawkets. Fifty years before Bethel's first permanent white settlers appeared, the Abenaki occupied a village on the banks of the Androscoggin River, where they cultivated ten acres of corn.[27]

Newcomers gradually and ungently shouldered the indigenes aside. The original township of 1768 was granted 24,278 acres. The population as of 1790 was a close-knit 362. Growth was agonizingly slow at first. In 1810, there were still only 388 residents. In the next 50 years, however, the population soared; the 1860 federal census found Bethel a town of 2,523.

Turn In, Turn Over, Turn Out

The Maine landscape bred not only trees but also oceans of mud in spring and clouds of ravenous black flies in June, followed by mosquitoes in August. The rhythms of western Maine life leap from the pages of the diary kept by Edgar Harvey Powers (1843–1894). The twenty-year-old bachelor commenced his 1864 entries with the wish "that I may do nothing during the New Year that will cause me a blush of shame to write in here." During January, Powers cuts timber in the forest and hauls it out on a sled pulled by steers. He preaches sermons and yearns to learn algebra— but no qualified instructor lives in the area. He attends a singing school.* A Mr. Morse comes to the house and cobbles him a pair of shoes in a

---

* A singing school is an informal session in vocal music often associated with a church favoring the a cappella tradition—or with rural congregations using the seven shape note system.

Late summer haying. Bean's Corner, Bethel, Maine, 1885. Photograph by Irving Kimball. Courtesy Bethel Historical Society.

single twenty-four hours. Powers courts the nubile Eugenia, who bestows encouragement in the form of a lock of her hair. He experiences at close range outbreaks of diphtheria, smallpox, and typhus, attends wakes and burials, and records snowfall, rabbit hunting, and a fox hunt.[28]

Bethel's settlers whittled away at the black walls of the forest. Sweat equity cleared and then broke ground for kitchen gardens, hay, grain and pasture. In 1825, the township had 564 acres in tillage; 1,208 in upland mowing; 1,053 in pasture; 2,136 acres of corn and 905 of wheat. Enumerators tallied 165 barns, 122 horses, 216 oxen, and 435 cows.[29] Locals termed a short night after a long day's farming "turn in, turn over, and turn out." Hay was a major export.

Meals were basic—dishes like fricassee of wild pigeon or pot pie of squirrel. If squirrels proved scarce, supper might be Cape Cod turkey— concocted from a salted whole cod hung in the woodshed for emergencies. "Good old yaller-eyes" (dried beans, soaked then baked in a glazed pot) were a staple—and a favorite of Andrew. Tender, savory "Bean-hole beans" were baked in the ground, clambake style, for twenty-four hours. A particularly savory dish was "salt pork and sundown": fried slices of salt pork with fried eggs—the hen fruit cooked in the fat without turning them over. Corn bread or breads made with mixtures of grains were staples. Rye and Injun (a dense, filling loaf combining rye meal and cornmeal) was common for both breakfast and supper, often served awash in creamy milk warm from the cow.

From dawn to dusk, and sometimes until after midnight, women were engaged in cooking and cleaning and child-raising. The complete house-wife knew how to dry beans and herbs, pluck geese, butcher beef, "put down" pork in brine, and simmer venison mincemeat, according to the reminiscences of Martha Fifield Wilkins in *Sunday River Sketches*. Apple slices threaded on string hung near the ceiling above the hearth; when dry, the slices were moved into an unheated storage area along with win-ter squash, carrots, potatoes, turnips, and pies baked a dozen at a time. Women scrubbed floors and tables with sand, painted or whitewashed their own walls, and braided their own rugs, dyeing the wool with bark and roots. Preparing lye and tallow for soap was an annual chore.

Health was a tenuous state of affairs. Epidemics of influenza, small-pox, measles, mumps, "throat distemper," and scarlet fever devastated families in the days before aspirin, vaccines, and antibiotics.* Minor ail-ments were treated by "yarbs"—wild herbs and ingredients such as mint, willow bark, slippery elm bark, and worts. Native Americans shared their skills in splinting broken bones with birch bark and closing wounds with the "baseball stitch."

Aching muscles and chapped hands earned dividends; soon Bethel's

---

* Throat distemper was also known as throat-ail and "putrid sore throat." It was particularly fatal to children. In Hampton Falls, N.H., in 1735, 20 families buried all their children following an epidemic of throat distemper. More than a sixth of all inhabitants perished. Another epidemic of this disease—possibly strep throat—blasted New England in the 1760s.

The Bartlett-Bean Ferry (shown here circa 1900) carried passengers across the Androscoggin River from 1830 to 1910. Henrietta Foster and her husband, Ira Hickford, ran the West Bethel Ferry, on the same river, from 1914 to 1936. Courtesy Bethel Historical Society.

settlers were able to afford luxuries. The first sofa was turned out by a cabinetmaker in 1821.[30] The first barrel of flour was trundled into town in 1824. Residents felt their settlement had finally come into its own when the first train of cars chugged over the newly laid rails of the Atlantic and St. Lawrence in March 1851.[31]

During this century, connections between Maine and Massachusetts continued to thrive. Proof comes in the form of a regular feature in the Lowell (Mass.) *Daily Courier*. As late as November 1895 the column "News from Maine Homes" remained a staple. It printed briefs about such topics of interest as the appointment of postmasters, the building of hotels, the output of starch factories and spool mills, and the populations of deer and bear.

In 1860, Bethel's 2,500 citizens averaged twenty-six years of age, with more than 80 percent deriving a living from agriculture.* The town boasted a lending library, one dentist, five doctors, twenty-eight teachers, and eight clergymen. Thirteen men worked for the Grand Trunk Railway (formerly the Atlantic and St. Lawrence). In the 1860 election, a son of Oxford County, Hannibal Hamlin, ran on the Republican ticket with a lanky country lawyer named Abe Lincoln. Both candidates stood for no further extension of slavery.[32]

D is a Drummer Boy

In 1860, the North was a region in transition. That year, for the first time, the value of manufactured goods surpassed the value of farm products. Three-fourths of Northerners lived on farms or in small towns, but the population was shifting to cities. [33] Exports from the Union were $331 million as opposed to the South's $31 million—most of which was in cotton.[34] The North had six times as many manufacturing plants as the South and nearly twelve times as many factory workers.[35] Of the joint population of 20 million, only about one percent were African-American [36].

Most Northern villages encouraged schooling, with males attending until age fourteen. Literacy rates remained significantly lower in the South until the late nineteenth century. Philip Sheridan was convinced that schooling spelled victory in the Civil War: "The little white schoolhouse made us superior to the South," the general remarked. "Education is invincible."[37]

The invention of the cotton gin served to keep the South agricultural. Just when slavery appeared to be on the way out, cotton prices dropped and world demand rose. The slave population quadrupled from fewer than a million in 1793 to four million just before the Civil War, and cotton was planted in Alabama, Texas, southern Kansas, and California.[38] The 1860 population of the South was eight million whites and four million African-

---

* In 2007, Bethel had a population of nearly 2,500, and wood products continued to be a major factor in the community's economic life.

Americans. Only a quarter million of the latter were free.

The four short months between Lincoln's election as the sixteenth president on November 6, 1860, and his inauguration on March 4, 1861, were tumultuous. In late 1860, four slaveholding states threatened secession from the Union. On December 20, South Carolina became the first state to secede. On January 9, 1861, the first shots were fired at the Union vessel *Star of the West* as it attempted to reinforce Fort Sumter at the mouth of Charleston Harbor. Jefferson Davis was inaugurated president of the Confederate States five weeks later, on February 18, in Montgomery, Alabama. Although still feeling his way in office, Lincoln refused to compromise. Letters influenced Lincoln's decision to accept Fox's plan for a naval expedition to the fort. The president called on Mrs. Abner Doubleday, whose husband was stationed at Sumter, and asked to see his letters. In one communication, Doubleday indicated that small vessels might get in with troops and supplies, if they attempted the run at night.[39] But negotiations failed when Fort Sumter was bombarded April 12 and 13.

The drumbeat signaling war between the states likely reached Andrew Bean's ears when Portland's newspapers reported the siege of Sumter, and Maine's Gov. Israel Washburn Jr.* proclaimed April 11 a "Fast Day, for Humiliation, Public Fasting and Prayer."[40] That same day, on the boards of the Portland Theatre, a gifted actor named John Wilkes Booth portrayed William Tell and Macbeth.[41]

Few people urged compromise. Attorney John A. Rawlins, a friend of Ulysses S. Grant, escorted Grant to a meeting at the Galena, Illinois, courthouse on April 16—two days after Fort Sumter fell. Grant did not speak. Rawlins proclaimed, "There can be but two parties now, one of patriots and one of traitors. . . . Only one course is left for us. We will stand by the flag of our country, and appeal to the God of battles."[42]

During the first year of the Civil War, men enlisted out of a spirit of

---

* Governor Washburn had strong antislavery tendencies. He convened the Maine Legislature on April 22 and advocated measures for the suppression of the Rebellion. During two terms as governor, Washburn was always prompt in getting troops for the Union.

Union infantryman, 1861.
Dover Civil War Illustrations.

adventure as well as patriotism. Following the Union defeat at Bull Run in July 1861, a call for volunteers yielded 91,000 men in just eighteen days. By November the Union Army had the 500,000 men it had requested—and 120,000 more. [43] For ragged immigrants in crowded city tenements, enlisting for thirteen dollars a month seemed to promise escape.

Initial predictions saw the war over in ninety days. But fighting continued without resolution, and additional troops were required. In July 1862, with the collapse of Gen. George McClellan's Peninsular Campaign, President Lincoln requested 300,000 three-year volunteers. The mood of civilians began to shift. As more and more coffins were unloaded at Northern railroad stations, early enthusiasm for enlistment waned. Soon it was necessary to establish quotas for states, cities, and townships. Enlistment was encouraged by revivalist-style rallies, newspaper editorials, and rousing verse and song. Educational publishers got into the act, issuing patriotic primers printed on cloth. *The Union ABC* marched to the tune: "A is America, Land of the Free, B is a Battle, our soldiers did see, C is a Captain, who led on his men, D is a Drummer Boy, called little Ben."[44]

Eradicating slavery was not uppermost in the minds of New Englanders; enlistees were more concerned with preserving the Union. It was less than a century since freedom from British tyranny had been won; Yankees were determined that the newly minted United States should not be ripped apart by secession. Lincoln, comfortable with ambiguity, gradually transformed the conflict from a political dispute to a moral crusade.

Bethel responded enthusiastically to the call for volunteers. Of its 2,500 population, 265 men were enlisted or commissioned. Seven more were drafted. Ten were killed or mortally wounded. Six died as prisoners of war. Another twenty-three succumbed to disease. Eight deserted. Only 128—fewer than half—were present at mustering out.[45]

The floundering economy kicked the stalled engine of war into gear. The rise of the antislavery movement encouraged the conflict, but economics, more than any other factor, moved the country to war. Men like Andrew, only too familiar with "the great scarcity of money," viewed enlistment as a respite from economic depression. Bounties dangling enticingly before their noses, men coveted a way to fund better futures—to put a down payment on land or a home. Each recruit was entitled to a federal bounty of $100 cash, and some states, counties, towns, and even businesses offered additional sums. In July 1862, the municipality of Deer Isle, Maine, offered a $100 bounty.[46] New York City recruiting posters advertised a cash county bounty of $300, a state bounty of $75, and a U.S. bounty of $302, plus $15 in "hand money" to "any party who brings a recruit."[47] The hamlet of Ashby, Massachusetts, voted to provide each volunteer with a revolver, a bowie knife, a Bible, and $10.[48] By the end of 1862, bounties skyrocketed; the Washington Cavalry of Philadelphia and Bucks County offered $162 to men who signed up to follow Capt. J. W. Hall.[49] In Chicago in December 1863, Mulligan's Irish Brigade offered a bounty of $302 to new recruits and a tempting $402 to men who had already served at least nine months.[50] In Cortland, New York, during the summer of 1864, bounties soared to an astounding total of $900 per recruit.[51]

Saddled with infantry's role of taking and holding ground, infantrymen suffered the overwhelming majority of the deaths and injuries in the war. Andrew prepared for this role by getting acquainted with a thirteen-pound rifle and heavy knapsack. Infantrymen learned to polish brass buttons and buckles. Clumsily wielding needles, they embellished their uniform caps with the number or letter of company and regiment, as well as an emblem. Andrew's cap bore the infantry emblem, a bugle or French hunting horn.[52]

Perhaps Andrew's most valuable military training was the nine steps for loading a rifle. Drill instructors reviewed those steps every day. If a soldier could not execute them properly and speedily, he would probably fall in battle. The steps began with holding the rifle vertically, butt on the ground, ready to load. Then came "handle cartridge," followed by "tear cartridge." (A soldier required at least two teeth—one on the top and one on the bottom—to tear open the paper cartridge.) Next in succession the solider had to "draw rammer," "ram cartridge," "return rammer" (to its clips along the gun barrel) before placing a percussion cap in the cone, at which point he could complete the order to "shoulder arms." A practiced regular could complete this drill in twenty seconds.[*]

The Putrid Venom of Secession

When the rockets' red glare lit up Fort Sumter in April 1861, Oxford County, Maine, contained one solitary military organization—the Norway Light Infantry. Educator N. T. True formed a contingent of Zouaves—known for their distinctive, colorful uniforms.[53] When Lincoln called for 75,000 volunteers to protect the nation's capital, Maine's share was a regiment of a thousand, with one company of a hundred from Oxford County. Eight Bethel men rushed to join its ranks, to battle what the *Oxford Democrat* labeled "the putrid venom of secession."

On Saturday, May 4, 1861, three weeks after the fall of Fort Sumter, Andrew Bean enlisted. He was mustered in for three years at Portland on June 24, 1861, as a private in Capt. Clark S. Edwards's Company I, 5th Regiment Maine Volunteer Infantry. Edwards (1824–1907) hailed from Bethel, as did two other 5th Maine officers, John B. Walker and Cyrus Wormell.[54] When news of the bombardment of Sumter reached Bethel, Edwards was in the midst of shingling his roof. This father of five immediately descended his ladder, secured the authority to form a company, and began gathering recruits. Unlike Andrew, the capable Edwards rose

[*] An excellent video explanation of this process may be found on the Web at www.nps.gov/rich/photosmultimedia/upload/ready%20aim%20fire%20flash.swf

through the ranks.[55] He was mustered out with the rank of brigadier general by brevet.[56] When Edwards spoke at the dedication of the 5th Maine monument in Gettysburg on October 3, 1889, he made no bones about the unit's actions at Gettysburg and elsewhere, declaring that the state of Maine "sent no better" regiment to the field, claiming for it the capture of six flags and more than two thousand prisoners.[57]

On May 6, attorney Mark H. Dunnell joined with the rank of colonel and took command of the 5th. During the course of the war, New England was to supply 14 percent of total Union forces: Maine, 71,745 men; Massachusetts, 141,785.[58]

Both William Lapham and Andrew Bean were thirty-three and Clark Edwards was thirty-seven—all considerably above the norm. The National Park Service puts the average age of Civil War soldiers at twenty-one.[59] Another source says they ranged from eighteen to thirty-nine, with an average just under twenty-six years.[60] Boys of fourteen and fifteen, not about to miss the fun, lied about their ages; even younger lads became drummers.

Other males in Andrew's extended family were quick to enlist. His cousins, Peter S. Bean and Sumner G. and George H. Holt; his sister Eliza's husband, Henry C. Foster; and his wife's brothers, Charles J. and John M. Hayes all served in the Union Army. Sumner Holt enlisted with the 15th Maine as an assistant surgeon; during his service, he succumbed to typhoid. Charles Hayes enlisted in the 16th Maine, was taken prisoner at Gettysburg, and confined in Libby Prison in Richmond, Virginia, for thirteen months. Peter T. Bean of the 16th Maine was also locked in the notorious Libby. While imprisoned, he was "glad to get a lean dog to eat," he recalled, and his clothing was worn away below the waist.[61] John Hayes served in the 27th Maine. Farnum Llewellyn Bean was one of twenty-eight Bethel men who lost their lives during the War between the States. He served in Company B of the 23rd Maine Volunteers. On Memorial Day in 1908, Bethel erected on Main Street a blue granite monument to its Civil War soldiers.[62]

The Union now and forever

The 5th Maine left for Washington, D.C., on June 26, and was feted all along the way. Near Boston, crowds turned out to cheer, wave handkerchiefs, toss bouquets, and deliver gingerbread. On June 27, the *Boston Herald* noted that the soldiers of the Fifth were "better drilled than disciplined." The article went on to note: "They perform any exercise in the manual of arms well, and march very competently; but on parade rest it was evident that they had not been told out to conduct themselves properly or didn't care to."

That same day, the regiment passed through New York City—a bigger city than most of them had ever seen before—where on the steps of City Hall they were presented by former residents of the Pine Tree State with their regimental flag, a confection of blue silk with orange fringe.[63] The *New York Times* noted its embroidered slogan: "The Union now and forever, one and inseparable."

Entering Washington on June 28, the men were brigaded with the 3rd and 4th Maine and 2nd Vermont under the command of Col. Oliver O. Howard as part of the Third Brigade, Third Division of the Army of Northeastern Virginia.* After less than two weeks' additional training, on July 11 they moved into Virginia.

Ten days later, on a sweltering July 21, the regiment was ordered on the "double quick" to Manassas. This was a disastrous march for the men of the 5th, many of whom collapsed from exhaustion, sunstroke, and dehydration. Those who made it to Manassas saw their first action: the First Battle of Bull Run. Colonel Dunnell noted in his report to Colonel Howard that the "best, stoutest, and bravest men failed, and fell by the roadside." Under Brig. Gen. Irvin McDowell, 28,450 Union troops engaged 32,230

---

* Oliver O. Howard served at Manassas; at Chancellorsville (where he lost about 20 percent of his corps); at Gettysburg; at Chattanooga; and in the Atlanta campaign. When Gen. J. B. McPherson was killed at Atlanta, Howard succeeded him in command of the Army of the Tennessee.

Confederate troops commanded by brigadier generals Joseph E. Johnston and P. G. T. Beauregard.

You are all green alike

Brigadier General McDowell hesitated to take untried men into battle, but impatient Union politicians and Washington's anxious citizens were desirous of a quick victory over the Confederates massed in northern Virginia. When McDowell protested his lack of readiness to Lincoln, the beleaguered president replied, "You are green, it is true, but they are green also; you are all green alike."

During the First Battle of Bull Run, the Union suffered 460 killed, 1,124 wounded, and 1,312 missing or captured. Confederate forces had 387 killed, 1,582 wounded, and 13 missing. Gen. Howard's Brigade, of which the 5th Maine was part, had 70 men put out of commission. Andrew's certificate of record (discharge paper) bears witness, certifying that his regiment "bore a gallant part in the battle of Bull run . . . losing 70 men in killed, wounded and missing."

Some of the Boys cryed

The First Battle of Bull Run took place on July 21, a sweltering Sunday. Exhausted troops were directed by inexperienced regimental commanders. It was a fiasco. Union casualties were 482 killed, 1,126 wounded, and 1,836 missing—a total of 3,444.* The Confederates counted 1,900 killed, wounded and missing. Andrew's superior, Capt. Clark Edwards, confessed in a letter to his wife, "I will own that after the Battle was over I sat down and shed a tear. Some of the Boys cryed as well as myself."[64]

Abner Small, a noncommissioned officer with the 3rd Maine, record-

---

* *The Civil War Almanac* (p. 60) gives slightly different figures: 460 Union men killed, 1,124 injured, and 1,312 missing; the rebels, 387 dead, 1,582 wounded and 13 missing. Sources are often in disagreement over Civil War casualties; reports and records were often incomplete. Henceforth in this work, the *Civil War Almanac* figures will be used unless otherwise noted.

ed his own impressions of Bull Run—his regiment's first engagement. Kept in reserve, Small's brigade did not arrive at the battle until three on that steamy afternoon:

> The brigade was now formed in two lines, the 4th Maine and 2nd Vermont regiments ahead, the 5th and 3rd Maine behind. Up through the trees Colonel Howard led the forward line, out of our sight; and we that were left waiting had a last anxious quarter hour. We felt that our numbers were very few and we wanted company. . . . Some cavalrymen, pelting for the rear, broke the ranks of the 5th Maine, and carried away some of the wreckage in their blundering flight. From off to the right a rebel battery opened fire, and the survivors of the unhappy 5th suffered more damage and disorder, a ball striking their flank. . . . The next thing we knew, we were in the field on the hill and facing the enemy. I can only recall that we stood there and blazed away. . . . The faces near me were inhuman.[65]

Maine's governor, Israel Washburn, paid the 5th a visit on July 30—perhaps to see for himself if reports of Bull Run were correct; and certainly to lift the men's spirits.[66] He visited again at New Baltimore, Virginia, on November 9, 1862.[67]

The Battle at Bull Run. Dover Civil War Illustrations.

Andrew does not write to Eliza and Henry until two weeks after Bull Run—and gives scant detail, despite the fact that he was cited for gallantry during this conflict. He received a promotion to corporal on August 1.[68] Perhaps he conveyed this news to his wife, and believed she had passed it on to other family members.

Relatives back home read about Bull Run in the *Oxford Democrat*. The August 2 issue reported that the 5th Maine was "all cut up." One Bethel soldier was wounded, and the captain's water boy, Charles Freeman, thirteen, was missing. In its coverage the following week, the *Democrat* shared the gratifying news that the water boy had been found, but went on to charge, "There has been some outrageously bad management in that battle."[69]

On October 10, Andrew was assigned to Gen. Henry Slocum's Brigade and encamped for the winter near the Virginia Theological Seminary below Alexandria. During that fall and winter the regiment stood picket duty and built fortifications; some of its troops skirmished with the enemy near Mount Vernon. Picket duty was usually assigned to a trio, who took turns sleeping.

The voices of women were sometimes heard in winter camp, but they were usually those of officers' wives or an assortment of camp followers and local women seeking laundry jobs.

During winter camp at Camp Franklin, Virginia, Andrew was promoted to the rank of second corporal in January 1862. Three months later, in April, as sopping roads solidified, the regiment emerged from winter camp and moved with the Army of the Potomac to the Virginia peninsula, where it was held in reserve during the siege of Yorktown. On May 7, the regiment took part in the Battle of West Point, Virginia, a minor skirmish. The regiment was then assigned to the 6th Corps, Army of the Potomac, and participated in the Seven Days' Battles. Within the space a few short months, these mostly inexperienced men had taken part in some of the heaviest fighting of the war.

To maintain the morale of Maine's enlisted men, the *Democrat* urged residents, "Write to the soldiers . . . [for] many a rough cheek has been wet with tears when a letter has been received from those at home and who by their letters gave a pledge they were not forgotten."[70] The 5th had a sense of humor that leavened its service. When the men were sent in May 1862 to repair roads to Richmond, they erected a sign: "Gorham, Maine, 672 miles; Richmond, 20 miles."[71]

On September 1, the 5th Maine again marched to Manassas (Second Bull Run) and covered Gen. John Pope's retreat from that field toward the District of Columbia. The regiment was assigned to the Maryland Campaign and took part in the battles of Crampton Gap and Antietam in September 1862.

Suffering frequent illness, Andrew witnessed much of this action from the sidelines. A search conducted by the Bureau of Pensions in October 1893 turned up no medical records for him. However, the search revealed that Andrew "appears on Returns" as serving from September 1861 to February 1862 as company cook; in August and September 1862 in the commissary department; in October 1862, again in July, August, and September 1863, and October 1863 to April 1864 with the quartermaster department.[*] These returns total nineteen months, more than half of his thirty-six-month enlistment.

The dead covered more than five acres of ground

The period from May 4 to June 15 of 1864 became known as Grant's Overland Campaign. Gen. Robert E. Lee lost 40,000 men—half his strength. Lee, 57, also lost some of his best subordinates. General Grant lost 12,000 men.[72] Eighteen thousand Confederates were buried in Hollywood Cemetery, where a ninety-foot pyramid memorializes them today. The nightmarish forty-day campaign was called "a funeral procession." A Massachusetts private said of it, "All of us see the frail threads

---

* "Return" is used here in the sense of "official report." Clark Edwards's papers reveal that he acted as a quartermaster in terms of obtaining food. He would have known if Andrew were shirking duty.

that our lives hang on upon, and that more vividly day by day."[73]

According to the official record of the 5th Maine, the regiment served at Cold Harbor June 1–12, 1864. It is unclear whether or not Andrew Bean was present for this engagement, which was part of the Overland Campaign.

Their three-year enlistment concluded, members of the 5th Maine who had not reenlisted as veteran volunteers boarded the steamer *John Brooks* for Washington. Standing at attention on the dock, they were read a June 23 letter from Brig. Gen. Emory Upton noting their "valor and patriotism in the field," and remarking that they had been reduced from over 1,040 men plus recruits to "but two hundred and sixteen."[74]

Upon reaching Washington, Andrew and his fellows camped on the grounds of the Smithsonian Institution until they were ordered to Portland, Maine, arriving there June 28. The men were mustered out on July 27. Andrew must have written letters during this time—but none survive. It's little wonder that some correspondence never reached its intended destination. On the Union side alone, 45,000 letters were dispatched in the East; twice that many were sent from the Western Theater.[75] Union postmaster general Montgomery Blair strove for an effective mail service to and from military posts. But he also instituted compulsory payment of postage by the sender.[76] This provision meant that soldiers in the field who lacked stamps could not send mail.

Andrew Bean's thoughts on bravery and risk-taking elude us, but he does not seem to have actively sought dangerous assignments. He was honorably discharged on July 27, 1864, at Portland. His discharge papers, signed by Brigadier General Edwards, describe him as five foot ten, with a light complexion, brown hair, and blue eyes.* The Company muster-out roll states that Corporal Bean was due $38.15 for "clothing not drawn" as well as a U.S. bounty of a hundred dollars.

---

* The "Copy of Honorable Discharge" gives Andrew's age as thirty-three. This may be an error by the clerk who filled out the form, but it seems to be in Andrew's hand. He swore to its accuracy before a notary public. This may indicate that he gave his age as thirty when he enlisted, perhaps deliberately to appear younger.

Andrew's birthplace, agricultural Bethel, was undergoing big changes. It was nursing a reputation as a destination for tourists from southern New England. In the 1860s, three large hotels operated at Bethel Hill
Common.[77] Guests gawked at natural wonders like Screw Auger Falls
and Greenwood Ice Caves. Hiking and fishing also attracted visitors. The
Grand Trunk Railway station, built at West Bethel in 1865, welcomed
tourists and trophy hunters and shipped out potatoes, hops, apples, grain,
wood, and wood products such as spools and dowels The Grand Trunk
Railway was one of the most important and heavily traveled railway lines
in Canada and New England. It linked Montreal with the nearest ice-free
port, in Portland, Maine. The first through train between Montreal and
Portland crossed the border at Norton, Vermont, on July 1, 1853.[78] Despite
this flourishing economy, opportunities were too few for returning veterans—especially those with itchy feet, who now had a much wider view of
life than when they left the farm.

Never are we less gay

There was the need, as well, for veterans to recover, to rid themselves of
the stresses of battle and anticipating battle, to lower the volume of their
days. Disembarking from the ship of war, men stumble, seeking their land
legs. General Joshua Chamberlain of Maine expressed the mixed feelings
of veterans as they made their way home following Lee's surrender at
Appomattox:

> Now on the morrow, over all the hillsides in the peaceful sunshine, are
> clouds of men on foot or horse, singly or in groups, making their ear-
> nest way as by the instinct of the ant, each with his own little burden,
> each for his own little home. And we are left alone, and lonesome. We
> miss our spirited antagonists in the game, and we lose interest. The
> weight is taken out of the opposite scale, and we go down. Never are
> we less gay. And when we took up the long, round-about march home-
> ward, it was dull to plod along looking only at the muddy road, without

scouts and skirmishers ahead, and reckless of our flanks. It was tame to think we could ride up to any thicket of woods we pleased, without starting at the chirrup of those little bluebirds whose cadence was so familiar to our ears, and made so deep a lodgement in our bosoms too, sometimes.[79]

Andrew had to battle his way back to existence in the everyday world where bluebirds are feathered avians—not bullets.

Following the death of his sister Eliza in 1867, Andrew took care of her children, Henrietta and George. He acted quickly to assume this role; Eliza died on August 20, and Andrew was named guardian in probate court on September 3.[80] Andrew and his second wife, Lizzie, four years his senior, had already moved from Maine and purchased a large house at 212 Tenth Street. (The dwelling stands there still, although somewhat changed in exterior appearance.) Andrew accepted a position with a Lowell mill. Andrew's rough map titled "1896 layout of street" shows 11.5 acres including a barn where he housed a buggy and a sleigh, and kept livestock.

A mortgage deed dated September 19, 1856, conveyed to Daniel Cummings Andrew's land in Albany: "a part of lot No. 65 in the fourth range, said Land contains half an acre & lives in the angle of the County Roads leading to Bethel & Greenwood." Cummings paid $175 for the land. However, the deed allowed Andrew to pay off a promissory note and recover the property. He did so on November 22, 1861.

When he had been previously obliged to mortgage his Albany property, how was Andrew able to afford urban acreage in Lowell? Did Lizzie bring a sizeable dowry? Like Eliza's 1863 diary, an 1869 ledger and receipts open a window on Andrew's household and daily existence. The ledger, bought at Johnson Merrill on Merrimack Street, contains notations for January through April only. Pages are allotted to merchants J. M. G. Parker, Joseph Holtham, O. A. Buzzell, Patrick Mars, P. Hirshfield, John A. Lewis, Daniel Kelley, McGoverin, Joseph Lamere, G. A. R., and John Cain. Tallies reveal it was Bean's custom to pay his bills in cash in full at the end of each month. But occasionally, as in the case of McGoverin, he allowed the bill to run up during two successive months to $22.93, and then paid only $7.70 in cash.

In the case of Parker, Andrew seems to have owned the premises. He charged small amounts (ranging from 44 cents to $4.60), and then canceled them out at the end of each month with the sum of $20 for "rent of shop." Should his total charges be less than the rent, he took the remainder in cash. At the end of March, for example, he had $5.89 coming to him in cash.

Most of the ledger lines that could have shown what he was purchasing from these merchants are left blank. However, at Hirshfield on April 19, 1869, Bean recorded expenditures of $6.50 to "by clothes for Geo." and another $6 to "by Pants."

The receipts are penned on small slips exactly like those printed in modern receipt pads. A lone receipt reveals that Bean was lighting his dwelling with gas. His Lowell Gas Light Co. bill for the month of January 1869 totaled 900 cubic feet of gas, at a cost of $3.18.

Receipts for comestibles bear the names of E. S. Hunt (a wholesaler of meat and lard), A. L. Waite ("commission merchants"), Levi Hancock & Son (butter, cheese, and produce), Litchfield, Edwards & Co. (commission merchants at the corner of Market and Shattuck who sold butter, cheese, eggs, dried apples, beans, and produce), and G. N. & E Nichols (dealers in "country produce generally"). These are significant; the quantities prove that Bean was running a boardinghouse and indicate something of the daily fare. Boiled potatoes, fried eggs, and baked beans seem to have been favorites.

For instance, in January Andrew went to David Perham, a dealer specializing in pure cider vinegar (produced at the Perham farm in Chelmsford) and purchased 41 gallons. This commodity must have been intended for putting up fresh food—perhaps pork. On January 14, he purchased a bushel of peanuts, a bag of lemons, and a barrel of pickles. In February he bought 20 bushels of potatoes from Waite; a barrel of onions, 5.25 pounds of cheese, and 15 dozen eggs from Litchfield, Edwards; a bushel of dried beans from Levi Hancock; plus rumps, leaf lard, necks (not further identified), and pork from Hunt; and additional cheese from Nichols. On the February 5 receipt from Hunt for rumps, two barrels are listed—one empty, which indicates preserving is afoot. On February 26, Andrew purchased 48 pounds of turkeys from Hancock, paying $11.15. In March, he bought a bushel of apples from Litchfield; 11 pounds of butter, a single bar of Pears soap, and 25 dozen eggs from Waite. The Pears soap must have been for Lizzie—rather than the boarders.

Receipts for his 1894, 1895, 1896, 1897, and 1898 taxes show the tax rate rising from $17.40 to $18 per $1,000 of property. By 1894, Andrew had prospered sufficiently to add to his Lowell holdings. Handwritten attachments document that Andrew owned 12 acres of land on Tenth Street and 3.75 acres at the corner of Tenth and Christian. He was assessed separate amounts for his house, barn, horse, and four cows. He paid a $1 poll tax to both state and county. His total tax bill for 1894 was $176.07. Settling this bill two days late, he was charged seven cents interest.

Whatever his financial standing, Andrew was determined to collect the pensions due him and Eliza's offspring. He hired John L. Andrews, a "Government Claim Agent" and "Relief War Claim Agency" at the corner of Court and Tremont Streets ("up one flight") in Boston. From handwritten notes on Andrews's business cards, it appears that Eliza began using this agent before her untimely demise, and Andrew later followed suit. Andrews promised clients, "No charge until the money is collected."

Subsequently, desiring a lawyer closer to home, Andrew consulted Lowell attorney John F. Frye about probate and pension services. Among Andrew's miscellaneous papers, he retained handwritten receipts from Frye & Moore dated August 1, 1868, and April 20, 1870. The first was for $21.73 "in full for probate and pension services to date." The second was for $5.00 "in full for services in obtaining arrears due children of H. C. Foster, & not in original pension certificate." It apparently took Frye two years to obtain the arrears due Eliza's children.

Complaining of an inability to earn a living by physical labor, in the

1890s Andrew applied for a service pension on several occasions. He had his letter of May 20, 1892, notarized.

> *Lowell, May 20th, 1892*
>
> *To the Hon. Commissioner of Pensions. Dear Sir:*
>
> *Yours of the 12th received. . . . I have been troubled a great deal with Rheumatism, which would go all over me and would at times have a palpitation of the heart. . . . I injured my left hand in October 1871 while working on an express wagon for a Mr. Pennimen [?]. Inflamation [sic] set in and I lost a great deal of the use [of] it ever since. I have nothing upon me due to vicious habits. And to the best of my knowledge and belief all my ailments are of a permanent character.*
>
> *Andrew J. Beane*

Andrew's pension anxiety may have been fueled by knowledge that his grandfather, Revolutionary veteran Daniel, was not granted one until just a year before his death.[81] Between May and December, Andrew was examined by a medical board—but he did not second their opinion.

> *Lowell, Dec. 15, 1892*
>
> *To the Hon. Commissioner of Pensions. Dear Sir:*
>
> *Yours of Nov. 18th received and I must say that I am astonished at the decision in my case, and I think there must be a mistake with the Board of Surgeons for I am down with the Rheumatism every little while, and there is something on me all the time. One of my hands is nearly useless. Five years ago I had a sickness and was very low from which I never fully recovered, and two years ago was obliged to quit work intirely [sic]. . . .*
>
> *[I] have several times been under the Physicians care with little expectations on my part of getting up again, and while this is my condition and I see others drawing pensions and earning money, I*

cannot but think there is a mistake in my case, and ask to be sent
before another Board of Surgeons . . . if it pleases you to do so, you
will oblige

    Yours with respect.

    Andrew J. Bean

Nothing but small jobs

Andrew set his jaws like a snapping turtle. He applied again in 1896 under the Act of Congress approved June 27, 1890, for an "original Disability Pension." In a declaration signed October 16, 1896, he claimed to suffer permanently from "asthma, kidney disease, mental affliction, pleurisy, impaired vision [in] both eyes, rheumatism, stiff joints, [and] General weakness of the body and heart disease." Now, over sixty, he declared himself totally disabled and stated his latest occupations as "nothing but small jobs."

Andrew's persistence eventually paid off. By January 1898, he was receiving a pension of eight dollars a month. Veterans were due an automatic increase in pension when they reached age seventy; Andrew applied for this increase on March 11, 1898.[82]

Decades limped past before the pension system caught up with the needs of potential pensioners. When the Civil War began, the nation had 80,000 veterans. When the war ended in 1865, another 1.9 million Union veterans were added to the rolls. In 1868, Congress authorized half-pay pensions to veterans' widows and to their children until they reached age sixteen. Until 1890, Civil War pensions were granted only to servicemen discharged because of illness or disability caused by military service.

The Sherwood Act of 1912, which awarded pensions to all veterans, came almost too late for Andrew. However, he speedily put his foot in the open door.[83] The act was signed into law May 11; on May 16, Andrew, eighty-three, presented himself before a notary public to attest to his military service. Accompanying him to witness the declaration for pension were his daughter and a third resident of 212 Tenth Street, Bessie Fraser. Fraser (probably the housekeeper) swore she had known the claimant for nine months.

The Bureau of Pensions sent him a questionnaire dated March 29, 1915, which was filled out in his daughter's tight script but signed, with obvious difficulty, by Andrew. The Sherwood Act was amended in 1918; with that change, Andrew began receiving forty dollars a month. (A pack rat in her own right, Mary Frances saved the "Pensioner Dropped" form dated March 22, 1919, that removed her father from the rolls after his death on February 12.)

As Andrew harangued the federal government for his due, his niece demonstrated her concern regarding money she felt should come to her and her younger brother. As a married adult, Henrietta became impatient with Andrew for failing to settle the inheritance she believed due herself and George. She confronted her uncle by post:

> *Lynn   [Mass.] May 6, 1907*
>
> *Dear uncle Andrew,*
>
> *I write these few lines to ask you if you dont think you can have a settlement with George and I?*
>
> *Dont you think it would be a relief to get this matter off your mind, dont you think you would live happier if you should settle it up now, not let it run on any longer.*
>
> *Our mother has been dead 40 years come August don't you think it would be a good plan for us all to work out the "golden rule" and fix this thing up on its lines.*
>
> *Mary Frances [Andrew's daughter] doesnt want any thing that belongs to us   if she is the Mary Frances I think she is   and doesn't need it [.] she has enough that she has earned with her own honest hands, to say nothing of what was left her, now uncle we have waited very patiently [.] you have got your mortgages paid off I un-*

derstand, and "Uncle Sam" is paying you over for what you did for him.

What is [if] had been my father [Henry Foster] that had been spared instead of you, and he had had the care of your daughter.

Please let us know what you can do as early as possible and oblige

Henrietta Foster Hickford

For a time, Andrew let the matter lie, but on July 23 he roused himself to write to the Department of the Interior, U.S. Pension Agency, requesting a complete accounting of payments for Henrietta and George. A speedy reply dated August 5, 1907, shows that a total of $1,313.65 had been paid. Henrietta's share was $516.33, George's, $797.32. Henrietta's final payment was made in 1874, George's in 1876. Pensions dried up when the children reached their sixteenth birthdays.

Andrew also queried the Commonwealth of Massachusetts, Commissioner of State Aid and Pensions, requesting an accounting of aid from the City of Lowell. An August 20, 1907, reply from this office shows $240 in aid for Henrietta and $338 for George. The accounting for state aid showed $1,508.31 for George and $1078.54 for Henrietta (including allowances for "sundry payments and charges"). On the sundry payment pages, Andrew asked to be recompensed for liquidating the debts of Eliza's estate ($105.86), plus his wards' board, clothing, and his "Services as Guardian." These records reflect a tight-fisted, rather than a generous, uncle. Considering the poverty of his early married life, it may have been impossible for him to resist counting pennies.

Touch not the cat but with a glove

Andrew's second wife, Elizabeth, is most likely the "Mr. E. T. Beane" to whom the Lewis Historical Publishing Company of New York City wrote on March 4, 1908, enclosing a "sketch of Beane family prepared for *History of Middlesex County*." Appended to the typed cover letter is a hand-written "heraldic description of Armorial Bearings" for Clan MacBean, Highland appellation, Clann Mhic Bheathain. The description is illustrated by a drawing of the "arms of chief," with a lion rampant gules and the motto, "Touch not the cat but with a glove" or "Touch not the cat without a glove."* The cover letter solicits the Beanes to subscribe to a forthcoming "history" and submit their family genealogy. "Please make prompt return, as we have a special page place for this and do not wish to see it removed therefrom," concludes the unsigned form letter.

Andrew's certificate of record, dated August 27, 1903, supplies a few facts about Elizabeth: she was a member and for three terms president of the B. F. Butler Relief Corps, No. 75, as well as a member of the Daughters of Rebekah and the Women's Christian Temperance Union.

By the 1880s, most Civil War veterans were able to submerge gruesome memories and overlay them with considerations of comradeship. Memberships in the Grand Army of the Republic and the United Confederate Veterans swelled, and popular magazines like *Century* brimmed with essays by participants in important past military campaigns. There were encampments, reunions, and battlefield commemorations where grizzled survivors were admired. At an 1879 encampment at Albany, New York, for example, a governor told the men assembled: "But for the Union soldiers, there would have been an end to the country."[84] As they aged and mellowed, veterans like Andrew basked in admiration—not only at reunions but also when they marched in Memorial Day parades.

Reunions at Gettysburg were well attended. At first, only Union veterans paced these Pennsylvania pastures and peach orchards, reflecting on unfaded memories and the Rebellion's outcome. In 1887, however, twenty-four years after the battle, the first invitations went out to Confederate

* A variant on this clan motto occurs on the title page of *The Clan MacBean in North America*. The variant is "Touch not a Catt Bot a Targe," or "touch not a dangerous cat without the protection of a small, round shield." This is a dramatic way of saying "Be prepared." "Targe" can also mean buckler, and the frame around the motto has a belt buckle attached, with a claw-like prong securing the belt.

Andrew Jackson Bean, from his Portfolio of Personal, Civil and Military History, presented to his daughter on Nov. 16, 1912. Courtesy Bethel Historical Society.

veterans. Veterans from Philadelphia invited Virginia vets from General Pickett's division to join them. A thousand members of the Philadelphia brigade massed at the Gettysburg train station to meet 160 former enemies from Old Virginny. J. T. Parkham of the 32nd Virginia held aloft the Stars and Stripes as the first shift entered the dining hall. All told, nine thousand veterans and their families visited the battlefield in 1887—most suffused with the spirit of reconciliation.[85]

Tens of thousands gathered at Gettysburg for the battle's fiftieth anniversary, in 1913. The Maine state legislature provided train fare for its veterans to attend. James B. McCreary, governor of Kentucky, was among those delivering remarks: "We are not here with battle flags, charging brigades, roaring cannon, rattling musketry, and dead and dying soldiers, but we are here with friendship and fraternity, good will and glorious peace."[86]

At an 1880 reunion at Vinton, Iowa, veterans from Northwest Maine, Illinois, Colorado, and Massachusetts joined their Iowa counterparts. Andrew is not listed among them. There was also a 1914 GAR Reunion at Lewiston, Maine. But Andrew must have attended an event at some point; among his effects are two of the postage-stamp-sized likenesses of their commanders that veterans commonly wore pinned on their breasts at reunions.

In 1888, 5th Maine veterans constructed a permanent meeting place, a Regimental Memorial Hall (now the Fifth Maine Regiment Museum) on Peaks Island in Casco Bay. Andrew Bean and Clark Edwards were members of the Memorial Society that planned the hall.[87] For decades, this "cottage" served as a vacation spot for veterans and their families.[88] Edwards spent many summer days here.

In his declining years, Andrew sported a picturesque beard and enjoyed traveling—sometimes touring the White Mountains with his daughter, Mary Frances, via the regular schedule the Boston & Maine Railroad had begun running by 1905. Several of Andrew's jaunts were memorialized with studio portraits of himself wearing a Civil War ribbon and medal on his sky blue jacket, posed against a painted backdrop.

Andrew's sole surviving child, Mary Frances Bean (1858–1931), never married. She earned her living as a teacher. The Rebellion had the positive affect of allowing more women to enter the teaching profession. In 1860 women made up only 25 percent of the nation's elementary and secondary teachers. But by 1880 they held 60 percent of the positions, a percentage that soared to 80 by 1910.[89]

In her final years, Mary Frances led a comfortable existence. She drove a 1929 Buick Brougham, had milk delivered by G. H. Richardson, heated her large house with coal, subscribed to two newspapers, owned twenty shares in the Southern Pacific Railroad, hired a gent to shovel her sidewalk, and employed a housekeeper, Julia Lapierre.[90] The Civil War veteran who lived a long life usually had living under his roof a dedicated spinster daughter. Mary Frances obviously took good care of her father— and, important for later historians, preserved his papers.

Eliza Howard Bean Foster (1835–1867)

Living on properties ranging from fifty to 160 acres, Yankee farmers prayed for husky sons to help with the back-breaking chores of domesticating beasts and taming glacial moraine. Ebenezer Shaw Bean (1781–1839) of West Bethel, Maine, sired ten children—six of them sons—by his first wife, Eunice Kendall Bean. When Eunice was carried to her final rest in the spring of 1825, Ebenezer was desperate for household help—and considered a replacement spouse the proper form of that help. Victorian social dictates required a widower to mourn for six months. Eleven months after Eunice was interred in West Bethel's Pine Grove Cemetery, Ebenezer married a local woman nineteen years his junior.* His second wife, Mary Holt Bean (1800–1868), soon began to produce offspring.

With a multitude to provide for, Ebenezer may have greeted the birth of his sixteenth child—a daughter, Eliza Howard Bean—at 11:00 on Sunday, March 8, 1835, with more chagrin than enthusiasm. But perhaps he put on a good face for the sake of Eliza's exhausted mother, Mary.

---

* Eunice Kendall was born in 1780. She died March 16, 1825, and is buried in West Bethel Cemetery.

The role of American women in the early 1800s was as tightly circumscribed as a Southern belle's waist. Upon completion of their appointed rounds of chores, females were allowed to read and scribble, but popular magazines like *Godey's Lady's Book* instructed them to look no further afield than home and hearth. "Our men are sufficiently money-making. Let us keep our women and children from contagion as long as possible," wrote Sara Josepha Hale, the widow editor of *Godey's*.

The virtues of the True Woman were deemed the opposite of those of the true man: "Man is strong—woman is beautiful. Man is daring and confident—woman is diffident and unassuming. Man is great in action—woman in suffering," proclaimed the catalog in *Ladies Museum* magazine.[91]

Women rarely left the home place except to attend church or the funerals of neighbor women worn out by childbearing. They were escorted everywhere. Females were considered simply unfit, both physically and mentally, for public life. "A woman is never truly her own master," argued Martin Luther in his criticisms of the German Bible. "God formed her body to belong to a man, to have and to rear children. Let them bear children till they die of it. That is what they are for."

The form of a union

Eliza's future seemed pigeonholed. On the one hand, she lived during a time when Americans were locked into a rigid notion about woman's role in society. Historians later dubbed this phenomenon "the cult of domesticity."

On the other hand, she lived during a yeasty period of social change, a period when the limits of a woman's world were tested, and the women's rights movement flowered. A vocal critic of the traditional domestic role allotted females was Margaret Fuller, author of the 1845 treatise "Woman in the Nineteenth Century." Fuller argued that man was inherently imperfect, and that he saw fit to place woman in an even more imperfect situation. Fuller promoted the perfection of the female spirit—that "immortal being" whom she judged deprived by law and society of its "nature to grow, as an intellect to discern, as a soul to live freely and unimpeded, to unfold such powers as were given to her" by the Creator. Fuller targeted the inability of males to acknowledge the importance of woman's soul as the root of much female suffering. Marriage, for example, "if it be only to find a protector, and a home of her own" was all too often a matter of "convenience and utility" rather than a "meeting of souls," she wrote.

From Fuller's point of view, the "convenience" of most unions deprived man of the spiritual bliss a complete woman would have the capacity to share. If a woman must "obey" in marriage, it was destined to be an imperfect union— "the form of a union where union is none." If a woman must obey, she is restricted from following the dictates of her unique mind, and subject to those of another. A chintz ceiling of obedience bars her from achieving perfection.[92]

Fuller was up against the law in all its stultifying, patriarchal rectitude. American law was based on English common law, summarized in the Blackstone Commentaries: "The very being and legal existence of the woman is suspended during the marriage, or at least is incorporated into that of her husband under whose wing and protection she performs everything." Or, to put it in the words of jurist William Blackstone himself, "Husband and wife are one, and that one is the husband." There is no doubt Eliza loved Henry. How free she felt has not been recorded, but his letters to her show a generous disposition.

Bean's Corner vs. Brunswick

In the early nineteenth century, Eliza's hometown of Bethel consisted of a handful of nodes of population, including Bethel Hill, Walker's Mills, North Bethel (Swan's Corner), East Bethel (Bean's Corner), and West Bethel (Gander Corner). The rustic pace of life was governed by seasons, the vagaries of weather, and the demands of crops and herds.

Life shifted into a higher gear in 1809, when Maine's first cotton mill was built in Brunswick. By 1810, Maine's population topped 228,700.

However, in 1815, a push for western migration, known as "Ohio Fever," infected the district. The fever burned restlessly until about 1870, substantially decreasing Maine's population, as did a birth rate that gradually declined over the length of the century.

Songs of innocence

Education in rural Maine was generally a domestic or private affair. Children were taught to read, write, add, and subtract by their parents— if their parents were literate. If the home housed educated older siblings, those sons and daughters provided lessons to their juniors. If educated outside the home, children attended classes in teachers' homes, churches, or one-room schoolhouses. Terms depended on the number of students who could pay tuition and the commitments of the available instructor. Until the age of twelve, students bent their heads over reading, spelling, writing, arithmetic, geography, and the lives of great men. Rote learning was the order of the day; spelling tests and recitations were popular. School terms averaged three or four months.

Children as young as six were set behind the plow or trudged off to the mills, cutting short their opportunities for education. Formal schooling for them was generally limited to reading, writing, and 'rithmetic—taught at a Sunday school on their single day off.[93] The rustic Currier & Ives ideal of hoop rolling, sleighing, and sledding was not available to many New England children in 1830, when 55 percent of Rhode Island's textile workers were children earning about 15 cents a week.

Maine's public school system did not coalesce until 1828, eight years after statehood. In 1836, Bethel's educational opportunities expanded when the doors of Gould Academy swung wide. In Gould's halls, young ladies plumbed the mysteries of Latin, Greek, and German. Eliza's name does not appear on Gould's class lists. She could have attended school at the structure today known as Albany Town Hall, built in 1848. Whatever her formal education, she must have soaked up the intellectual activity of Oxford County, commented upon by no less than Harriet Beecher Stowe.

Stowe had composed much of *Uncle Tom's Cabin* in Maine, where her husband, Calvin, was a professor at Bowdoin College. Stowe's letter to *The Portland Transcript* was printed on September 25, 1852. She was particularly impressed by the women whose homes she had visited: "I can assure you, by the by, that these [educated] women are yeomen house-keepers, and that you will never taste the Latin and the Greek in sour bread or bad butter. . . . The fact is, that sterile soil and a harsh climate though not good for growing anything else are first rate for raising men and women. . . . The long cheerless winters here are powerful educators, both physically and morally—physically in the amount of oxygen and vitality which they form into the system, intellectually in the leisure which they force on one for intellectual pursuits."

Stowe's comments foreshadow Eliza's fate: "But I must add to what I said about the Maine women and girls, one drawback. . . . the want of an appearance of robust health. The young girls are fair, sparkling, intellec-tual-looking, but they are wanting in physique. They look like the forest flowers—very fair but as if a breath might wither them. . . . Can we not see in this fact the reason for the predisposition to diseases of the lungs which is constantly the terror of every parent in New England, and which seals every year hundreds of her fairest for the grave?"

Mad, wicked folly

With the tenacity of a virulent microbe, war bred in the shadow of finan-cial crisis. The South owed $300 million to Northern merchants—a debt that had to be written off almost totally.[94] To raise funds for its war chests, Congress levied an income tax in August 1861 and enacted luxury taxes in 1862. Leather, wood, and cloth were taxed as raw materials, and license taxes were levied on occupations.[95] The crisis resolved itself, and by 1863 the Union was riding an economic boom. The need for ordnance stim-ulated coal mining and steel manufacturing. The demand for uniforms, blankets, and tents invigorated textile mills.

The Rebellion cracked the status quo like an egg, and women began to loosen gender's constricting corsets. In 1837, Massachusetts schoolteacher Mary Lyon founded Mount Holyoke College, one of the first four-year institutions of higher learning exclusively for women in the United States. Vassar flung wide its doors in 1861. Other colleges (for instance, Oberlin in 1833) became co-educational, and women began seeking higher education in greater numbers. By 1870, about one-fifth of American college and university students were women.

Hand in hand with higher education went a call for women's rights. In 1848, the United States' first women's rights convention assembled in Seneca Falls, New York. Elizabeth Cady Stanton led in drafting a feminist answer to the Declaration of Independence— a "Declaration of Sentiments" pleading for the end of discrimination against women in all aspects of society: "We hold these truths to be self-evident: that all men and women are created equal. . . . The history of mankind is a history of repeated injuries and usurpations on the part of man toward woman, having in direct object the establishment of an absolute tyranny over her." Three hundred women and men signed this declaration.[96] Male philosophers like Thomas Higginson agreed with Stanton that the situation of women could be compared to that of slaves.[97] Conversely, Queen Victoria pooh-poohed the notion of Women's Rights as "mad, wicked folly."

Commenting in the *North Star* on the general public's reaction to the Seneca Falls convention, Frederick Douglass wrote, "A discussion of the rights of animals would be regarded with far more complacency by many of what are called the wise and the good of our land, then [*sic*] would be a discussion of the rights of women."[98]

Ebenezer would have wished Andrew, the oldest son of his second marriage, to be afforded the best possible education. Andrew, in turn, might have instructed Eliza in the rudiments of reading, writing, and arithmetic. Eliza's older sister, Jane, a long-time teacher, may also have had a hand in Eliza's education.

A reward for achievement in sewing. Henrietta Foster received this pink and white cup when she was twelve. Photo by Fernand L. Chandonnet.

Songs of experience

Eliza's life pulsated with the industrial development of her time, with the charge that the cotton gin, the factory, the steam engine, and the power loom sent through the warp of American life. When she was born, homespun ruled fashion. But the perfection of the power loom made domestic printed fabrics widely available and affordable. By the 1840s, women were purchasing commercially printed fabrics to sew.

The American cotton industry geared up in Rhode Island in 1790 with the first yarn spinning mills. Here Samuel Slater earned the title of Father of the American Industrial Revolution. However, two Massachusetts cities, Waltham and Lowell, share the crown as the first sites where power looms wove cloth.[99]

By the 1820s, the New England landscape was studded with four- to six-story-tall textile factories where virtually all workers were young women, each earning two to three dollars a week. (Supervisors—all men—received twelve dollars.)

As the number of slaves working Southern plantations continued to grow, the production of "Negro cloth"—coarse fabric used for field hands' clothing—became increasingly profitable. But gradually demand increased for finer fabric in a variety of patterns.

Like many of her Yankee contemporaries—young, single women from rural backgrounds—Eliza chose to leave the family fireside for the advantages of cash wages. Textile industry historian Paul Rivard called the act of taking work at an urban factory "an initiation, equivalent to young men going out to sea."[100] The primary motivation for many young women was purchasing a dowry.[101] In some mill towns, a large part of workers' pay came in the form of goods from the company store, but Lowell's Boott Cotton Mills paid cash.[102] It is likely that Eliza's parents encouraged her choice, because her departure meant one less mouth to feed.[103]

Politician and ship owner William King established Maine's first cotton mill, in Brunswick, in 1809. By Eliza's teen years, mills operated at Saco, Augusta, Lewiston, Woonsocket, and Winthrop as well. In 1810, an estimated one million yards of linen or partly linen homespun were being laboriously produced on Maine's domestic hand looms.[104] But as the century progressed, Maine's "manufactories"—"factories"—began to outshine domestic production.

In July 1851, shortly after turning sixteen, Eliza packed her reticule. Her destination was bustling Biddeford. After the building of the Pepperell Manufacturing Company on the banks of the Saco between 1850 and 1855, Biddeford counted eleven separate factories plus the usual assortment of related structures—dye houses, bleacheries, boarding houses, offices, tenements, and brickyards.[105] Pepperell alone sprawled over fifty-six acres.*

Maine's population in 1851 stood at 583,169. At the peak of textile manufacturing in Biddeford, twelve thousand people were employed in the industry. Inexperienced workers shuttled bobbins and cans of yarn and

---

* Pepperell Manufacturing, a cotton textile firm, operated in Biddeford from 1850 to 1928. It was named for Sir William Pepperell (1696–1759), colonial entrepreneur. Pepperell, J. P. Stevens & Co., and West Point Manufacturing merged in the twentieth century to become West Point Stevens. Among the more than 1,000 volumes of Pepperell records housed in the Harvard Business School library, "Wages and Duties" gives a job description for fly frame girls in the main carding room: "Run 10 frames, or an average of 170 spindles each, 8x4. They set up their roving, oil top rolls and spindle, and doff, and average 77 hanks per week on 1.92 hank roving @ 8 cents per hank."

New England textile mills of the nineteenth century. The **Pepperell Mill** (above), in Biddeford, Maine, employed many young women in its operations. (Courtesy Maine Historical Society.) **The Boott Cotton Mills** (right), in Lowell, Massachusetts, was nicknamed "the mile of mills." Photograph by Fernand L. Chandonnet.

Newspaper ad from the *Lowell Courier* **promoting milling supplies** from one of many New England suppliers.

roving among the spinning frames, and replaced filled bobbins and spools. Men labored as machinists, loom fixers, expressmen, and machine operators, but the fair sex—ages fifteen to twenty-five, mostly—accomplished the bulk of the work.[106]

Eliza probably entered Biddeford clad in homespun dyed with lichen. She would have stood out like a sore thumb until she could afford more stylish garb. She soon found employment at Pepperell Company. Because her mother was a talented hand weaver, Eliza may have been able to transfer her knowledge of that craft to machine production. She was assigned to the weaving room of Mill No. 2, with lodgings at the boardinghouse of Mrs. Cleaves, the supervisor or "matron." One Pepperell boardinghouse was a regular barracks: 420 feet long, four stories high, containing 256 rooms.[107] Girls were required to live in company boardinghouses, to be punctual for work and regular in church attendance.

Mill girls were paid once a month. The average mill girl labored for less than two years, earning $450 to $600 per year.[108] Certainly she yearned for the fine paisley shawls, lace fichus, and plumed bonnets beckoning from shop windows, but she was expected to exercise thrift. The amount she could put aside from her cash wages eked out the earnings of the family farm, went to help a brother further his education, or was reserved for her own dowry.

Weavers worked by the light of whale-oil lamps and were warmed by cast-iron stoves.[109] They operated two or three looms at a time. Close attention was necessary to prevent defects or unevenness in the fabric. The job required good eyesight, hand-eye coordination, keenness, and "substantial grace under pressure."[110] Milking a cow, one could lean into a warm belly and nudge the animal into position—even take the opportunity to sit back on the three-legged milking stool and pet the waiting cat; with a machine loom one has no such companionable relationship. Dangers included breaking leather belts, the flying ends of which could gash—or kill. Clothing could also be drawn into the machinery by belts, removing arms before the loom could be shut down.[111] Sanitary facilities were one privy per floor; waste dropped into the millrace.

About the same time that Eliza left western Maine to earn cash, wealthy New Englanders packed gear for trout fishing, tramping trips, or trophy hunting in the White Mountains. As an adult, the popular author Lucy Larcom (1824–1893) spent several summers in Bethel—enjoying the quiet and scenery of the western gateway to the Presidential Range. Prized for her flexible rhythms, easy rhymes, and strong moral tone, Larcom knew well the din and dangers of Lowell's mills. Her autobiography, *A New England Girlhood* (1889), records memories of her idyllic infant life and education contrasted with her stint as a factory girl.

Larcom's widowed mother ran a boardinghouse, but made the mistake of feeding her boarders with too lavish a hand. When the cupboard grew bare, her blue-eyed daughters were sent to work in Lowell's Lawrence Mill, rising at five, during winter months breaking ice on their basins to bathe. At age eleven, Lucy changed bobbins on spinning frames. She pocketed a dollar a week over her room and board—a sum she handed over to her mother with alacrity. Lucy's excruciatingly long days in the mill left her with a lifelong aversion to loud noise and a wish to escape cities for sanctuaries where she could observe nature.[112]

Although factory work netted women cash income, historian Rosalind Miles believes the shift from home to industrial production had damaging consequences for females. Among those consequences was the loss of partnership status, gained when wife worked alongside husband—digging, sowing, reaping. On the home place, women had control over what they produced—perhaps extra eggs, straw braid, or baskets that could be marketed for "pin money."[113] Women also chose their hours of work and could take breaks—or switch from task to task—as they wished.

"With the shift from an agricultural to an industrial economy, from country to town, from home to factory," Miles reasons, "women lost the previous flexibility, status and control of their work. In its place they were granted the privilege of low-grade, exploited occupations, the double burden of waged and domestic labor, and the sole responsibility for child care that has weighed them down ever since."[114]

After some years in Biddeford, Eliza sought a "better situation." She headed south, to a destination eighty-five miles away, in another state. Most likely she rode bone-rattling stagecoaches to Portsmouth, lodged overnight, and then boarded the Portland, Saco & Portsmouth railroad for Lowell, Massachusetts. She disembarked, dusty and dehydrated, in the busy "city of spindles."

Eliza hired on as an "operative" at Boott Cotton Mills—a riverfront complex nicknamed "the mile of mills." The factory bore the name of Kirk Boott, an ambitious man who had his finger in many local pies. Lowell was erected on the site of a village called East Chelmsford and home to only two hundred inhabitants in 1820.[115] The spot was renamed Lowell in honor of Francis Cabott Lowell (1775–1817), the Boston merchant and clever industrial pioneer who memorized details of power looms during his 1811 tour of England and Scotland.*

In prehistoric times, the Pawtucket Falls area served as a spring fish camp site for the Pennacook Confederacy, an alliance of the Nashobah, Pawtucket, Pennacook, Souhegan, and Wamesit Indians. Fish camp was a combination tribal reunion and marketplace. Salmon and other fish were caught and dried, trading partnerships reinforced, and marriages arranged. These seasonal activities continued until Europeans infiltrated the gently rolling hills and valleys in the mid-1600s. In due time, industrialists would find these same rivers and hills an ideal site for factories driven by water-power channeled by manmade canals.

Geography was destiny for Lowell. It was bisected by the Merrimack and Concord Rivers—winding, willow-shaded water roads for Native Americans as well as canoeing enthusiasts like Henry David Thoreau. The 110-mile Merrimack, or "place of swift current," drains a watershed of more than four thousand square miles. Gathering speed as it flows out of southern New Hampshire and angles through northern Massachusetts, it aims like an arrow at Newburyport. Plunging cold and clear over rock ledges at Lowell, the river drops more than thirty feet in a mile, providing a perfect site for water-powered enterprise.

Lowell's site was recommended by its proximity to the Middlesex Canal. Completed in 1803, this twenty-seven-mile water route connected the Merrimack River with Boston's Charles. The waterway simplified the delivery of raw materials and foodstuffs inland as well as the transportation of manufactured products to the coast. Lowell was patterned on the "Waltham system" devised by Francis Lowell: mills were large, built

---

* When Francis Cabott (sometimes spelled Cabot) Lowell returned to his native Massachusetts from abroad, he and Paul Moody designed and constructed the first power loom in America—an improvement over the Lancashire loom. Lowell then founded the Waltham mill which, after his death, sparked the idea of founding Lowell as a perfect, harmonious industrial town.

The Boott Cottom Mills today has been restored as a museum; in Eliza's day, the complex was a self-contained village. Photograph by Fernand L. Chandonnet.

at major waterpower sites and powered with canal networks. Named for Francis Lowell's original 1815 mill in Waltham, Massachusetts, the innovative system aimed to integrate under a single roof the series of tasks necessary to convert bales of raw cotton into bolts of fabric. Locked in their neat stone conduits, canals gave an impression of peace and order. But as soon as giant wheels began to hum, shuttles to travel right and left and leather belts to squeak, the system relied on the nerves and sinews of young spinsters.[116]

Because Waltham's site had physical limitations, the Boston Associates began to scout for a mightier power source. On a cold day in November 1821, Kirk Boott, Patrick T. Jackson, Warren Dutton, Paul Moody, and Nathan Appleton—the Boston Associates—were "perambulating the grounds" of East Chelmsford. Fewer than a dozen houses stood there.

Nevertheless, as snow sifted around the partners' ankles and Pawtucket Falls drummed the granite riverbed, the quintet was able to imagine the scene peopled with twenty thousand inhabitants in their lifetimes. Within a year the associates owned four hundred acres and had chartered the city's first cotton mill, Merrimack Manufacturing Company. Irish laborers trudged from Boston to dig canals and raise roof beams. By 1826, the town had 2,500 residents and prided itself on an international reputation for humane working conditions.

By 1860, more than 270,000 female operatives were employed in Northern industries—not only textile milling but also shoe and clothing manufacture, and printing and publishing establishments. More than 135,000 labored in New England, accounting for 65 percent of the region's industrial labor.[117] The remaking of New England from an agricultural economy to an industrial one was well under way.

Living on the Boott

Boston Associates' goal was to produce printed calico suitable for home furnishings as well as shirting and dress goods.[118] Their ambitious enterprise, Boott Cotton Mills, was chartered in March 1835.[119] Four mills were planned under this umbrella title. Masons speedily mortared tons of red brick, and two mills roared into production in June 1836. All four Bootts were completed by January 1839, although the supporting canal system continued to expand through 1848.

Practically a city unto itself, Boott embraced a counting house, storage for raw cotton, picker houses, card rooms, a repair shop, an elevated railroad, 910 looms, 32,036 spindles, and eight rows of brick boarding houses between Amory and French Streets. The three-story boardinghouses measured an impressive 150 feet long by 36 feet deep. In 1842, the company employed 950 female and 120 male operatives and cut from its looms 9,360,000 yards of cloth per year.[120]

A separate weaving mill (No. 5 Mill) was constructed close to the Merrimack in 1847–48, leading to a 60 percent increase in Boott Mills' total output between 1849 and 1851.[121] By 1859, the annual output of the mills had reached an astounding 15,600,000 yards, although production soon dropped during the Civil War because of shortages of raw cotton. Boott Mill continued operating until 1956-57.[122] To the delight of today's tourists, Boott Mill preserves a complete nineteenth-century mill yard within a unique national–state park established in 1978.[123]

Existence for Eliza was "living on the Boott"—working twelve hours a day, six days a week.[124] At the boardinghouses for unskilled, unmarried workers, linens were washed and meals were prepared, but the mill girls were responsible for their personal laundry. Beds were commonly shared.[125]

Nine-year resident Rev. Henry A. Miles produced a profile of Lowell published in 1845. The chief mills operating then were Merrimack Manufacturing Company, Appleton Manufacturing Co., Lowell, Middlesex, Suffolk, Tremont, Massachusetts, and Boott. Miles's guidebook supplied information on the moral and intellectual advantages of the city, details on how calico was printed, and statistics collected from agents, operatives, and boarding house matrons, as well as worshipful sketches of notables like Francis Cabott Lowell and Kirk Boott.

On average, an unskilled worker pocketed $1.50 to $2 per week above the fee for room and board of $1.25 to $1.50. Actual earnings averaged between $160 and $190 a year most of the time between 1825 and 1863, with a low of $129.73 in 1861.[126]

When Eliza took up residence in Lowell, the mills churned out calico, broadcloth, wool flannel, cassimere (a wool fabric with a subtle woven-in pattern) and satinet (a mixed weave of cotton and wool). One mill wove wool carpet. Here, mill hours were longer than in Maine. In Massachusetts, New Hampshire, and Rhode Island, an eleven and three-quarter-hour day was common. The adoption of a ten-hour day did not come until 1874.[127] Bells rang to pry the mill girls out of bed, send them to their posts, and escort them home.

The tyranny of the bell did not sit well with young women who anticipated a measure of independence as they latched the pasture gate behind them. Half the women workers in Lowell stayed less than a year, while men averaged just over two years.[128]

With whom did Eliza work? An 1845 tally of one Lowell factory found a total of 173 "hands": 21 from Massachusetts, 45 from Down Maine, 55 from New Hampshire, and 52 from Vermont. When all eight factories were considered, however, a historian found that 7 percent of these employees were Irish. The origin of hands changed quickly; by 1852, over half of the mill girls were foreign-born.[129] The supply of immigrant labor made it possible for mill owners to reduce wages and allow working conditions to deteriorate without closing shop.

Among Eliza's contemporary operatives was Harriet Jane Hanson, who moved to Lowell from Boston. To supplement the budget of her widowed mother, Harriet began her career as a spindle girl in 1834 at age ten. Her autobiography, *Loom and Spindle* (1898), describes her experiences as a mill worker until age twenty-three.

The earnings of mill girls, Hanson notes, often went to rebuild the barn, paint the farmhouse, or modernize its kitchen. However, she wrote, "The most prevailing incentive to labor was to secure the means of education for some *male* member of the family. To make *a gentleman* of a brother or a son, to give him a college education. . . . I have known more than one to give every cent of her wages, month after month, to her brother, that he might get the education necessary to enter some profession."[130]

Compared to Britain's "dark, satanic mills," Lowell was a Sunday school picnic. Praises for its social idealism were sung by visitors ranging from frontiersman Davy Crockett to President Andrew Jackson. The *Essex Gazette* called Lowell "a fairy scene. . . . with immense prospects of increasing extent and boundless wealth."[131]

Lowell's fame as a utopian manufacturing community grew exponentially following the 1842 visit of British author Charles Dickens, who set forth his observations in a volume titled *American Notes*. During his American Tour, Dickens coined the phrase "the almighty dollar." He gave

Lowell short shrift—only thirteen paragraphs. At least two of those are padded with gratuitous recitals of his personal opinions concerning proper female dress and deportment. Supposedly incognito, he visited three mills—a woolen factory, a carpet factory, and a cotton factory:

> I happened to arrive at the first factory just as the [noon] dinner hour was over, and the girls were returning to their work; indeed the stairs of the mill were thronged with them as I ascended. . . . These girls . . . were all well dressed: and that phrase necessarily includes extreme cleanliness. They had serviceable bonnets, good warm cloaks, and shawls; and were not above clogs and pattens [wooden platforms attached to footwear to raise shoe leather above mud or water]. Moreover, there were places in the mill in which they could deposit these things without injury; and there were conveniences for washing. They were healthy in appearance, many of them remarkably so, and had the manners and deportment of young women: not of degraded brutes of burden. . . . I cannot recall or separate one young face that gave me a painful impression.

Visiting in winter, Dickens witnessed nothing of the sweltering conditions of summer, when windows were often nailed shut—because the looms worked best when warm.

Cross, lazy, and nasty

How did Eliza learn of Lowell? Perhaps from another girl in her hometown. Perhaps from her reading. In the evenings, New Englanders often gathered near the hearth to snack on apples such as Russets, Ribstons, or Normandies[132] or on freshly popped corn. Sitting as close as possible to the lamp, women knitted, mended, or darned. Men nursed pipes or whittled. Literate family members took turns reading aloud from the leather-bound family Bible, volumes of collected sermons, or the widely serialized works of popular authors.

On such occasions, Eliza, her brother Andrew or her sister Jane might have perused Dickens's *American Notes*. The 1843 Maine edition of the

Farmers Almanac and the *New England Gazetteer* also puffed Lowell.[133] And there was a more personal, autobiographical piece as well. At the request of the Proprietors of Locks and Canals, Nathan Appleton in 1858 published a thirty-six-page pamphlet, *Introduction of the Power Loom, and Origin of Lowell.*

Laboring in a mill year upon year differs markedly from a brief tour. Consider, for example, Barilla Taylor. In October 1843, Barilla, fifteen, waved goodbye to the family farm in Maine. Reaching Lowell by stage, she signed a one-year contract with Hamilton Manufacturing Company. In July 1844 she wrote home describing her overseer, Augustus Lord, as "not terribly clever." She also mentioned a fellow worker, Ann Graham, who had "got her hand tore off" in the carding room. At first, Barilla lived in a company boardinghouse with about thirty other females. When her friend Else developed personality conflicts with two women, she and Barilla packed their slender wardrobes and moved elsewhere. The second boardinghouse keeper was "cross, lazy, and nasty" and served disgusting coffee. Barilla moved again.

By her second year on the mile of mills, Barilla entertained dreams of going west. But before she could make that move, fate intervened. Hamilton payroll records for July 1845 show that she worked only fifteen days that month, and someone else signed for her wages. Barilla died on August 22, 1845. The cause of her death was not listed in the *Lowell Vital Records.*[134]

The most common causes of death among the mill girls were consumption (a lung disease, often tuberculosis), cholera, and typhoid fever. Most deaths clustered, hornets buzzing a rotten pear, around the heat and humidity of August.[135]

Mill work was crushing to body and soul. Rosalind Miles notes, "The hours themselves would not have been so different from the workload of a home-based woman. But the forced pace of the labor, with the inability to break off, to rest or to vary the work in any way, made it a mental as well as a physical torment."[136] The average age at which mill girls died in Lowell in 1846 was 20.68 years.

Apologists, like the Rev. Henry Miles, went to great lengths to prove that mill girls had "comparatively light" work.[137] If they fell ill, Miles unashamedly wrote, it was their fault: "Some come with the seeds of disease already growing within them, and they find that their constitutions would soon break down by continued labor. Others, freed from the guardianship of parental care, are greatly improvident in their diet, or dress, or exposure to cold and damp air."

Neither Dickens nor Miles mentioned the phenomenon of a splintery factory floor thrumming with a hundred looms as if it were the deck of a ship at sea. One operative described the din "as of crickets, frogs and jewsharps, all mingled together in strange discord." New hands shrank toward the walls, feeling that "the sight of so many bands, and wheels, and springs in constant motion, was very frightful."[138]

Six years after Dickens's visit, Lowell had grown into the largest industrial center in North America. Annually the city's looms produced 50,000 miles of cloth—enough yardage to sash the equator twice around. But Lowell's very success spelled difficulties for its mill girls. Its early profits spawned competition and textile prices fell. To keep dividends high, mill owners cut labor costs and required their employees to tend more machines at a faster pace. Fingers or arms were sometimes lost to the works. If hair tangled in a machine, an operative could be scalped.

Lowell's first strike came in 1834 when operatives objected to a 15 percent wage reduction. Two years later, growing competition persuaded mill owners to again slash wages, reducing them by a dollar a week.* This incited 1,500 girls to stage a "turn-out." They bravely paraded the boulevards waving handkerchiefs and singing words put to a popular tune:

> Oh! Isn't it a pity, such a pretty girl as I—
> Should be sent to the factory to pine away and die?

---

* Another source gives a rather different version of this story: the strike was against a proposed rent hike; the mill owners rescinded the proposal after the strike (www.transported.org/lowell-factory-girls-of-the–19th-century).

> Oh! I cannot be a slave,
> I will not be a slave,
> For I'm so fond of liberty
> That I cannot be a slave.

The owners responded to this protest by increasing the number of frames and looms girls were required to watch, and overcrowding the boardinghouses, stuffing as many as eight operatives into a room.[139] Increased competition degraded the system that had formerly seemed ideal. Traveling in England and Scotland, Francis Cabott Lowell had been deeply affected by the impoverishment of the working classes. But Francis Lowell was no longer alive to see what his Waltham system had become.

A community of itself

At their lodgings, weary mill girls generally enjoyed the respite of pleasant surroundings. "The life in the boarding-houses was very agreeable," wrote Harriet Robinson. "Each house was a village or community of itself. There fifty or sixty young women from different parts of New England met and lived together. When not at their work, by natural selection they sat in groups in their chambers, or in a corner of the large dining-room, busy at some agreeable employment; or they wrote letters, read, studied, or sewed, for, as a rule, they were their own seamstresses and dressmakers."[140] This bustling sisterhood ameliorated homesickness and bore fruit in relationships which endured when the girls quit the mills and became wives and mothers.

The boardinghouse was a keystone of the Waltham system. By erecting housing at their own expense, by limiting lodgers to employees, and by installing at the head of each lodging a matron of tried character, mill owners satisfied rural fathers that it was safe—even beneficial—to send their innocent daughters to town. Factory owners made much of the fact that the majority of their supervisors were married men with children. Parents were assured that their daughters would learn discipline and be superior

Dana Russell Fox (left) and Mabelia Foster Fox. Courtesy Bethel Historical Society.

wives and mothers as a result.[141] Mill owners argued that they were not only providing upscale goods for the nation, but also giving employment to women to "save them from poverty and idleness."[142]

Where did Eliza board? She may have boarded at #45 Boott Corporation. This boarding house unit was inhabited almost exclusively by women from 1849 to 1884—twenty-five to thirty of them at a time, under the thumb of one keeper, Mrs. Amanda M. Fox, a hard-working widow.

Life at #45 is reflected in Amanda Fox's 1895 probate inventory. It listed 13 bedsteads, 14 feather beds, 59 chairs, 7 stoves, 5 tables, 7 flat irons, 4 bureaus, 9 steamer trunks, 10 brooms, and various fruit jars and "chamber crockery."[143] Assuming the usual number of female boarders and only thirteen bedsteads, that works out to a minimum of two females per bed, assuming Amanda slept alone. If Amanda's children lived at home or she required a bed for guests, boarders' beds become more crowded.

Her daughter, Diana, was born about 1839.* Her son, George, followed in 1841. For a few years, the children may have shared their mother's bed or been tucked into a trundle.

With whom did Eliza share her bed? Odds are good that she battled for covers with another farmer's daughter much like herself. But there were other possibilities. In 1844 the Boott employed 816 women including forty "supposed to be Irish" and forty-three illiterates.[144] As many as eight girls shared a room.[145]

Amanda's establishment is of particular interest because it was home to Dracut farmer Dana Russell Fox during the workweek. This cohabitation was made possible— that is, respectable—by the fact that Amanda was his aunt; she was the widow of Dana's uncle, Joseph Varnum Fox, who died in 1843.

Dana's wife, Mabelia, was the older sister of Henry Foster—and this may be the link that spawned Eliza and Henry's meeting and courtship. Dana was born in Plymouth, Vermont, as were Mabelia and Henry. Mabelia and Dana were married in Plymouth in 1851, their union indicating that the Fox and Foster clans socialized in Vermont. A letter Mabelia wrote to Henry dated January 27, 1855, refers to Dana's address during the week as "Lowell Boott Corp., #45."** Dana most likely held the position of supervisor—and it is entirely possible that Henry visited his brother-in-law Dana at Boott and first caught a glimpse of Eliza here.

Harriet Robinson described the main floor of a typical boardinghouse as boasting a "best room. . . . to entertain callers in; but if any of the girls had a regular gentleman caller, a special evening was set apart each week to receive him. This room was furnished with a carpet . . . and with the best furniture."[146]

Usually, the first floor housed not only a "best" room, but also private quarters for the housekeeper as well as a communal dining room, a washing and storage area, and a commodious kitchen. The unpaved backyard

* Diana L. Fox died in 1867 (Jeffrey Hooper, e-mail, June 25, 2008).
** The United States did not institute postal delivery in rural areas until the end of the nineteenth century—so Dana had to wait for mail delivery to Dracut.

was threaded with clotheslines—to be avoided when making a hasty bee-line for the well or privy. Nicer back yards had the luxury of boardwalks and were landscaped with elderberry bushes and grape arbors. By way of a curfew, doors were locked at 10:00 p.m. There was scant leisure time.[147]

In the boardinghouse, plain meals were served on stark white iron-stone. Breakfast was hearty, usually meat, hash concocted from the previous day's leftovers, fish, potatoes, and porridge. Lunch might be pie—savory or fruit—something that could be gobbled in a hurry. For dinner, boarding houses ladled out New England boiled dinner (corned beef simmered with root vegetables)[148] or bread with gravy.[149] Big yellowware bowls of applesauce, pickled beets, and baked beans provided a treat for the eye and also for the taste buds.

At home

During Eliza's lifetime, the American diet was seasonal and often nutritionally unbalanced. Science had not discovered vitamins; methods of preserving foods by canning and freezing were just coming on line. Because of spotty nutrition, the average age of menarche in the United States was 16.5 years in 1840; with improved diet, the average age of first menstruation declined to 12.9 in 1950. In colonial America, the average age of marriage ranged from 19.8 years to 23.7 years. In the mid-nineteenth century, when most American families lived on farms, the average age of marriage was 20 for women and 22 for men. Forty-three percent of Victorian women bore between five and nine children; 17 percent gave birth to ten or more.[150] But as industrialization made its demands felt, men and women began to postpone marriage until later in life, to delay childbearing and to limit the number of offspring.

Eliza Foster is not listed in the 1851 Lowell city directory. There is, however, an 1853 listing for a "Bean Eliza, Mrs., boarding house, 4 Bleachery." A September 1859 doctor's bill documents her address as 12 Chestnut Street.

Girling it

In rural areas, church services, singing or quilting parties, and husking bees afforded arenas for courting or "keeping company." "The Paring (or Apple) Bee," published in the *Lowell Offering* in 1845, describes typical hometown frolics, all of them celebrated in "the spirit of agrarianism and hilarity." Those country amusements included sewing parties, tea parties, candy-making parties, sugar-camp parties, parties for cracking nuts and parching corn, huskings, quilting bees, and spinning frolics.[151]

Kisses and cuddles could be snatched in shadowed nooks when the workday was done, but heterosexual relationships were generally circumspect. Courtship usually precluded sexual intercourse. Informal courtship was known as "girling it" in the eighteenth century; it took the form of innocent socializing across looms or brief frolics in currant patches. After leaving the family home, young adults like Eliza and Henry had less restraint from parents—more freedom to woo unsupervised and choose mates as they wished.[152]

Lowell afforded courting couples not only the banks of the Merrimack, but also a network of elevated stone walkways and footbridges bordering canals. Here they could meet after church services to exchange confidences and stroll discreetly arm-in-arm. Spending time together in this manner was called "walking out."

From his study of mill girls' letters, Thomas Dublin estimated that on average, female operatives hired on at age sixteen and a half and continued to work for five and a half years. The operatives were likely to wed men closer in age to themselves than their rural counterparts. A contemporary observer calculated in 1845 that the average length of time women were employed in mills was four to five years. Eliza's life fits these patterns.[153] Another pattern growing common at the time had to do with choosing marriage partners. Had Eliza remained on the farm in Maine, the men courting her would have been known to her kinship circle. With her residence in Lowell, parental control over her suitors declined; it is probable that none of her Maine relatives had met Henry and, before their marriage, knew of him only through her letters.[154]

Five years after she began working in the Biddeford mill, Eliza, now a comely twenty-one, wed Henry Charles Foster, twenty-two. The couple was joined on December 5, 1856, by the Rev. D.C. Eddy of Lowell's First Baptist Church. Perhaps to satisfy a landlord's sense of propriety, Eddy wrote out a marriage certificate in his own hand. At some later date, the couple acquired an official certificate of record of marriage. On this second, more inclusive, document, Henry's occupation is given as painter—that is, house and sign painter. Eliza's occupation is given as "at home." How delighted she must have been to leave the thundering mill for the solace of her own parlor.

The couple feathered their nest with a table, six chairs, and a rocking chair from E. B. Patch, dealer in secondhand furniture. They stocked up on cups, dippers, and pots. No record of their bedroom furniture or bedding survives, but iron beds were in vogue at this time because (unlike wooden bedsteads) they lacked crevices in which dust, dirt, and bedbugs could hide. Eliza probably hemmed her own sheets of linen, cotton, or Swiss twilled calico. By 1857, these fabrics were being woven wide enough to allow sheets without seams.

Their dwelling lacked indoor plumbing and central heating. Eliza may have begun keeping house two or three stories in the air, but she knew all about chopping wood and toting wood and water from her earthbound youth on the farm. A rent receipt dated September 1, 1857, signed by Amos Merriam, shows Henry paying $4.75 per month. Receipts for June and July of that year are for $3.25, so perhaps the fall saw Henry and his bride moving to larger quarters in anticipation of expanding their family.

Parents of this era did not expect all their children to live, but Eliza's flourished. She and Henry welcomed two offspring: Henrietta, or Etta, born June 14, 1858; and George Arthur, who arrived on October 17, 1860. Most births took place at home, with experienced older women assisting.

Life expectancy predictions for whites in 1860 ranged from 41 to 43.6

Foster family portrait, made in Lowell during Henry Foster's spring 1864 furlough. Clockwise from top: Henry (aged 30) and Eliza (29) ; Henrietta (almost 6); George (3). Courtesy Bethel Historical Society.

years. Although separate figures were not calculated for women, and dependable records are mostly lacking outside New England, childbirth was known to claim many women in their prime. At the beginning of the nineteenth century, the typical American woman experienced seven to eight live births in her lifetime. The death rate in childbirth was one woman in every 154 live births—a rate 83 times the year 2000 maternal death rate. In 1850, infant mortality per 1,000 live births was 216.8—more than 20 percent. In 2000, by comparison, the rate had declined to 5.7 infant deaths per 1,000.[155]

Prenatal care was rare, and the recommended diet was insufficient. Dr. William P. Dewees's *A Treatise on the Physical and Medical Treatment of Children* (1825), the first American textbook on pediatrics, assured pregnant women that they could successfully carry a child to term without increasing their daily intake of food or appeasing any extraordinary cravings for sardines and pickles. Pregnancy often resulted in malnutrition of the mother, a low birth weight for the baby, and the subsequent non-thriving of both. In Eliza's case, her two pregnancies may have set the corporeal stage for her early death.

Clues to other aspects of Eliza and Henry's daily lives survive. Magpie Eliza saved letters and pocket diaries as well as paid grocery bills, receipts for poll tax paid by her husband—all manner of fascinating scraps. A running tally with grocer Theodore E. Parker kept between December 26, 1861, and January 6, 1862, shows Eliza's purchases of molasses, granulated sugar, crackers, wheat, rice, saleratus (a form of baking soda), pepper, oil, raisins, soap, camphor, peppermint extract, and stove polish, among other items—to a total of $4.24. The previous bill—November 5 through December 26, 1861—includes tea, butter, a barrel of flour, and nutmeg to the tune of $18.04.

Shadows in the dusk

At the time when Henry and Eliza were raising their young family, talk of Southern secession—and a resulting civil war—occupied the newspapers and the minds of the citizens. Still, the nation's newly elected president had neither experience of nor admiration for war. At his inauguration on March 4, 1861, Abraham Lincoln declared that he would not accept secession—yet he hoped to resolve the national crisis without warfare.[156]

But he could not avoid action the following month, when the Confederacy fired on Fort Sumter, South Carolina. Lincoln decided to resupply the island-like garrison. Assistant Secretary of the Navy Gustavus Fox argued that Sumter should be readied to do battle, but Lincoln, anxious to avoid armed conflict, decided to send non-military supplies only. However, even barrels of hard tack were sufficient for the South's purpose. From the mainland, Confederates fired on the fort on April 12, and Sumter's commander, Major Robert Anderson, eventually surrendered and evacuated the garrison in the relief steamer *Baltic,* with Fox on deck. Emboldened by the eventual fall of Sumter, four more states joined the Confederacy, leaving Washington, D.C., a vulnerable island washed by a secessionist sea.

On April 15, Lincoln, realizing there was no turning back, ordered Secretary of War Gideon Welles to call out the militia. Recruits were to be men from age eighteen to forty-five, standing at least five feet three inches, and possessing physical strength and vigor—able to serve ninety days "unless sooner discharged." Governors were assigned quotas. The Bay State was to supply two regiments comprising 74 officers and 1,486 men. Gov. John Albion Andrew of Massachusetts speedily replied: "The quota of troops required of Massachusetts is ready. How will you have them proceed?" Massachusetts demonstrated its patriotism by exceeding its quota, furnishing 3,736 men.[157]

Lowell residents felt a personal affront when the 6th Massachusetts was mobbed in Baltimore on April 19. Nine civilians and four soldiers were killed. Eventually the city raised a monument on Merrimack Street to the first Lowell boys killed in the Rebellion, Luther C. Ladd and A. O. Whitney.[158]

Three short months proved unequal to healing the rift between the

North and South. In fact, three months was insufficient even to train militia as troops. Lincoln soon realized his army was vastly undermanned, and, on July 1, 1862, he requested 300,000 more men.

Defending the capital

Between the attack on Fort Sumter and the Battle of Bull Run, there were only a hundred days. Washington, D.C., the nation's capital, sat uneasily between two states—Virginia and Maryland—considering secession. If it had fallen to the Confederates in those hundred days, American history might have been very different.

When the Civil War was reaching a full boil in the spring of 1861, Washington was a project in the works. Unpaved streets served only 63,000 residents.[159] Faced with the threat of invasion, however, it became the most heavily fortified city in North America. The incomplete U.S. Capitol was turned into a temporary military barracks. Thomas Walter, the architect in charge of the Capitol's dome, was irritated by "about 100 drummers all the time drumming." At the peak, about 4,000 volunteers were billeted in and around the Capitol. Walter wrote to his wife, "The smell is awful. The building is like one grand water closet. Ever[y] hold and corner is defiled." Brick ovens were built in the basement, and began baking 58,000 loaves of bread a day. The ovens were finally removed in October, when smoke damage was detected in some books in the Library of Congress—also housed at the time in the Capitol.[160]

The swampy Mall, an open area between the Capitol and the Executive Mansion, metamorphosed from a public park into an armed encampment complete with lines of flapping tents, latrine trenches, and cooking fires. Soldiers bedded down at the Navy Yard and in the House and Senate chambers. A private was amazed that "hogs run around the street just like dogs." Nevertheless, newcomers, including Clark Edwards, enjoyed sightseeing—ogling the grand marble buildings, touring the Executive Mansion, the Smithsonian Institution, and the Patent Office.[161] H. G. Otis Perkins, who trained with Andrew Bean, wrote from Washington on July 3, 1861, complaining, "The flies are as thick as mosquitoes."[162]

On the day of Lincoln's election, the city had only one river fort. The Army of the Potomac was charged with the defense of the District of Columbia, and the muscle of volunteers like Andrew Bean allowed fortification to begin. Maj. Gen. John G. Barnard, father of Washington's defenses, ordered innovations such as thicker walls and vertical post revetment. The new forts were built by constructing a wooden framework and digging a trench on the outside. The excavated soil was rammed into the frame and topped with turf. Finished walls could be twenty-five feet high and eighteen feet thick.[163] By the close of the war, the defenses of Washington totaled 68 enclosed forts with 807 mounted cannon and 93 mortars, 401 emplacements for field guns, 20 miles of rifle trenches, miles of military roads, and a telegraphic communication system.[164]

An average of 20,000 men from the Army of the Potomac were stationed here at any given time, and $1.4 million of the Union war chest was lavished on these extensive field fortifications and defending the capital.[165]

How long, O Lord

The lives of ordinary Americans like Andrew, Eliza and Henry were blown off course by this storm of national events. Although battered by a hail of bad news, Henry took his time enlisting. He did not join when the 6th Massachusetts was brutally set upon in Baltimore.* He did not follow in

* The man considered the first combatant killed in the Civil War was Sumner H. Needham of Maine and Massachusetts. Needham was born in Norway, Maine, but his family moved after his birth to Bethel; it is possible that Eliza knew him because his sister Melinda married a Bean of Bethel. Early in the spring of 1861, Sumner Needham enlisted in the 6th Regiment of the Massachusetts Volunteer Militia. Four soldiers were killed on April 19, 1861, as that regiment passed through the streets of Baltimore, marching a mile to the railroad depot. The first shot killed Needham. The other soldiers whose names are known are Addison O Whitney and Luther C. Ladd, both of Lowell (Donald W. Beattie, *A Distant War Comes Home*, p. 89). The deaths of these men would have been a great motivation for Henry to enlist. According to another source, Needham, aged thirty-three, was beaten with a paving stone and died eight days later, "the first mortally wounded man in the Civil War." Needham was buried in Lawrence (Kathryn Skelton, "Sumner Henry Needham: 'I sense there will be trouble today,' " *Sun Journal*, Lewiston, May 24, 2009, A–1.).

the footsteps of his brother-in-law, Andrew Jackson Bean, who signed up in May. He continued to hesitate in June when West Virginians declared themselves separate from Virginians and joined the Union. He bided his time in July after the Confederate victory at Bull Run, with its chaotic and dispiriting retreat of federal troops. The North was especially incensed with rumors of Confederate atrocities at Bull Run. The July 24 *New York Times*, for instance, alleged, "They Make Targets of the Wounded Soldiers, Mutilate them with Knives, and Fire at the Hospital."[166]

Henry had good reason to stay home: he was no longer in his first youth; he had a wife and two small children. He held a good job in a slumping economy. But all around him men were enlisting; his friends were enlisting. Rodney and John Marean Bean, older half-brothers of Eliza, had enlisted. [167] The very air in the streets seemed to vibrate with the necessity of preserving the Union.

Long and hard, Henry weighed his options, until he could no longer resist the call to demonstrate honor and duty—indeed, his very manhood. He became a member of Company A of the 26th Regiment of Infantry, Massachusetts Volunteers, enrolling on October 18, 1861, to serve three years. Within weeks, he was headed for the Gulf of Mexico.

War's reality was hardly that of shining ranks marching toward each other on grassy pasture. It was hunger and thirst and suffering. It played out on thousands of muddy back roads, on dozens of fronts, in snake-infested wildernesses and swamps, in feints, charges, and retreats. Bruce Catton describes it as a series of "related segments": "Here it was a battle in which ill-equipped armies learned their trade in blundering action; there it was a matter of shadows in the dusk, neighbor ambushing neighbor, hayrick and barn blazing up at midnight with a drum of hoofbeats on a lonely lane to tell the story, or a firing squad killing a bridge-burner as a warning to the lawless. The separate scenes were monstrous, confusing, ever-changing; put together, they might make a horror planned neither in Washington nor in Richmond."[168]

A tender farewell scene. Detail from John Bodwell's Testimonial of Service certificate, State of New Hampshire, Feb. 22, 1867. Collection of Ann Chandonnet.

Will outlive her husband

Unselfishly, lovingly, Henry's letters stress again and again that he desires Eliza and the children to be comfortable, to enjoy themselves. He urges her not to worry about paying her bills, to provide for herself. So Eliza prepares for a long, cold winter. On December 16, 1861, she shops for an "airtight stove" plus the necessary stove pipe (sold by the pound), two pipe elbows, a stove damper, and some zinc—perhaps sheets of it to place beneath the stove to insulate its hot metal legs from the wooden flooring. The purchase may have been made possible by Henry's enlistment bounty. However, Eliza's stoves led short lives. Eliza must "carry out" the parts of an old stove in 1863 and replace it.

Eliza's 1863 diary reveals that she often felt alone. Her loneliness was assuaged by visits from friends and relatives, by shopping trips, household chores, and the demands of childcare, custom sewing, and correspondence. Dipping, redipping, and wiping their pen nibs, women on the home front could easily eat up an hour a day composing letters to loved ones. Most often they would not take up their pens until the close of the day, when they were already exhausted and had poor light to write by.

"Love is a passion full of anxiety and fear," Penelope writes in a letter to the absent Odysseus. "Who would have thought a day could be so long?" The average Northern woman did not tote a gun or man barricades, but she battled for survival nevertheless. One of the hardest crosses to bear was silence: "[N]othing could make those on the home front more apprehensive than not hearing from their men, and if a longer than usual period elapsed between letters the women naturally imagined the worst."[169] Dread grew as silence oozed from one dreary day to the next.

Eliza was an average, hard-working housewife and mother. For inspiration she had the examples of other daughters of Maine, particularly Harriet Beecher Stowe and Dorothea Dix. She did not, as far as we know, emulate those exalted examples. Nor could she. She lacked the leisure, the social standing, and the education to emulate them. Nor was she a woman in the activist Amazon mold of Frances Watkins Harper, Elizabeth Cady Stanton, or Susan B. Anthony. She did not provide intelligence to the Union army as did Sarah E. Thompson of Tennessee and the formidable Pauline Cushman.* She did not, as did some fifty women, including Frances Clayton, disguise herself as a man and carry a gun.** She did not join a sewing circle producing havelocks to protect Yankee necks from Southern sun.

Following the reenlistment of most of Henry's company, the men were rewarded with a furlough. Henry wrote to Eliza from New Orleans in mid-March 1864 saying he hoped to be home soon. On May 6, having spent thirty days sipping the sweetness of family, Henry wrote from his temporary quarters at Camp Meigs, eight miles from Boston. He expected to remain there for several more days, and requested that Eliza rendez-

* Cushman was an actress who served the Union Army as a spy in 1863. Thereafter known as the "Spy of the Cumberland," she appeared in P. T. Barnum's show.
** It is estimated that more than four hundred women served in the Civil War.

Sewing havelocks for the Union troops. *Harper's Weekly*, June 29, 1861.

vous with him. The following day he wangled an unanticipated leave to visit Lowell once more, and took along his regimental acquaintance John McIver. The Scots-born McIver flirted with Eliza, and Eliza—charmed, perhaps grateful for his attentions—responded. Henry's overwrought reaction to this innocent exchange erupted in several hasty letters written as he was shipped back south.

Victorian woman was expected to be chaste, in thought, word, and deed; by modern standards, she was sexually repressed. She was to be virginal until married, and thereafter faithful to the marital bed and, blessedly, a mother but never a sexual aggressor. A Victorian woman "could only be eligible for goddess status after having been declared legally dead and sexually spiritualized."[170] In his 1857 work, *The Functions and Disorders of the Reproductive Organs*, William Acton assured readers that women were by nature sexually passive: "Love of home, children, and domestic duties are the only passions they feel," Acton assured readers.[171]

It seems far-fetched that Henry could actually believe that McIver had cuckolded him. But his lines seethe with vexed potential, fueled by the infidelity he has witnessed among his Union comrades. The *possibility* haunted him. The ten dollars that Eliza generously handed McIver becomes comparable to the handkerchief in *Othello*—a symbol of betrayal, a suggestion that festers and grows, that swells in the husband's fevered imagination until it becomes undeniable proof of evil deeds.

As the months of Henry's reenlistment crept past, Eliza grew increasingly confused about her future. She looked to sources other than friends and prayer for clues. With Queen Victoria and Mary Lincoln consulting spiritualists, what could she lose following in such eminent footsteps? At some point around early 1864, she had her horoscope told.

> "Eliza H. Foster [was] "Born under the constellation Aries. . . . is sympathetic. . . . Has loved a man before her Husband—has two children. . . . married in her 20 year, married a man that she loves more than he does her. Will outlive her husband and will marry the 2 [second] time. Has had to look out for her own living —has worked hard[,] has

not had a strong constitution. Will have a death in her family in last of [illegible] 1864 or 1865. She is very secretive. . . . Friday [is her] lucky day. Married on Friday. Look out for August & July, unfortunate months. Married [next] on Sunday evening [.] Her 2 [second] Husband will be a man that is well off. . . . Will be married twice before she is 40 years old. Will have three more children. . . . Will leave Lowell in her 31 year. . . . Will settle in the South West. Will mary [marry] a Farmer for her 2d Husband. Will lose one of her Children—younger one of three. . . . Be careful in your 36 year."

The horoscope's prediction that Eliza would "outlive her husband" suddenly became fact. During the Third Battle of Winchester, on September 19, 1864, Henry was badly wounded in the left knee. He succumbed two days later. Delay in receiving treatment may have contributed to his death.

Sharpshooters in the forest. Detail from John Bodwell's Testimonial of Service certificate, State of New Hampshire, Feb. 22, 1867. Collection of Ann Chandonnet.

The last full measure of devotion

Third Winchester was part of Gen. William T. Sherman's Shenandoah Valley Campaign. Sherman began by destroying the Confederate granary in the fertile Shenandoah so thoroughly, that, in his own phrase, "a crow would have had to carry its rations if it had flown across the Valley."[172]

Maj. Gen. Philip Sheridan planned Third Winchester carefully, relying on information from a resident spy, Quaker and teacher Rebecca Wright.[173] Sheridan's Army of the Shenandoah numbered 39,240—vastly outnumbering the 20,000 Confederates. At 3:00 a.m. on September 19, Sheridan's troops began their advance. Fierce fighting lasted all day.[174] The battle did not go precisely as Sheridan had wished; nevertheless, the Union was victorious. The Union suffered 5,020 casualties in this fierce battle, while the Confederacy suffered 3,610.[175]

The din of hard-fought battle was captured by Henry M. Stanley of the Dixie Grays. Stanley describes early dawn at Shiloh when bullets "hummed and pinged sharply by our ears, pattered through the tree tops, and brought twigs and leaves down on us."[176] As the battle progressed, "The world seemed bursting into fragments. Cannon and musket, shell and bullet, lent their several intensities to the distracting uproar. . . . I likened the cannon, with their deep bass, to the roaring of a great herd of lions; the ripping, cracking musketry, to the incessant yapping of terriers; the windy whisk of shells, and zipping of minie bullets, to the swoop of eagles, and the buzz of angry wasps."[177]

Although debate continues over casualty statistics, about 5 percent of Union and 11 percent of Confederate troops died in the war. An estimated 250,000 wounds from bullets, shrapnel, and other airborne missiles required the attention of Union physicians, compared to only 1,000 cases of wounds from swords and bayonets. Amputees on the Union side alone numbered 30,000, and medicine was sufficiently advanced to keep almost three-quarters of them alive.[178] Infection, blood loss, and shock carried off many brave souls.

News of the war. Engraving from sketches by Winslow Homer, from a *Harper's Weekly* front page.

The success of French army Capt. Claude Étienne Minié's bullet, the minié ball, multiplied casualties in the first years of the conflict. A non-rifled musket could send a bullet only about seventy yards. With a rifled barrel and a minié ball, however, the average soldier could hit a target at two hundred yards. Close-order assaults led to slaughter where combatants toppled like lines of blue or gray dominoes. Officers trained in pre-minié tactics were slow to change their ways.

"As time went on experience taught soldiers new tactics adapted to the rifle," James McPherson explains in *The Battle Cry of Freedom*. "Infantry formations loosened up and became a sort of large-scale skirmish line in which men advanced by rushes, taking advantage of cover offered by the ground to reload before dashing forward another few yards."[179] But the tactical changes came too late for Henry and thousands of others.

How quickly news of Henry's demise traveled from Virginia to

Massachusetts is unclear. But it did not take long, as F. A. Wilmot wrote to Andrew on Wednesday, September 28, 1864, informing him, at Eliza's request, of Henry's death.

The Union directed its quartermaster corps to care for and bury remains.[180] However, neither North nor South notified relatives about the deaths of enlisted men. Neither side compiled official lists of the dead after battles—although war correspondents often made their own enumerations of officers killed and wounded, and these lists were published. Non-coms pinned slips of paper bearing their names to the backs of their jackets before battle—in hopes that comrades in arms would notify their families.

Eliza's white-hot grief would have been tempered by the fact that Henry died for a cause greater than himself. Her grief may also have been assuaged by the fact that the victory at Winchester was greeted with jubilation throughout the North. Referring to the battle and its impact on the November elections, James Garfield used a rhetorical metaphor: "Phil Sheridan has made a speech in the Shenandoah Valley more powerful and valuable to the Union cause than all the stumpers of the Republic can make."[181]

How did she get the news? By 1858, boxes for mail collection began to dot the sidewalks of big cities, but house-to-house postal delivery still lay in the future. Eliza customarily walked to Lowell's post office to mail outgoing and retrieve incoming missives. Consequently, she may have opened there the envelope bringing notice of Henry's death. If she was alone in that echoing public space, she doubtless stumbled back home, threading her path through a maze of tears. To relieve families of such stress, postal officials initiated the first free home delivery of city mail before the close of the war.[182]

In whatever manner Eliza received the dreadful tidings of her husband's passing, and however she found the strength to relay those tidings to young Etta and George, she would have begun mourning rites as soon as possible. Her first act may have been to fashion black armbands for the children to wear in public until she could dress them in black head to toe. Midnight borders an inch deep were applied to handkerchiefs. Chandeliers, gilt mirror frames, and front doors of private dwellings were draped in bunting and crepe, the official "habiliments of woe."

Habiliments of woe

Respect for the dead necessitated a public show of grief. When Queen Victoria lost her beloved Albert in 1861, she donned a mourning cap and dressed in widow's weeds until her own death in 1901—setting the ultimate standard for bereavement. American and European women who lost loved ones were expected to wear unadorned black cotton, wool, or dull black silk dresses. When a husband died, his widow was expected to dress in black for at least two years.

Anticipatory mourning—gruesome as it seems to modern sensibilities—was prevalent. As a soldier left home to report for duty, family members would ceremoniously snip a lock of his hair. If he died in battle, that lock was braided into memorial jewelry or placed in a locket. The rigorous mourning of the time also favored needle "paintings" of weeping willows, weeping family, and tombstones or monuments.[183]

A loving mother, Eliza was surely concerned about the war's psychological effect on her children. Her contemporary, Margaret Junkin Preston, commented that it was "sorrowful" to watch children enact battles, take prisoners, build fortifications, perform amputations, and hobble about with a cane as if missing a limb. "It is sad indeed," Preston wrote, "that they must learn such things in their very infancy."[184]

The stresses of Eliza's domestic responsibilities were increased by the understaffed and inefficient Pension Bureau. The cogs of Union government moved "slow as cold molasses" to provide for both the wives of prisoners and the widows of the dead. In fact, the majority of women and children who applied for pensions never received any financial assistance.[185]

"Many families of Union soldiers. . . suffered grievously," wrote Hannah Geffert in the *Journal of Women's Civil War History.* "No government insurance check or pension payment cushioned the blow when a soldier was killed, and if a man was taken prisoner his pay stopped until he rejoined his outfit. Early in the War, a Connecticut newspaper reported that auctioneers were helping soldiers' wives sell their furniture 'where necessity compels the sacrifice.' Two years later a war widow in Hartford and her two children were found weak and destitute, having eaten little more than a few potatoes in the preceding week. Nearly three fourths of the charity cases in Connecticut cities during the winter of 1864-65 were military families."[186]

True, Eliza did not have to endure the effects of enemy invasion, occupation, blockade, destruction, displacement, and defeat as did her Southern counterparts. Nor was she destined to endure the dozen hard-scrabble years of Reconstruction that would beleaguer Confederate women. But she had lost her heart's own darling, her Henry. The romance and love that sustained her had drained from her life.

All Old Land Marks Are Swept Away

In the unsettled months following the war, newspapers lauded women and urged them to be strong, to lead. A *New Orleans Times* editorial of August 5, 1866, stated: "[T]he persistent crisis demands from our women more of a peculiar, and persistent heroism, than the battle field or crowded hospital. . . . Now, if ever, her countrymen need her aid. They stand bewildered and perplexed on the threshold of the great change, where all old land marks are swept away. . . . More than ever now is she called upon to be the comforter, the assistant, of the father, husband, son and brother, who go from her roof to unaccustomed toil. Let her voice be to them a trumpet note of hope and encouragement! . . . To the tender, loyal heart, and gentle hand, belong (we firmly believe) the strongest and clearest mark to be made upon this chaotic page of our eventful history."[187]

Economic inflation dogged the conflict, with prices for goods increasing 100 percent while wages grew only 50 to 60 percent. Eliza, even with a sewing machine, was unable to generate sufficient income to remain home with Henrietta and George. She had no choice but to return to the mills.

Some Northern women, however, teetered on the verge of starvation. "Many who were eligible for aid meted out to soldiers' dependents or to a part of the men's pay or to a widow's pension waited an interminable period before receiving compensation, and some did not know what they were entitled to or how to go about applying for it," writes Mary Elizabeth Massey in *Bonnet Brigades*.[188]

The wages of women doing piecework at home increased the least: "The most pitiable case was that of the seamstresses, thousands of whom were employed in making army clothing, some hired directly by the government, some by contractors under a vicious system of contracting and sub-contracting," found Lawrence F. Gross. "In the Philadelphia Armory in 1861 women were paid by the government seventeen and one-half cents for making a shirt; three years later, at the very time when prices themselves were highest, only fifteen cents. . . . In the middle of 1864 a woman in New York, using a sewing machine and furnishing her own thread, and working fourteen hours per day, made four pairs of cotton drawers at four and one-sixth cents each, or sixteen and three-fourth cents per day; another woman got five and one-half cents for making a pair of canton flannel drawers, and succeeded in making two per day."[189]

Pride, respectability, and notions of gentility embroidered the economic picture. "Nine-tenths of the sewing women were Americans who preferred to stick to the needle and starve rather than engage in domestic service, which was more remunerative, and thus put themselves on a plane of equality with the negroes and the Irish."[190]

An Oversight of the Burial

On November 5, five weeks after Henry's death, Eliza applied for a widow's pension. She was obliged to swear that she "had not, in any manner been engaged in, or aided or abetted the rebellion." Claim No. 37.424 was granted on January 30, 1865. The Department of the Interior awarded Eliza eight dollars per month, back-dated to September 21, 1864, "payable at the Pension Agency Boston." Surely having to travel to Boston to collect would have been inconvenient as well as an expense. Moreover, she had to apply separately for aid for the children, available until each turned sixteen.

There was also the matter of the bounty Henry anticipated after re-enlisting. According to his letter of January 11, 1864, he expected to receive two thousand dollars. Eliza tried to collect this sum, according to Andrew's letter of March 21, 1867. Her brother consulted John Andrews, an agent whose client instruction booklet lists among services provided the collection of "Arrears due to deceased pensioners."

Although Eliza searched no battlefields, as some widows did, seeking remains, she, too, trod the shadowed valley of grief. But she must have been urged from that seductive defile by the pressing need to care for and provide for Henrietta and George. Another cause that put steel in her backbone was recovering Henry's body.

The State of Massachusetts diligently applied itself to helping unite the living with their dead. From March through August 1862, wrote the state's adjutant-general, many of the Massachusetts dead who had served in the Army of the Potomac were embalmed and sent home for internment in family graveyards. Furthermore, the Massachusetts Association was formed "to secure . . . proper care for the wounded and disabled, and decent interment for the dead." The governor appointed Gardiner Tufts the agent for Massachusetts in Washington, to grease the ways for this organization's efforts. Tufts, commissioned on July 18, was instructed to visit all fifty-four hospitals in the District of Columbia and Fairfax and Falls Church, Virginia, in person, sending a weekly report. Tufts "was to have an oversight of the burial of the dead, and, when requested by their friends, to have the bodies forwarded, at the expense of the parties requesting it."[191]

This was an admirable effort—as far as it went. It was useless to Eliza because Tufts gave his first attention to the wounded, and did not attend on the Battle of Third Winchester.

Haunting memories

Eliza's supervisors probably never uttered the term byssinosis—even if they knew the term. Byssinosis, or brown lung disease, was caused by "fly"—a noxious combination of loose cotton and dust that filled the air at textile works, especially in the carding room. Breathing in fly over an extended period of time—like breathing in coal dust or asbestos—resulted in diminished lung capacity for many employees.[192] Inhaling fly could precipitate daily nosebleeds.

Illnesses among mill workers seemed to cluster particularly around August and September. The incidence of "bowel complaints, dysentery, typhoid and fevers" increased during these months—perhaps because of the heat and spoiled food, perhaps because some workers did not have time to gulp down breakfast before reporting to work.[193] Occupational hazards specific to male workers included testicular cancer from spindle oil.[194]

Mills were Petri dishes for infection. "The fastest way to draw the thread through the ceramic eye in the side of the old-style shuttle was using a quick, sucking 'kiss.' If the person who performed this operation had a communicable disease such as tuberculosis, the second weaver was in line to contract it. In any case, lint, dyestuffs, and other foreign matter were inhaled, hence the name 'kiss-of-death' shuttle. It is no wonder, then, that 70 percent of textile operatives died of respiratory disease at a time when only 4 percent of Massachusetts farmers died from this cause."[195]

Describing Lowell in 1845, Rev. Miles hedged on the subject of illness among mill operatives. He noted that the Massachusetts House of Representatives had been petitioned for a reduction of work hours for matters of health. However, in March 1845, a special committee was told by a Dr. Kimball, "an eminent physician of Lowell," that there was "less sickness among the persons at work in the mills than . . . among those who do not work in the mills."[196]

Although her livelihood was long associated with cotton, Eliza might by now be weaving wool. Boott was able to acquire sufficient cotton during the Civil War, but it also looked to the future; at the end of 1864, Lowell factories altered their insurance so they could work with wool.[197]

Look out for August and July

The widowed Eliza struggled to keep up with domestic chores, collect her pension, and pay her bills. Chronic ill health—perhaps migraine headaches, perhaps the first stages of tuberculosis—plagued her. The fastest seamstress working twelve hours a day, six days a week, could not earn more than two to four dollars weekly for her efforts. In March 1864, the *Washington Chronicle* delivered an editorial, "Woman and Her Work," arguing that the plight of women who worked an entire day to stitch a shirt by hand and netted only twelve cents should make citizens blush with shame. Incensed over the situation, the editor suggested that behind woman's sad state was society's refusal to permit them to hold any but the most "limited range of occupations," so that only "teaching and the ill-paid needle" were considered respectable pursuits.[198] Caught between an economic rock and a hard place, Eliza was forced to return to mill work as she mentions in her letter of March 7, 1865.

Meanwhile, the Rebellion was grinding to a halt. On April 9, Lee and Grant met at Appomattox Court House and the Army of Northern Virginia surrendered. At noon on April 14, the Stars and Stripes once again fluttered above Fort Sumter. That same night, Lincoln was assassinated at Ford's Theatre.

On April 19, 1865, Massachusetts governor John Andrew was scheduled to deliver an address in Lowell on the occasion of the dedication of the memorial for the three men killed in Baltimore on that date in 1861. Because of mourning for Lincoln, Governor Andrew requested that the ceremony be postponed. On June 17, mills closed, and a cavalry company and the old 6th Infantry regiment joined the somber parade. Andrew delivered his address from the balcony of the Merrimack House—trying to show how "history at last had brought them [Maryland and Massachusetts] into close and cordial harmony."[199]

The warmer months of 1865 must have been especially trying for Eliza as her women friends embraced their returning husbands. Between the first of May and the first of August, 279,034 veterans resumed civilian life. By August 7, the total had tripled, to 640,806.[200]

The federal government, however, proved inefficient in handling registration and disbursements for pensions. The lot of widows like Eliza was captured in *Frank Leslie's Illustrated Newspaper* on April 7, 1866, in a drawing titled "Women Wait for Pensions at the U.S. Pension Office in the New York Custom House." Exhausted, several women seat themselves on the grimy curb, heedless of their skirts.

A year later, Eliza visited Maine and began to consider remarriage. At the time, Eliza corresponded with a Sam Wily or Wiley, a widower with two children of his own.* But in two letters written in April 1867, Andrew let her know in no uncertain terms that he disapproved of Wiley.

As a result of Eliza's visit and her wish to return to Massachusetts, Mary Holt Bean finally surrendered home and possessions and moved to Lowell to live with Eliza and the children. At the same time, apparently, Mary Frances Bean took up residence with Andrew and Lizzie.

A few months later Eliza, aged thirty-two, grew ill and succumbed to what her death certificate labels "phthisis"—a term used to describe any wasting disease but usually indicating tuberculosis of the lungs.

Tuberculosis was known as consumption because it "consumed"—shrank, devoured, wasted—its victims. In the nineteenth century, physicians knew little about the mechanism of infection. The medical community was unaware that tuberculosis was spread by aspirating dried sputum circulating in the air or by contact with pus from lesions. Historian Robin Young notes that "in the 1830s, once the disease set in, 50 percent of the victims died within five years of onset; 20 percent remained chronically ill, and the rest recovered."[201] Tuberculosis then accounted for one out of every four American deaths. Victims sometimes languished for years with night sweats and diarrhea, stomach pain, vomiting, and wracking cough.

* There are Wileys and Willeys listed in *Clan MacBean*, but no Sam.

These figures changed little until after 1870, when cities began to concern themselves with modern sanitation.

The decline in Eliza's health is documented by ten surviving photographs. Eliza was a pretty, winsome girl and an attractive woman who enjoyed having her image preserved. In what seems to be a photo of her in her early teens (fig. 1), she is dressed in a closely fitted gown with a gold chain necklace at her throat, a black band on her right wrist, and two gold rings on her right hand. Her face is plump, youthful—emblematic of good

5

6

Portraits of Eliza Bean Foster, various dates. Courtesy Bethel Historical Society.

7

health. Her gaze is somewhat tentative. Perhaps this delightful portrait was posed in Biddeford, paid for with some of her first mill earnings.

In a tintype photo perhaps taken a few years later, a fur piece—likely a photographer's prop—drapes Eliza's shoulders and her loose gown (fig. 2). Her hair is elegantly dressed, and her lace collar is accented by a large cameo brooch. In what may be an engagement photo (fig. 3), Eliza wears her lustrous hair barely parted and arranged in two large side puffs, accented by curls that hang to her shoulders. The ribbon around her neck holds a pendant, which appears to be hand-colored gold. The fabric of her dress has wave-like figure, perhaps a jacquard weave; the sleeves have two layers, and the shoulders of the dress protrude over the fitted top of the sleeves.

In a photo with her baby daughter on her lap (fig. 4), perhaps taken in 1860, she has assumed a matron's coiffure—the ear curls banished. The material of her dress is a broad stripe, and her earrings are conspicuously large. Her expression is serious and her face somewhat drawn. Her hands display three large, dark rings—perhaps memorial jewelry plaited of hair. At the same sitting, she had a second pose taken of her alone, with different collar and earrings (that photo is not shown here).

A family portrait, taken when Henry was on leave in the spring of 1864 depicts the parents standing behind the two children, steadying their heads during the long photographic exposure (see page 63).

After Henry's death in September 1864, Eliza used photography to document her new role in life. Perhaps she mailed copies to relatives to demonstrate just who she had become. In one pose, she wears mourning dress, cape, and lace veil (fig. 5). Her expression is mournful, but her face is full and seemingly healthy. Her coiffure is soberly parted in the middle, the puffs of hair are somewhat restrained. In another photograph, apparently somewhat later, she wears a more somber veil plus a black hat tied with a large bow under her chin, which seems less broad (fig. 6). She had no mirror (she writes that hers was broken); perhaps she wished to see herself as others saw her.

In the final portrait, she no longer wears black (fig. 7), a clue that dates it to late 1865—at least a year after Henry's demise. Eliza poses listlessly, expressionless, hugging Henrietta to her side as if she needed support. Eliza's face is pinched, and her eyes sunken; she is obviously ill. Even her distinctive, dark eyebrows are fading from view. On the reverse of this photo, Etta later inscribed, "My poor, poor Mother."

Science and sense

"Consumption"—a term applied to a wide variety of lung complaints including tuberculosis—took a high toll among mill workers as well as enlisted men. Tuberculosis cost the Union army 6,497 men; many additional cases were discharged in questionable health with the victims succumbing later. No reliable treatment was known at the time. Ordering bed rest, medicos claimed that they could cure not only "Consumptive difficulties" but also cholera, dropsy, scrofula, asthma, St. Vitus' dance, pleurisy, nightmare, inflammation, and "Suppression of Urine" with remedies made from "harmless vegetables."[202]

In the year of Eliza's death, Lowell *Daily Courier* advertisements touted a multitude of patent medicines and supposed cures. On May 21, 1867, for example, C. A. Richards & Co. was selling Extract of Rye, a remedy able to "carry its lubricating and fattening effects to the lungs." Extract of Rye was said to "throw off disease" better than "common whisky." On August 12, 1867, Dr. P. B. Trask recommends China root tonic and Cherry Balsam, a medicated vapor.

Decades later, the *Courier* continued to accept advertisements disguised as news items. Such items attracted attention with enticing titles like "No consumptive will die so long as he can digest and assimilate food." Such a piece, published Nov. 8, 1895, put the blame for illness on the patient's diet: "Consumption is starvation, slow or rapid, as may be. The first symptom is, not necessarily a cough, but a tendency to lose flesh, to grow thin. Stop this tendency now . . . Increase the flesh and the danger is past. What is needed is an especially-prepared food. . . . Such an article is the Shaker Digestive Cordial, made by the Shaker Community of Mt. Lebanon, N.Y. . . . One may have consumption and not die of it. This is science and sense. The success of this new remedy proves it." Countless sufferers like Eliza wasted their earnings to subject themselves to disgusting and useless remedies in their desperate fight to live.

Tuberculosis reached its destructive peak at the end of the nineteenth century, when it carried off one-seventh of the human race. As late as the

1940s, this fiendish malady continued to cause more deaths than any other contagion. Fulfilling Harriet Beecher Stowe's prediction, Eliza succumbed to consumption on August 20, 1867.

The Factory Girl As I Knew Her

Too late to benefit Eliza, Massachusetts passed a ten-hour workday law for women and children in 1874. In 1905, almost four decades after Eliza's death, the Rev. George Whitaker of Lowell delivered a series of talks titled "The Factory Girl As I Knew Her Nearly Forty Years Ago." He eulogized an idealized character, perhaps more out of nostalgia than reformist sentiment. Whitaker noted that mill employees attended church regularly and "were devout."[203]

> She was nearly 13,000 strong, which constituted more than half the female population of the city, whose entire population was 40,928. She was not a native of Lowell—except in small proportion. She came here to earn her daily bread from Nova Scotia, Maine, New Hampshire and Vermont. Her home was in the corporation boarding house, where as many as 100 boarded together in some houses and six occupied the same room. . . .
>
> The factory girl was usually bright, earnest and self-reliant to a good degree," Whitaker continued. "She became an earnest worker and interested in all questions involving a cultivated mind and religious life. . . . Her life was laborious and earnest, but her ideals were high, and her Christian work commendable and wholesome. Her good influence will long remain."[204]

Rev. Whitaker was not the only one to memorialize Lowell's factory girl. In 1882, Ben Butler became governor of Massachusetts. In his inaugural address, Butler had stated one of his hopes for the future of the state: protection for working women and children.[205] He had not forgotten those spirited mill-girl conversations he had heard as a boy around his mother's boardinghouse table.

HENRY CHARLES FOSTER (1834–1864)

HENRY CHARLES FOSTER, WHO WOULD IN DUE TIME marry Eliza Bean, entered the world on July 14, 1834, in Castleton, Vermont.* His parents were Samuel Foster and Clarinda Patterson Foster. The surname Foster may derive from "Forster" or "Forester"—common in Scotland and the north of England, and perhaps originally from the Old French *forestier*.[206] A compilation of English surnames in 1601 and 1602 finds the name existing in the counties of Hampshire, Buckinghamshire, Lancashire, Middlesex, Nottinghamshire, Durham, and Yorkshire, as well as in the city of London.[207] An alternative ancestor to the English name stems from the Old French *forceter,* or scissors-maker. The American line spawning Henry begins with Benjamin Foster, who in 1699 was granted land in Kittery, on the Maine bank of the Piscataqua River.[208]

Castleton nestles among the rocks and rills of Rutland County, seven miles east of Vermont's border with New York State. It was chartered in

* On his record of marriage, Henry's birthplace is given as Castleton. However, his infantry discharge certificate dated January 1864 gives his birthplace as Plymouth, Vermont—a locale thirty-seven miles away, in a different county.

1761, with settlers beginning to trickle in during the spring of 1767. Slate and marble quarries pocked the landscape, while farmers raised cattle and sheep. In the second half of the nineteenth century, tourists visited Castleton to enjoy its lakes and scenery—just as they frequented Andrew Bean's hometown, Bethel, Maine.

Like Maine, Vermont was linked to Massachusetts by the textile web. Before the Civil War, sheep farming was common, with flocks ranging in size from fifty to a hundred head. However, as the demand for wool increased during and after the war, sheep farmers in the American West and Australia began to supply fleeces and Vermont's farmers shifted to dairy herds. Vermont butter and cheese were soon moving by railroad to Boston.[209]

In 1845, when Henry was eleven, Samuel Foster died and was buried in Plymouth Notch, leaving the family in dire straits. The older offspring soon dispersed. William, for example, married in 1847, Mabelia in 1851. Henry's mother went to live with her married daughter, Clara, in Poultney. In Clara Lynch's household resided Moses Lynch, Clara's widowed father-in-law. In what was likely a marriage of convenience, Henry's widowed mother and Moses wed.

Nothing is recorded of young Henry's education, although his penmanship demonstrates prolonged instruction. He could have been apprenticed to a house painter. As a teen, Henry could have attended the academy in Cavendish, twenty miles away.[210] The Foster correspondence proves all family members were literate—although mastery of spelling varied considerably.

By February 1856, Henry, now a skilled painter, had moved to Lowell, where he would soon meet Eliza Bean. The couple wed in December of that year. The newlyweds proved a sociable couple who spent a good deal of leisure time "calling"—visiting friends. The evidence for this is not only the constant stream of friends and relatives (some of whom stayed the night) cited in Eliza's 1863 diary, but also the existence of an engraved card: "Mr. & Mrs. H. C. Foster, Lowell Mass." The lower left corner bears two names, one above the other: "Henry C. Foster. Eliza H. Bean." Less expensive than wedding invitations (or, indeed, a wedding), these "wedding cards" acquainted old friends with new unions. The Fosters' address during 1857 is unknown, but their address for September 1859 is recorded on a receipt by Dr. John C. Dalton for his house call at No. 12 Chestnut Street in Lowell.

White with cotton and dark with slaves

Seven years and two children after his marriage, Henry enlisted in the Massachusetts infantry.* The seeds of the Civil War were sown long before Henry's own birth. One might almost say they were inadvertently broadcast by Eli Whitney, the Yale graduate and mechanical genius who invented the cotton gin, a device that ginned, or removed seeds from, cotton bolls. Whitney, son of a Massachusetts farmer, observed cotton cultivation while teaching in Georgia. He said his invention was inspired by watching a hungry cat trying to pull a chicken through a fence—and able to extract only feathers, a paw full at a time.[211]

Whitney also juggled notions concerning interchangeable parts and efficiency. His ideas affected how factories operated, how firearms were produced, and how costs were estimated. He patented his gin on March 14, 1794, but his patent was not validated until 1807. He hoped to make his fortune with this invention, but the gist of the device was soon circulating beyond his legal reach. The gin was able to remove seeds fifty times faster than a field hand. It had the nation-shaking effect of turning "the South white with cotton and dark with slaves."[212]

Colonial Yankees filled their coffers producing rum that was traded for slaves. Generations of rum profits were soon poured into factories. Since cleaned cotton could be produced faster using Whitney's gin, cotton prices

---

* Not all records of his service are dependable; for example, a roster of "Lowell's Civil War Soldiers and Sailors" at the University of Massachusetts Center for Lowell History is both incomplete and erroneous: it shows his rank at mustering out as private, places him in the 32nd Infantry, and gives his date of discharge as June 29, 1865.

dropped and demand rose. Southern agriculture exploded. The slave population boomed from under a million in 1793 to four million just before the Civil War, and the value of a plantation field slave multiplied from $200 to $2,000—while his life span dwindled.[213]

The war gave slaves new opportunities to flee their masters. These runaways forced the North to define the dimensions of freedom. What had Jefferson meant by "justice and liberty for all"? Black journalist and abolitionist Frederick Douglass assumed that fighting for the Union would give African-Americans the right to citizenship: "Once let the black man get upon his person the brass letters 'U.S.', let him get an eagle on his buttons and a musket on his shoulder and bullets in his pocket, and there is no power on earth which can deny that he has earned the right to citizenship in the United States."

In 1861, Gen. Benjamin Franklin Butler opened the door for fighting blacks when he declared three escaped slaves "contrabands of war." Warring with doubts, headaches, and sleepless nights, Lincoln seconded Butler's motion in an article of war passed on March 13, 1862.[214] But these actions did not make life easy for black soldiers.* Their pay was lower than that of their white counterparts. They were not allowed to hold officer rank. They were often treated with skepticism and ridicule, and given the more tedious and dangerous assignments.[215]

Butler's adopted state, Massachusetts, was slow to take a firm stand on slavery. In September 1862, more than a year after Henry enlisted, the Republican State Convention met in Worcester. Convention president A. H. Bullock stated he had learned much since Sumter, including the fact that "African slavery on this continent is so intimately connected with the war, that the two things can no longer be considered apart." The committee on resolutions adopted a resolution that "as slavery was a principal support of the rebellion, slavery should be exterminated."

* According to David Blight's *Race and Reunion*, 188,571 African-American soldiers and sailors served in the Civil War. About 137,000 died, more than 90 percent of them of disease. This 20 percent death rate was 3 percent higher than the death rate among white troops (p. 193).

In humility and mud

Born in Maine, John A. Andrew (1818–1867) graduated from Bowdoin College in 1837. After moving to Boston to study law, Andrew helped organize the antislavery Free Soil Party in 1848. He was elected to the legislature in 1858 and to the first of five terms as governor in 1860. Energetic and efficient, as soon as he took office in January 1861, Andrew sensed war in the wind and prepared the militia for duty. When on April 15 Lincoln called for troops to protect the nation's capital, two Massachusetts regiments were mustered on Boston Common the following day, and on April 17 were on their way to Washington.[216]

Spurred on by untarnished memories of Revolutionary triumphs, the Bay State moved quickly to raise its assigned contingent of 15,000. A town meeting in Weymouth agreed on a bounty of $150 per volunteer. Governor Andrew encouraged five hundred men from California, as well as runaway slaves living in Buffalo, New York, to join Massachusetts regiments.[217] The adjutant-general of the commonwealth, William Schouler, received fevered inquiries from all over the state, seeking recruiting papers and guidance in organizing regiments. Between July 8 and August 1, Schouler wrote more than five hundred letters to towns like Haverhill, Worcester, and Rockport. Among those letters were instructions to the Hon. H. Hosford, Mayor of Lowell. To Hosford he wrote, "Should Lowell furnish its quota, and other towns should fail, to Lowell will be the honor." Another correspondent inquired specifically about commissions. Schouler replied matter-of-factly, "Let Lowell fill up the companies, and then the commissions will come."[218]

Enlisting was easy. Training was cursory. When Maj. Gen. John C. Frémont received reinforcements in Missouri at the end of July 1861, he called his new regiments "literally the rawest ever got together . . . entirely unacquainted with the rudiments of military exercise."[219]

The Massachusetts legislature convened an extra session in May to discuss matters including uniforms, commissions for regimental and line

officers, a home guard, and aid to dependent families. A bill giving aid
to the families of volunteers permitted any town or city to raise money by taxation to aid parents, wives and children under sixteen of any
Massachusetts man in military service. The aid decreed was one dollar
per week for each parent, brother, sister, child, or wife "who, at the time
of his enlistment, was dependent on him for support." Total aid was not to
exceed twelve dollars a month.[220]

Henry Foster was mustered in as a private on October 18, 1861, to
serve for three years. Unlike many enlistees, he could write and read, and
his education and manners probably made him stand out among his fellow enlistees. Nearly as soon as the regiment completed basic training,
Henry received promotion. His rank advanced from private to corporal
on December 1, 1861, while he sailed for Louisiana aboard the transport
Constitution. The promotion was retroactive to November 1.

This or none

There is no evidence that Henry enlisted to free the slaves. His surviving
letters never mention slavery. Like so many of his contemporaries, when
he uses the word "nigger," it is usually in a slighting or derogatory context.
Until he was stationed in New Orleans, Henry was doubtless unfamiliar
with both African-Americans and slavery except in print. The North had
liberated its slaves shortly after the Revolution. Northerners argued that
there should be no shackles in "the land of the free," and many had positive impressions of the courage demonstrated by black soldiers and sailors
during both the Revolution and the War of 1812.[221]

On the other hand, some Northerners were vehemently opposed to
blacks in uniform. John Dunban, a member of the 77th Pennsylvania
Veteran Volunteers, was stationed in Victoria, Texas, in the fall of 1865,
when he expressed his opposition in a letter to his family: "There are negro troops around here. The citizens say that they want us white troops to
stay until the negroes are all un armed for they say that they cannot trust
a negro. They are quite uneasy. They wants to get rid of them day before

"View of Decatur Street River Front and Lugger Landing from Roof of Custom House," salt print by Jay D. Edwards, c. 1860. Collections of the Louisiana State Museum; used by permission.

yesterday. I was talking to an old man on this subject, and he said for his part that he was tired of them and was advising them to go North. I told him that we would kill them if they would come up there."[222]

Henry took up arms to preserve the Union. That prime motive is demonstrated again and again by what he writes, as well as by his choosing stationery headed "This or none" for his letter of October 23, 1862.

New Orleans was a cosmopolitan city of 700,000 when Henry stepped ashore. Its residents included about 4,000 Jews—the seventh-largest Jewish population in the U.S.[223] About 38,000 of the residents were foreign-born traders and businessmen from places like Poland and Ireland. And there was a large, sophisticated, free black community—many of whom initially enlisted on the Confederate side.[224] In this melting pot, seditious language and actions were rife. Smugglers dealt in goods like quinine, percussion caps and shoes. Unscrupulous characters masqueraded as city police in order to gain entrance to homes and confiscate property.[225] Under the constraints of the Union blockade, its citizens were anxious and hungry. Some slaveowners could not feed their slaves.[226]

In New Orleans, Henry's days were divided between picket duty and guarding C.S.A. prisoners. On April 27, 1863, Henry was promoted to sergeant, with the rank retroactive to March 10. He was discharged January 1, 1864, at New Iberia, Louisiana, a necessary formality before he could reenlist as a veteran volunteer. It was not patriotism as much as a powerful sense of duty and camaraderie that sealed his decision to reenlist. His oath of identity paper dated Franklin, Louisiana, January 10, 1864, describes him as twenty-nine years of age, five foot nine, with a light complexion, blue eyes, and dark brown hair. Reenrolling on the same day was a blue-eyed, Scots-born carpenter, John A. McIver, who would become Henry's friend.

Although letters from kin infrequently reached him, Henry wrote home long and often during the next three months. At last leaving behind the backwaters of Louisiana, Henry marched into the thick of things. His first three years of infantry service afforded him scant experience in battle.

Third Winchester

Union troops began assembling around Winchester, Virginia, in early September 1864. During the Third Battle of Winchester, on September 19, the 26th Massachusetts marched with the 2nd Brigade, 2nd Division, 19th Corps. During the initial phase of the battle, Henry and his compatriots fought in the First Woods, where Henry was severely wounded in the left knee. The Union infantry had bogged down in Berryville Canyon during that morning of fierce fighting.

Winchester nestles in the Shenandoah Valley, seventy-five miles northwest of Washington, D.C. The Valley Pike (today's Route 11) funneled armies north and south. Built at a strategic crossroads in a fast-growing region, the town changed hands more than seventy times during the war. The valley was a fruited plain, a cornucopia of grain and grist mills linked to the East by roads and railroad. Stonewall Jackson said of the Shenandoah, "If this Valley is lost, Virginia is lost."

For most of the war, Winchester was in Union hands, but the prevailing sentiment among residents was Confederate. As the Frederick County Courthouse in Winchester changed hands, soldiers (prisoners or patients from both sides) inscribed their names, drawings, and curses on the walls.

After suffering the knee wound on September 19, Henry grappled with awful death for two days. He may have had no medical attention for some time after being wounded, as he fell into Confederate hands. Henry may have received neither food nor water as he waited. He finally reached a Union hospital, where surgeons amputated his leg on September 21. He died during the surgery or shortly thereafter.

The war to combat wounds

Throughout the war, mortality from disease and wounds was higher than that from bullets and bayonets. Fairly reliable mortality numbers for the Union armies give totals of 67,000 killed in action, 43,000 lost to wounds, and 224,000 to disease.[227]

The care of Union wounded had improved greatly after the fall of 1862 when Jonathan Letterman was commissioned medical director of the Army of the Potomac. Letterman instituted a better medical supply plan, organized an ambulance corps, and reformed the field-hospital system. He also advocated triage—prioritizing casualties by severity of wounds. Not all these improvements went into effect overnight, but his new system showed its worth at Fredericksburg in December 1862.[228]

Letterman's enthusiasm and determination could not erase all suffering. Countless horrific wounds were caused by big, soft lead bullets fired at short distances. The minié ball, a .58 caliber bullet weighing an ounce or more, could hit a target a mile away.[229] When the minié was fired, the hollow base of the inch-long bullet expanded, hacking and mutilating tender flesh.[230] In battle, minié balls "could fill the air like swarms of deadly insects, ripping gruesome wounds wherever they struck. Battlefield amputations were the most common surgery. . . . Doctors, many with minimal training and no credentials, simply removed mangled limbs and tried to stop bleeding. Then the second war would begin—the battle to survive disease and infection."[231]

Henry did not win that second battle.

Referring to Third Winchester, Walt Whitman wrote," The papers are full of puffs [spin], etc., but the truth is, the largest proportion of [the] worst cases got little or no attention. We receive them here [in Washington, D.C.] with their wounds full of worms—some all swelled and inflamed. Many of the amputations have to be done over again."[232]

When Confederate general John Hood was wounded in his right upper thigh at Chickamauga, minié bullets destroyed five inches of bone. The Union Army recorded almost 175,000 gunshot wounds to extremities during the war, leading to 30,000 amputations. Three-quarters of the patients survived.[233] Location of the wound was an indication of chance of survival; knee amputations carried a 58 percent fatality rate.[234]

A Warrior's Shroud

Shortly after Henry's demise, his faithful comrade Charles Henry Richardson found and identified his body, supervised his burial, and wrote to Eliza of the circumstances. (Richardson's letter appears on pp. 417.)

It is possible that, to spare Eliza, Richardson hedged on the facts. Without Richardson's searching for his friend and identifying him, Henry's remains could have been unceremoniously dumped into a pit. Because of the thousands of wounded, almost every substantial edifice in Winchester had been turned into a hospital, so Richardson—himself wounded—covered a great deal of ground in order to render his friend this final favor.

Last rites and proper burial were important to Victorian sensibilities. But they were often impossible on the battlefield or even for days after a battle.

A sensitive man, Clark Edwards of the Fifth Maine makes many references in his letters home to the screams of the wounded, to lack of medical care for the wounded, and to sleeping close to the wounded or dead. He sometimes brings aid to the wounded himself.[235] Memories of the wounded bring on shudders and tears, he writes to his wife. In order to make sure the dead are properly cared for, Edwards sits by the bedside of one dying man for whom his superior has personally purchased a metal coffin and, on another occasion, orders and oversees the burial of a wounded Rebel incinerated alive in a hospital by his own comrades.[236]

Richardson specifies the surgery Henry received, to assure Eliza that he received medical treatment—even if it was delayed. His reference to Henry's interment in a "warriors shroud" was surely intended to reassure her that he had been buried with a respectful covering. She would have read or heard reports that many soldiers who fell on the battlefield were liberated of uniforms and boots by desperate survivors in tatters or by the enemy. Abial Edwards repeatedly documented the Confederates' treatment of Union wounded: "The Rebels robbed all of our wounded they could even striping them naked" and "the Rebels . . . robbed our dead & wounded of all their valuables."[237] When burial details were insufficient or entirely lacking, thousands of casualties lay on the bloody ground until their remains were nearly skeletal—and then were thrown into mass graves, helter-skelter. In an era long before DNA testing, the remains of many were never identified. At Salisbury National Cemetery, in North Carolina, for instance, 99 percent of the 12,000 Union dead were unidentified.[238]

If their comrades were not present to name them, the dead were identified by photographs, diaries, or letters carried in knapsacks or bestowed about their persons. Anxious to have their identities known, soldiers took the precaution of inscribing their names in pocket testaments. Others affected the gold and silver pins advertised in *Harper's Weekly* and *Leslie's*. Soldiers who wore rings often scratched their names and units inside.[239] Others scratched their names in the lead backing of their belt buckles.[240]

Neither North nor South provided soldiers with identification tags or "dog tags," a system that was not adopted in the U.S. until 1914 and

Brass stencil of Henry C. Foster's name, used to identify his uniforms and belongings. Courtesy Bethel Historical Society.

World War I. Union sutlers hawked identification disks of brass, pewter, or lead, bored with a hole for a lanyard or neck chain. The most popular medallion featured an eagle, a shield, and the increasingly ironic phrase "War of 1861" on one side. For a small fee, a sutler hand-stamped the soldier's name, regiment and company on the reverse.[241] Hometowns and even lists of engagements were added to some disks.[242]

Soldiers fallen in battle could sometimes be identified by stencils inked onto their clothing, commonly inside the right sleeve. Both Billy Yank and Johnny Reb used metal stencil plates to mark their belongings—jackets, canteens, haversacks, and personal items such as camp desks or folding checkerboards.[243] The basic marking kit consisted of two plates, a stencil brush, and a bottle of permanent ink. Some stencils gave both the soldier's name and regiment. Henry's bore only his name.

In the dark days immediately after the shock of widowhood, Eliza may have been given some comfort by the knowledge that the desperately contested battle of Third Winchester proved a turning point in the war. In the long run, it marked the decline of Confederate power. Eliza's successful campaign to bring Henry's remains to Lowell must also have been a comfort.

In several letters, Henry had urged Eliza to buy a small farm in Dracut, the sprawling rural community north of Lowell. Perhaps she chose to postpone such an important purchase until he could be at her side—or perhaps she delayed because she was reluctant to leave her circle of friends, and anticipated that being closer to her conceited sister-in-law Mabelia would prove a poor substitute for their warmth. Perhaps she had had enough of the drudgery and isolation of farm life during her childhood.

A Superabundance of Chronicles.

Letters penned by the Fosters, the Beans, and their extended kinship circle are time capsules of social history. The correspondence records information ranging from weather to field work, from travel plans to intimate thoughts. These exchanges, supplemented by Eliza Foster's 1863 diary and Lewellyn Bean's diary, bring to life the human dimensions of a New England family in the nineteenth century, on the verge of, and in the midst of, the war that split their nation asunder.

Before the war, it was work that motivated the family to travel. For example, in the spring of Henry's twentieth year, he left his home state of Vermont to seek employment elsewhere. Proof comes in the form of May 1854 letters addressing him in Fulton, New York—letters from his mother and his older sister Clara. Though these letters do not spell out Henry's business there, the 1850 census identifies his oldest brother, David C. Foster, as a Fulton resident, suggesting that Henry was most likely working with him as a carpenter or house painter.

> *Poultney [VT]   Sept. the 2   1854*
>
> *Dear Son*
>
> *As it has ben [been] so long since we received your letter I think you must about give up looking for one from us for I had from you but I can tell you it was received with much pleasure and gratification to hear from you all once more. When you wrote to Clara you wrote that Chalon [Henry's older brother] was writing to me so we watched the post office all summer but no letter.[244] We are all well as usual here now. Dana [Fox] and Mabelia and their*

little Lucinda has been here and gone holme [to Dracut, Mass.] last week. They did not stay here but a week then Chancy and Clara [Lynch] went over the mountain with them and they went to Ludlow and tok [took] the car. I was in hopes to hear how they got home before I wrote but I thought I would not wait. They went up to Davids and McMaes and all round. Old Mr. Spaulding is dead and Michael Madden, and George Potter has got back from California and Isaihas [sic] has moved up to the old place where his father used to live you know up in the woods there up above the lime kill [kiln]. Well and Lovina has come over here again and wants to stay all winter and allways if we will keep her. Well I must tell you something about the times here for they are rather hard for poor folks and we have a great many here that are dependant on the farmers for all they have to eat. Butter is 20/cents pound and Potatoes 100 Doll. [$1.00] Per Bushel but we sell them for 90 cents. It is Because there has bee[n] such a drought. Some of our potatoes that are on the dry ground that was planted early are not bigger than walnuts and only 2 or 3 in a hill. We could sell I dont know how many bushell every day but we cant. We only supply 4 or 5 familys and I am a fraid we shant hold out at that long but we begin to feell encouraged. When we got up this morning it rained and it rained all the forenoon so that it begins to look more like live [sic]. I never knew such a drought before and most every one say[s] so here. . . .*

I feell very anxious for you all that you might do well and be happy here and (on eternily). . . .

Write all of you.

[Clarinda Patterson Foster Lynch]

The earliest document in the families' paper trail is, however, not a letter but a sheet of factory rules collected in July 1851. Eliza Bean

---

* Boston & Maine did not construct the Hampden Railroad to Ludlow until the early 1900s, so Clara probably refers here to a stagecoach rather than a railroad car.

saved her copy of Pepperell Manufacturing's General Regulations—guidelines that included even directives for her after-hours activities. Pepperell's broadside stipulates that "ten hours of actual labor should be a legal day's work." Such details supplement the capsule biographies in previous chapters.

The majority of the extant letters of this mid-nineteenth-century trio are transcribed here. In the documents that follow, original spelling is reproduced exactly. Editorial intrusions have been kept to a minimum; the use of "sic" has mainly been restricted to the first occasion of a common error, and bracketed interpolations have been used sparsely.

Clarinda Patterson Foster Lynch. mother of Henry Foster. Courtesy Bethel Historical Society.

Hard Times for Poor Folks

Henry's married sister, Mabelia, was a faithful correspondent. Her chatty prewar letter supplies interesting details about sibling relationships, health, moral values, and the New England economy. Mabelia's injunction to her brother to be "good . . . prudent and steady" typifies the tone of women's letters to absent male relatives. Women not only feared for their loved ones' safety but also fretted that the men would acquire bad habits such as drinking, gambling, and whoring. After the war began, "mothers, wives and sweethearts sensed that military experiences would change them [their men] but hoped that the change would not be for the worse. Many also worried lest they abandon their religious training instilled in youth."[245] While her attorney husband Theophilus served the Confederacy, Harriet Perry beseeched him in this cautionary vein: "Don't forget your prayers my darling—read your Bible[,] every things [*sic*] depends on our heartfelt petitions—I desire above [all] things for you to be a model man in all things, especially in being moral & religious—Try to live every day for Heaven."[246]

Dracut Mass Jan. 27th, 1855

Dear Brother

I am seated with pen in hand to address a few lines to you and glad of [the] chance to answer a letter from you, for I had given up ever hearing from you again. I was very sorry that you could not come and see me for I had partly made up my mind for it [the visit] but disappointment is [the] lot of us all. I hope it will be so that we shall meet some time. My health and also Danas and Lucindas is very good at present and such a rogue you never see as L is. She is in all manner of mischief. She is as sly as a Fox.

I don't think of much news that will interest you only it [is] very hard times. Provisions of all sorts are very high. Flour is 13 dollars per barrell and other things in pportion [sic]. Hard times for <u>poor</u> folks. The factorys [mills] are dismising many of the employes [sic] and beggary and robery [sic] are the effects of it and I dont know what our country is coming to if matters go on as they are now. The people are geting waked up [to the truth of the situation] some here but not quite so much as they ought to be. Tell Chalon [Mabelia and Henry's older brother] that he need not entirely forget his sister if [although] he has got a family to look after for I should be very *happy to hear from him or see him either and so [to] give my love to them will you and tell [them] to write.*

I have had a letter from Mother [Clarinda Patterson Foster Lynch] since you went away from there. The small pox has raged to some extent in this town and Lowell but I believe it is abating somewhat now. It has been fatal where it has been.

It is geting late and I must close for I cant think of any more to write. Be a good boy Henry and prudent and steady and come see me as soon as you can. I shall be glad to see you any time. Write soon. This from your sister and well wisher

M B Fox

It has been some time since I wrote this letter and not having an oportunity [sic] of sending it I thought [I] would write a little more. I received a letter from Clara last week. She was better than when you were there but not well [enough] so she has not tried to do her work. It is very pleasant here to [too] hot for most part of the time. It is very hard weather here this winter rain and snow [,] snow and rain all the time. Pretty much of the time no sleighing. . . . News I have not much now only Dana has drove off a cow [to its new owner] that they sold for 50. dollars yesterday, and some go higher than that. . . .

The sly Fox was not long for this world. Born October 22, 1852, Lucinda Ardelia Fox died on August 30, 1855. Reading between the lines of a letter written by Henry on November 23, 1862, Mabelia and Dana lost another infant at that time: Henry Foster Fox, born June 7, 1862, died September 19, 1862.

Our Life Is But a Shadow

By February, 1856, it is clear Henry has shifted residence again, this time to Massachusetts, because his sister Clara addresses him there. Her letter seems to suggest he moved to Lowell during the previous week. She is familiar with Lowell because she spent ten years there, as her letter of February 6, 1857, confirms. In an admirably even hand and a most sisterly tone, Clara cautions him about urban temptations, invoking the admonition of Ecclesiastes 6:12.

Feb. 16, 1856 [Poultney, VT]

Dear Brother Henry

How do you do this afternoon. We are all well here as usual and it is most a delightfull day. It really seems like spring but I tell you it has been cold enough here most of the time for two months. Oh! Dear there is such a noise I dont know what I write for Chancy has just brought home the [window] sash for our new house and is fixing to paint them and they all have a word to say about it and I am very tired to [too].

We recved [sic] your letter one week ago and was very glad to hear from you for we have been very anxious about you or I have at any rate for I know a little something about the society of Lowell and I know too that there are a great many temptations laid in the path of young men that are not in the way of ladies but till there is no necessity of being lead astray if you are guarded as you should be, by the grace and love of God and if you are not do seek to be immeadiately [sic] for life is so uncertain it is dangerous to delay. There are a great many dying around us and we must die sooner or later and it is of the utmost importance that we be prepared for our life is but a shadow that soon passeth away and is no more. . . .

Your Sister C. F. L.

On August 23, 1856, Henry's mother appends some petulant lines to a letter by his sister Clara:

Dear Son

As C thinks she cant cant write any more I thought I would finish out this half sheet We received a letter from Chalon dated the 14 [?] of July. He writes he has got up [erected] his house and moved into it in May so he went to work for the State again and has worked there all Sumer [sic] but about 4 weeks and he works on his house nights and mornings. He says he has considerable time to work. He wanted I should tell him where you was so it seems he has not had no letter from you since you were there to Lowell. . . . As he seemed to express so much Shame to himself for not writing in so long a time perhaps he has writen to you before this time. He said he would wite [write] one a month but we have not had none yet. He sent a paper about 2 weeks ago but what is the matter you dont go and see your Sister [Mabelia] oftener. She complains of you because you don't come there [to Dracut]. We are expecting a letter from her soon. I must stop.

From your Mother and well wisher O Henry be Steady do.

[Clarinda Foster Lynch]

Where Thou Lodgest

Nineteenth-century courtship leaned to the circumspect. For instance, when Noah Blake courted Sarah Trowbridge in 1805, he handed her a Bible verse at Meeting. He used The Second Epistle of John as his envoy: "And now I beseech thee, lady, not as though I wrote a new commandment unto thee, but that which we had from the beginning, that we love one another." Noah waited impatiently for an answer. Sarah kept the lad on tenterhooks until the following Sunday, when she passed him a folded paper at the conclusion of service. Reaching the privacy of home, Noah opened the note, which read only, "First chapter of Ruth, 16." Jittery Noah had to ask his mother for the Bible box to research that reference. Fortunately for the eager suitor, his mother knew the verse by heart: "Entreat me not to leave thee, or to return from following after thee: for whither thou goest, I will go: and where thou lodgest, I will lodge: thy people will be my people, and thy God my God." When he heard those encouraging words, Noah didn't stay for dinner; he made a beeline for Sarah's house.[247]

Henry Foster and Eliza Bean, at mid-century, likely had a more direct courtship from the outset. Henry obviously sent Clara some inkling of his growing intimacy with Eliza, for his sister jests with him on the subject. On October 31, 1856, she wrote, "Well Henry as it is past the season for harvesting Beans I hope you will go over and see Mabelia and tell her what is in your letter so I shall not have to write all these particular[s] to her." In her next letter, dated December 19, Clara whistles the same tune: "How does your Bean come on. It [it's] rather bad weather for Beans though."

"Bad weather" notwithstanding, Clara was already behind times. On December 5, 1856, Henry wed Eliza Howard Bean, an event of which he quickly informed Clara and his mother. Clara replies:

> *Poultney [VT] Dec. 20th 1856*
>
> *Dear Brother*
>
> *We recved your letter one week ago last night and although I had but just then written to you which letter you have probably recved before this still I thought I would write again and not wait so long as I did before. We were very much surprised to hear that you were married, but every body will do so and you thought you would follow the fashion and I hope you will never have cause to regret the step you have taken either of you. From what you wrote it would seem as if you both have had sufficient time and opportunity to become acquainted with each others tastes and habits so that you need not be decved [deceived] and I trust it has not been the object of either of you to decve. If you have you will have to suffer the consequenses your selves. Oh: Henry do try to be a faithful and loving Husband but while I thus entreat you I fear that you lack one at least of the principle prerequisites to enable you to be such an one as you should be and that is the grace of God in the heart. If your wife is not already a Christian I hope you will make up your*

minds deliverately [sic] and with one accord to seek for that Pearl of great price without which you cannot enjoy the things of this world as you can with it. Henry excuse the plainness and ernest maner [manner] with which I address you and remember that I am your sister and consequently feel a deep interest in your welfare and a strong desire for your happiness. . . .

Forgive me if I have trespassed upon your patience and although these lines have been written with a trembling hand and throbing [sic] heart do not I beg of you pass them unheeded by as an idle tale. . . . hopeing that you and your wife will write to us often for although you do live in Lowell we shall claim her as one of the family though she may not think she is.

Clara

Reaction from Henry's mother to her son's marriage is conspicuous by its absence.

A Good Long Letter Write

Don't go to the theatre lecture or ball
But stay in your room tonight.
Deny yourself of the friends that call
And a good long letter write.

Write to your dear old mother at home
Who sits when the day is done
With folded hands & downcast eyes
And thinks of her absent one.

Don't selfishly scribble "excuse my haste"
I've scarce the time to write
Lest her brooding thoughts go wandering back
To many a bygone night—

When she lost her needed sleep & rest

And every breath was a prayer

That God would leave her darling babe

To her tender love and care

Don't think that the young and giddy friends

Who make your pastime gay

Have half the anxious thoughts for you

That your mother has to-day.

The duty of writing don't put off

Let sleep and pleasure wait—

Lest the letter for which she has waited & longed

Be a day or an hour too late

For your sad old mother at home

With locks most all turned white

Is longing to hear from her absent one

So write her a letter tonight.

—Sarah H. Hamblin, South Waterford, Maine.*

Andrew Jackson Bean was an educated man with the skills to teach school, fell timber, milk cows, drive a sleigh, construct barns, and perform marriages. He doted on his pretty younger sister, Eliza, and she valued his opinion. In a span of ten years (February 1857 to April 1867), he wrote her at least twenty-eight letters—several addressed to both Eliza and her husband, Henry Foster. The occasion of the first surviving missive was to announce his marriage—to a woman apparently well known to Eliza.

Poverty was the major excuse cited by Andrew for his sparse early correspondence; there were many occasions when he simply could not

---

* The poem, transcribed here from a printed slip of paper interleaved in the diary of Lewellyn Bean, was widely copied in the newspapers of the day. Numerous variants survive.

Letter from Andrew Jackson Bean, written "In Camp Near White Oak Church, April 21, 1863." Courtesy Bethel Historical Society.

afford postage. A secondary hobble on his communication was his embarrassment at owing Henry and Eliza money. Third, it is likely that some writings by Andrew's hand sank forever in the whirlpools of the wartime postal system.

Clarinda, Clara, and Chauncey (Chancy) are three cogs in a well-oiled clockwork of correspondents who urged Henry and Eliza to travel north. Henry's widowed sister, Amanda Wood Foster, had struck a similar note in 1859. To work as a nurse in this era was considered inappropriate, unfitting, unwomanly—in particular for young, single women. Stubborn, self-possessed Amanda, no longer in the bloom of youth, dared to move beyond nursing: she practiced hydrotherapy, an alternative medicine. (In her letter of June 6, 1858, Clara Jr. wrote of Amanda: "She is in New York City studying medicine.[248] Her address is No. 15 Laight Street. She left her Children at Plymouth [;] Nellie with Mrs. Spragues and the other two at Thomas Moores.")

As Yet We Have Been Quite Happy

Less than two months after Eliza married, Andrew tied the knot. Andrew's letters are generally not introspective, but in the following he expresses loving concern for his mother and renders a candid summary of his own character.

> *Lynn, Mass., February 22, 1857*
>
> *We board on Crosby St. Tell us if you are going down home [to Maine] this Spring.*
>
> *Dear sister Eliza*
>
> *If you have not heard from home lately I suppose that you do not know that I have a wife [married Feb. 3] & it may seem strange to you too but it is no more strange than true for I have a wife to love & serve. Though dear sister I may be a tyrant & a fool yet my desire & prayer is to be a man indeed which is no small thing at the*

present times. We should have written you before but have been
putting it off because we did not know how long we might stop [stay
in our present location]. It was not because we have not thought of
you often. Mary & I wish very much to see you & Henry before we
go to A. if we go this spring but you know that Mary does not like
to live in Albany very well & I am sure I should as live some where
else if Mother was willing. I never will leave or neglect our dear
mother so long as she clings to me. If I could get a nice situation here
I should like [to stay] I think but I do not think that I like making
shoes well enough to work at it [for a long time; permanently].

   *A.J. Beane**

Writing from Lynn, northeast of Boston, Andrew was likely commenting on the fact that men in the shoe industry had to labor 16 hours a day to earn $3 a week. (Women worked the same hours for $1.)

Massachusetts' footwear industry put its foot down in colonial times and took giant strides until it became a leading industry in the state. For centuries, shoes had been fashioned at home. Subsequently, a specialist, a shoemaker, made the entire shoe by hand at a small shop. When industrial sewing machines capable of stitching through leather were invented, shoe-making was taken over by factories. Among migrants from rural to urban areas of New England before the Civil War, 55 percent of the men sought shoemaking employment.

The McKay sewing machine—which rapidly stitched uppers to soles—entered the market in the second year of the Civil War, 1862. With this mechanical helper, one man could produce several hundred pairs of shoes a day, whereas by hand one man could sew only a single pair a day. When steam power was applied to the McKay, great factories sprung up thick as dandelions. The *Lynn Reporter* declared: "Operatives are pour-

---

* Andrew occasionally leaves a wider than customary space to indicate a pause in the locations where other correspondents might use dashes (or sometimes a colon or semicolon). These spaces have been retained here.

ing in as fast as room can be made for them; buildings for shoe factories are going up in every direction; the hum of machinery is heard on every hand."[249]

Andrew enclosed a letter from his new bride, Mary Frost Brown Beane:

> *My Dear Eliza,*
>
> *Andrew has just written you a few lines. He is sitting here by the window wishing he could see you & your husband. Well E— we are married & boarding at D Bells. As yet we have been quite happy only Andrew thinks much of his absent friends & more especially [sic] his Mother. You well know he is peculiarly Meshed [connected] to his friends from having so long stood at the head of all their pleasures or struggles in life. We do not for certainty yet know how soon or at least the time of our leaving Lynn for Albany, but we wish very much to see you & your darling husband as you no doubt esteem him. We wish you could come out here & see us. Can you do it. Perhaps you can or will & then we can talk over the whole we wish instead of writing. I must stop writing as our last ½ sheet is full & Eliza you must excuse neglect in not writing before & answer soon. Much love to all especially yourself & husband.*
>
> *Mary Beane*

Andrew next writes from his home state:

> *Albany, Maine, July 13, 1857*
>
> *Eliza*
>
> *How do you & Henry do. Here I am in our chamber [bedroom] with little Ebenezer though he is asleep & Mary is eating dinner.*
>
> *We were to see Austins wife [Andrew and Eliza's sister, Mary Bean Pingree] yesterday. She is quite sick. We were to see Ephm's [his brother, Ephraim] folks. Austin is at home or rather to work for Frank Cummings & boards at home with Mother & Mary.*

Austins wife received your letter but she is not able to answer it. Eliza I do not know what to say to you about her but there is one thing certain. She cannot live long as she is now for she does not eat or drink scarcely a mite & she does not say any thing. She may get better. I have not heard from her to day. She has been growing sick for a week.

I am in a hurry so you must excuse this hasty letter. If I thought that Mary [Austin's wife?] would not get better in a few days I should say come & see her while she lives but you know she has been so before when she lived in Steve Needham's house.

Write just as soon as you get this & tell me where & what Street & what No. you live for I have for gotten.*

A.J. Bean

Little Ebenezer, born June 7, was five weeks old at the time Andrew wrote the sentences above.

In his next letter, Andrew is despondent:

Albany, [ME.] May 21, 1858

Henry & Eliza

I suppose that you think it strange that I have not answered your letter before. Well some of the time I have been so poor that I have not had enough to pay postage & at other times I have been so poor in spirits that I could not write.

Hard times never reached us till after you left Albany but I was lucky once I had a chance to get some sade [shade] trees for Bethel Hill folks so that I earned me a Bbl. of flour in 2 days &c [indecipherable] I have swaped horses with S.P. Haskel & got a cow to boot so to have milk.

---

* If Andrew did not know her address, this letter was perhaps posted to Dana and delivered by hand to Eliza.

Henry & Eliza Can Mother have a home with you. It seems hard to me but she will be better off I think though it does not seem to me as though I could let her go from me. I have thought it best for her to sell at auction her things that she does not want to carry for she needs the money. If there is a town meeting the 7th of June I [think] they could be sold. I do not turn Mother out of doors forgetting that I am indebted to her for her hard labor for past years & if I have any property left I [will] do what is right, though I do not know [as] I could [spare] a dollar for her now. Henry would it not be better for you to meet her in Portland say the 8th or 9th of June next. Well write just as soon as you get this.

Yours

A.J. Bean

Henry's mother, Clarinda, chides about both visits and more frequent communication, in a postscript to Clara's letter of June 6, 1858:

I want to hear from my Children often as convenient. I dont expect to as often as the Widow Hawkings does from her [hers] about once a week or 2 at the most. I hope you will be a making your calculations to come home next fall for I cant have you put it of [off] any longer than any howe.

Andrew's next letter speaks of having to sell a mill. Whether this is a gristmill, carding mill, or fulling mill is unclear. Fulling mills used hammers to shrink and raise a nap on woolen goods woven at home. In the early 1800s, these mills commonly operated beside gristmills and sawmills perched above swift New England streams.[250]

Albany, Maine, August 4, 1858

Dear brother & Sister

I do not know what you think [of me] by this time. I know I should have written before but I have not for many reasons.

We are well at present & hope you are the same though wife has been very sick for a few days. Had Dr. three times. Had a hired girl two weeks. Mr. Morses's folks little boy died in just a year since the one died last year.

I hardly know how to begin my story of report but such times of trouble as there has been in Pingree's neighborhood I hope never will be enacted again. Austin's wife [that is, Andrew's sister, Mary Pingree] is to Augusta in the Hospitle. A. Grover carried her there a week ago last Monday. Eliza if you were here I could tell you all about it but cant write half. Pingree's folks have not the least feeling for Mary in the world & old Mrs. Johnson & her folks are not much better. She swears that there is nothing the matter with Mary &c &c. Pingrees folks care for nothing only rum & fighting among themselves. To make a long story short I suppose that you want to know why Mary was sent to Augusta. Mr. Grover is one of the Selectmen of Albany. He heared [sic] that Austin was putting his property out of his hands & was going off to leave Mary for the town to take care of so he just goes to him & makes Austin secure the town for her board at A. for six moths [months]. Then some thought that she had better not go & some thought another thing. Mr. Mitchell took her to his house & kept her two weeks then Grover took her to A. as I told you. Sewel [Suel] is at Ephraims with Mother. Austin is at his fathers with Henry. Such gossiping as there is in among the folks around here I hope God does not suffer in any other place & the worst of all with me just now is poverty. I new [knew] nothing of hard times till since you left here. I am trying to sell mill to be taken down & moved off & shall lose two or three hundred dollars but if I can do that I can get out of debt & have some thing left. Hedghogs eate one of my big belts in two in the mill. I have raised my house up three feet. Here comes Mary & Ebenezer up from below [from the basement or root cellar? from visiting at a house down the hill?]. He is a smart little fellow runs all round gets up in the chairs &c.

He wants to see Uncle Henry & Aunt Eliza with that little cousin.
What is her name.

Now Eliza do not let any of this trouble you. Mary [Pingree] is
better of [off] where she is than she possibly could be about here.
You have something to live for now. Strive to live for yourself child
& husband whom we all love. Eliza do not let <u>one</u> opportunity
pass without doing your best to please him whom you have taken
[pledged] to protect as long as you live. Remember that he is nearer
to you now than any one else. Do not confide in any one but Henry.
Have no secrets that you are not willing that he should know. I am
happy to know nothing but you are all that he can wish & if you are
I doubt not but that Henry is one of the best of husbands. May God
bless you Eliza. Do not take pattern by me but be good. I can truly
say that I think my wife loves me for she is the same now the clouds
of adversity lower [used in the sense of "appear dark and threaten-
ing"] around me. She strives hard to assist me though you know
she & I think differently about many things. Here comes Ebenezer
climbing up into my lap & you see his [pen] marks.

It is the poorest haying that I ever saw. I should write you a
great lot more but am in a hurry. It rains today & I have got to do a
good deal. Write just as soon as you get this.

Rece [receive?] this from loving brother

A. J. Bean

Andrew's letters illumine the extended kinship circle of the Bean, Foster,
Fox, Holt, and Lynch families as well as their regular movements among
Vermont, Maine, and Massachusetts. His letters and those of the Lynches
often tell of neighbors who have made the exciting trek to California or are
"clearing a space big enough to turn around in" in the Michigan woods.
Zest for adventure and an appetite for elbow room were important facets
of early American psychology.

In 1858, while Andrew was having difficulty making ends meet in the country, in the city Henry was thriving at his vocation, house painting. In fact, he was doing so well that his brother-in-law asked to become his apprentice:

> Albany [ME] August 6th 1858
>
> Mr. Henry Foster
>
> Dear Sir
>
> I will send you a few lines to let you know that I am well and all the rest of the folks about here. My wife [Mary Bean, sister to Eliza and Andrew] is insain and I have sent her to the insain hospital for six months. I have given my boy [Suel] to Ephm for his one [own?] and I being in want of imployment want to know iff you can not take me as a printice and learn [teach] me the traid to paint and pay me what I can ern. It will not take me long to get [master] the traid But iff you donot think it best get me some other work.
>
> Write as soon as you get this.
>
> John A Pingree

On the reverse of the sheet, John Pingree's plea continues:

> Well Henry I will write a little more. I will work one year or five with you for I am dun farming at present. I will work in the factory iff [sic] I had a chance. Iff you will do the Best you can for me when I come I will bring you some Beas hunney when I come and what more I can Bring. I think you and I can do well painting. I am in a hurry for work so good Bye.

She Is Only a Lent Treasure

When posting this request, Pingree seems unaware that Henry had new responsibilities in 1858—responsibilities that would make it unlikely that he would take on an apprentice and provide room and board. On June 14, Eliza gave birth to their first child, a daughter. Half of children under the age of five did not live to see their sixth birthday. Because of the cruel realities of infant mortality, sister Clara strikes a cautionary note addressing Henry and Eliza a month after Henrietta's arrival.[*]

> *Poultney   July the 19 1858*
>
> *Dear Brother & Sister*
>
> *. . . Henry do not place your affections to[o] strongly upon your little girl for remember that she is only a lent treasure for you to train up and make meet [worthy] for the kingdom [of] heaven and Oh let it serve to draw your mind from the things of earth to those of a higher nature. We expect of course that you will love her. I should if I had any but it seems to be ordered other wise in regard to me, but I am glad to see others happy in life if I am not but oh Henry and Eliza do be good and then you will be happy.*
>
> *We went up to Emils yesterday. They are well and all the Cousins as far as I know. I want to see you very much and I hope you will come and see us if you can posibly this fall. . . .*
>
> *Good bye*
>
> *C. F. L.*

Clarinda pins another postscript to the coattails of Clara's letter of July 19, 1858:

> *Dear Children*
>
> *. . . I am making cheese now days. I wish you could have some of it. You did not say anything about coming up here. It seems if I could not give up but that you must come this summer or fall. I now [know] it is heard [hard] tims but if you can save enough to come I*

---

* In the nineteenth century, mothers were frequently held accountable for the deaths of their infants. One physician announced that most infant death resulted from "ignorance and false pride of the mothers. Children are killed by the manner in which they are dressed, and by the food that is given them as much as any other cause" (Collins, *America's Women*, p. 126).

hope you will. I want to see the litte [little] grand Child [Henrietta]
you know and I cant without you come up here.

C. Lynch   Mother

In the following letter, sister Clara sends several wistful, welcoming and jesting paragraphs to Eliza. Although the child is nearly two months old, she still lacks a name. It was common not to name newborns until they seemed sure to thrive.

[Poultney, August 5, 1858]

Eliza

How do you do. I was very glad that you thought to write to me although we have never seen each other yet. You are my baby Brothers wife and some how seem rather near to me, but I hope the time is not far distant when we shall see each other. I am very sorry you cannot find a name good enough for your little darling. What are you going to do with the next if you are troubled for a name for the first, but perhaps you think there will be no trouble about that after the first one is named. Excuse my nonsense.

I suppose you must be very lonely to have Henry away so much especialy nights. . . .

[Clara]

According to Clara's October 30, 1858, letter to Henry and Eliza, Amanda Foster returned from New York earlier that month. Amanda's intention was to return to the Big Apple the following April to complete her studies in alternative medicine. "Then she will graduate and take her diploma and be ready to go into practice I suppose. Her Brother Allen is going with her this time," Clara writes.*

A couple of months earlier, Chauncey had dispatched an encouraging

* Amanda and her first husband had four children: Lois Amanda, Nellie Alma, Elsie, and Lydia Clarinda. Elsie was apparently stillborn; Lois died before her second birthday. Amanda was widowed in 1855.

word from Vermont, but quickly bogged down in a peevish dissertation on misuse of alcohol.

> *[Poultney] Aug 5th 1858*
>
> *Dear Brother*
>
> *I Now take my Pen in hand to write a few lines to you to let you know that we are wel as usual, But my hand trembles So Bad I do not know as you Can Read it. We Received Your letter yesterday. We was glad to hear that you was well and think of Comeing to Vermont. You ask how I prosper. I hardly know what to say, in an-swer. My health has been as good as I Could expect under Existing Circumstances. I have had to work very hard this summer for Silvester [his brother] has or Did not work here, But [only] 3 Days, before haing [haying] Commenced Since last March, so you can guess something what hard time I have had, though you nor any one else Cannot know what trials we have to Pass through. Father [Moses Lynch] and Silvester have to have their Bitters all the time.** *They have used or Poured Down over half a Barrel of that adulter-ated stuff that they get out to the Bridge, Since the first of March last. S[ilvester]. Sayes he should [have] been Dead Before Now if he had not used it, But I can-not Belve [believe] that it Does him any good nor Can any one of us But Father, nor Can we belve that it is an advantage to Father to use it as he Does. Some may think Perhaps that we are unbelver [unbelievers], So we are   in the use of liquor. At the Commencement of haing [haying] I weighed one hundred & nine and a half Pounds. I have not worked quite as hard sice [since] we Commenced haing. . . .*
>
> *I go to West Poultney to the Seminary, with Butter about once in two weks. I was there last week. Uncle Lashua [?] as we used to*

---

* Bitters is an alcoholic "tonic" or mixer flavored with bitter herbs, such as gentian. The *Massachusetts Spy* of January 3, 1838, featured an advertisement for Cordial, Stomachic, Detergent Bitters, a powder to be dissolved in wine or boiling water—to "strengthen the stomach, procure an appetite, and assist digestion."

Call him was very Sociabl, more so than Common. The Sem looks as though it Should Be Painted again inside for the Paint is wore off in many Places. . . .

I wish you would Come to Vermont this fall. . . . I have some work in Reserve for you When you Do Come. Our Parlor is not Painted. . . . I will Pay you for the paint and for Putting it on as soon as I Can. I Dare not say that I wil Pay as soon as the work is Done. The Reasons I will tel you when you Come.

I must go and help milk, so good by for this time.

Chancy Lynch

Illness and death are common threads in these letters (see Andrew's of June 30, 1859, for example), as they are in literature of the period. The short life of Phila Bean Sturtevant of Sunday River, Maine, demonstrates the pain and suffering common before the introduction of modern medicine. In the summer of 1861, an epidemic struck, and within six weeks five of her children, aged three to eleven years, had died. Soon Phila herself fell victim to the disease and bid a final farewell to her husband and infant son.[251]

As the year 1858 drew to a close, Andrew's financial struggles continued.

Albany, November 21, 1858

Henry & Eliza Brother & Sister

I certainly thought when I received your letter that I should write long before no [now] but I could not get the money. I kept thinking that I should get it & that I would send it but I have not had any money since you left. It took me all summer to get enough to live on. I have not done a thing to the house. We live in the chamber just as it was when you left but I have built a little barn 24x24. Got the floor laid & partly boarded enough so that I keep my two [?] cows mare pig & hens in it. I hewed the timber myself. Got Crosby to *frame on Cr. [credit?] got boards & planks on Cr. I have seen harder times [since] you left than before as to a living but I am earning some money now & just as soon as I get it you shall have your pay. I have two schools I have kept two weeks. The one in Uncle Uriah Holts & this one at Town house [Albany Town Hall] 8 weeks each. I shall get about $80 in both.*

*Eliza I am hoping to be able to pay you a part if not all in Jan [January]. Here comes Ebenezer. I wish you could see the handsome little fellow. He loves me very much. Lays his little arms round my neck every night since his little sister [Mary Frances] has taken his place at his mothers side. Our little girl is four weeks old to morrow morning. Is a nice little thing not so large as Ebenezy was. I should have written before but you see that I must have been very buisy in mind & body for we had Sophronia Upton [a hired girl] only two weeks. Mary has got along alone since & I have kept school but I board at home ride in gig.** There has been a great many changes here since you left. Mrs. Morse's folks lost their boy in July. Mr. Sperry & Sloans have gone to California. Abby Frost died & Mr. John Cummings. Seth Kimball buried to day. Mr. Wm R. Pingree died about two months ago & I was to marry him to Mrs. Smith that has been keeping house for Mr. Hunt to morrow eve. Mrs. John Marshall has a little girl about two weeks old.*

Austins wife is at Augusta [in the asylum] yet. Mr. Grover heared from her not long ago. She was about the same as when she went there. Austin has gone off with a Mrs. Bacon. She left her husband & child on Bethel Hill. She was old Asa Youngs daughter so you see how much character Austin has got or ever had. If he ever

* Uncle Uriah Holt, Andrew's uncle on his mother's side, was the father of two Holts, Andrew's cousins, who served in the Civil War: Dr. Sumner Holt and "Judge" George Holt. The Holt residence in Albany was located across from the town hall at Hunt's Corner.

** That is, he was commuting to his teaching job. Unmarried teachers often boarded with the families of students.

comes where you are I hope you will treat him as he deserves. We
have had a week of very cold. No sleighing but a little snow.

Write just as soon as you get this.

Do not blame me for not writing before.

Yours A. J. Bean

Severe back pain from farm chores sometimes kept Clara lying awake
night after night. Amanda Lydia Wood Foster recommended hydropathic
treatment, which gave Clara relief, as Chauncey tells a skeptical Henry.
Hydrotherapy, an alternative treatment of stiff joints or disease, was popular from about 1835 to 1880. Harry Weiss and Howard Kemble were able
to identify 241 individuals who practiced hydrotherapy in the nineteenth
century. Hydropaths treated their patients by soaking them in hot tubs,
then putting them in cold ones, and massaging them in "wave-baths."

The rich would sometimes "take" these cures for a year or more, and
no less figures than Catharine Beecher and Harriet Beecher Stowe were
treated by hydropaths.

[Poultney] March 12ᵗʰ 1859

Dear Brother

. . . [A]bout the time Amanda was here She [Clarinda Jr.] Could
not hardly lift a pail of water without herting her Back. Now she
can lift 3 pails of watter & Not hert as Bad as one used to. Is Not
this in favor of Hearing [adhering] to Amanda's advice. . . .

Chancy Lynch

To fill out the sheet and save the price of a second stamp, Clara adds to her
husband's letter:

Dear Brother and Sister

How are you this beautiful Sabbath morning It [is] so delightful
morning. The blue birds are singing all around and all nature seems
to join in one general song of greatful Priase to him who reigneth

over us and shall we not strive to bear some humbe [humble] part
in this great and glorious work of loving and prasing [praising] God
and doing good to our fellow mortals around us. I fear that we but
faintly realize that 'tis not the whole of life to live nor all of Death
to die:

Now Henry Amanda intends to visit you when she leaves New
York on her way home and she wishes to know where you live so
that she can go right there. She cannot tell exactly the time but it
will be probably between the 5ᵗʰ and 10ᵗʰ of April. . . .

[no signature]

The next letter tucked away in Eliza's cache came from the hand of
Amanda Foster herself. Peripatetic Amanda had recently visited Henry
and Eliza in Lowell as planned.

Woodstock [VT] June first 1859

Dear Brother and Sister

I presume you think I have forgotten what I promised in regard
to writing to you but I have not. I have thought of you a great many
times since I got home but have not had leisure to write any except
what I have been obliged to. After we left your place we had rath-
er an unpleasant time. It was very cold before we got very far. We
found snow and ice quite plenty. From Ludlow to Plymouth Notch
[a distance of about twenty miles] the Stage wheels were loaded
with snow or mud so that the horses could hardly move. The snow
was two feet deep in the road most all the way up the mountain.
We got to Fathers that night just after dark, I went home the next
Friday, did not intend to practice any under three or four weeks but
was called upon three times the first week, one case detained me
two nights and two days, I have had considerable practice and first
rate luck so far. I have two patients that are coming to stay with me
three or four weeks apiece and take treatment.

I had a letter from Clara [her sister-in-law, Clarinda Jr.] last week. She said Mother [Clarinda Sr.] was lame [limping; suffering from arthritis]. She said she had just had a letter from you. Chauncy and Clara talk of coming over the mountain before long to make a visit.

When are you coming to Vermont? I shall expect you this summer or fall. How is Henrietta? Does she walk yet? I will send you a Water Cure Almanac and a Catalogue of the Hygeio-Therapeutic College [of New York]*. Please read them and tell me what you think of the doctrines therein taught. I will send you the first extra number I get of the Water Cure Journal. Perhaps you would like to take it a year. I will get it for you for fifty cents. The postage will be six cents. It is printed the first of each month. It is worth twice what it costs to any family.

You see what a hurry I am in by my writing. I leave out nearly half the words, I have been interrupted twice by persons who called for advise [sic] and treatment.

The children are well and happy. They go to school every day. They were very much pleased when I got home. The weather is fine and the grass[,] grain and corn look well. Henry[,] you know Orren Wood's Ellen, well she married a young man by the name of Pratt about a year since. Last winter they went up to Bridgewater to a Cotilion [sic] party. He thought he would try a little rum and he did so and had to be led out of the hall by Ellen and one of her Brothers. That made a fuss but she went home with him and staid a while, however they quarreled pretty badly, after a while her Mother sent for her to come home and make a visit. She told her husband when to come after her; he went at the apointed [sic] time,

---

* The Hygeio-Therapeutic College of New York, chartered in 1856, went out of business by 1867. It was founded by health reformer Russell Trall, M.D. During this period there were water cure establishments in several states, including Dr. Robert Wesselhoeft's Water Cure Establishment, at Brattleboro, Vermont.

staid all night[;] next day, got his horse ready, to start for home,
when she went to the door and told him she wouldn't go home with
him and he was obliged to go without her. She has lately gone back
to her husband. Isn't that nice to get married and unmarried and
married over again in one year? Please write soon.

   From your Sister

   Amanda L. Foster

Andrew, continuing in dire straits, frets over money he has borrowed from
kith and kin.

   Albany [ME], June 30, 1859

   Henry & Eliza

   I hardly know what to say for myself or for [as to?] you but dear
brother & sister if you knew my circumstances & my unpleasant
feelings this evening you would not you could not blame me for any
of my neglect if so you see fit to call it.

   It has worried me dayly because I could not pay you. Last night
I sold my cow to pay the man a debt & to get five dollars towards
paying Uncle Jacob for a berrill of flour that I got last month. I
expected to have had some money of Parker Dresser this month
for some timber but have not. O Eliza if you & H had my feelings
you would pity your brother. All that I can say is God have mercy.
I have been waiting to hear from your family this long while & the
only reason why I have not written before is I thought I should get
the money to send you but I will send it just as soon as I can.

   I do not know what you know about things down here but you
will be surprised to hear of many things you have not heard of
them. It is very sickly in this town at this time. Father Brown died
very suddenly I suppose you know. Val Jewett died Joseph York died

yesterday. His wife is very slim. Old Mrs. Abbott they thought was dying one morning this week. Mrs. Stephen York is nearly gone. Two of Mrs. Morse's little girls are very sick. Lois Mitchell they do not expect to live. Her sister is sick too. Mr. Coomb's little boy is sick today. Mother is keeping house at H. Cummings & taking care of Mary [Pingree, back from Augusta].*

Mary [his wife] was quite smart [healthy, able] for her a few days ago but alas she is not so well this week. She has been very low since you saw her but God only knows what is in store for us. Be so kind as to write us all the news as soon as you get this.

A.J. Beane

Mrs. Rily Pingree is sick. One of her girls has been sick. Mr. Hunt has a very nice wife. Carter Holt has bought Leonard Town's stand. He is married.

Mother wants to hear from you very much so you must write.

Barker [Rebeckah or Rebecca?] Holt is merried [married]. Uncle Uriah's Sarah [Holt] is keeping school & George is in Boxford or near Andover, Mass.

It is quite cool to night & I will go to bed with little Ebenezer & Mary Frances.

A.J. Beane

North Bethel saw an epidemic of smallpox in February 1863. The identity of the particular sickness mentioned above is not specified by Andrew. However, before aspirin was available in 1899, many folk succumbed to fever alone. One dreaded warm weather ailment was "summer complaint," or cholera infantum, thought to be the result of heat interfering with digestion but usually simple food poisoning—common before pasteurization and refrigeration. Infants were particularly prone to summer complaint. In

---

* Extreme thinness was often a symptom of advanced tuberculosis—the reason it was called "the wasting disease."

an ordinary year in this era, 50 percent of the deaths reported would be of children under five years old.

In his next letter, Andrew delivers Maine news and requests help for a relative compiling a genealogy.

Albany [ME], August 21, 1859

Eliza

I received your letter last night & was very glad to hear from yu. I think it the very best plan that I have thought of. I went out to see Mother & Mary this morning. Told them what I thought of about it & they are willing to go to Lowell if you think proper & best for all and I certainly do.

The town of Albany took Austins property to take care of Mary [Pingree] with & Mother has a dollar per week &c &c. Ephm [Ephraim] as I told you is not allowed to speak to Mother or Mary. Mother comes to our house on good terms with my wife now &c &c but you know it is impossible for me to do the first thing if I was able but I am poor poor indeed. I have not told you before but I have given up my mill all together. Moved the machine to Grover's & lost five hundred dollars just as sure as I am writing you this letter.

I can not express to you my feelings in my adverse circumstances. I am having a very hard time of it indeed is all that I can say.

I think now that Mother & Mary will go to your place as soon as they can get ready if you think best. I have been thinking of the coming cold winter but if they can have a home with you I am very glad or at least I think that they had better go and stay this winter & see how they like. Mary is quite smart for her now.

Wm. Kendall [a cousin] has a little boy. Walter Brown too & Gils folks have one 2 weeks old. We are here to L. Mason's from Gils. I send this to Bethel by Walace.

Eliza please write me you [your] age when you we [were] mar-

ried by whom how many children whe [when] born &c &c.

Aunt Hannah wanted me to let her know all about our family in this respect for there is to be a book printed with all the Holt race in it.* I will find out all their coming so as to tell you next time.

A. J. Bean

Love to Henry &c

My Sheet Is Full

Ignoring changes of season and state lines, the family's correspondence flew back and forth at unpredictable intervals. Chauncy and Clara were dependable correspondents. Between May 1854 and February 1865, the couple wrote twenty-five letters to Henry or Henry and Eliza; some of the letters bear additions by Clara's mother.** In the following example, Chauncy and Clara lack cash for traveling, and drought plagues them. As a household economy, Chauncy experimented with making ink*** from elderberries. Clara continues to request visitors, but her tone has turned from sweetly playful to sourly critical:

[Poultney] Sept. 16ᵗʰ /[18]59

Dear Brother & Sister

. . . Oh: how I do wish you and Mabelia with your companions and Children would come up here this fall. . . . The last we heard from Chalon he was better they thought. Well his health was bettter

---

* The "Book with all the Holt race" is *A Genealogical History of the Holt Family in the United States*, which would be published in 1864 by Daniel Steele Durrie.

** The majority of these letters add little to the narrative of Henry and Eliza, and are omitted here.

*** Most ink at this time was prepared by combining iron sulfate and tannic acid (from oak galls). People experimented with extracting iron from nails covered with vinegar, mixing this solution with tannic acid immediately prior to use. A well-prepared ink of this sort could not be erased.

*[sic] for he had got so he could saw and fit their wood for the stove
and go of [off on] errands some. They wrote that they had heard
that Asa was married last winter in Whitehall and was still boat-
ing. I think he might hve [sic] come and seen us if he got so near as
that but I don't suppose he cares anything more about us now than
he does any body else. I think it is very wrong for people to neglect
each other so untill they lose all interest and affection too for one
another. My sheet is full. Write soon and come and see us if you can.*

> *Clarinda [Lynch]*

Eliza and Henry answered Amanda's letter promptly, but she waited five
months to reply.

> *Woodstock [Vt.] Dec 26th 1859*
>
> *Dear Brother and Sister*
>
> *I received your letter in July but have neglected to answer it, not
> because I have forgotten you but for want of time. . . .*
>
> *I have considerable [medical] practice and that you know takes
> up time, and then the children want considerable attention and
> besides I have a large number of correspondents, but they have all
> been sadly neglected of late. However I have a little more time to
> myself now, and will try to make amends for past neglect. I am well
> and so are the children, we havent been sick a day since I came
> from your house, the girls go to school every day. They have got to
> be great [i.e., grown-up and/or large] girls, they can knit their own
> stockings and can sew very well, the two oldest have each of them
> pieced a bed quilt. They want me to give their love to Uncle Henry
> and Aunt Eliza and tell you to bring little cousin [Henrietta] up
> here. Why havnt you been up this fall? I have been expecting you
> and Mabelia would come in the fall, or fore part of winter. Are you
> not coming up this winter?*
>
> *. . . I had a letter last week from Chancy and Clara; Clara has*

got to be quite fleshy. Mothers health isnt very good. She is troubled with Rheumatism a great deal. . . .

My plants grow finely that I got at your house. Tell Mabelia I will write to her soon.

Please write soon. I want to hear from you very much. I wish you a merry Christmas and a happy New Year. We have fine sleighing now.

Amanda L. Foster

What luck did you have with your birds [?].

Weary Dragged Down

Albany [Maine], January 23, 1860

Brother & Sister

Henry & Eliza

I was very glad to hear from you.

We are all well as usual except our dear Mother. She has a very bad finger. Her little finger on her right hand has been sore for about three weeks so bad that the Dr. cut it open long ago & since that it has burst open it self near her hand. It was so bad that she could not rest night nor day. It is some better. Mary [his wife] is quite smart. Does the work. Takes care of Mother &c. Sewel is there with them. Ephm [Andrew and Eliza's brother] took Sewel of Austin before he went off as his own child since that time because Mother had pay for taking care of Mary [Pingree]. Johnson's folks or some one else have put the devil [?] into Ephm's head & he turned the poor little fella off & throwed him on to the town. Ephm has talked foolish & saucy to Mother & Mary & has said a good many foolish & saucy things about different things but then he must answer for his own faults you know. Ebenezer has waked up so I must see to him. You would laugh to see the old fella [two and a half years old].

He can tell a good story. Little Sister can run all around. It is half past ten at night. There is a singing at Town house. I am tired & weary draged [dragged] down from the cares of my schools. I have kept one in Uncle Uriah's Dist seven weeks board at home & did my choars &c. I have kept [a school] here two weeks. This is the third week.

Mrs. York has lived along till this time. No one thought that she could live so long. They thought today that she could not live but a few hours. I have had 41 scholars here. We have had fine weather lately. I have not received that miniature [of Henrietta?] yet but have heard from [about] it.

Eliza Ebenezer waked up last night so that I could not finish this but I will do it this night so to send it to Bethel tomorrow.

Write me all the news &c &c.

A.J. Bean

Albany Me.

Andrew is by now the father of three. His next letter contains both good and bad tidings.

Albany, Oct. 22, 1860

Henry & Eliza Dear Brother & Sister

I suppose I know that you have wondered many a time why I have not written you before. This is my reasons I have thought you better off than myself so I neglected to do it though I have thought of you often. We are pretty well at present.

We have three children Ebenezer, Mary-Frances & Andrew Jackson. The little Son [Andrew] was born Aug. 7ᵗʰ last. [The] 9ᵗʰ Mary took cold & was very sick for a few weeks. You must know that I had a sorry time of it. I stood by & over her day & night. If I had not she would not have been living now.

I have said a good deal to her [our?] Mother [to] go to Lowell but there are so many obstacles in the way I do not know as it is possible for her to do so. I expect that Mary has written you all about their circumstances which are very embarising to us all.

Eliza I should have paid you the rest of the note before now if I could have done so. I am want of a Bbl. [barrel] Of flour now but I have not the money to get it either.

Write soon & I will answer.

A.J. Bean

I Live on Letters from Wife & Children

Four years and nine letters after his first to Eliza, Bean traveled to Portland to volunteer for Capt. Nathan Walker's company of the 5th Maine Infantry. He enlisted on May 4, 1861, and was mustered in on June 24. Pay of eleven dollars a month was scant financial encouragement, but enlistment provided a socially and patriotically acceptable way to "get away from it all"—all the depressing facts and perhaps accusatory faces of home.

"I live on letters from wife & children," Andrew writes in 1862. Soldiers on both sides shared his feelings. Confederate cavalryman Theophilus Perry told his wife, "I want a letter every mail. I do not feel right when I fail to get one. I should kiss one."[252]

Diaries, letters, and verses written during the Civil War are plentiful. By 1891, at least one veteran, G. W. Burnell of Wisconsin, believed that all the war's stories had been committed to paper. "The future historian will not be troubled for lack of chronicles," Burnell wrote. "His trouble . . . will be their superabundance."[253]

In his *Life of Billy Yank*, Bell Irvin Wiley found that letter writing by soldiers was "one of the most pervasive of camp diversions." A civilian visiting units in the fall of 1861 reported that regiments—a thousand men—regularly mailed an average of six hundred letters a day. One

Yankee reported writing 164 letters in 1863, 109 of which were addressed to relatives and 55 "to other friends." In addition, he penned 37 letters for men in his company who were illiterate. He received 85 letters.[254] Clark Edwards wrote to his wife twice a week.

Andrew is not a lively writer like Warren Goss of the 2nd Massachusetts Artillery, nor does he have the nose for news of Henry Morton Stanley of the Dixie Grays. He does not share Edwards's love of books, architecture, and flowers. He is plain-spoken, generally brief—and frequently seems more concerned with eliciting news from home than with sending news. Yet each letter adds unique details to the canvas of the War between the States.

Because his regiment, the 5th Maine Volunteer Infantry, was active in the Eastern Theater, Andrew Jackson Bean should have had a front-row seat to dramatic and historic scenes. During numerous actions, however, Andrew took a back seat, assigned to detached service. Illness confined him to the cook tent or to commissary duty with quartermaster William Fenderson for significant periods of time. He mentions serving in the cook tent in June and July of 1862, serving "yet" as commissary in February 1862, and again being assigned to Fenderson in October 1962, May 1863, and July 1863. His duties would have included digging fire pits, collecting fuel, stoking cooking fires, and carrying water, as well as actual meal preparation.

Despite its limitations, Andrew's war correspondence looms large in terms of the written personal records of Bethel's soldiers. Only two other letter collections are known today;[255] in addition, H. G. Otis Perkins and Walter H. Farwell of the 5th kept diaries.

In wartime, letters were central to morale. Andrew pleads for mail again and again: "I wanted letters often . . . to cheer me on"; "Write just as soon as you get this." He and his brother-in-law, Henry Foster, exhibited an unquenchable thirst for news from home, for reassurance that they were both loved and remembered.

Nearly a year passed before Andrew wrote to Eliza again. During that period, he enlisted, underwent training, and participated in his first en-gagement—Bull Run, the battle that made the Rebellion only too real for North and South alike.

Andrew did not write to Eliza and Henry about Bull Run until two weeks after the fight—and relayed very little.

> *Camp in Via [Virginia] near Ft. Ellsworth, Sunday, August 4, 1861*
>
> *Dear Sister Eliza & Brother Henry*
>
> *Do you know that I am a Soldier & did you feel anxious about me after the great battle at Bull Run 2 weeks ago to day. I have thought of writing to you often. I hope this will find you all well as it leaves me so that is as well as any one could expect after pass-ing through the fatigues that we all have under gone. I thank God often for saving me in that battle where they fell on all sides of me & cannon balls struck all round me. I have just been to supper fine bread, beef, [and] coffee. I have washed my drawers [underwear], footings [stockings] & c & self to day & c.*
>
> *I feel here as though I wanted letters often from friends to cheer me on to strengthen my faith in Gods goodness to guide, direct, & preserve all things. I get a long here very well. All officers & pri-vates use me first rate. I am in Co. I. Maine V. M. 5th Regt. Enlisted the week that the Regt. Left Portland [the week of June 24]. Have been pretty well all the time but the march on double quick to the battle & retreat all most used me up.* ˙ *The sight on the battle field is more than I can describe. You have seen it in the [news] papers. Remember I belong to Maine 5th Regt. Co. I, so you can keep track of me if you wish by the papers.*

* According to Hardee's manual, the double quick step is the same as the charge. It covers 33 inches of ground per step and requires 165 steps per minute. This would mean a man would cover just over 150 yards in a minute—on relatively flat terrain with no obstacles.

> *I have not heared [heard] one word from you for a long time &*
> *know not where you are. (Fall in Co. I, so wait a short time)*

[The letter continues:]

> *Monday before sun rise August 5th*
>
> *Dear Sister*
>
> *I had to leave this as you see for dress perade & c. I was so tired*
> *& sleepy last eve that [from] my been [being] on guard [the] night*
> *before that I thought I would finish this this [sic] morning so to send*
> *it to day. I have just waked up. Am siting [sitting] on my blanket yet.*
>
> *Henry & Eliza write me just as soon as you get this all about*
> *yourselves [and your] dear little Children &c. Direct [address in*
> *this manner]*
>
> *Andrew J. Bean*
>
> *Washington, D.C.*
>
> *Maine V. M.*
>
> *5th Regt. Co. I.*

Here begins a gap in Andrew's paper trail, one that can be partially bridged by a report from Camp Vernon, Virginia, dated September, 1861, by Bethel volunteer Simeon Sanborn. He cheerfully informed his kin that "Old Jeff [Jefferson Davis] has not gotten me yet," and that grub and camp were pleasant: "We have plenty of peaches, watermelon and muskmelon and any quantity of grapes. I have eaten about a half bushel today. Have got a nice place for camping. It is on a high hill [where we] can see all the ships and steamers pass up and down the river. We have plenty to eat and drink whiskey twice a day if we want. I don't draw my ration [of whiskey] very often and I think if the rest of the boys did not draw so much of theirs it would be better for them."[256]

Away Down South

Away down South in the land of traitors,

Rattlesnakes and alligators,

Right away, come away, right away, come away,

Where cotton is king and men are chattels,

Union boys will win the battles,

Right away, come away, right away, come away.[257]

Letters home from combatants ooze poignancy, even while soldiers display brio and merriment in camp. Deciphering their faded lines leaves a sweet-and-sour taste in the mouth. In his love letters, Henry repeatedly pledges wholehearted devotion to his wife and family, but he is not always as sure of Eliza's fidelity as he is of his own.

As the correspondence begins, Eliza and her children reside comfortably at No. 31 High Street in Lowell. She is hedged about with a group of women friends, some of whom she may have met at Boott Mills, some of whom (like Rose) she had known in Maine. Several of these consoling companions were married to other members of Henry's Company, and shared news from the front as well as tea, religious attendance, and sympathy.*

One persistent annoyance was financial: Eliza had difficulty collecting the government allotment due her. (The allotment was a portion of military pay, regularly deducted.) Henry attempted to smooth her financial path in a letter written November 18, 1861, to Lowell's Rail Road Bank. He had the letter endorsed by his colonel, E. F. Jones, in order to make the request as official as possible. (The endorsement appears to be made with a rubber stamp.)

---

* Sharing letters was common during the war. Daniel P. Mason of New Hampshire mentions in a March 1863 letter from Camp Parapet (north of New Orleans) that he and William Sams Jr. shared their letters from home. He mentions receiving twenty-two letters from his mother, one from an uncle, and seven from others during that single month.

To the President

of the Rail Road Bank

Please pay to the order of Henry C. Foster Private in Co. A 26th Regt. Mass. [indecipherable] 10 ten dollars to be drawn monthly (as per allottment [sic] Roll) By Eliza H. Foster

Henry C. Foster

Dated Nov. 18th 1861

Camp Chase

Lowell Mass.

Assembling his profile of the average Yankee soldier, Bell Irvin Wiley found that Union pay was frequently in arrears, and, to add to the soldier's frustration, that home-relief services were often poorly administered.[258] In 1863, a soldier correspondent at the Virginia front complained in a dispatch, "The shameful neglect of the proper officials at Washington to pay our brave soldiers has been the principal means of causing the wholesale desertion in the army."[259]

Henry's letters of December 25, 1862, as well as January 12, January 24, February 1, March 6, and July 22 of 1863 yield details about continuing difficulty with pay and/or allotments. Aggravatingly, other men in the regiment sometimes pocketed double pay. Even when Henry was on furlough, wages were not forthcoming. Eliza's brother Andrew cites a similar allotment difficulty in his letter of December 24, 1863.*

Although Henry's prose lacks elegance, it is capable of a muscular subtlety. Now and then he rises to a near-eloquent phrase. Eliza must have delighted in affectionate sentences such as "Husband & Wife should never tire of loving, or rather their whole life should be one continued courtship . . . " (letter of June 3, 1864).

---

* Soldiers' not receiving pay was hardly a new phenomenon. In 1779 Sergeant Samuel Glover, a veteran of several Revolutionary battles, and unpaid for fifteen months, led a mutiny of veterans. He was shot for his audacity.

Henry C. Foster in Union infantry uniform, in a photograph likely taken in New Orleans during the summer of 1862. The "A" for his company is visible on his hat. Courtesy Bethel Historical Society.

An engaging aspect of Henry's correspondence is the fact that his writing vocabulary gradually increased. In a single letter, he might put to use three or four words he had never employed before. For instance, in his letter of May 16, 1863, he uses *authority, aggregate, integrity, decisive,* and *justified.* Six days later, on May 22, 1864, he employed *beset, hymen's altar, admonitions, rectitude,* and *boon.* Such growth shows an active and inquisitive mind—a mind striving to master new forms of expression. This increase in vocabulary may reflect study of newspapers or attendance at religious services.

Henry's spelling is inconsistent, though he is quite regular in his use of *of* for *off* and *to* for *too.* On occasion he learns how to spell a word that he has been misspelling—such as *vermillion.* It appears, as in his long letter of July 6, 1862, that he quizzed men around him to spell the "hard words"—but often failed to check the "easy" ones. In addition, his writings contain their share of comma splices, sentence fragments, and run-on constructions. The editorial "*sic*" typically follows the first instance of an idiosyncratic spelling (such as *goodeal*) so as not to interrupt the flow more than absolutely necessary.

Further peculiarities include the repetition of words (*Kiss. Kiss, the the*), and the fact that Henry has not made the acquaintance of the question mark. Paragraph breaks are generally lacking—likely to cram the most words onto a page of scarce stationery. Here the editors have added paragraph breaks at obvious junctures in order to organize the material for the reader's ease.

More often than not, Henry, like Andrew, uses a wide space to indicate what he might have punctuated with a dash. Such gaps have been preserved. Most of all, Henry's letters shed light on matters of home and family. Far from the comforts of his own fireside, concerned about his wife's health and the well-being of his children, Henry repeatedly fought depression. In his correspondence, he grapples with fate as if it were a doppelganger—or an angel. However, his temperament is cheerful at bottom, and, in the long run, his letters float on a buoyant optimism. Even when leisure afforded him opportunity for deep introspection, Henry was continually sustained by his positive feelings about the future as well as an unyielding faith in God. (One of the most eloquent expressions of his faith occurs in his letter of December 6, 1863—with its repeated *hope hope.*) Further psychic sustenance trickles down from his conviction that the Union must be preserved.

Civil War combatants relied on letters from home to reassure them that all was well and to lift flagging spirits. Henry uses the word "despondent" when wondering why letters are not arriving from his wife. One soldier, William Henry Ruse, wrote to his beloved Maggie in Adamsville, Ohio, that it would be amusing should their letters speak to each other as they passed on the road. Soldiers lacking established relationships with the fair sex often ran lonely-hearts advertisements to entice correspondents and ease their solitary lot.[260]

Henry would certainly second the sentiments that Confederate first lieutenant William Steele expressed to his sweetheart, Annie McFarland: "The only pleasure I now see is in perusing your very precious letters."[261] A Union soldier, John Dunban, told his family, "I almost wear my letters out a reading them. I get them pretty wear [well] learned by heart."[262]

These tented fields

In his next letter, Andrew writes little of battle.

> *Camp Franklin, Via [Virginia] Dec. 1st, 1861*
>
> *Dear Brother & Sister*
>
> *Sunday Eve*
>
> *In accordance with the promptings of my feelings & love for you I write you this short letter to inform you of my health & location So as to receive the happy message from you of the like character I hope.*
>
> *Notwithstanding I have passed through many hardships as found in a Soldiers life & O the loss of little Jacky [his younger son, born August 7, 1860, who had died September 3, 1861, in Albany, Maine] my little name sake I have been strengthened beyond measure only as God can do. Though I sit here in my tent weeping bitter tears of agony yet God is good & I am in good health at this time.*
>
> *Maine 5ᵗʰ Regt. is in Gen. [Henry W.] Slocum's brigade & in Gen. [William B.] Franklin's division & we are just Est [east] of fort Ward.**
>
> *Dear Sister Eliza,*
>
> *Let me congratulate you as I have done before for having so good a husband. Love him well. Be a Christian woman & mother to*

---

* Fort Ward, in Alexandria, Virginia, was erected to protect Washington, D.C.

the Children of the husband you have chosen for life.

Train the little ones in the ways of wisdom & truth. Love each other dearly & forget not to ask of God many rich blessings. He is able. It is late. Time I was asleep but have been writing to wife & Children. So I pen these few lines hoping they may find you & I [will] receive an answer shortly. Tell me (if all if any) [news of any?] that I know that are in the Mass. Regts.

Write as soon as you receive this & I will tell you more particulars of a Soldier's life next time.

Yours truly

Corp. A. J. Beane

Washington D.C. Maine V.M. 5ᵗʰ Regt. Co. I

Between August 4 and December 1—the dates of Andrew's two letters above—the Eastern Theatre churned with battles at Carnifex Ferry, West Virginia (September 10). Cheat Mountain, West Virginia (September 10–15), Santa Rose Island, Florida (October 8-9), and Balls Bluff, Virginia (October 21).[263]

Camp Franklin   Va.   February 3ʳᵈ, 1862

Monday eve

My Dear Sister

I have neglected to answer your very welcome letter duly received dated Dec. 8ᵗʰ 1861 but I have not forgotten you and your family in prayer to God for your guidance and protection—that you may be a Christian, virtuous wife, and mother.

Respect your self and dear little children. Be all to your husband that you Should be and feel that in so doing God is your best friend.

I am very glad you told me of Henry's Regt. and Co. &c I have looked for a letter from him [for] some time. I know you must feel very bad but be good and put all your trust in God. I remember you showed me Gen. Butler's house [in Lowell]. Tell Henry to write me or give me his address and I will write him.

I remember Rose. Glad you have a friend so near. Tell George he ought to be out in Secesh [country] to use his rifle & pistol.* *Where is Tinker and family. Yes Mary [his wife] lives in our house with Ebenezer & Mary Frances alone. O God have mercy. My dear little Jacky's body lies under the cold cold snow but God is good yet I am sad and sorrowful.*

Pray for yourself in secret. It is so pleast [pleasant] to feel that God is your friend in deed.

We have had very dull rainy weather here for a long time and mud ankle deep. Two or three inches of snow last night an [and] today. We have had about the same twice before but the snow lasts but a short time.

I am Commissary for our Co. yet [still] & help the cook. I am excused from all other duty. It has been more sickly of late than in Dec. Sergt. Dolloff [Levi W. Dolloff of Bethel] Died in our Co. last month.** His wife was in Lowell a short time since but is [now] in Gorham N.H. His body was sent there. I am quite well as usual. I bless God for health. O Sister—He is good.

We are in Gen. Slocom's brigade & Gen. Franklin's division above Alexandria near Ft. Ward.

Eliza write me just as soon as you get this. Kiss [the] Children for Uncle A.J. Tell me all the news.

Receive this from your loving brother

Corp. A. J. Beane

---

* "Secesh" is an abbreviation of "secessionist," used derisively by Northerners for both the Confederacy and its inhabitants.

** Levi Dolloff died at Camp Franklin on January 16, 1862.

Wife of My Bosom

Although he considered putting his thoughts on paper a hardship, Henry Foster wrote more than seventy letters to his wife, Eliza. The letters commence on the day he enlisted in the Twenty-Sixth Massachusetts Volunteer Infantry—September 21, 1861—and conclude shortly before his death exactly three years later.

From references within these surviving letters, it is certain that additional missives were created—but went astray. For example, in December 1861, Eliza was able to forward to her brother Andrew Bean the specifics of Henry's enlistment and whereabouts. But the letters that carried to her the original news of Henry's being stationed on Ship Island, Mississippi, and then on the Louisiana mainland, have disappeared. Some of the difficulty with mail delivery stemmed from the sudden cleaving of the postal service into Union and Confederate organizations.

Henry had a cheerful and confident temperament. His first dispatches exhibit a buoyant, easy-going ebullience that must have been soothing to his anxious spouse. The tone is often pious—but it is not a false piety.

Eliza shared Henry's missives with friends and relatives. However, she did not simply hand them over willy-nilly. She read them aloud, keeping to herself the portions she deemed too intimate for sharing.

As might be expected, Henry's letters are repetitive: commenting on the progress of the war, reporting his own health and the health of other men from home, inquiring about family health, relaying his emotional state, remarking on human frailty or his faith in a higher power, expressing loneliness or frustration with the tardiness of his pay.[*] These subjects

---

* Henry's brother-in-law, Andrew Bean, seems to have been paid on a more regular basis than Henry, but himself complains about lack of pay in his letter of April 21, 1863. Bicknell, adjutant of Andrew's regiment, wrote of a two-month payday on September 12, 1861: "For weeks many had been without a penny. They affirmed that they would not even know the color of gold. . . . Why, we seemed to feel richer then than at any other day we had ever seen in our lives. Twenty-six dollars! What a lot of little necessities it would buy." Clark Edwards fretted dozens of times about lack of pay.

are common to combatants throughout written history.

Harrison Otis Perkins of the 5th Maine Infantry wrote to his father from winter camp near Petersburg on January 22, 1865: "The government are oweing me most five months pay & we dont [*sic*] expect to be paid unto the first of March then they will owe me 6 months pay. I would like to have you send me $10.00 if you have it handy."[264]

The Western Theater

As historian Henry Steele Commager pointed out in the mid-twentieth century, the military aspects of the Civil War have always "attracted disproportionate attention," and "the literature on the fighting in the East, especially in Northern Virginia, is far more voluminous and more interesting than that on the fighting in the West."[265] The letters of Andrew Bean and his brother-in-law, Henry Foster, help to balance the literary record by supplying firsthand reports of ancillary aspects of war such as pay, grub, and morale. Henry's letters from New Orleans help to flesh out the western front.

In the 1860s, the American West was defined as the territory between the western slope of the Appalachian Mountains and the Mississippi River, as well as the trans-Mississippi Theater, west of the Mississippi. The Western Theater brought to national attention leaders like Ulysses S. Grant and William Tecumseh Sherman as well as James B. McPherson and William Rosecrans. Confederate generals who served there included Braxton Bragg, Albert Sidney Johnston, Nathan Bedford Forrest, and John Bell Hood. (Henry's regiment was among several inspected at New Orleans by Sherman on February 19, 1863, and he mentions both Rosecrans and Bragg in his letter of June 29, 1863.)

That Imperilled But Still Radiant Flag

By the beginning of 1862, Massachusetts had sent more than 30,000 men to follow "that imperilled but still radiant flag." Regiments and batteries were stationed in front of Washington and at Fortress Monroe; five regiments were at Annapolis, ready to take part in General Burnside's expedition against North Carolina; one regiment and a battery waited on Ship Island. Meanwhile, the wounded trickled home: "The 'empty sleeve' was seen daily in our streets; and maimed veterans hobbled up the steps of the State House on crutches, on their return from distant hospitals, to show their honorable discharge papers, and tell in modest words of their toils and dangers."[266]

Between the writing of Andrew's previous letter (February 3) and the following one (April 16), the 5th Maine broke winter camp. When spring marching orders were given, the troops abandoned their cozy, semipermanent winter quarters. Marching orders were typically preceded by the issuing of three days' rations, and the men would scurry to cook food to carry with them.

John D. Billings, a Bay State soldier, renders a droll description of an infantry cook on the march: "That man who seems to be flour and grease from head to heels, who needs no shelter nor rubber blanket because he is waterproof already, perhaps, inside and out, . . . who shuffles along with 'no style about him,' is the cook, perhaps, for the regiment, probably for headquarters, certainly not for Delmonico [i.e., any fine restaurant]."[267]

> *Camp Franklin Va. April 16ᵗʰ, 1862*
>
> *My Dear Sister*
>
> *Eliza*
>
> *I rec'd your letter this eve with pleasure. It finds me well at present though we have had rather hard marching & bad weather of late—yet God is very good to me.*
>
> *I had a letter from your husband [Henry Foster] yesterday dated March 21ˢᵗ. He was well. Said he had had but one letter from you then. He had written you as often as once in two weeks. He feels badly. It is too bad. I live on letters from wife & children.*

Henry is a very good husband. I trust he loves his wife & children of course.

I know that rumor said that our letters would go no farther than Washington but it was only a story. I guess when Uncle Sam does not allow his boys to write their families I shall ask for a discharge on account of ill usage.

Eliza We have been out beyond Manassas & stoped 7 or 8 days. We had a hard march & very bad weather indeed. We came into camp here Sunday P.M. [April 13] We were 40 miles from Alexandria on the rail road toward Richmond [the Confederate capital]. We expect to go down the Potomac to join [Gen. George] McClellan. We did not think of coming back here when we left but such are the fortunes of war.

Dear Sister Do not forget your God at any time. It is so good to be good. Pray to Him often when you are alone with those dear little ones remember the absent father who loves you all so well.

I wish I could see your children. Eliza I forgot to mention in my last letter about the pictures you spoke of. You have mine have you not. I should like Henry's that you said you would send me. Can you not send me a copy of yours I used to see.

It is bed time now & I must close this & write Henry to night So Be a good wife & mother. Be a Christian & all is well.

From your loving brother

Corp. A. J. Beane

Direct as before

Rebels in Sight

It is unclear from the previous letter whether Andrew fought at Shiloh. Nothing is heard from Andrew about the Battles of West Point or

Mechanicsville—both of which took place on May 7, 1862—until the following:

> *Mechanicsville Va. June 3ʳᵈ, 1862*
>
> *My Dear Sister*
>
> *I am pretty well for this hot weather. I was very glad to receive your letter dated May 23ʳᵈ. Yes dear Sister Our Regt was in the fight at West Point & I was in our Co. at the time so I was out with the Regt. [i.e., on the battlefield] all day. We lost but one killed & three to four wounded in our Regt. None in our Co. Thank God for my life for the bullets flew thick & fast. Many of us must [would] have been killed at one time if we had not huged [hugged] close to [the] ground. We were in thick wood. Eliza please write me oftener. I should like to see your little ones very much. I have longed to hear from Henry for a long time. Of course dear Sister you think a great deal of any thing Henry sends you.* That is right. Love him dearly. I too wish the war was over that I might meet my dear family & stand with them at little Jacky's grave. This is Sorrow yet how rich the consolation to know that his little spirit is an angel in Heaven.*
>
> *My wife is teaching School in our Dist. Commenced this week Monday. Boards at home & takes Ebenezer & Sister in to School of course. Rest of our folks well. Gilberts folks got a little girl. Eliza here we are within 5 miles of Richmond.** Rebels in Sight. We one side of stream & rebels the other. You will learn more by news papers than I can tell you of particulars &c of the general movements of the armies.*
>
> *I have been looking for a letter from Henry. I have not had one since I wrote you. This little village [Mechanicsville] is at four cor-*

---

* Eliza seems to have told her brother about the clover blossoms or the poems which Henry sent her. Soldiers often copied verses from *Waverly* magazine.

** The Confederate capital was only a hundred miles south of Washington, D.C., the Union capital.

ners of roads. Our men drove rebels from it a little more than a week ago. Shelled every building till rebels were glad to leave. When we shall get into Richmond I can not tell. We can hear fighting every day. Some times on our right & some times on our left. Our batteries have shelled the hill over across from here but got no answer.

I must see about dinner for I am in cook tent again So I will close by Sending you a brothers love & prayer.

A. J. Beane

Direct as before & write soon.

Eliza I was so busy I could not get this in to mail the other day.

I am pretty well.

Yours Truly

A. J. Beane

Write Soon

In the preceding letter, Andrew, like many of his comrades, links heat with ill health. John Dunban of the 77th Pennsylvania Veteran Volunteers, who was assigned to guarding mules, makes the same assertion as he writes from Camp Jackson near New Orleans in July 1865, "In all my life I never felt such hot weather. There are a great many sick. The sickness all begins in the head & pain in the bones. It is called dumb ague. They shake but none die. There are as high as 17 men sick in our Company of 36 men. I think that it is all caused by the heat. It would be an impossibility for any of us to work out in the sun here. It is work enough for us to cook and keep the graybacks [lice] and musketoes away."[268]

Union forces wormed their way within sight of Richmond's church steeples in 1862, but the city did not surrender until April 1865.

Andrew penned his next letter to Eliza from Harrison's Landing near Charles City, Virginia. During July and August of 1862, General McClellan headquartered on the grounds of Berkeley Plantation at Harrison's Landing. The plantation was soon alive with 140,000 Union soldiers, their cooking fires and chatter. When Andrew was not perched upon a beef barrel, there were dried beans to bake—and pots to scour.

The West Gulf Blockading Squadron

Henry, meanwhile, was assigned to the West Gulf Blockading Squadron scheduled for picket duty in and around New Orleans. As he bided his time on Ship Island, however, he was in the dark about this assignment, as were many others, because—in an attempt to keep plans secret—navy secretary Gideon Welles did not mention New Orleans when cutting orders for David Farragut, and Lincoln's orders to Benjamin Butler intimated he was to invade Texas.[269]

Picket duty was a dangerous assignment, particularly when opposing lines were very close. At Cold Harbor, Daniel Chisholm of Pennsylvania wrote in his diary: "…the fighting [was] going on continuously. They were using solid shot, shell, grape and canister and small arms. At nine O'clock our Regiment went on picket we had to fight our way to the Picket line. Both armies was like hornets. We dug holes with our bayonets to protect ourselves and more than one poor fellow was shot before his little dugout would protect him."[270]

Henry's regiment, the 26th Massachusetts Volunteer Infantry, remained on Ship Island from December 3, 1861, to April 15, 1862. Butler liked to have Massachusetts men around him.* Regiments from other states were recruited, among them the 21st Indiana,, the 4th Wisconsin, and the 6th Michigan, until Butler's invasion force numbered 15,255 men.[271]

A boomerang-shaped barrier island about eight miles long and less than a mile wide, Ship Island repeatedly played strategic roles in history because it provides the only natural, deep-water harbor between Mobile

* One of the immediate effects of Lincoln's issuing of a preliminary Emancipation Proclamation on Sept. 24, 1862, was that Butler was able to enlist black troops. As part of his plan for his Louisiana command, he formed three regiments of African-Americans, many of them free men who had prewar militia experience. These regiments included black officers (Longacre, *A Regiment of Slaves*, pp. 9–10).

Bay and the Mississippi River. At the climax of the War of 1812, for example, the island figured in naval battles between Great Britain and the United States. Harbor and anchorage lie at the western tip of the island—composed chiefly of blowing sand, biting insects and salt spray—but conveniently only seventy-five miles east of New Orleans by way of lakes Borgne and Pontchartrain. The federal government began constructing a brick fort here in 1856. The still incomplete structure was taken over by companies of the 4th Louisiana Infantry in 1861; they named it Fort Twiggs after Confederate general David E. Twiggs. The Confederacy set fire to the fort as they abandoned it in September 1861.[272]

After Farragut's flagship dropped anchor at Ship Island on February 20, 1862, the Union Navy used the island as a supply depot and repair facility for Farragut's fleet; coal was stockpiled and machine shops erected. New Orleans was now under pincer attack—from upstream, where Grant, John Pope, and Andrew Foote were pressing the offensive—and downstream, from the Gulf.[273] In April, spring flooding of the Mississippi swept away a boom and other obstructions placed by the Confederates, and Farragut's fleet began its run upriver on the intensely dark night of April 23. With Farragut clearing the way, Butler headed for New Orleans. The citizens, who had been so convinced the city was safe, panicked. Cotton was carried to the levee to be burned, banks transferred $4 million elsewhere, and citizens fled. Ashes from the cotton still sifted about the waterfront when Butler arrived on May 1.

Emancipation Proclaimed

In June 1862, President Abraham Lincoln revised a draft of his Emancipation Proclamation, but realized it was not yet the proper moment to make it public. He met with his cabinet on the last day of December, specifically to discuss this document. Finally, he signed the groundbreaking document on January first, to mostly enthusiastic reception. But even after the final proclamation freed slaves in states in rebellion, many slave owners failed to tell their charges about their new status.[274] Rather, hundreds of African-Americans were informed they now had the status of indentured servants, and must work seven years for their freedom.

Henry's attitude toward blacks rarely surfaces in his correspondence. In his leisure time in New Orleans, he had the opportunity to visit Congo Square on the edge of Treme Plantation, a verdant Sunday afternoon meeting place for black slaves since the late 1700s. In the mid–1800s, the site, also known as Beauregard Square, was paved with cobblestones. Free blacks assembled here to market goods, socialize, drum, and dance the Flat-Footed-Shuffle and the Bamboula. Henry dreamed of a restored nation, but he did not limn a dream of a race-blind democracy.

Gustavus Vasa Fox

Henry was doubtless unaware that the assignments of the West Gulf Blockading Squadron were being plotted by a fellow Yankee, Gustavus Vasa Fox. Born in Saugus, Mass., Gustavus Fox (1821–1883) was the son of a couple born in Dracut. After a decade and a half in the Navy, he became an agent for Bay State Mill in Lawrence. When war was in sight, he offered his services to the newly elected Lincoln. The position of assistant secretary of the Navy was created for him.

During the Rebellion, Gus Fox was among the Navy's most influential officers. His background, intelligence, and persuasive powers combined to form an ideal naval administrator. At age seventeen, Fox went to sea as a midshipman. He sailed in the Mediterranean, off the coast of Africa, in the Gulf of Mexico, and with the East Indian Squadron in the Pacific. His participation in the Coast Survey and navigating the lower Mississippi in the 1850s, plus his stint as the captain of a steamer that plied the triangle from New York to Havana to New Orleans, gave him experience that proved crucial to mounting a successful blockade. His genius for troubleshooting lent spine to his experience.

To keep blockading squadron commanders on their toes, Fox sent them word of suspicious vessels. To encourage them, he shared reports of successful blockade runners. The squadron's assignment was ambitious:

Gustavus Vasa Fox. Engraved portrait from *Narrative of the Mission to Russia, in 1866* (1873).

blockade more than 3,500 miles of shoreline and patrol more than 3,600 miles along the Mississippi and its tributaries. It seemed impossible, but, prodded by Fox and well supplied, the blockade worked. Fox was gratified at the depth of its support: "The North seems to respond to every call upon it, men, money, ships, engines, munitions, all come forth with the alacrity of Alladin's Lamp."[275]

A glutton for long hours and hard work, Fox earned Lincoln's trust. On a lighter note, he may have been one of the only persons of his gender to waltz with Lincoln. The occasion arose when Ben Butler and Silas Stringham's squadron took control of Fort Hatteras, North Carolina, on August 29, 1861. Butler reached D.C. late at night with the good news, and hastened to the executive mansion in the company of Gus and postmaster general Montgomery Blair. "Lincoln appeared in his nightgown and slippers, looking even taller than he did in public, and when Fox announced the victory, Lincoln grabbed the pudgy five-foot naval assistant around the shoulders and whirled him about the room in the strangest victory dance ever witnessed by Butler."[276]

As the conflict gained momentum, Fox played a critical role in the Navy's success at New Orleans, Mobile Bay, and Fort Fisher. Writing a diplomatic pass for him in 1866, William H. Seward said, "It is universally acknowledged that the professional experience and abilities of this gentleman have materially contributed to the recent triumph of our arms in his branch of the service."[277]

Even Southern schoolbooks acknowledged the success of the blockade. A geography primer written by Marinda Moore mopes: "Q. What is the present drawback to our trade? A. An unlawful Blockade by the miserable and hellish Yankee Nation."[278]

New Orleans was an important river port as well as an interstate rail hub. It had great strategic value to the Confederacy, although it was located geographically well away from Virginia, where most of battles of the war occurred. By late 1861, the Union had sufficient ships to do more than continue the coastal blockade, and Gus Fox suggested that if the Mississippi were opened, troops could move east and push the Rebels into the Atlantic. Fox received approval from Lincoln for this gambit, and intelligence was gathered about the forts that protected New Orleans, Jackson with its 74 guns and St. Philip with 52 guns—both well-stocked and serious obstacles to upstream traffic.[279] Commodore David Dixon Porter plotted a way to breach the forts, and recommended his foster brother, David Glasgow Farragut, for the job. Fox and Porter both built on Secretary of the Navy Welles's "Anaconda Plan"—designed to strangle the Confederacy by a combination of coastal blockades from Chesapeake Bay to the Rio Grande as well as seizure of key sites along the Ohio and Mississippi.[280] The blockades prevented cotton, rice, timber, and other valuable commodities from exiting Southern states and being exchanged for food, ammunition, ships, and other supplies needed by the Confederacy.

Meanwhile, in Richmond, Jefferson Davis considered New Orleans secure. After all, Island No. 10, Fort Pillow, Memphis, and Vicksburg guarded the city on the north, and Forts St. Philip and Jackson on the south.

For the base of operations of what became known as Mr. Lincoln's Brown Water Navy, Farragut chose Ship Island. His fleet anchored offshore on February 20. By April 18, the fleet's mortar schooners had been camouflaged and were ready to bombard Fort Jackson, the stronghold near the mouth of the Mississippi.[306 to 381]

The 26th's adjutant-general, William Schouler, described the 26th's departure:

Many of the officers and men of this regiment [originally] belonged to the Sixth Regiment in the three months' service, which was attacked in Baltimore, on the 19th of April, 1861. The twenty-sixth left Boston in the transport steamer 'Constitution,' on the 21st day of November, 1861, for Ship Island, Mississippi. This was the first loyal volunteer regiment that reached the Department of the Gulf. Its field officers were Edward F. Jones, of Pepperell, colonel; Alpha B. Farr, of Lowell, lieutenant-colonel; and Josiah A. Sawtelle, of Lowell, major,—all of whom were officers in the Sixth Regiment in the three months' service.

Henry's first surviving letter to his wife was mailed in April from this Western Theater.* His military service took place chiefly backstage in this enormous arena, but mighty forces swirled around him—forces battling for control of Texas, New Mexico, and the vital Mississippi.**

In December 1861, David Farragut had been assigned command of the West Gulf Blockading Squadron with orders to capture New Orleans. Although a Southerner by his birth in Tennessee, Flag Officer Farragut was fiercely loyal to the Union. Raised in New Orleans and married to a Virginian, Farragut became a midshipman in his teens and served during the War of 1812 under Oliver Hazard Perry.[282] At age sixty, Farragut was anxious to make his mark and considered the challenge of the lower Mississippi the apogee of his career. After his success on the Mississippi and at the battle of Mobile Bay in August 1864, he was promoted: "I have now attained what I have been looking for all my life—a flag [that is, the right to fly an admiral's flag from his ship]—and having attained it, all that is necessary to complete the scene is a victory. If I die in the attempt,

---

* Other battles were going on further west, in New Mexico Territory, where both sides wanted to secure the natural resources of the remote territory. For details, see "The Battle of Glorieta and Union Victory in the Far West" by Don E. Alberts, *Hallowed Ground*, Winter 2007, pp. 2–26. Alberts calls the Battle of Glorieta "the Gettysburg of the West." For details about the war in Arizona, see "Clash at Picacho Peak" by Jim Head, in the same magazine.

** It was not until late in 1864 that Henry finally came ashore at Virginia, in the Eastern Theater.

it will only be what every officer has to expect. He who dies in doing his duty to his country and at peace with his God, has played out the drama of life to best advantage."[283] Congress rewarded Farragut with a $50,000 bonus—equivalent to several million dollars today.[284]

Henry sent poems but did not burden Eliza with the difficult conditions on Ship Island. When Major S. C. Gordon, a surgeon with the 13th Maine, took the steamer *Mississippi* from Boston in February 1862, many of the men suffered from pneumonia following measles. They were exhausted from confinement below deck and eating badly cooked rations. The men were in poor shape when they dropped anchor on March 2. For the next three months, diphtheria was the scourge of the island—a thousand cases in four regiments. Gordon cited as the "real disease" of the Department of the Gulf homesickness, or nostalgia. "Many a poor fellow suffered to an extent scarcely to be believed."

As Henry passed the time on Ship Island, Anaconda slowly tightened its coils. Union Major General Pope's men took fortified Island Number 10 on April 7. At the Mississippi's mouth, Farragut ran the gauntlet of fire from Fort St. Philip and Fort Jackson and from a small Confederate fleet. Farragut's fleet appeared before New Orleans about noon on April 25. "The crowds on the levee howled and screamed with rage," resident George Washington Cable wrote.[285] The mayor declined to surrender the city, so on April 29 Farragut sent in marines to raise the Stars and Stripes.[286] Lt. Col. John Broome, commander of the Marine Corps detachment aboard Farragut's flagship, described being struck and spit upon as he made his way to City Hall to hoist the flag. ". . . the scene of excitement on this occasion. . . was intense, nearly every one seemed like an escaped lunatic, and there were thousands of infuriated men, in the streets we passed through."[287] Broome succeeded in his mission, and Farragut was then able to pen this short-but-sweet dispatch to Welles: "Our flag waves over both Forts Jackson and St. Philip and at New Orleans over the custom-house." Gus Fox congratulated Farragut on the "magnificent execution" of his attack.[288]

On June 3, Fort Pillow and the nearby town of Memphis, Tennessee, were taken by Union troops. Louisiana began a downward spiral. The wealthiest Southern state before the war, it sank to the rank of poorest by 1880.

The Darkness Before Me

While Farragut gilded his reputation, Henry was camped with thousands of his fellows on cheerless Ship Island. Although the accompanying letter did not survive, we know that Henry wrote from this posting because Eliza preserved a poem he copied out by hand, with "Ship Island April 8th, 1862" inscribed at the top right-hand corner.

> *Wife of my bosom the midnight hangs o'er me.*
> *And shadows and silence encompass our camp.*
> *Oh dark is my heart like the darkness before me*
> *Wife of my bosom, while lonely I tramp.*
>
> *'Tis not that I falter or fear the sad morrow*
> *When true men give battle to rebels forsworn*
> *But the heart of each soldier may have its own sorrow*
> *And 'tis thinking of thee, love, that makes me forlorn.*
>
> *Wife of my bosom in god's blessed keeping*
> *Our lives are still mingled though parted are we*
> *As he watches with mercies*
> *Wife of my bosom o'er thee and over all.*

I dare the wild conflict these lines must be rendered

And faith in my bosom now brightens with morn

By thy prayers in the past I have still been defended

And he whom we trust will not leave thee forlorn.

Eliza: Truly, Yours

In the envelope with his copy of the poem, Henry enclosed a sprig of flowering clover and a newspaper clipping of "She Was All the World to Me." The rather lugubrious stanzas of this second poem—obviously much influenced by poets such as Edgar Allan Poe—were copyrighted as sheet music in 1864, words by "Dr. Duffy" and melody by Stephen Foster. But the verses themselves circulated for some time before being set to a tune.[289] The phrase "Wife of my bosom" became commonplace; both Hawthorne and Poe employed it in short tales.

She Was All the World to Me

In the sad and mournful Autumn,

With the falling of the leaf,
Death the reaper, claimed our loved one,
As the husbandman the sheaf;
Cold and dark the day we laid her
'Neath the sighing cypress tree,
For though nothing to another,
She was all the world to me.

In the month of song and blossom,
In the month when tender flowers
Spring from Earth's maternal bosom—
Waked to life by gentle showers;
As I wandered close beside her

'Neath the spreading greenwood tree;
Fair, I said, and radiant maiden,
You are all the world to me.

Then the rare and bright-eyed maiden,
In the month of song and flowers,
Rosy-lipped and beauty laden—
Curtained by the twilight hours—
Gave her hand into my keeping
'Neath the spreading greenwood tree;
And she said, with eyelids drooping,
You are all the world to me.

Bright the visions round us floated
On the quiet evening air,
For to them whose wife is loving
There is beauty everywhere.
Long we stood, yet scarcely spoke we,
'Neath the spreading greenwood tree,
Sometimes hinting, always looking
You are all the world to me.

But there hovered near a spirit
Darker than the bird of night,
And it touched her drooping eyelids,
Covered up her eyes of light;
Then with careful hands we laid her
'Neath the sighing cypress tree;
And my heart with hers is buried—

She was all the world to me.

Nothing Like Taking Things Cool

In the following long letter, Henry's vocabulary expands to embrace *conjecture* and *licentious*.

> *Quarantine Station   Miss. River [La.]* *
>
> *July 6th, 1862*
>
> *My Dear Wife*
>
> *How do you & the children do this morning. I am well this morning & trust these words will find you all enjoying the same blessing of this world. I received your letter this morning dated June 20ᵗʰ & am thankful to receive such happy messages from one I love so fondly and more so to learn that you are well and pray that you may all be blessed with health during my absence & for time to come. I also received 2 papers and I was glad to get them for we have had no news from the armies in Virginia since 7ᵗʰ of June and it seems as every thing depends on the success of McLellan [sic] now as the rebels have concentrated most of their force there & I fear it will be a hard battle, but I have all confidence in our brave Gen. & his men, but I pray that the good results may be brought about without the loss of so many lives as has already been sacrificed. Gen. McLellan no doubt has some good object in view by waiting and I hope strategy may do more than hard fighting as it has done in a great many cases.* **
>
> *You have got more news from the Missisippi [sic] River than I can tell you, for all I know is what I got from the papers you sent me. The N.O. [New Orleans] papers are not allowed to print any news about the war and I notice other papers do not tattle quite so much*

* At this spot on the Mississippi below New Orleans, soldiers were detained before going to their final assignment, to make sure they were not infectious. Able-bodied men were assigned to load and offload cargo while there.

** Nicknamed "the young Napoleon," Gen. George McClellan, a veteran of the Mexican War, was at this time engaged in the Peninsula Campaign.

about affairs that is none of their business, and I am glad they are suppressed somewhat, for they have done more hurt than good to the country. The 26ᵗʰ Regt. has been going up the river for a month past but [this company?] have not got started yet but next Friday if nothing splits I suppose we shall get under way but don't know where we shall stop and it is no use to conjecture but wait.

There is nothing like taking things cool I find in this life and especially in the Army for if I did not [try to remain calm] I should be in a pickle all the time and fret myself to death. There is plenty of men in this Co & no doubt in all other's (for people are about the same all over the world) that worry worry all the time, and nothing else ails them and they are whining around, sick cant do duty. They will eat enough in one day to last them 2 and be sick the next. It makes it pretty hard for those that are well. I have been on guard every other day for nearly 6 weeks but the duty is not very hard and I [would] rather feel well and go on guard every day than be sick or think I am sick as a good many do but may I be pardond for so thinking. It is not for me to judge of others, but take thought of my own faults. I fear some of our men give away to despondency to [too] much. They are homesick. They all thought the war would be over before this time and they should all be at home & they cant think any different, foolish men. I pity them but it does not good to talk to them for they will not reason. Some of them got started for home before they left ship island and have been going home ever since but they are still here yet and no more prospect about going home than there was when we first landed on ship island but what [what's] the use to fret. This is a trying world and these are trying times.

This [war] is a great school and the best place to learn human nature in the world and if ever I was disappointed in any person I am in some men in this Company. Men that you would think was the most brave and enterprising and would dare most anything *when we were in Camp Chase [in Lowell], here they give up all energy and ambition and are more like a little pevish [sic] child, than like a stout hearted brave man as they should be, but I am thankful such men are not plenty in this Co though there is quite enough, but I tell you men will show their true nature here if anywhere and some men do not try to check their nature nor their appetites* They think they must eat their rations or else they will get cheated. I come very near gitting into the same channel myself, but I rallied my spirits and see that it would never do. I had got something to look out for, and I am now as cheerful as a cricket only when I have to wait to [too] long for a letter.*

Sunday 3 o'clock

Kiss Kiss How I would hug you wouldn't I.

Sun shining brightly & quite cool. The steamer Fulton has just passed up the river from N.Y. 26th ult so I hope we shall get some more news. The steamer Roanoke went up 4th of July day. We got the mail by her. The (Blocke) Island went up the 2d. We have not got her mail yet for by some mistake it was put aboard of a steamer and sent up the river where some of the troops are stationed as though they were afraid we should get it to quick. They did not have a chance to put it aboard some sailing craft so it would take it 2 months to come so they had to send it up the river. Slight blunder that is all but soldiers are supposed to grumble and I think they have reason to some times to [too]. It will be down in a day or 2 and I hope I will get lots of letters and papers. Write as often as any of them if you don't write so much. I would like to hear from you every day. Steamers are coming quite often now & I hope the [Mississippi]

---

* The gobbling of rations is well documented. Men were issued two or three day's rations at a time—commonly the day or evening before a march or battle. Troops were to cook their rations and carry them along. However, many felt that they might have to leave their haversacks behind or could not reach their rations when pinned down by enemy fire. Therefore, they bolted the lot.

river will be open soon then our mail will come quick.

Willard did not get any mail this morning, but it is strange that Chancy's folks do not write to me.* I have not received a letter from them since I left ship island. By the way you think their baby was born with close [clothes] on don't you.** I thought as much. Well they ought to have a baby some way after trying so long. The last letter I got before this one was dated May 23d so you see it is almost a month between them, but there may be a lot of them in that other mail.

Well Eliza what kind of a 4th of July did you have. I will tell what kind of one we had. We had roast pig for dinner and fried dough-nuts for supper. 7 of us patched up [pooled their rations] and made a pudding out of soft bread, milk, eggs, and sugar. Well perhaps it want [wasn't] good but I notice it disappeared pretty quick . . . it was quite rainy here all day. Salutes were fired at the forts, otherwise it [was] no different from any other day. We should have had target shooting had it not rained. We have not been paid off yet, and I guess they have forgot us this time. I am going to write to Andrew right away. I wish I had wrote before now.

Eliza dear do not let any vain tattlers or licentious talk trouble in you the least for they have no grounds whatever. I trust we both have clear consciences and know each other well and we must be true to each other as any lovers ever could be. I think I know who you have reference to in your letter, but I think she is beneath you at least in one respect, but such persons can not enjoy themselves [without demeaning others]. They are to be pittied. The worse is their own and may God have mercy on all such evil minded persons.

---

* Willard's identity is unclear. Two men with the surname Willard appear on a list of Lowell's Civil War Soldiers and Sailors: George K., an infantryman with Co. C., and Ira P., an artillery man with Co. L.

** "Born with clothes on" suggests an under-the-counter—or unacknowledged—adoption. In some contexts it simply indicates "not right or true; odd."

Tell sisy [Henrietta] & georgy to be nice little children, and be good to every body and remember Father & he will come home as soon as he [can] and take them to a good long ride but do not disappoint them by making them think I shall come quick. Tell them they must wait paitiently a good while for papa don't know how soon he can come home. I hope we shall get paid soon for I am afraid you need the money. We shall get 4 months. The story about taking out the state pay [money sent directly to wives and children] is all gammon [literally, fat meat; figuratively, nonsense, humbug] started to get up some excitement among the men so they could have something to talk about.

Well I close for this time for I have come to a dead halt for want of words. The time that I was unwell Comerford came to me and said he was writing. *Asked me if he should say any thing about my being sick. I would rather he would not for I thought I should be well in a few days. So I was. So you see how kind he was in granting my request not to write. I asked him today about it. He stammered. Some said he guessed he did get it in to the letter some day. He was very sorry about it. This from your ever true husband.*

H. C. Foster

Adhesive postage stamps had come into use about ten years previously but were often in short supply during the war. In lieu of postage for the above, Henry's chaplain endorsed the envelope with "A soldiers letter" and his signature. The postmark is New Orleans, July 11.

New Orleans was a crucial prize because of its importance as a commercial center and shipping port. On January 31, 1861, months before the fall of Sumter, secessionists thumbed their noses at Washington by occupying the United States branch mint and customs house there. *Harper's Weekly* illustrated the event in its issue of February 16, with an image of

---

* Pvt. William H. Comerford is mentioned more than a dozen times in Henry's correspondence to Eliza.

"Gov. Thomas H. Hicks, of Maryland, Hon. Joseph Holt, Sec. of War/the Custom House at N.O., Seized by the State." This act of defiance occurred during the Great Secession Winter, when Lincoln was still president-elect, anxious to hold off the spread of slavery but unwilling to act boldly.[290]

Immediately after the fall of Sumter, Lincoln proclaimed a blockade of Southern ports. As early as May 27, the Union man-of-war *Brooklyn* anchored off Pass a l'Outre at the eastern entrance to the Mississippi. The result was striking: "The river front at New Orleans, heretofore crowded with sailing ships, often three abreast, from all parts of the earth . . . was now comparatively a deserted and dreary waste. The 'forest' of sailing vessels, the masses of piled up freight on the wharves, the vast army of workers . . . had passed like a dream away."[291]

During the winter of 1861–62, the Confederates believed the Mississippi impregnable. New Orleans was defended by 10,000 troops under Gen. Mansfield Lovell. A New Orleans journal boasted, "Our only fear is that the Northern invaders might not appear. We have made such extensive preparations to receive them [assembling a home guard, etc.], that it were vexatious if their invincible armada escapes the fate we have in store for it."[292] As late as April 27, 1862, the *Daily Picayune* assured its readers that news from down river was "of a very favorable and gratifying character."[293]

Andrew and the Fifth remain engaged in Virginia:

> *Camp near Harrison's Landing Va. July 26th, 1862*
>
> *My Dear Sister*
>
> *I was very glad to receive your letter dated June 22nd. I should have answered it ere this but about that time we had other business to attend to just before the retreat & through the weeks hard fighting as you have seen by papers.*
>
> *I was tough [healthy] all through that till about [July] 4th. I have been sick most of time since of Diarrhoea & kidney complaint. I got some milk to eat for 3 or 4 days & got well. I guess you will*

laugh but you know I love milk best of any thing except Browne Beanes. So you see I am pretty well now for me in my situation but a Soldier's life I do not like. I wish to be with wife & Children. I had a letter from Henry about [the same] time I got yours dated May 26ᵗʰ. I have not answered it but will in a day or two if I am well &c.

I am Commissary & in cook tent yet. None of our <u>Co</u>. were killed but several wounded.* Our Lieut. Col. was killed & Col. wounded. Several of [the men from] the other Co's. were killed & wounded.

Peace I pray for peace. Let the North send forth her noble sons enough to put down this rebellion at once or we shall all be killed or die of disease.

Eliza Please write me just as soon as you get this & let me know if you have heared [sic]from Henry lately. Kiss the Children for Uncle Andrew. Forget me not in prayer to God for He alone is able to give & take.

I had a letter from Sister Mary this week saying that they are well &c. I have written them today.

Old Mrs. Abbott is dead. I was very glad you sent me the paper for it was just what I wanted. Postage Stamps are the hardest to get. Wife sent me six but this is last one but I guess I can find some before I want to write again.

From your brother

A. J. Beane

According to Dr. S. C. Gordon of the 13th Maine, the phrase "He doesn't have the guts for it" derives from the fact that many Union troops had to be dismissed from service because their systems could not adjust to life in the deep South.[294] Diarrhea flourished because troops knew little about the importance of hand-washing or the maintenance of field latrines.

---

* Here Andrew may refer to the Battle of Malvern Hill, which took place July 1, 1862. One of the wounded may be James C. Ayer, who died Aug. 7, 1862. Clark Edwards's letter of July 5, 1862, reports that 65 privates were casualties.

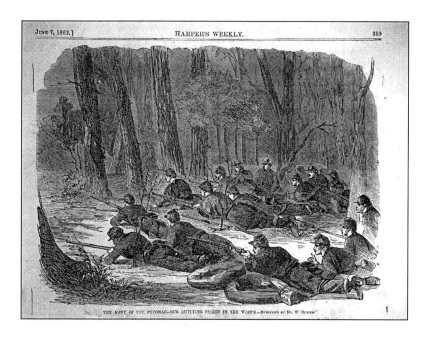

JUNE 7, 1862.]   HARPER'S WEEKLY.   359

THE ARMY OF THE POTOMAC—OUR OUTLYING PICKET IN THE WOODS.—Sketched by Mr. W. Homer.

Army of the Potomac—An Outlying Picket. Engraving from sketch by Winslow Homer in *Harper's Weekly,* June 7, 1862.

The Sanitary Commission prepared pamphlets to instruct soldiers in personal hygiene as well as the excavating and use of latrines, but soap and water were often lacking. About 64 percent of all troops were affected by diarrhea and dysentery in the first year of the war, a rate of infection which increased to 99.5 percent in 1862.[295]

The typical dose prescribed at sick call for diarrhea was "blue mass" or "blue powder"—a mixture of mercury and chalk. Opium and strychnine were also used to treat dysentery.[296]

Generals as well as infantrymen suffered. Thomas P. Lowry wrote of General Lee, "At Gettysburg, R. E. Lee had terrible diarrhea and was always popping into the bushes to have another exhausting and crampy bowel movement."[297]

Andrew seems to have escaped more serious illness, although many of his fellows contracted pneumonia during the winter in Virginia. The blame

was assigned to rainy weather. Pneumonia was often compounded by typhoid fever, malaria, smallpox, or measles. Bacteria and airborne germs
were not understood. A board of inquiry called by General McClellan ruled
that malaria resulted from the noxious fumes of low-lying areas, and that
typhoid was caused by overcrowding tents and overworking soldiers.[298]

Writing from camp under such conditions, Andrew desires to have
Eliza's visage with him:

> *Camp near Harrison Landing Va. Aug. 1st, 1862*
>
> *My Dear Sister*
>
> *I was very glad to receive your letter this morning dated July
> 25th. I guess you have got my letter ere this & I am glad you wrote
> me this one. I had a letter from Henry [received on] July 27th dated
> July 15th.*
>
> *I was glad to hear that he was well & had such good quarters
> in New Orleans.*
>
> *I had a letter from wife & children this morning. They were
> well. This is last day of Mary's school.*
>
> *Eliza when I think of it for a moment it seems as though I could
> not live without seeing wife & children but this [mood] will not do.
> I am here & can not get away.*
>
> *Rebels opened on our transports in river & camps this side of
> river last night near 12 [midnight] from their batteries on the other
> side of James river. Killed some me [men] & horses I hear. I could see
> flashes of cannon & shell.*
>
> *Let the North send an Army large enough to put down this re-
> bellion at once & not let us all die, get killed, or taken.*
>
> *It should have been done ere this. Cant you send me a little
> cheap copy of your miniature that you used to have.*
>
> *Please write me soon. I answered Henry's letter.*

Yours truly

A. J. Beane

Oak Grove—the site of many clashes between opposing pickets and the spot where Andrew wrote his next letter—was located south of the Richmond and York River Railroad. The jousting blossomed into full-blown battle on June 25, 1862, but McClellan gained only six hundred yards at a cost of more than a thousand casualties. Oak Grove was the first of a series of engagements called the Seven Days' Campaign—one of many efforts by the Confederates to keep the Federals out of Richmond.[299]

Five Hundred Cannon

After a victory at Harpers Ferry in September 1862, Stonewall Jackson joined Lee's forces at Antietam Creek to make a first attempt to move the war onto Northern ground. The Battle of Antietam was fought along the banks of a creek near the town of Sharpsburg, Maryland—only about forty miles from Washington, D.C. The battlefield was sandwiched between Antietam Creek and the Potomac River. The fierce conflict lasted fourteen awful hours on September 17, 1862, and proved the single bloodiest day of the war. One hundred thousand men and five hundred cannon blasted away at one another through thunderous din and blinding clouds of smoke. Isolated in a cornfield, the 1st Texas regiment suffered more than 80 percent casualties. When night fell, there were more than 20,000 dead or wounded. Clara Barton moved among them, nursing the wounded by lamplight.[*]

* During the Civil War, New Jersey teacher Clara Barton became one of the first women employed by the Patent Office in Washington, D.C. Some forty men in the 6th Massachusetts had been Clara's students, and their mothers asked her help in sending boxes of food and clothing. Barton soon began actively soliciting donations of foods like fresh lemons to combat scurvy. Within six months, she ran three warehouses. She distributed preserves, soap, and foods such as fresh bread at military hospitals and to ships and trains carrying wounded men from the front. Finally she got permission to visit the battlefields themselves, passing through the lines with wagons of supplies. She soon began assisting in operating rooms.

Maj. John H. Brinton, a Union surgeon, described the horrific aftermath:

"During the battle, the Surgeons of the different divisions established their field hospitals in the farm houses with their barns and out-buildings scattered over the field of battle, which extends some six miles irregularly along Antietam Creek. . . . As soon after the fighting as was possible, the wounded who were scattered over the vast area . . . were taken charge of. . . . The scene was a busy one. Men were actively engaged in collecting the wounded, ambulances were hurrying to the rear, many of the slightly wounded were staggering to hospital-wards, and burial parties were busy digging long burial trenches.* The evidences of the battle were everywhere, bullet marks on corn, twigs, and fences, trees shattered in their trunks, and the dead scattered far and wide."[300]

If Andrew dodged bullets in the Antietam Campaign, there is no record in these surviving letters.

Imagine All the Kisses You Can

From the phrase "You see I am not in N Orleans now" in his next letter, it appears that Henry wrote to Eliza from New Orleans—and that letter was lost. He now writes from an outlier protecting one approach to the city.

Lakend [Lake End, LA., near New Orleans] Oct. 1, 1862

Dear Eliza

How do you do to day & how do you get along & how are the children. I am well to day. You see I am not in N Orleans now. This Co. [Company A] is on detached service again. We are 7 miles from the city at the south end of Lake Ponchertrain [Pontchartrain]. This has been a summer resort for New Orleans big folks [high society], but is pretty much deserted now. It is a very pleasant place & I am

---

* Burial parties were composed of men who had fought all day but could still walk and dig. They were too tired to do much more than cover the bodies, sometimes erecting boards at the head of each grave, with a name carved into the board.

pleased that we were sent here.* I think Co A is lucky again. I had rather be her [here] than to be under the nose of all the big officers. The rest of the Regt. is in the city. G. Co's at the Custom house.** The rest in different places. This is one of the out posts. We are quartered in a large hotel. There is another Co here now but expect they will go away in a day or two. We left our quarters in the City night before last about 6 oclock [sic] marched 1-1/2 miles to the depot took the cars [railroad cars] and rode 16 miles & through the blunder of somebody we got to the wrong place. We stopped about 1 hour & took the next train back to the City. Arrived back at 9 oclock stayed in our old quarters over night, had breakfast started again at 7 oclock marched to another depot ¼ of a mile & took the cars again. Went to Carrollton*** 8 miles than changed cars for this place 5 miles farther. Arrived here at 8-1/2 oclock, all safe. So you see we got considerable railroad travel. The first since I left Boston. How long we shall stay here I cannot say. Direct your letters as before. A mail come to day but I got no letter.**** I got a paper from you of Sept. 6th. I think I ought to have got a letter but there was another steamer come in this morning with a mail that we have not got, so I hope to get a letter yet.

---

* What Henry calls "Lake End" is probably Milneburg, where Pontchartrain Beach would later be located, at the end of the "Smokey Mary" train line, the second oldest railroad in the United States. Development of Milneburg began in the 1830s. The hotel is probably the Washington Hotel.

** The custom house (or "Customs-House") was an Egyptian Revival style building begun in 1848. The vast, unfinished building covered a city block. It was designed to combine the functions of a customs house, mint, courthouse, and post office.

*** While Carrollton today is a neighborhood of New Orleans, at this date it was a separate township, incorporated in 1833. Its African American residents clustered along the river.

**** The Union Navy had mail service far superior to the postal service for land troops. Large mail steamers such as the *Rhode Island* and *Ocean Queen* could carry as many as 400,000 letters and 2,000 packages to men in the blockading squadrons.

Good news comes here of union victories. They say the rebel army is all cut to pces [pieces]. I hope it is a decisive battle for it is time this bloody contest was stopped & I hope & pray that it soon will be, but oh how many a good life has been sacrificed, to punish the deluded, & wrong minded. I don't know what to call them, they are like a spoiled & humored [over-indulged] child. They have allways had their own way & they think they always must, but we are a strong nation & we must preserve our nationality & the unruly must be brought to Justice & Law. We must have a government.*

[October] 2nd

Good morning dear ones at home. Oh! That I could see you this morning. This is a fine morning here, all is quiet & peaceful seemingly, but this life, the soldiers life is a very unnatural life, but I hope & still hope, it will soon end & we may once more be permited [sic] to return to our peaceful home's away from musquito's & swamps, to good old N.E. among the hill's [sic], but God only knows, our destiny. We must trust in Him all we can. I am thankful for his many blessings & his goodness & I always mean to be greatful [grateful] & sin as little as possible. Eliza be hopeful & cheerful as you can. Keep good courage. Oh I hope you had a good visit. I suppose you are at home by this time aint you. Tell Sisy [Henrietta] and George that Papa is out to the lake now keeping a Hotel. We have got our recruit from Lowell, that is all & 7 in N.O. We have but 4 or 5 sick in the Co. now. All in good health & spirits hoping soon to be home. Well dear E good bye for this morning, from your true & loving husband. Give my respects to all. Yours ever.

Henry C. Foster

The recreational complex at the west end of Lake Pontchartrain was known

---

* Henry may be referring to the Sept. 19 battle at Iuka, Mississippi. Northerners under Union General Rosecrans overwhelmed the Confederate forces of Gen. Sterling Price. On Sept. 21, Union troops retook the town of Mumfordsville, Ky.

for its fine dining, bath houses, pistol gallery, and pleasant garden.[301] It is a comfortable post for Henry:

> *Lakend [La.] Oct. 6ᵗʰ, 1862*
>
> *My Dear Family:*
>
> *I seat myself now to write you a few lines, to in form [sic] you I am well & hope these lines will find you all enjoying the same great blessing. We have a writing desk rigged up here in our room & it is so long since I wrote on any thing but a board in my lap that I don't make it go very well you see, but I will get the hang of it after a while I guess. We have a room about the size of our sitting room & there is 7 of us in it so you see we have plenty of room. The other Co is gone that I spoke of in my other letter so we have the whole house now.*
>
> *This is the best place we have had yet but it is nothing but swamp any where in this part of the country. There is not much danger of the enemy here for they cant get here without coming through the swamps which are impassable, except they cross the Lake & the gunboat New London, takes care of that. The rebels know her to [too] well to venture very near her, 400 hundred of our men went up the river a few days ago, & captured a drove of cattle 1500 & all the droviers, & took them to the City [New Orleans]. They have been ever since last May driving them from Texas.* * Sad affair for secesh, but I think they are in rather hard luck all around just now.* ** What do you think dear. Our boats were fired into coming back from a battery on shore & 3 men killed, but the gun boats soon shelled them out.* *** We are very anxious for news from Virginia. Oh!*

---

* The Handbook of Texas Online credits Texas rancher William H. Day with "driving herds to Louisiana markets" in 1862, but says nothing about the cattle being captured.

** An abbreviation of the word "Secessionist," "secech" was used derisively by Northerners for both the Confederacy and its inhabitants.

*** The gunboats *New London*, *Josiah Bell*, and *Uncle Ben* were all part of the Union's West Gulf Blockading Squadron.

I hope the battle has been decisive there. It seems as though if they are used up there that the war will soon end but God only knows when it will end. I pray that it may be soon. We have had no news since the 20th ult. It is a long time since I heard from you not since the 8th Sept almost a month. I was so disappointed not to get a letter last mail. I hope I shall this one. The mail is expected to day. I wish I knew that [you] are all well & how you get along. I suppose you are in L. [Lowell] by this time, and got your money I hope.

We have just received news that Mr. Gilpatrick is dead.* I just asked the capt. And he did not know what day he was buried. He said he should write to his [that is, Gilpatrick's] wife to morrow & he thought it best for her to receive the inteligence [sic] through his letter than to have you tell her & she will no doubt get the letter as soon as you will get this, but in case she should fail to get his letter, you can tell her, but you had better wait as long as you think proper, but if she asks you, of course you must tell her as you cannot avoid it, very well. Poor woman she will feel very bad no doubt. Mr. Gilpatrick was very much broken down, by drinking, I think & the fever & ague took hold of him very hard. He has been in the General Hospital ever since we come to the City & he would [have] recovered there if any where for they have the best of care in that hospital. We have 2 men there now Mr. Blackmer & a Mr. Wilson, not the one that comes to see you.** Mr. B. I saw a few days before we left the City. He was able to walk about the City but he has lost one of his eyes entirely. I believe he can see but a little out of the other. Please tell May [Mrs. Blackmer?] this. Give my respects to all. I send you all my love, & best wishes & kisses for you & the children, from your

Henry

---

* Pvt. John Gilpatrick of Lowell.

** Mr. Blackmer is Warren A. Blackmer. Three men with the surname Wilson had enlisted in Henry's company: Franklin T. Wilson, Josiah H. Wilson and Justus B. Wilson.

Please write often as you can dear Eliza.

In the following, Henry, hungry for news, again wonders why mail from home does not reach him.

Lakeend [La.] Oct. 13th 1862

Dear Eliza:

I will write you a few lines to day so that you may know I am well & I hope you & the children are also well. Oh could I but see you to day & be with you but it cannot be so, & we must abide by events that seperate [sic] us so far, but dear ones I trust the time is not far distant that we may again embrace each other but we will try & wait with good cheer. I do not see why I do not get a letter I am sure. It seems as though I never should get one again but I hope I shall soon. The 8th of Sept was the last one Mr. Wilson had. The 27th his wife wrote that you had not got home [to Lowell] then. I do want to hear from you so bad. It seems as though you must have written. There is 6 or 7 letters that I have not heard from besides some things I sent by the one of the band [a band member going on furlough]. I hope you will get them all. I directed only 2 letters to Albany [Maine] the rest to L. as you said. I am afraid you will not get them all, but I hope Mr. Holt will not fail to send them to you.

It is very pleasant & quite cool here to day. We have had several days' cool weather so that we needed our overcoats on to keep warm. It seemed really good I assure you to pass a few days without sweating our gizzards out. This seems like a real fall day. It little seems as though there was any war, from the appearance of things here in this quiet place. I try and give you a description of the place as near as I can. I am going to put the whole of it on a piece of paper. There is 2 hotels here. We occupy one & there is some 4 or 5 stores or rum shops.

We are all in pretty good health now. There is 2 of our Co in the Hospital at the City. 3 or 4 sick here. We have lost 8, in all. 12 been sent home. 11 enlisted in N.O. so we have got a pretty strong Co now. We have to go on guard once in 2 or 3 days, & duty is easy. Much more so than in the City. You spoke of going home [to Maine] with Mr. Merrill & staying. What Merrill is it. Eliza do as you think best & stay where you can enjoy yourself the best. You know I would like to come & be with you as much as you would like to have me but it is impossible. I would not try as hard as some have to get discharged, for all that my life is worth. Quite a number have made them selves sick and fretted so much that now they are good for nothing & never will be. They are object of pity really. Well it seems that Hussey enlisted after all, & Merrill to [too]. I wish them good success & a safe return home.

Eliza I think this war will be over this winter but we cannot tell. God only knows but I hope for the best & trust to an All wise & reuling [ruling] providence for all good. I trust this war is not in vain, but there is so much wire pulling [pulling strings; getting someone to use influence on one's behalf], & so many men striving to do any thing but right, that it looks dark some times, but all will be well, if we only have faith & persevere to the end. We consider all those persons, who stay at home, more because they are cowards then anything else & slander those that sacrifice the comforts of home and everything to save their country & their own homes even. I say they are beneath contempt, poor miserable scamps, to make the best of them, & let [tell?] things for what they are. They ought to be kicked by cripples till they could not use their toungues [sic]. I would like to get a chance at them. It is no use to notice such contemptible scape gallows [guilty parties who have not yet eaten their just desserts].

Oh by the way lidy [lady], if you see a good farm that suits you just pitch in for it that all. I will be with you as soon as it is possible for me to do so. I hope & pray that my life may be spared me to return again to my family for your sake & feel that it will be, but our lives are in the hands of our Maker, & he will do what seemeth Him good.

We have the same old fare as ever salt horse & ham fat, & hard bread [hardtack].* We have soft bread [freshly baked bread] ½ the time & potatoes the same. Mr. J. Thompson's health is very poor.** The Doc. told him he was in consumption [tuberculosis] but I hope he will recover. Do not mention it to his wife. Mr. Sawyer & son are well & W. [Willard? Wilmot?] & all that you know. Accept this from your husband with all his love which is fathomless for his wife & children. Kiss them & tell them to remember Father & be good. Father will come home as soon as he can.

Good bye yours, ever, Eliza.

Henry C. Foster

In his next letter, Henry instructs Eliza how to handle importunate merchants with whom she has run up bills.

Lakeend Oct. 23d 1862

My Dear Wife & Children,

How do you all do to day. I trust you are well. I am well as usual. I received a letter from you yesterday & was very glad to learn you were well, for it had been a long time since I had heard from you. It was mailed Sept 30ᵗʰ. I should have got it before but it was detained on the way. I was getting quite uneasy about you. I was afraid you were sick or something had happend [sic] to you. Oh how glad I was to learn you wer [were] well. I had a letter from Vt

---

* Hardtack was a durable cracker, often called a "worm castle" because it was commonly infested with vermin. Packed in barrels, it was a basic ration for sailors and soldiers. It could be eaten dry, dipped in coffee, crumbled and fried into "doughnuts," or used to thicken soup. A soldier's ration was ten hardtack per day.

** "Mr. J. Thompson" is probably James G. Thompson, whose death is mentioned in the letter of Nov. 16, 1862. "Mr. Sawyer" is not listed among the men who initially signed up for Company A.

Letter of Henry C. Foster, Oct. 23, 1862. Courtesy Bethel Historical Society.

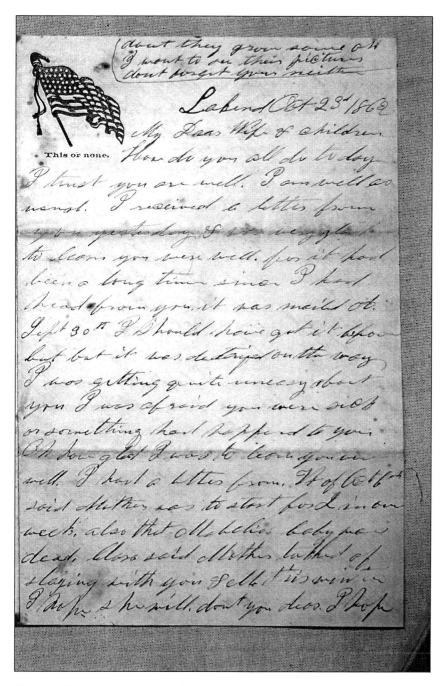

The pages shown here are 4 and 1 of a conjugate leaf folded in the center.

of Oct. 6th. *Said Mother [Clarinda] was to start for L in one week,*
also that Mabelia's baby was dead. ** *Clara said Mother talked of*
staying with you & M. this winter. *** *I hope she will, dont you dear.*
I hope you will all have a nice time. I should be very happy indeed
if I could be there to [too], but I have entered into a contract with
U.S. this time, that I cant get out of so easy so we must be patient as
possible, till he [the federal government] gits ready to let me off, but
this is a much more serious affair than I ever thought it would be.
As you said I think there is a good many will learn a good lesson if
they live to get through it.

Eliza I pray that you will not let people worry you. I feel it a [as]
much as you do although I do not have to be there under their nose.
The scamps. If there was any decency or humanity about them they
would treat a woman deacent [decently] at least I think. I do not
owe Soures [?] one cent & I am so sure of it if I was there I would
busst his eye for him. Don't you pay him a cent. I hope you will show
them how spunky you can be & tell them all to hunt for their pay,
if they cant be satisfied to get it as fast as you get it. Eliza I beg of
you to use your money for your own convenience first (for all leting
them have it). Let them know you don't care for them. You will say it
is all very well [for] me to talk, as long as I am away. Eliza it makes
me feel bad & it makes me mad to [too] when we are doing the best
we can to pay them [tradesmen] & here I am exposing my life & de-
priving myself of the comforts of home & family to save our Country
from ruin, & trying to sustain the liberties we have always enjoyed
& which they are now enjoying & the stinking cowards are staying

* This would have been a letter from Chancy or Clara. Mabelia would not have written herself because she would have been recovering from the birth and had Daniel Dana, aged six, to care for.

** The infant mentioned here, Henry Foster Fox, appears in *Descendants of Thomas Fox*. Mabelia bore three children who died soon after birth. Henry Foster Fox, born on June 7 and died on September 19, was one of the three.

*** Clarinda or "Clara" is sister to Henry Foster and wife to Chauncy (Chancy) Lynch of Vermont.

home abusing defenceless [sic] women. I would like to boot their asses. Still I hope as much as you do that we shall get them payed [paid] sometime. I think they will get a few of my sentiments when I do get home., if I should be spared [i.e., granted] that great boon of again being restored to my family, which hope & pray I may be.

Eliza I beg of you to be sure and make yourself comfortable & prepared for the winter, before anything else. It is your duty to do it for your own sake and the children also. These are trying times, and it is your duty to look out for number one first, so it is every ones duty, & I believe it is what every one goes in for now a days. Eliza get you [your] wood & coal &c for the winter, first. I shall be payed again soon I expect but it will be some time before you will get it.

If you think it proper to buy a stiching machine or if it will be any advantage to [you] can you get work enough to pay without doing it to cheap, or for little or nothing. I supposed there is a great demand for [seamstress] work is there not. I guess you have enough to do to take care of the children don't you. How is Sis [Henrietta]. Is she [a] good girl. I think she is & how is George. Dont they grow some. Oh I want to see their pictures. Dont [sic] forget your [yours] neither.

Well I have a few words more to write you, so I will take this haf [half] sheet which you sent me. Perhaps you thought this would be as much as I should want to write on, or at least as much as you would want to read unless it's better. I know I scrible a goodeal [sic] that aint of much account but you must consider from whence it comes. I do not have much of interest to write you except to tell you that I am well so I scrible of [off] something to fill up [the page]. You must excuse all mistakes &c. You said I could imagine how you feel towards me. I don't know. I expect you feel that I am ungreatful & unfeeling but Eliza I always tried to do the best I could, & I thought best to do as I have done. If I have done wrong towards you please forgive me.

You know I love you. I love my family, as husband or father ever could love his family, but I may not possess so free a manner of communicating it as some but it is not my fault. You have my best wishes, & I hope will imagine all the kisses you can. I would send you a cargo if they would do you any good. I shall go and see Dr. Holt [Eliza's cousin] if I can.* The 15th Regt is at Carrollton, 6 miles from here. I shall be very glad to see him but a soldier don't have a great deal of time to run around you know. Give my love to Mother, Mabelia & send it to Mother Bean & Mary &c. Mr. J. Thompson [is] very sick. We don't expect he will live but a short time. Mr. Sawyer & son, Mr. Comerford & Willard are all well.** Please write often. Write all the particulars &c. Mabelia did not tell me about the money so I did not know any thing about it. Write me a good loving letter wont you lidy [lady]. I feel lonely & homesick some times but I keep the best courage I can. . . .

H.C. Foster

Henry penned the first page of the above on stationery printed with a full-color Stars & Stripes plus the legend: "This or none." Embossed or decorated envelopes or stationery were popular; the New-York Historical Society preserves almost 500 envelopes related to Civil War events or personalities.[302]

Bowels Are of More Consequence Than Brains

As he penned his next letter, Andrew Bean had been promoted from the cook tent to assisting the quartermaster. The quartermaster assigned quar-

---

* Dr. Sumner Holt is also mentioned in Henry's letter of July 31, 1863.

** Mrs. Comerford seems to live downstairs from Eliza, and the two women share news from their respective husbands' letters. Henry refers to Mr. Comerford again on Nov. 16 and Dec. 10, 1862. See also his letters of Feb. 15 and May 16, 1863.

Sawyer is either Pvt. Barnard H. or Pvt. Edward A. of Henry's Company A. Henry mentions Sawyer again in his letters of Nov. 16 and Nov. 27.

ters and stores and distributed clothing and equipment. Men too ill to march into battle but fit enough to handle light duty in camp were tasked with these chores.

> *Camp in Oak Grove near Sharpsburg Md. Oct. 22, 62*
>
> *My Dear Sister & family*
>
> *I am pretty well at present though I have been sick indeed at times. I was glad to get out of Va. & I hope & pray that we may not have to go into that State again but I fear that we shall.*
>
> *I was glad you were in Albany [Maine] to see our dear old Mother when you wrote me last. God bless her in her declining years. Dear Dear Mother. I should have answered your letter long ago but you see we have been on the move all of the time since & I was so sick that I did not write any though I kept along. I have not been in hospital yet. I am with Quarter Master so I have a chance to take care of my self & live first rate.*
>
> *I had a letter from wife last mail & she told me you had gone home & our Mother with you. I am very glad you took her to Lowell &c. Now Eliza please write me just as soon as you get this all about your visit in Albany & if you called or visited at my house. Tell me how my wife & children were. How Ebenezer & sister [Mary Frances] look & appear. I love Ebenezer dearly dearly [sic] & sister too of course.*
>
> *Tell Mother to take care of your children so you can write me a good long letter. Tell me all the news.*
>
> *I had a very good letter from Henry but did not answer it for the same reason that I did not your letter.*
>
> *Tell me all about him & tell him all about me when you write him. I will write him soon.*
>
> *You have seen all the news of this Army the hard battles &c. Ah Dear Sister I have seen hundreds of dead rebels. Such is war.*

George Holt that lived with Mr. Green is in 16th Me. I saw him the other day. He told me that Charles Pressy was in some Regt. Do you know which one.

Eliza I got the box last winter that Mother & Mrs. Lovejoy sent me but articles do not come very well for we have moved round so much. Several boxes came the other day that were sent to Harrison's Landing. Cake in them was rotten &c. I would be so glad to have any thing from you. I have clothes enough every thing except mittens or gloves. If you can send me a nice pr. of gloves leather or woolen.

If we happen to stay here in Md. I should get any thing by express but you can send gloves miniatures & c in mail you know. Do them up so no one can see what they are.

Eliza Tell me how much that note is or how much I owe you for I have forgotten or send me the note so I can see. Tell me all about it at least.

Mother I wish I could see you. I hope I shall some time. I may not if God wills it so. Remember dear Mother that your loving Son forgets you not in pray [praying, prayers] to God.

We have had no fall rains yet but several frosty nights of late.

I have a tent by my self. Sleep alone in it. I have not undressed to go to bed a single time since I left my house. I must close so to go to rest for it is time. Eliza Please Do write just as soon as you get this. Direct

A. J. Beane

Washington D.C., 5th Maine Regt. Co. I. From your loving brother

Andrew does not name his illness in the above letter; perhaps it is the same as previously reported. Intestinal complaints were endemic and probably encouraged by the constant diet of fiber-rich beans. Some soldiers contracted typhoid fever, which accounted for 17 percent of all military deaths in 1861 and in 1865 killed 56 percent of all those who had contracted it. Soldiers from the rural western states were especially likely to contract measles, chicken pox, mumps, and smallpox. As if that were not enough, men often suffered from scurvy because of the lack of fresh vegetables and fruits in the military diet.[303]

Lest any reader suspect Andrew of malingering, hear this testimony from Major S. C. Gordon, given in 1898: "[In June 1862] the dead march could be heard at almost any hour of day or night. . . . It was estimated that nearly five hundred men, in the four Maine regiments, either died or were disabled to a great degree from diphtheria alone."[304]

Andrew's immediate superior expressed satisfaction with him both as a man and as an infantryman. Clark S. Edwards wrote to his wife on October 5, 1863, "The Boys are all well as usael that is Wormell Littlehall Russell Orin Brown Bryce [Clark's brother] & Andrew Bean.* I hope you may see as [that] he [Bean] is one of the best of fellows. I think he had fifty Dollars given him before he left from home. But *you need not mention it.* I give him ten Dollars. We have to be free in many cases."[305]

I Do So Much Want to See You

In the following letter, Henry dwells again upon financial matters:

> *Lake End Nov. 5th 1862*
>
> *My Dearest Ones: at home.*
>
> *What shall I say to you to day. I have so much I want to say, if I could see you, lidy. I guess [we] would have one chat wouldn't we. Well, I am well to day for the first & best thing & I pray that my family may be all well, also, Mother Bean included, & Mother*

---

* Edwards is referring to Lorenzo D. Russell and Orin S. Brown of Company I. Orin Brown was mustered into Company I on June 24, 1861, and taken prisoner May 29, 1864.

Foster & all the rest of the folks. Perhaps you will want [to] know how I know that your Mother [Mother Bean] is with you, for you did not give me a letter this mail, at least I did not receive one. The last One I received was Sept. 30th. I was some disappointed you may judge not to get one, but I hope I shall get one soon. I received one from M. [Mabelia?] of Oct. 20th. She said you had got home a week or more before that & had been over to her [to Dracut] & the rest of the folks. I suppose you were all well for she did not say. Frank Wilson had 3 [2?] letters.* His wife wrote that she had been to see you. I asked him if she wrote anything about my folks. He said yes they were all well & you were fat as butter. I am glad of it & I hope it is so. I should [have] thought you might wrote me a little bit of a letter, but I will not complain for I know you have to much to do. Oh I am so glad your Mother come home with you for you will not be so lonely. I hope you will take comfort together. I wish you all well a thousand times well.

I hope you have money enough so to be provided for this winter. We were payed again yesterday for 2 months. We expected to have got 4 month's so there is 2 month's due us now. I want to send you some money. If we had got 4 months pay I should, but now I dont know when we shall get payed again & I am afraid I shall need it. I dont know but I can buy tobacco as cheap here as there. I dont know but I shall have to leave of [off] using it it is so scarce & high but I am so lost without it but I have done without once & I can again if I try hard. I have thought some of selling my watch & send you the money. I could get $12.00 dollars for it most any time & I guess more but I hate to part with it. It has been worth a thousand times its value to me for good watches are scarce in these diggings and mine has stood what no other one in the Co has, except the Capt. Ship I. is a hard place for a watch. Every watch in this Co. stopped on Ship Island by getting sand in them but mine never has

* This is probably Private Franklin T. Wilson.

stopped except it run down, but it needs cleaning & regulating as it never was regulated you know. I could sell it pretty well but it has served me so well I hate to part with it & I am afraid I could not get another as good. I know the value of having a time piece especially when on guard so to know when to relieve guard & if they are not relieved just on time they will blame the Corporal. I used to lend it to him some times, but I made up my mind I would not lend it to no man so I will not for some dont know how to use a watch. I hated to refuse a comrade but a man has to look out for number one a little. I find I am thought just as much of, but Eliza I want to do all I can to help you.

How much will a stiching machine cost. Oh! Well I wont say any more about it this [time?]. If you think best to by [buy] one do so. I dont know but it wold [would] be the best thing you can do. I hope you will get my 2 month's pay soon.

Oh! I do so much want to see you & the children. Does Etta & George grow. How I wish I could see them. When will this war end. Do you hear from Andrew. I have not for a long time. Do write often and tell me all you can think of.

Please accept this from your true & loving husband.

H.C. Foster

Kiss E. [Etta and] G. Send their pictures & yours. Tell me all how Mother likes Lowell &c. Give her my love.

Once federal troops occupied the Crescent City, African-American refugees began trickling in. Some were encouraged by masters unable to feed them to seek food at Union army camps. Others abandoned their masters and headed for the camps. John DeForest, an officer with the 12th Connecticut Volunteers, was surprised that former slaves would assert their rights, and wondered in his letters what would happen to plantation society in Louisiana and Virginia. He sympathized with the men, but was not sure what would become of them. On July 13, 1862, he wrote, "As to the Negroes, they are all on our side, although thus far they are mainly a burden."[306] Some Union officers hired former slaves as camp servants. DeForest was unofficially offered the colonelcy of an African-American regiment, but declined. He later served at Third Winchester.

From winter camp, Clark Edwards wrote to his wife on November 10, 1862, on the subject of slavery: "I said when I first enlisted that I would not leave my <u>home and all</u> to come here to fight to do away [with] slavery in the state where the constitution had planted it. No that was not my motive, it was to establish one government once more on the constitution and there let it remain."[307] His statement reflected the thoughts of thousands of Yankees.

For his part, General Butler saw good use for able-bodied African-Americans. On Sept. 27, he oversaw the mustering in of the first of three regiments of Louisiana Native Guards, containing both former slaves and men from the state's free black population. On March 3, 1863, *Leslie's* devoted its front page to "Scenes in Louisiana," with a large engraving of pickets of the First Louisiana Native Guard watching the New Orleans, Opelousas and Great Western Railroad.[308]

Often in letters to Eliza, Henry strums the theme of marital infidelity—especially following his 1864 furlough. The subject gnaws at his liver—perhaps because he sees so many instances among his comrades. See his letters of January 12, 1863, and June 5, 1863.

As winter sets in, Henry reassures Eliza that rumors she hears about Union troops "starving" are false:

Lake End [La.] Nov. 16th, 1862

My Dear Wife: Eliza

I take this opportunity to write you a few lines in answer to a letter I received from you last Wednesday dated Oct. 24th. I was very thankful to get it, but sorry that you did not feel well when you finished it. I hope you will not be sick. I am afraid you work to hard. Do not work so hard. Get some one to do the hard work, such as sawing wood & getting in wood & c. I was glad to hear that you were all so well & the children to. Oh I want you [your] pictures so much. Do send them wont you. You can send them in a letter.

As for sending a box it costs so much that I guess you had better not. There is many things I should like but I can get along without them. I should like some of the apples you have there so plenty [plentiful] for one thing but you must eat for me. We have to pay 5 cents apiece for them here & rotten at that. Yesterday I swaped 3 large loafs of bread (one of them is a days ration) for 5 apples. We have good bread & potatoes 2 or 3 times a week, fresh beef 3 & 4 times a week, salt horse & ham the rest of the time. Pretty fair living for soldiers eh. This does not look like starving to death does it. The stories you hear have no truth, 9/10 are fake.

Mr. Thompson died about 2 weeks ago.* I forgot to mention it in my last letter. In fact I did not write so much as I intended to. Mr. Sawyer is at the Hospital now also Willard, but they are doing well. Mr. Comerford is well & all that you know I believe.

As for Capt Dickerman he is not liked in the Co. by but few men, for what reason none can hardly tell.** He has always used [treated] me well, & I have nothing further to say more than that. He lacks energy & confidence in himself.

This is a very bad country to live in. My health has been good so far & I am thankful for it, too, & I try to be as careful of it as I can. I have to go on guard every other day now but the duty is easy. I get along as well on guard as off. I dont know how long we shall be here. There is no signs of moving. The talk is now that Col. Jones is coming back again.*** We expect to get paid again soon. I hope so dont you. Oh, I want to see you so & the children. How they must

* Pvt. James G. Thompson of Henry's company.
** George M. Dickerman.
*** A Private Edward F. Jones appears on the company roster.

have grown. I dont know as I should know them now. Things begin to look a little as though this war would end some time dont they. The rebels begin to be pretty skeered. According to the latest news it seems our Army is making some pretty big moves. I hope they will be decisive in some way but we have been disappointed so many times. All we can do is to hope.

Monday Morning [November] 17ᵗʰ

It is a rainy morning & I have got to go on guard so I will finish this & send it. I have not got the letter you said you were going to write the next day after you finished the last one. We are expecting a mail now in a day or two. Tell me if you hear anything from Andrew. He must have been in a great many battles if he is alive. I have heard nothing from him since he was at Harrison's Landing [i.e., July and August]. Write me all how you get along &c. How your health is. Do you have the sick head ache [migraine?] as you used to. Is those bunches on sis much now.* I can imagine George running around, little chub. Take good care of your Mother, & make her stay as long as you can.

Have you got a stiching machine yet. I send you 5 dollars last mail. I will help you a little, I hope. I dont need much money here.

The 15ᵗʰ Maine Regt. is at Pensacola. Went last summer so I have not seen Dr. [Sumner] Holt & don't know as I shall.

Most all the men are receiving miniatures.** I dont get any. I suppose times are pretty dull in L. are they not. I am glad provi-

---

* One meaning of "bunch" is swelling. Bunches in the throat are mentioned several times in contemporaneous Vermont diaries, and apparently refer to infected adenoids or tonsils.

** Daguerreotypes, ambrotypes, tintypes, and cartes de visite were forms of photographic "miniatures" available to the American public. The carte de visite was affordable to most families by the 1860s and became very popular during the long separations spawned by the war. Some soldiers in winter camp took advantage of their leisure to pose for photographs, and compiled albums of their comrades.

sions are so plenty. I hope you will get along comfortable this win-
*ter. I think we will be at home in the spring. I pray God may spare
all our lives, that we may meet again. May God bless you all, &
protect you in my absence. From your true & loving husband*

    H. C. Foster

Salt horse was beef or pork preserved in casks of brine. The meat often
proved coarse and unappetizing, leading servicemen to suspect that its true
source was equine.

Henry again reminds Eliza about sending miniatures of the family:

Lake End   Nov. 27ᵗʰ 1862

My Dear Wife & Children

*I once more take my pen to commune with you. I trust you are
all well this Thanksgiving morn. I am well as usual. My health has
been very good all the time. I received your letter day before yesterday of the 29ᵗʰ Oct. I expected to find some pictures in it but imagine my disappointment when I opend it and found something else,
but I hope they will come sometime. These are very nice pens. This
is one I have writing with now. I had 3 letters this mail. One from
you & one from Mother & Mabelia & one from Chancy & Clara. I
wish I could have letters every day. It does me so much good to hear
from home & friends. I had no idea that Mother Bean was going
home so soon. I thought she would stay with you all winter. I hope
she will not go. Eliza keep up good courage. I pray for a better time
coming when this war will be over. I think it will be over this winter.
I went down to the City yesterday & went into the Hospital to see
Willard. He is agoing to get his discharge. He is pretty bad. He is all
swelled up and they cant do anything for him so they are going to
send him home & 7 or more out of this Co.*

* From evidence in her 1863 journal, Eliza purchases some provisions from the
Fox farm. She pays for the food and firewood—but perhaps she pays less than she
would on the open market.

Mr. Sawyer is very sick in the hospital with a fever. He will be discharged if he gets to go home & there is a lot out of Co D that are going home. It is astonishing how this war uses up men. Oh that it was ended, but I cannot end it. If I could you better believe it would be ended pretty quick. The Capt. [Dickerman?] is quite sick now. I asked him about Mr. Gilpatric's pay.* He said he would see. That's the answer one usualy [sic] gets from him, so that is the most I can tell you about it now. I shall have to stop now for I must go on guard to day. I [will] try and get time to finish this during the day as the mail goes Saturday. It is a frosty morning here. I wish I could be at home and eat a Thanksgiving dinner with you to day but as I cannot I shall have to put up with soldiers fare. Oh I am heartily sick of this war & so is every body unless it is some that are making plenty of money. I hope the removal of Gen McLellan [McClellan] will be of some benifit.** We have news up to the 19ᵗʰ of this month throgh [sic] rebel sources. It seems the Army of the Potomac has not done much yet, but it is no use to be discouraged for it only makes the matter worse. The past cannot be recalled. If it could I think I should not be a soldier, but as it is I have got to make the best of it.

I hope you will not worry. I trust you may be comfortable & look forward with hope & be cheerful & happy as you can. I am thankful that we are spared thus far & I pray that we may be spared to meet again. It is my daily hope & prayer that I may be restored to my family, again. Do not give up hope for it is everything. These are trying times indeed, but they will be better some time. Oh if I could see you how I should like to talk to you, but we must wait with patience. The time will soon roll round. I dont know hardly what to

* Pvt. John Gilpatric[k].

** George B. McClellan (1826–1885) became commander of the Army of the Potomac after the disaster at First Bull Run (July 21, 1861). He led the Army of the Potomac during the Peninsular and Antietam campaigns. McClellan was relieved of command of the Army of the Potomac on Nov. 5, 1862; he ran for president against Lincoln in 1864 and later served as governor of New Jersey.

say I want to say so much. It makes me feel homesick to see so many going home but it makes me feel worse to see them sick. I had much rather be well & have to stay my time out than be sick even if I could get my discharge, but we cannot always have our choice, but I pray that I may have my health, & that you & the children are well. Be prudent & do the best you can & I will help you all I can. How nice it must be to have a door cut through from the sitting room to the parlor. Mr. Morey is getting good aint he. How did you go to work to get him to do it. Has May got his so to [got him to do so too] of course he has. I am glad you have got yours. What do you burn this winter wood or coal. I suppose wood is the cheapest though you did not tell me what you paid.

Tell Etta & George, that Father wants to see them very much. Tell them he is way out in Louisiana watching the rebels, & will come home as soon as he can. Tell them to be good children & re-member papa &c. It seems you had not heard that Mr. Thompson was dead as you did not mention it.* I told you in the last or next to the last letter. Does Sylvia hear from George.** Give my respects to her, & to Moreys folks & all the rest of our neighbors, &c. I suppose you have [sic] having winter there now aint you. We are having what they call winter here. We have some frosty nights, but warm days.

It grves [grieves] me that you think your lot is so hard dear Eliza. I hope you will not think so. Take courage & be true, & be sure that your husband will be. Let that be the least thing to trouble you dear wife. I trust you can confide in me, but Eliza many stories you hear are but to true. I know enough to make me shudder. Some men have degraded themselves beneath the brute, & they are get-

---

* Henry mentioned Thompson's poor health in his letter of October 13, and his demise in his letter of Nov. 16.

** This seems to be a married couple, George and Sylvia Huzsey or Hussey. His name is not listed in the roster of men enlisting with Henry on September 21, 1861. Henry's letter of October 6, 1862, suggests he was a late enlister.

ting their pay for it to. I know some that are most dead with the P4x [pox or syphilis]. I cannot have no sympathy for such people, but Eliza I never shall forget that I have a wife & children at home & I honor & respect them so much that I shall always be true to them. How miserable I should be if I was not, & I trust in you my dearest of all on earth to me. Times look dark some times but I always hope to look on the bright side. You have my best wishes with many kisses. Oh if I could tell you how much I love my family. Kiss the Children for me, & God bless you all, & protect you.

From your true & loving husband,

Henry C. Foster

How Different

Henry has not heard from Eliza since October 29.

Custom House, New Orleans   Dec. 10ᵗʰ 1862*

My Dear Wife & Children at home.

As it is a long time since I have received a letter from you I will not wait any longer, & thinking perhaps you would like to know how & where I am I write now to inform you &c. I am well & my health has been good, as yet & dear ones I wish I could know the same of you all. I hope and pray that you [are] well. Oh: how disappointed I was not to get a letter the last mail. I dont see in to it [I can't figure out the reason]. I have not received a letter from you since the 29ᵗʰ Oct. It is very strange. Most all the rest had letters. I am afraid you or the children are sick but Mr. Comerford had a letter & Willard also. They both said my folks were all well. I am glad the rest got letters if I dont. I am all most discouraged sometimes. I write about

---

* Many of Butler's troops were stationed in Jackson Barracks, downriver from New Orleans's French Quarter. However, Jackson would not hold all the troops, and the unfinished Custom House accommodated some of the extras.

four letters where I get one but I am going to keep writing so that you cant forget me. I should like to know if you received that money that I sent the 5ᵗʰ of Nov. The last letter I wrote you I sent you that miniature I had taken in Lowell. It was getting spoiled in my knapsack & I did not want it so I thought I would send it.* It will do for the children to play with, if nothing else and you cant say I did not send you anything can you.

We left Lake End last Friday the 5ᵗʰ. How different from 6 years ago that same day [their wedding day], which was the happiest of my life & I trust of both our lives. Although we are seperated [sic] from each other by space I am happy that we can commune with each other by letter. I know it is hard for you dear Eliza to have me away. It is hard for me to be away. Sometimes I think I would do almost anything to get out of the Army so that I could be to home with my family, but I dare not undertake the game that some have to get their discharge.** I ought to be more thankful that I have my health & that my life is spared thus far, from day to day, & while we cannot have it otherwise than it is I will be as cheerful as possible & try to be true to my family & I trust you will keep up spirits & not get discourage. Trust in God, who doeth all things well. I might worry & fret myself to death almost. I almost think some men have done it, but what good would it do. You know it does not better the matter any. I hope that I shall get home some time & I hope that it

---

* Abner Small of the 16th Maine paints a picture of the Union knapsack, revealing how Henry's miniature could have been soiled: "The knapsack . . . is an unwieldy burden with its rough, coarse contents of flannel and sole leather and sometimes twenty rounds of ammunition extra. Mixed in with these regulation essentials, like beatitudes, are photographs, cards, huswife, Testament, pens, ink, paper, and oftentimes stolen truck enough to load a mule." (A "huswife" or housewife is a sewing kit.)

** "The game": Some enlisted men shot off a finger or toe or feigned illness in order to be discharged.

will be soon & so long as we have hope we have comfort.*

I will tell you something about our quarters. We are in the Custom House. It occupies a whole square, & fronts on 4 streets. The U.S. have been 25 years building this house & it is not finished yet & no knowing when it will be.** *It is a large building. It is built of granite & marble. The principle street that it fronts on is Canal St. which runs from the river straight to the Lake [Pontchartrain]. It is very wide. It has a double track of horse railroad in the center of the st. & a wide street each side of that. The horse railroad only runs half way to the Lake. There is a canal also that runs to the Lake along side of this, 6 miles. We have pretty good quarters but not so good as we had out to the Lake.*

Willard is in the Hospital. I see him most every day he is out walking around. Mr. Sawyer died last week Wednesday the 21ˢᵗ. He died with the fever. He was sick about three weeks. I am not going to write much more this time. I believe my ink is poor. It is to [too] thick. It is the same you sent me. Oh I sent you the pen to [too] in the last letter as you spoke about swaping. I hope you may get it.

We expect to get payed again next Saturday.*** *You have never told me whether you received your money or not the last two payments. I suppose there is no doubt but you have received it before this time. I hope you have at least.*

This is a fine warm day here. It seems like May or June here, but we have cool nights & some rough windy days. It is a spendid [sic] sight to go up on top of this building and look around. We can

---

* At this stage of the war, enlisted men were not granted leave unless they were recovering from a serious wound or unable to recover from an illness. Following his reenlistment, however, Henry was granted a furlough.

** Henry is mistaken; construction of the Custom House began in 1848—only fourteen years previously.

*** Soldiers' not receiving pay was hardly a new phenomenon. In 1779 Sergeant Samuel Glover, a veteran of several Revolutionary battles, and unpaid for fifteen months, led a mutiny of veterans. He was shot for his audacity (Rosalind Miles, *Who Cooked the Last Supper?*, p. 172).

see everything in & around the City but there seems to be one thing
missing & that is hills & mountains. It is all one vast level as far as
we can see. This is a pretty big City. We have to shine up [for drill*
and parade] pretty nice here now. I tell you it takes us about all the
time. We have to have every thing look just so buttons shined shoes
blacked &c. We have to drill about 4 hours per day.

Well I guess this is enough for this time. You have a true hus-
band's & Father's true love, with this. Give my respect to all. Do
please write, Eliza.

Your husband

Henry C. Foster

Kiss & love my dear children. May God protect you all.

Harbor no expectations of newsreel-like combat descriptions from the
pens of the ordinary infantryman. The individual witnessed a microcosm:
"The soldier on the battlefield who is doing his duty knows but little of
the general movements of the battle. . . . To him, his regiment or at least
his brigade, is the whole army. And generally he cannot see far even when
he has time to look. He fights in a cornfield where the tall stalks wave
above, or where hedge fences and clumps of trees, houses, barns, and even
chicken coops limit his view."[309]

Another veteran, Wilbur Fisk, agrees: "You never need to ask a private
soldier for general information. He is the last man to get that. His circle
of observation is very limited. He sees but little of what is going on, and
takes part in still less."[310]

To receive pay, soldiers needed to be present to sign the pay rolls once
each month. The camp's paymaster operated much like a civilian, often
dressing as one except when distributing cash from his two-hundred-
pound iron money chest. Payment was irregular at best. The Smithsonian
Institution comments, "Although soldiers were to be paid every two weeks,

---

* New Orleans was one of only nine cities in the United States at the time with
a population over 100,000.

A private in the Confederate Army. Dover Civil War Illustrations.

pay was often months late. As a result, many families became destitute, leading desperate soldiers to desert the ranks to care for loved ones."[311]

Paymaster Josiah D. Pulsifer left an account of hazards in the field.[312] On July 19, 1864, he wrote to his wife about distributing $100,000 to three regiments: "Our paying was interrupted by shells & minnie [minié] balls thrown as near our quarters as the enemy could guess. I saw one shell strike the ground and explode. . . . This shell I spoke of bursted within 20 feet throwing its fragments very near."[313]

During the winter, when roads were impassable and most fighting ceased, troops generally camped in one spot for months—an opportunity for more reliable paydays, "whereas regiments campaigning in the field often complained that the army's paymasters could not find them, or, having found them, feared to join them at the front."[314]

Writing to his parents, Samuel Oscar Chamberlain of the 49th Ohio described difficulties with his pay that echo Henry's. February 23, 1862: "…we have been promised our pay every day for about a month."[315] August 19, 1862: "…we are looking for the paymaster as 4 months are nearly due us."[316] November 2, 1864: "We expect to get our pay soon but don't know when."[317] November 20, 1864, at winter quarters in Pulaski, Tennessee: "…a few minutes ago we got orders to get ready for our pay and that looks like marching so we think or we would not get our pay so late in the evening."[318] In 1865, Chamberlain was forced to borrow money from his parents.[319]

I Am Corp. Just the Same

Henry continues in good health, although many other members of the regiment are ill.

Custom House, N.O. Dec. 14ᵗʰ 1862

I am Corp. just the same as I have been but it looks so straining [arrogant, boastful?] on my letters don't you think so.

Dear Wife:

How do you & the children do to day. I am well & trust & hope you are all the same. I received a letter from you to day through the P. Office. Had to pay 3 cts on it. Was over weight. Was dated Nov 26 & 28ᵗʰ. I thought the pictures had come this time sure but I was disappointed again, but I was so glad to get it & learn that [you] were well. I received one from M. [Mabelia] also. I think you had better not send so much [blank] paper as you have to pay extra postage as I can by [buy] paper here very reasonable. I wrote you a letter the 10ᵗʰ but I dont suppose it has gone yet.

Willard has gone to the Charity Hospital. He has been examined by the board of Drs. & approved of for a discharge so I suppose he will go home soon. I was up to see him yesterday. He looks very pale but he says he feells pretty well. He dont know what the disease is. Mr. Comerford went to the Hospital day before yesterday. He is not very sick but was unable to do duty. The rest of the men are pretty well. My health is good thus far & Dear Eliza how thankful I am that it is. I hope it it will continue to be & my family also. Health is worth everything. I cannot see very well here [in the dim light of his quarters] so I dont follow the line [printed on the stationery?] very well I guess.

We have news here from New York to the 2ⁿᵈ of this month. I have read the Presidents message. Oh I think it the best I ever read. If the people would only hear [adhere?] to it what a blessing it*

---

* "The Presidents message" is most probably a reference to Lincoln's Preliminary Emancipation Proclamation, issued on September 22. Lincoln declared that all slaves in rebel states would be free as of January 1, 1863. Two days after the proclamation, on September 24, fourteen Northern governors met at Altoona, Pennsylvania, and declared their support for emancipation.

would be to the country. I hope & pray that Congress will act upon it & endorse it & stop this war. It seems to be his great object to stop this war & blood shed & save the union also. I presume you have read it. If you have not I want you should.

Oh I am glad that you & the children were well. How much do you suppose I want to see you. So much that I would see you pretty soon if it was in my power to, but I cannot so I will be as patient as I can till that that blessed time comes, & I trust and pray that I may be spared to return to my family, & that you may all be blessed & comforted & protected in my absence.

I cannot say much about this war. It is a dreadful thing but when it will stop I cannot say, nor no one else save One that knows all things. It is rather a dark future, & discouraging but I hope to bare [bear] up through it all. I have not sold my watch & I guess I wont for I need it every much. We are expecting to [get] paid every day. We have signed the pay rolls. I aint going to write much this time, only to answer your letter. I hope [you] will get all my letters. I was in hopes your Mother [Mary Holt Bean] would stay with you this winter. She would be so much company for you & the children. I hope Mother Lynch [Henry's mother, Clarinda Foster Lynch] will

Mary Holt Bean, mother of Andrew and Eliza. Courtesy Bethel Historical Society.

be with you & I hope you will have a good time and enjoy your selves as well as you can but remember your true husband & Father. Our future happiness depends on our confidence in each other. Have

*courage & I will try to. Tell Etta & George to remember Father, & be
good to mama. A thousand blessings & comforts to my family from
your true & loving husband.*

 Henry C. Foster

 (leave of [off] the Corp. I have got sick of it. Say nothing.)

Though the following letter bears neither date nor location, it seems to
have been written around the time of the previous one. Henry gives the
same address at the close of the letter as would have reached him at the
Custom House.

 [December 1862 ?]

 Dear Eliza,

 *In regard to sending a box I think it not best for it costs so much
& it will not really be any benifit to me, for I get along well on soldiers rations. You know I never was very particular what I had to
eat. I like good things as well as any body but if I dont have them
it is all the same to me, as long as I get wholsome food & enough of
it & I can say that we have enough & that is good enough. We have
soft bread [freshly baked bread as opposed to hardtack or "hard
bread"] all the time and beef steak 2 a week & potatoes 2 or 3 times
a week, & we have some salt meat and baked beans, & there is
enough given away in this Co. every day to feed 15 men well. Any
man that will find fault with the living that we have in the Army
ought to go hungry a while don't you think so. I should be very glad
to receive any thing from you Dear lidy [lady] but we must econ-
omize the [these] trying times but I do want all your miniatures
[photographs] & I guess I will get them pretty soon by what you
wrote. Oh! I have a thousand things to say to you but I dont know
which to say, nor where to begin but I close for this time.*

* Henry may be sensitive to the fact that most of his company remained at the
rank of private. Obviously he wrote about his promotion to corporal in a letter to
Eliza that has been lost, since she was using that rank in his mailing address.

So good by sweet ones. If I am sick Dear Eliza I will tell you of
it. I will not keep anything from [you] if I can help it and I hope you
wont from me. Write as often as you can. Tell me all how [you are].

[to] Eliza H. Foster

Henrietta Foster

George A. Foster

Yours with Love

New Orleans under Benjamin Butler was a changed city. Because his father had succumbed to yellow fever, Butler was a stickler for municipal
sanitation. On his initial tours about New Orleans, the general witnessed
rotting garbage, open sewers, and fetid ponds on which animal carcasses
floated. He attempted to stave off disease by having the town's garbage
removed and the sewage ditches flushed daily. He also ordered a quarantine station established at Plaquemine Bend, fifteen miles south of the
city.[320] Although Jefferson Davis issued a proclamation in December 1862
declaring Butler an outlaw and ordering any Confederate office fortunate
enough to capture the portly "Beast" to hang him without delay, Butler's
martial law cleaned up the streets, scoured away street gangs, and helped
ward off the annual scourge of yellow fever.[321] Few residents gave Butler
credit for levee repairs, street cleanup, or his sponsorship of the United
States Relief Commission, which by November was feeding more than
34,000 locals weekly.[322]

Custom House N. Orleans Dec. 25th 1862

Dear Wife & Children

I wish you a mery christmas this morning. Oh that I could
be with you to greet you by word & lip but dear ones such cannot
be to day. When will it be. We will hope that boon will be spared
[granted] us, some future day. Never despair but hope on one. Last
night was Christmas eve. Shortly past nine oclock we were greeted
with the sound of two guns announcing a mail steamer, & I went

to sleep thinking of a letter that I should get to day for a Christmas present, but Oh [how] apt are we to be disappointed for no letter came to me. Eliza can you imagine my feelings. I thought I should get the miniatures to [too], but, no I must wait. I will be as patient as possible. I have not heard from any one at home since the 28ᵗʰ Nov. I cannot believe but what you have written. Well dear ones, I mean to render good for evil by writing you, to inform you that I am well to day & I hope & pray that you are all enjoying the same great blessing. It seems more like a May day here than like Christmas. I suppose there is plenty of snow in L. is there not. I shall not write much this time only to let you know of my whereabouts &c.

Gen [Benjamin] Butler left here yesterday for the North. Gen [Nathaniel P.] Banks arrived a week ago last Sunday with a large body of troops.* They have all gone up the river. That is the most I can tell you about it. The 26ᵗʰ is still in the Custom house. How long we shall stay here I cannot say, but there is no prospect of moving very son [soon]. We are not payed yet but expect to be soon. By accounts our Army has been repulsed again on the Rappahannock. It is rather sad news for Christmas but nothing is strange now. What will be the result who can tell. The rebels are desperate, & I have some fears, sometimes. It looks dark but I trust all will be well. God doeth all things well. We must put our trust in Him. Let us ever dear wife look to Him for support, & protection & obey His Laws. Oh I thank Him for His goodness, & may I ever live to praise His name. May his blessing ever rest upon you & our dear children.

I trust you are all well to day. I felt pretty sober [disconsolate] when I did not get any letter. I hope to get one soon. I will close. The boys [of Company A] are all about the same [as] when I last wrote

---

* Fresh from defeats by Stonewall Jackson in Virginia, Banks was sent to replace Butler in December 1862. In May and June of 1863, Banks's army besieged the Confederate garrison at Port Hudson, which had rugged natural and manmade defenses. With the aid of Farragut's warships and news of Vicksburg's surrender to the Union, Banks was able to take Port Hudson.

you. Give my [love] to all. Accept my, a true husbands & Fathers true love & affections. Be cheerful & take courage in the future. A thousand blessings to you all. Kiss the dear children for me. I wish you again a merry Christmas & a happy New Year & bid you good bye.

H. C. Foster

Your husband & Father, ever remembered &c

On New Year's Eve, Henry is still awaiting his pay:

Custom House [New Orleans] Dec. 31ˢᵗ 1862

Dear Eliza

I will now answer your good letter which I received last sunday date the 7ᵗʰ. I [was] very thankful to receive it I assure you also 2 papers & a letter from Mabelia & Mother. Oh how glad I was to learn that you were well though I fear you were not well if you had such a bad cold. I hope you got well of it soon.

My health is good as yet & has been thus far. What a blessing it is. I tell you I appreciate it above all things. God is good to us. How grateful we should all be to Him for the kind blessings we receive from day to day, but how few realize it.

This is a beautiful morning here but quite cool. This is the last day of the year. Who can tell where we will be at the end of another year. No one but we must hope. Oh Eliza it seems a long time to look ahead to the end of my enlistment but the time will roll away. At present I cannot expect to get home much short of it but still I have hopes that I shall. We will take courage & prepare for the worst & hope for the best, but Oh I hope ere another year rolls away, that I may have the joy of being at home with my family. I feel low spirited some times, but I hope to bear up through all to the end, but on the other hand I can but feel thankful that I have been so much favored, when compared with some other troops in the ser-

vice. I have not much time to write this morning. This [is] mustering in day, at 8 oclock but the mail closes at 12, so what I write I must write quick. The talk is as soon as we are mustered we shall get paid. I think it time we were any how.

    Well E. I don't know as I can tell you much news & perhaps it is not necessary for Mr. A. will give all information required. Mr. Comberford is in the hospital but he is not very sick so to be about [that is, ambulatory]. Wilard the same. There is 15 in the hospital and a number sick in quarters so our Co [100 men when originally mustered] is pretty smal [sic] now. One of our sergents has gone home 2 more are sick in the Hospital and will no doubt be discharged so I have some prospect of promotion if I behave myself, but I never had put myself out in the least for it. The most that worry me is being competent for the place assigned to me, but I must do the best I can. If they put me in to it[,] it is not my fault you know. I cant write any more now as the Company is falling in. We have been mustered & the Col. told us we should be paid this afternoon, for 2 month ending Nov. 1st so we shall have 2 months due.

    Dear Ones I will close hoping this will find you all well & comfortable. Tell me how you get along. I wish you could get my pay oftener & quicker. Do you have any trouble in gitting your money from the City now. Oh that I could be with [you] to day. Seems so I could see you & the Children in the nice sitting room. What do you have to pay for wood. I hope you may all be well, & get along well. You imagine me, sitting here in the Custom house on a broken chair with a stool to write on, under these little roofs. The building has no [permanent] roof on, so between the stories is small roof built that come clear down to the floor so it seems like an old fashioned country chamber sleeping under the rafters. Our quarters are dry and warm but rather dark but I have no fault to find with them.

    I guess you will think this is written in a hurry & so it is. Now good bye & may heavenly blessings rest upon you always. Oh I am

so anxious for those miniatures [photographs] that I can hardly
wait, but I think they will come next time though you did not say
anything about them. I hope you have not forgot them. My love and
best wishes to my family. Give my respects to M. & c. [Mabelia and
children?] From your true & loving husband & Father, ever

 Henry C. Foster

During 1863, Massachusetts did not slacken its efforts to provide troops. More than 11,000 volunteers were mustered in for three years' army service, bringing the total furnished for the war at that point to 63,359. In addition, 16,837 nine months' men and 3,736 three months' men registered for service. Massachusetts also enlisted more than 17,000 for naval service from the beginning of the Rebellion to December 30, 1863. On January 1, 1864, Massachusetts had 36 infantry regiments in service.

Here the written record is enriched by Eliza's surviving diary. She dotes on Henry's letters and those from Andrew, as they do on hers.

Mrs. Eliza. H. Foster. Lowell. Mass. Book, 1863

Back home in Lowell, at the outset of 1863—the year that Henry so ardently hoped would bring him home to his wife and family—Eliza Foster began making entries in a small "diary and memorandum book." The pocket-size journal, printed in Boston, provided blanks for activities and appointments, as well as end pages for financial notes.

At the beginning of the Civil War, important industries such as cotton, woolen, and paper mills and manufacturers of shoes and overshoes were largely dependent on female workers. According to an estimate by the director of the 1860 census, women performed 25 percent of the country's manufacturing. Females worked outside the home in the manufacture of jewelry, gold pens, watches, ready-made clothing, matches, perfumery, fireworks, flavoring extracts, and hats and bonnets.[323]

As the war continued, cotton mills in Lowell and Lawrence began hiring almost anyone who applied. The "quality of the operatives declined, mill work became for the time less respectable, and many women whose place was naturally in the mills refused longer to remain there, but went rather into dressmaking and similar vocations."[324] Eliza's employment history followed this pattern.

Six years into her marriage, Eliza opens to the first page of her diary. On the one hand, Henry's enlistment has put her life on hold for three years. Both of them—she as a wife, he as an infantryman—have yielded up control of their lives to others. Fifteen months of Henry's term of service have now elapsed, approaching one half of the total. The days sometimes seem endless. On the other hand, comforted by old Maine acquaintances as well as the Fox family, Eliza seems reasonably content—if sometimes overburdened by the physical tasks she must accomplish single-handed:

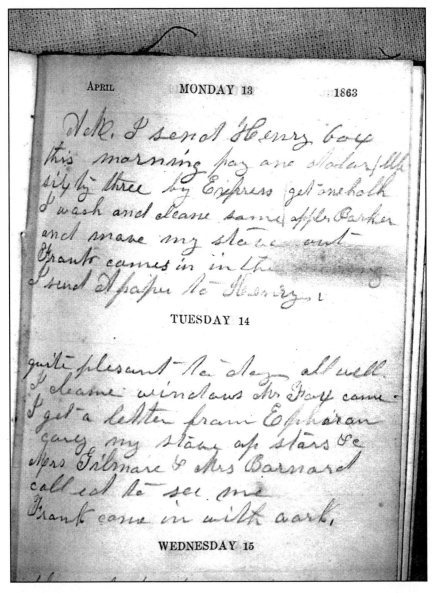

Eliza Bean Foster's notebook. Monday, April 13, through Wednesday, April 15, 1863.

chopping wood and bringing it in, carrying water for drinking, cooking, bathing and laundry, and toting out hods of ash. On the economic front, she wrestles with inflation. In 1840 Lowell, a dozen eggs cost 10 cents; an entire chicken, 15 cents; and a carcass of mutton, $2.[325] Between 1860 and 1863, living costs had increased by more than 50 percent.[326]

Eliza's diary bears comparison with the 1863 diary kept by Rachel Cormany, wife of a Union soldier from Pennsylvania. Alone with an infant while her Samuel was away at war, Rachel often complained of depression, loneliness, and boredom. However, her spirits soared when she was able to attend Bible class or to enjoy "a sweet season of prayer" at the end of a day of baking, ironing, and mending.

Exchanging photographs is a constant theme of letters and diaries. After a trip to France, in 1851 Mathew Brady had introduced the collodion wet-plate process, which made it possible to produce a good glass negative from which an unlimited number of paper prints could be made. Brady sold his studio portraits for $5 to $150. But about 1858, he perfected the inexpensive carte de visite (CDV) process, which Eliza and the general population gratefully embraced. Measuring about two and a half by four inches and usually bearing a headshot or other portrait pose, the carte de visite was traded among enlisted men and officers and reverently mounted in gilt-trimmed albums.

Like many diaries harboring good intentions of regular entries, Eliza's begins with plump daily notes—but these become meager and infrequent as the year progresses. The longest gaps are nearly a month—from the end of April to May 23 and from November 6 to December 3. In general, however, Eliza registers every letter from her husband, Henry, and every occasion of her writing to him. Even deliveries of meat or purchases of molasses or sewing supplies warranted a note.

Eliza's diary reflects both the spread of education and the explosion of diary keeping in the nineteenth century. Diaries served as aids to introspection as well as records of notable events, health, weather, visitors, and "how it all turns out."

In the following transcription, marginalia have been moved to the end of the day's entry. Figures and notations from the Cash Account and Bills Receivable pages have been moved to the diary proper, where they are integrated in chronological order. Eliza's handwriting is small and regular, though her entries lack introspection. Her spelling is often phonetic, and while her vocabulary is inferior to her husband's, she generally manages to express her feelings on paper adequately. Spelling and punctuation generally follow the original here, but capital letters have been added to indicate the first words of sentences or thoughts. Every effort has been made to identify persons mentioned.

On the same day Eliza began her diary, January 1, 1863, the Emancipation Proclamation went into effect—freeing those slaves residing in states still engaged in open rebellion against the Union. "The moment came," President Lincoln declared, "when I felt that slavery must die that the nation might live."

Thursday, January 1, 1863: *Welcome the happy new year and who can tell what another year can or will bring fourth [forth] I hope and pray that before a nother [sic] year roles [rolls] around that the dearest to me will be at home with me.*

Mother Lynch [Eliza's mother-in-law] is her [here] with me now. I spend the day at home We go out on the street I get cotton cloth 8 yds & Jockey Club 17.*

Bills Receivable, January 1: *One year rent, $13.50, "paid in full." Mr. Stickney [a grocer on Tilden Street] due $7.30 for milk.*

Eliza also records a debt of $18 due to grocer E. T. Parker, and another debt to E. Leavejoy of $10.54.** These are large amounts, considering that

---

* This entry may refer to a contemporary sporting paper named for the Jockey Club founded in Paris in 1834. The Club organized the Prix du Jockey Club, a horse race first run in 1836 that was the equivalent of the English Epsom Derby. During the Civil War, interest in horse racing revived, and new racetracks were built in Washington and Boston.

** Mrs. Lovejoy appears to have been Eliza's neighbor. She is mentioned as pairing with Mrs. Bean, Eliza's mother, to send a care package to Andrew Bean; see Bean's letter of Oct. 22, 1862. In his letter of May 9, 1863, Andrew mentions William H. Lovejoy and his brother Aaron. Lovejoy is mentioned on April 4, 1867, as well.

her regular income at the time was \$32 per month—\$20 from Henry's allotment and \$12 from the City of Lowell.

Saturday, January 3: *What splendid weather this is I spend the day at home all well I get a letter from henry [sic] dated Dec. 25ᵗʰ & go down to Mrs. Hussey a few moments in the evening*

One qt. of molasses

Sunday, January 4: *what splendid weather this is Mother goes to meeting with Mrs. Cameford***

Monday, January 5: *how plesant it is who can tell what another day may bring fourth*

I wash & ian [iron] etc

Bake. Mr. & Mrs. Fox [Dana R. Fox and his wife Mabelia] came and Mrs. F. staies all night.

Tuesday, January 6: *Not so plesant but as the day pases it stormes*

I stay at home in the morning and wash Leave George with rose [a friend, also known to Andrew] and go out with Mother Lynch and Mrs. Fox

They get their pictures taken

I get one copied for Mother 25 cts

Wednesday, January 7: *Stay at home except run out to get that picture of Henrys and a paper*

What pleasant weather

---

* A George Huzsey is mentioned by Andrew in a letter dated July 12, 1863, and a "Hussy" in his letter of Feb. 3, 1867. The enlistment of a Hussey is mentioned in a letter of Oct. 13, 1862, by Henry. Mrs. Hussey's first name may be Sylvia, as Henry refers to George and Sylvia in one of his 1862 letters. In his letter of August 6, 1864, he refers to "Hussy" and "Syl" as a pair.

** The 1861 Lowell city directory lists William H. Comerford, painter, residing at 90 East Merrimac Street, who may have been Henry's pre-war employer. The CWSS spelling is "Camerford."

Thursday, January 8: *how plesant   All is well that ends well Mrs. Hayez [same as Husey, Hussey?] & Rose I & Agnes goes a herin [?] in the after noon Get hats*

Mrs. Fox goes home from her [here]

The new hats were intended for greeting Lowell's own Gen. Benjamin Franklin Butler on January 10. Hats of the day included the Godey hat (a three-piece bonnet with a round brim, a Conestoga-wagon–shaped body, and a frill at the neckline) and the Empire (worn on the flat of the head in front of a chignon). The Godey was fashioned of straw or cloth, tied under the chin with silk ribbons. The Empire bonnet was suitable for church. The simpler prairie bonnet was popular throughout the nineteenth century. Eliza probably made her own hats as a rule—but wanted something in the latest mode to honor Butler.[327]

Friday, January 9: *How plesant   We are all well*

Mrs. Hayez [Husey?] & I go Berin [a department store?] again get hat Got home & how tiard

I maile a letter for Mother to Henry

Saturday, January 10: *Quite plesant all day until night.*

Snow & then raine

Gen. Butlar [Butler] comes home I go out to greet him.

*Get one half pound Tea to Parkers**

Benjamin Franklin Butler

A one-time pro-slavery Southern sympathizer, Maj. Gen. Benjamin Butler had been placed in command of the Department of the Gulf when it was created during the winter of 1861-62. The task of the department was to take command of Mobile, New Orleans, Baton Rouge, and Galveston

* The shop of Theodore E. Parker, grocer, was located at 65 E. Merrimac Street, according to the 1861 City Directory.

as well as the lower Mississippi and Texas. When Butler called for troops needed for this action, New England enthusiastically furnished 1,400 men.

Eliza's admiration for Ben Butler had two taproots. First, she would have seen him as Henry's ultimate commander in New Orleans. Second, though born in New Hampshire, Butler was embraced as a son of Massachusetts. His recently widowed mother moved her family to Lowell in 1828 and undertook

Gen. Benjamin F. Butler. *Dover Civil War Illustrations.*

managing a boardinghouse—as did the mother of Nathaniel Banks, another Civil War general. Bone-tired and frustrated, the mill-girl boarders aired complaints around the dining table, where little pitchers had big ears.[328]

After attending Exeter Academy, Benjamin Butler graduated from Colby College at Waterville, Maine,[329] then studied law with attorney William Smith of Lowell. A stickler for researching precedent, Butler was admitted to the bar at age twenty-one. Butler's sympathies for operatives' complaints meant that his first legal clients were factory girls pressing charges against employers. Advising mill girls to take action not by strike action but by retaining him to plead their case to the state legislature, Butler crusaded for employment concessions and shorter hours.[330] In 1851, the state legislature passed a compromise bill instituting a workday of eleven hours and fifteen minutes.[331]

Although a skilled trial lawyer, Butler had no military experience at the outset of the Rebellion. Like many of his fellows, the "political general"proved a poor administrator and leader for the Union. Henry refers to Butler several times—usually in a neutral tone—in letters from Louisiana.

On the occasion that Eliza is writing about, Lincoln had recalled Butler from Louisiana after eight months for tactlessness and ongoing disputes with New Orleans consuls. However, Butler's Northern public found little fault with him. He flaunted his mug from Washington, D.C., to Massachusetts in triumph, gathering formal votes of thanks from the House of Representatives, state legislatures, and the city of New York.[332] As Lincoln slowly changed his mind about Butler's usefulness, Butler held out for promotion that would satisfy his ego. In October 1863 he consented to return to his old command at Fort Monroe.

Eliza's Diary:

> **Sunday, January 11**: *Quite plesant Stay at home all day*
>
> *Mother & I wash ian etc.*
>
> *Mrs. Fox comes over and staies*

Wash day was such a trial that cookbooks of the period often printed instructions on how to manage it efficiently. For example, *Jennie June's American Cookery Book* (1866) gave directions for laundering white flannel baby garments, knitted wool socks, laces, needlework, tablecloths stained with coffee, and muslin print dresses. The author, Mrs. J. C. Croly ("Jennie June"), shunned newfangled devices, declaring that "few machines [had been] invented, to rival the stout arm, and strong hand of the professional wash-woman." But Mrs. Croly did allow that washing day was "the dreaded event of every household, large, and small; . . . proverbially associated with wretchedness and discomfort."[333]

> **Monday, January 12**: *I send a letter to Henry No. l one [sic]* ˙
>
> *Quite plesant wash ian*
>
> *Mrs. Fox comes over I get a letter from Henry dated Dec. 31 & get a frame for Henry photograph 73 cts & send it to Clara & she dear to Chaney [Chauncey Lynch]*

* Henry and Eliza numbered their letters, to track those lost in the mails.

Dearest of All on Earth

Tucked away in the dim attic of the Custom House, Henry seems to be bearing up fairly well, although he suffers from homesickness. In his second letter of 1863, he compares his lodging to a prison of stone.

No. 1 1863 Custom House N. Orleans Jan 12ᵗʰ 1863

Dear Eliza

How do you & the children do this morning. How I wish I could be with you to day, or if I could know even that you are all well. I hope & trust you are, & may be so. My health is good, & I feel first rate as far as bodily health is concerned, but I have some home sick days, when I think what a distance I am from home, but I feel that all will be well in good time & I content my self as best I can.

I received a letter from you yesterday dated 29ᵗʰ Dec the only one from you written in Dec. If you have written every week it is strange where they are. I also received the papers. I think there must be a mail that started be for [before] this that has not arrived, yet, for there was not a great many letters come. I shall look sharp for the box I tell you I hope I shall get.

It grves me that you feel so bad dear one. Think nothing of dreams. Do not let them trouble you if you can help it. You know I never believed much in them. I have had dreams myself that would have a bad impression on my mind, but I always bash [banish?] such things, as quick as possible. I dream of being with you almost every night, dear one. I have many pleasant ones, some are not so pleasant. Where our mind is there will our thoughts be. O what a joyful day it will be, should we all be spared to meet again on earth & should we not, we will trust all to God, in eternity: what a comfort it is to trust in Him, and ask His blessings & Oh! How thanful [thankful] should we feel, for His goodness towards us, that we are spared from day to day to enjoy the light of His blessings, but we must not trust all to our Heavenly Father. We must trust in ourselves also.

I hope that I may do right & I ask Him to teach me to do right in all things, but Eliza, the Army is a trying place, for a person. It requires a pretty strong mind, to guard against the temptations that beset us, not that I am or pretend to be any better than my comrades with me, but I do not think I shall fall into the vices that some have, & I pray that I may be pardoned for all that I to [do] amiss, unmeaningly [i.e., unintentionally]. What can men think of themselves & family to do as they do. They cannot thinks [sic] but little of their wives. I should never want to see home if I had degraded myself in the way that some have, but Eliza you know your husband.* Can you confide in him. Never mind what the world says as long as you have a clear concience [sic]. I hope there never will be any jealousy between us.

Dearest of all on earth, never be free with all & yourself, but do right. That is all either of us can ask. Be firm & faithful, & your husband will ever be so to you. Be cheerful & happy as you can, and we will hope the time will soon come that I shall be at home. The time will soon slip away if we are spared though it seems a long time to look ahead, but the time will surely come if we will wait. Yes Eliza we will be as contented as possible. I hope this war will soon end but there is not much prospect of it just now but as it [is] the darkest hour just before day, so it may be the day of peace is dawning on our Country.** I pray that it may be so.

---

* Henry seems to refer here to troops who resorted to the services of prostitutes, a common occurrence during the Civil War. Henry Steele Commager cites a Civil War doctor who found that the Union army treated 250,000 cases of venereal disease. The Union army even organized legal prostitution in Tennessee during 1863, and an 1864 letter from City Point, Virginia, remarks that officers believe that, barring the outlet afforded by prostitutes, soldiers would become rapists.

** "Darkest hour": "The darkest hour is that before the dawn" appeared in the *English Proverbs* anthology edited by William Hazlitt.

I presume you will hear that Galveston has been recaptured by the rebels ere you get this letter but I don't think they will hold it long.* Gen Banks is here now. Most of his troops have gone up the [Mississippi] river. We have to do guard duty at his headquarters every night. I cannot tell how long we shall stay here but there is no prospect of leaving. We were paid the last day of Dec for two months, up to Nov 1ˢᵗ. The pay rolls are all made out for 2 months more up to Jan 1ˢᵗ & we expect to get paid in a few days. I do not see why you do [not] get my pay but it is probable that government is keeping it to speculate on. I wish I could break the allotment roll. I would and send it to you for you would get it quicker.

Well this sheet is full and I will stop.

From your true & loving husband

H. C. Foster

May heavenly blessings rest on you all forever.

HOME

Eliza's Diary:

Tuesday, January 13: *7 o'clock Mother Lynch goes home to day Mrs. [name not given; perhaps Mabelia, perhaps Mabelia's mother-in-law,**] goes to depot to see her [off?]*

Mrs. Fox goes home in the afternoon

This is a plesant day

Wednesday, January 14: *I will clear up & set things to rights*

*   In 1862 Galveston had the best port on the Texas coast and was the state's second largest city. The Union had been blockading the port since July 1861. Butler's original orders from McClellan included securing New Orleans and environs, and then supporting the navy in expeditions against Baton Route, Berwick Bay, Galveston and Mobile. But he had only 15,000 men, and the swamps were full of trigger-happy partisans.

** Mabelia's mother-in-law is Hephzibah Peabody Fox (1789?–1883). Widowed in 1857, she was probably part of Dana's extended household.

as I am left alone againe Well I don't accomplish much The time
semes long to me although we are well

Thursday, January 15: *This day has past What a world this*
it seames although this world ought to be in morning [mourning]

Eliza may be reacting here to despondence, to gloomy winter weather—or
to news of the First Confederate Congress, which convened at Richmond
on January 12 for its third session. President Jefferson Davis spoke op-
timistically on the state of the Confederacy, an unwelcome message to
Union ears.

Friday, January 16: *Warm and raney all day*

I go in Mrs. C. a moment & Roses [Rose has a shop of some
kind, and Eliza often visits and/or trades there.]—Mrs. May steps
in with a lb. of meat

Saturday, January 17: *All is well What a blessing it is to have*
good health & how much we ought to appresiate is at the present
time while alone & no one to care for me now

Sunday, January 18: *I stay at home all day or at least after I*
get up about ten Frank cals [calls] in to see how I get along & Mrs.
*Husey & Charley in the evening**

Monday, January 19: *welcomes the washing day & I have a*
large wash & I have a lode of wood come one card [cord?] and one
food—I get it in

I get a pease of beef to boil & pork 37 [cents]

* Henry's Company A includes a Private Frank S. Berry, a First Sergeant Frank
Grout, a Private Frank Howard and a Private Franklin T. Wilson. The identity of this
Frank remains conjecture; he could be back in Lowell under a medical discharge.
He is most likely Frank Wilson (referred to in Henry's letter of Nov. 5, 1862, and
again on Oct. 6, 1862, indirectly, as "Mr. Wilson"— "not the one that comes to see
you)". At any rate, the diary shows he is someone Eliza trusts implicitly as she does
not mind his dropping by often, unaccompanied. Frank sometimes calls simultaneously with Willard, which reinforces the suggestion that he had been a member of
Company A.

A letter to Henry from his sister and Eliza's sister-in-law, Mabelia Fox, reveals more about the extended family:

Dracut [Mass.] Jan 19ᵗʰ 1863

Dear Brother

How do you do this beatiful [sic] Monday morning. I hope you are well. We [are] all well as usual this morning for which I fell [feel] truly thankful to God and as I was waiting for my clothes to boil I thought I would sit down and converse with you a little while through the silent medium of my pen. Dana has just started with a load of wood for Eliza   hard wood *. I was there last Monday and stayed all night and went to the depot with Mother Tuesday morning. I have not heard from her yet. I was there the day Ben Butler made his speech but I did not go to hear it. Mrs. Comerford did though so that was just as well as if she aint the greatest bag of news I ever saw, she shook hands with him want [wasn't] that great. She will tell of that a long time same as she did when she shook hands with the soldiers and bid them good by [sic] so many times when they left Lowell. She is a curious woman   I think any way.

. . . We have not had any snow here this winter hardly. It is very sickly in Lowell and other places too with scarlet fever and canker rash.**

Well Brother I have after so long a time got my picture for you but it looks so that I am most ashamed to send it to you but E says it looks just like me. I am very poor [in health] and that makes me look very long [in] my face and you know I am no beauty any way, but I cant help it. I heard E read your letter that was dated the last

* With its compact grain, hardwood burned more slowly than soft wood. In other words, Mabelia is assuring her brother that Eliza is getting the best wood for her heating and cooking purposes.

** Precisely what ailment is meant by "canker rash" is unclear. Canker usually refers to contagious sores in the mouth; however, it may also describe any invasive, ulcerous, spreading sore.

day of Dec. You said you recved a letter from me and Mother and there is one that I sent before Thanksgiving that I conclude you have not got for Mother did not write in that but I am going to keep writing whether you get them or not. Perhaps you may get some of them sometime. I hope you will keep up good courage if you can. Trust in the Lord who is your help and strength. God is good to those that trust in him. Try to do your duty in every place. Dont mind what other say to you. They have not got your sins to answer for nor you theirs. Neither can they do yur [your] duty. You alone can do it....I know it by experience. I will close. Good by from your loving sister,

M.B. Fox

Eliza's Diary:

Tuesday, January 20: *Verrey plesant—but I am tiared I have another lode of wood the same as the other & I got it in I have company Mrs. Maanez [Maines?] & Mrs. Heanley just caled*

Wednesday, January 21: *I am still at home how lonely it is to stay at home so much and then againe how plesant it is to have a home to stay at & I go over to see Mr. Gerld to here [hear] a [letter] from Henry Dear he spoke well of him*

Thursday, January 22: *quite plesant although some storm. I go into Roses & to see Mrs. Moery [Morey?] How slim he [Mr. Morey] looks [on his death bed, apparently] How sad to see that poor man pas [pass] away and leave his family. Helyn stops to Tea with me*

Friday, January 23: *It is quite plesant I stay in all day I am thankful that we ar [are] well I fix my old dress in the after noon Mrs. Hanley comes and stay to tea.*

I nit a cap for her or learn [teach] her how

Some suger & one bar sope.

Saturday, January 24: *Things go on about the same Time pases but what a world is this*

Here I Am Sitting on a Drum

In his next letter, Henry describes some rare rest and recuperation,—a night out at the theater.

No. 2 Custom House N. Orleans Jan 24ᵗʰ 1863

My dear Family,

I take this opportunity to write you a few lines to let you know that I am well to day, & I trust you are all well, & I hope you may be well & prosperous, during my absence from you. I did not get any letter from you last mail. I received one from Mother & hr miniature. She said you were all well but [did] not know as you would send that day [January] 9ᵗʰ. I am waiting as patient as I can for those pictures. I think Mothers looks very well indeed, but she has grown old since last I saw her.

Well my health is good & I have been well all the time but I feel homesick being shut up here in this stone house. It is equal to a states prison almost but we will be patient wont we dear one & hope for better times to come, & I hope it will come soon.

Willard was here to day from the hospital. He is getting some better. I guess he will not go home in a hurry. He is night watch now in the hospital, & gets extra pay so he says. Mr. Comerford is pretty low now. He has a diarhea [sic] which has run him right down. Ed Sayer [Sawyer?] is just come out of the Hospital, for duty. He has been in ever since we come from the lake.*

---

* Henry refers to Lake End, the summer resort on the south end of Lake Pontchartrain where he was stationed in 1862.

Oh I must tell yu. I went to the nigger show last evening.* It was first rate. One of our men paid me in [paid for Henry's ticket]. It is the first time I have been to any thing of the kind since I have been here. It really done me good. It livened me up & I almost forgot I was a soldier. Ned Greene is one of the troupe. He sung & whistle [whistled] the mocking bird & sung the indian song.** I thought I was in Huntington hall for a moment, but dear one you was not by my side to cheer me.*** This only made me sad again. I have many sad moments thinking of you & the dear little ones. It is hard but we ought to be thankful that we are spared, from day to day. I am for one very thankful that I have my health, & I hope hope on for the time to come when we can meet again if we are permitted by a kind providence to do so. I hope you will not feel sad but be as cheerful as possible. I know it is hard for you to be left with two smal [sic] children to take care of & to be tied up so much. They require a goodeal of care, but Oh D Eliza you have their laugh & prattle to cheer you, & help to make the long & dreary time more pleasant by

* Generally for men only, and serving alcoholic beverages, variety shows juxtaposed entertainment ranging from operatic arias to animal acts, banjo players, acrobats, mathematicians, bicycle acts, bird-call imitations, soft-shoe numbers, feats of magic, and recitals of Shakespeare. (By the 1880s, entrepreneurs developed the variety show into vaudeville—which banned alcohol, and welcomed an audience of both sexes.)

The Ethiopian Serenaders was one popular Negro minstrel group of the time. Other popular groups included Christy's Minstrels, the Bailey Troupe, Hood's Minstrels, Buckley's, the Virginia Minstrels, the New Orleans Minstrels, the Star Minstrels, and the New Orleans Serenaders and Operatic Troupe.

** An index to American sheet music issued between 1820 and 1860 lists nineteen songs with "Indian" or "Indian's" in the title, including "The Indian and His Bride," "The Indian Girl's Song," and "The Indian Mother's Lullaby." Folk music indexer Jane Keefer believes the song Henry heard is most likely "The Little Mohee," a British ballad originally titled "Indian Lass." The British lyrics included a verse about New Orleans. It is listed in the Laws' Native American Balladry index as H8 (personal communication with Keefer, Feb. 2, 2007).

*** Huntington Hall was a large civil space in Lowell. It seems that Eliza and Henry had attended entertainments there—perhaps during their courtship and before the birth of Henrietta.

their cuts [cutups, i.e., clowning, joking, attention-seeking behavior] & pranks.

Oh how I wish I could look in & see you, today, dont you think I would.

I hope you have got your money ere this. It is discouraging & makes me mad to [too] to see how government affairs are managed. We have not been paid again yet since 31 Dec but it [there] has been talk about it ever since every day. They owe us for Nov & Dec.

Well Eliza here I am sitting on a drum, belonging to one of our drummers that is in the hospital. I believe I have told you about our quarters have I not. Our duty is not very hard. The talk is now that our Co is going back to the lake again. The people there, in that vicinity have got up a petition & signed by over one hundred names, to have our Co go out there again. We have had no orders to go yet. Col Farr is acting Brig. Gen. now & Major Sawtelle is in command of the Regt. Ther [there] is no signs of the Regt leaving the City that I can see. I read in a paper that the 5th Maine Regt was sent home or what was left of it only 25 men. Andrew [a member of the 5th Maine] has had a narrow escape if indeed he has escaped, but I fear he is one of those missing but I pray that he may have been spared. This sheet is full & the last I have now, so here is a husband & Fathers love to [too] for his family & may God bless & spare you all, & protect you.*

H. C. Foster

Eliza's Diary:

Sunday, January 25: *Quite plesant This a day of sadness to Mrs. Maerz [Morey?] as her husband has passed away camly & plesantly We are all well*

---

* Col. A. B. Farr, who would later sign Henry's discharge papers in Franklin, La., on Jan. 10, 1864.

Monday, January 26: *All well to day*

Mrs. Heanley caled a few moments Get her cap reddy to send

Henry's next missive analyzes a complaint Eliza has expressed about Mabelia's behavior:

Custom House   New Orleans Lou. Jan 26ᵗʰ 1863

My Dear Family, at home,

My greatest consolation & hope. The thoughts of you comfort & strengthen me more than anything else on earth. Thy dear names are ever dear to me. I received your letter of the 11ᵗʰ, this day with the greatest of joy to learn again that you were well. I hope you are all well to day & I pray that you may all be well & comfortable during my absence—but dear wife of my bosom it is sad & grves me to hear that my sister [Mabelia] treats you so. I do not doubt for a moment but every word you have told me is true, for I know her well enough for that. I am very glad you have told me as much as you have & if there is more please tell me. It will make no difference in my opinion of her. I know she is passionate & reasonable to & I might say foolish, but it will not make the matter any better. It is strange that a woman of her experience & professions [of Christianity] should be so petty & unreasonable expecially to children. She ought to consider that they are such. She has had enough to do with children to know how to treat them, but she is what she is, but she is my sister & I will respect her as such. I shall never mention a word to her or any one else but you while I am away. She nor mother did not say a word about any trouble. M's letter [letters] seem to be written with good feelings towards my family though she seldom mentions you or the children, except to say that you were over there or something of the kind. If it is her game to twit [reproach, taunt, tease] my family of being poor, & being held up by her, we will have a settlement some day, though let the matter rest now for it would be of no use for me to write anything to her.

She would jaw you [verbally criticize] about it, & that would make you feel still worse, but dear one I think you are sensible enough not to take what she says to heart. I have always keep [kept] my peace with her to save trouble. She has rather a narrow mind about some good many things. She thinks every one must do just to her fancy. There is the trouble & if they do not, there is a muss right of [off]. I hope you will give her as good as she sends thats all. Do not worry about it for a moment. I know it is a very disagreeable thing. I am sorry, that she should treat you so & if she is what she professes to be she must be sorry to for it is a weakness for any one to lose their temper thus. I am glad you have told me. Why did you not tell me before I left home. Ah Dear one can you ever forgive me. I ought not to ask you why you did not tell me, you had but little chance to tell me & you was afraid it would make me feel bad and do no good. It might have done some good. I did not think she would be so low as to twit you of being poor. Whose fault is it, if we are poor. Surly [surely] it is not your fault. She has seen the day that she was poor as any body, but what is poverty, compared with a contented mind. Riches do not constitute happiness by any means, at least I fear not with her but I will not judge.

Be of good cheer dear one. Think not to much of such trifling things, but tell me all. Strange that a sister should be so thought less, but it is her nature & she does not try to check it.

Well the mail closes at 6 oclock. It is 5 now so I will finish this as quick as possible.

Oh tell me where you got your news that I was Sergent. I was Sergeant that is Acting one day, thats all. Chas. Richardson was promoted in Field's place. It belonged to him. He acted sergent all the time in Comp C. I am first Corporal now & have the promis[e]*

---

* Charles Richardson, mustered in as a corporal in Henry's company, shared a tent with Henry at Baton Rouge in the summer of 1863. Field is probably David C. G. Field.

of the next promotion. Whew, Whew!! That is I have it from Sergent D. the Orderly. The Capt. does about as he says. He expects to be Lieut soon & so on & so on. I will not make to much calculations on it for I may be disappointed you know & that would be bad wouldnt [it]. I hope for the best & that the war will be over some time & soon to.

I am well to day. Hope this will find you all the same. Give my love to all but take what you can yourself first. Kiss the dear little ones for me. Tell [them] to remember Father & be good &c. Good night dear Eliza, Henrietta & Georgy from your loving & true husband

H. C. Foster

Eliza's Diary:

Tuesday, January 27: *All well and at home here I wish you was at home to night Henry dear one*

Wednesday, January 28: *Mr. G. C. Moerz is berred today*

I go to the funeral

Leave Ette [Etta, her daughter Henrietta] & George with Thompson [wife of Pvt. James G. Thompson?]

Thursday, January 29: *The day is quite plesant Good news for me The alotmant role [roll] has come*

I get a letter from Henry No 1

Friday, January 30 [1863]: *Verrey plesant All well*

I go to the Bank draft, $40, dolars from the first of July 1 to Sept first & go in the field

Get two papers from Henry dated Jan 15,

Are all quite well now & [Rose?] Heasey has got a boy born 6 ½ [pounds]

Allotments were seldom up to date—on both sides. In his three-year war diary, for example, Henry Chambers of North Carolina often mentioned his empty pockets. On March 5, 1862, he went to regiment headquarters to get his pay for November and December—twenty-two dollars. A Confederate private's pay was eleven dollars per month in 1862, and usually late.[334] At the beginning of the war, Union privates were also paid eleven dollars a month, plus a clothing allowance. This was raised twice—to thirteen and then to sixteen dollars, but depreciation meant that the value of the amount actually declined.[335]

Another Confederate soldier, Randolph Shotwell, bitterly decried the economic situation: "As to purchasing clothes, the private soldiers did not have an opportunity of so doing once in six months, as their miserable pittance of $12 per month was generally withheld that length of time, or longer—(I only drew pay three times in four years, and after the first year, I could not have bought a couple of shirts with a whole month's pay." Shotwell concluded that going unwashed, fighting vermin, and being embarrassed in public combined to undermine the Rebel soldier's self-respect and efficiency.[336]

Henry continues to look for mail:

> *(No. 4) Custom House N. Orleans Feb. 1ˢᵗ 1863*
>
> *Dear Ones At home:*
>
> *I will write a few lines to you this morning, as my thoughts are ever with you. I am well to day and I hope this will find you all enjoying the same blessing: Oh that I could see you all and be with you to day, but it is not so and we must content ourselves to be seperated for a time. I hope it will be a short time but make up our minds to the worst for it may be a long time yet.*
>
> *We are expecting a mail every day now. The steamer Creole was to leave N. York the 21ˢᵗ but she has not arrived yet.˙ The steamer*

* On at least one wartime voyage, the *Creole* carried flour as well as mail from New York to New Orleans. The *New York Times* often mentioned the arrival of this vessel because it carried the latest news, only a week old, from the Department of the Gulf.

Marion leaves to morrow morning direct for N. York, so I hope you will get this pretty quick. I am going to send a paper to [too].

Mr. Comerford is quite low. I saw him yesterday. He looks very bad, but do not say anything to her [Mrs. Comerford] about it. He was paid of [off] in the hospital his full pay for 2 month up to Jan. He asked me to take $20.00 and send it to his wife & write a few lines as he was not able to write. I said to him, I had better give this to Arnold and let him send it. He said no he [would] rather I would send it so I did so. I wrote a few lines concerning the money and his sickness. Perhaps she will show you the letter, but if she dont you need not feel jealous in the least. The Regt has not been paid yet for those 2 months Nov & Dec. Whether they will break [cancel] the allottment altogether, I dont know but I hope so for I had rather send the mony home, than have you bothered so & not get it. It is a nuisance anyhow, but I hope you have got [it] ere this. I am sorry I have said so much about the miniatures for you must be short of money. I thought you must have got my pay. I dont know what to think of the times. I am discouraged almost but I will try to do my duty & serve my Country to the best of my ability but a soldier ought to have his pay for all any one else. Here we are. What can we do. All we can do is to hope that it will come some time and I am not much concerned but what it will be paid. I have all confidence in the government yet & I hope it never will be changed.*

I saw Willard yesterday. He is not quite so well. He has the shakes again. He missed it trying to watch. I guess he watched 4 night [nights] only. I saw a letter that Mrs. Sawyer wrote to Sergt. [Bradford S.] Norton requesting him to write to her concerning Edward as she had heard he was dead, but that is a false report, and she has no doubt got letters from him to the contrary ere this. Ed. is with the Co now doing duty though he is not very tough. We have 11 men in the hospital now.

* This could be Private William Arnold.

I cannot write you a very long letter this time though I have enough I want to say to you but where shall I begin. How is the little dear ones. Oh I can imagine their little talk & their plans & play. Does George talk plain. Who does he look like, now. Any like his Father. I guess he looks more like his Mother dont he. Etta is almost 5 years old aint she & you sweet one are most 28 years old. How time flies on, but Eliza do not be impatient. Take the events of life as calm as possible. Your lot is a hard one it is true. Oh I hope it will be better. I hope the time is not far distant when I can be with you, where every true husband ought to be with his family but look of [at?] the thousands that have gone forth (feelling a sense of their duty) to save one nations fame, but it seems foolish after all, for kindred & brothers to be arrayed in hostility but I can not help it. What is done cant be undone.

Well dear Ones here is a husbands and Fathers gratitude & love to you for enduring the privations & sorrow of being left as you are for a time. Hoping the time will be short that we are seperated, I will close.

My heart & hand is with you ever.

H. C. F.

Here is a specimen of N. Orleans money. The one with a hole is played out. The other is good. They are picayunes 5 cts.

Eliza's Diary:

Sunday, February 1 [1863]: *All well This is a day of rest I write to Henry*

Monday, February 2: *All quite plesant I send a letter to Henry No. 3.*

Tuesday, February 3: *Quite dul to day All well I go out & get*

---

* The picayune was the former Spanish half-real of Louisiana. The coin had little value, so the word has come to designate any trivial object.

*my money to day of city, 12 dolars Leave the children with Mrs.
Hensey [Heasey? Hershey?]*

Carey out my hods [buckets of ash; coal scuttles]

Get a letter from henry 4 cts [postage due] No. 2

Wednesday, February 4*: I am not well today Got colde going
with out [?]*

*Get a letter from Henry No. 3. He is well What a blessing it is
to know that he is well*

Thursday, February 5*: How sick I am   It is hard but who can
tell what another year may bring forrth What splendid wether for
Feb.*

Friday, February 6*: I will try and wash some today although I
am not well I will cleane up and [indecipherable]*

Another Northern wife struggling at home alone, Cora Beach Benton,
reports to her husband (serving with a New York artillery company) that
her shoulders and arms ache after she has done the laundry. In addition to
keeping a school to supplement her income, she regularly stays awake until eleven p.m. or later to write to her husband Charles, sew for her growing children, or mend. "Saturday I had my washing and cleaning to do, and
the consequence was I had to work till after dark," she writes on Nov. 27,
1864. "I was almost too weary to live. . . . This morning when I opened
my eyes, my first thoughts were lines of Mrs. Browning's poem. 'We are
so tired, my heart and I. We're very tired, my heart and I.' .... I have had
no chance to rest yet—I did not expect to have."[337]

Eliza's Diary:

Saturday, February 7*: I all well What a happy thing this is
to have good health aint it I twist some yarn today Mrs. Hensey &
Mrs. Chase calls today I bought [?] dollars worth of hunny*

Sunday, February 8*: I write to mother and Henry today I wish
that I could see him today*

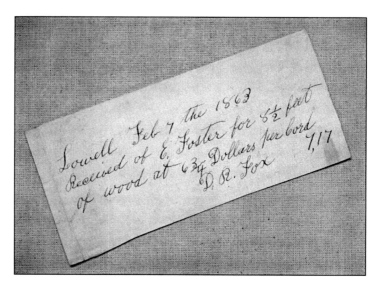

Receipt for Eliza's payment for supplies, signed by Dana Fox, February 1863. Courtesy Bethel Historical Society.

Frank comes in to see me

Monday, February 9: *All well I maile a letter to Henry. This morning letter No. 4 [from Henry].*

I wash and how tiard The children are well I am better now

Financial problems continue to dog the Fosters, because Eliza is not receiving her allotment (her portion of Henry's monthly wage). Henry has not yet heard of her windfall of January 30.

(No. 5) Custom House N. Orleans Feb. 9th 1863

Dear Wife & Children:

As I am permited once more to commune with you by letter I will improve the time by answering your ever welcome letter which came to hand yesterday. What joy it is to me to receive your letters, & Oh I am glad that you were all well. I am well to day & my health is very good indeed for which I feel truly thankful.

I mourn the loss (with you all) of Mr. Morey, for he was a kind *honest man & good citizen.* I never saw a man that I loved better than I did Mr. Morey. I am very sorry that I could not have seen him again alive, but such is the way of all the earth. We know not when we shall be called away from the buisy [sic] scenes & troubles of this life to another world. I hope he is happy. Mr. Morey had some curious traits in his character, you know, but he was a good man nevertheless. No doubt he has left his family enough to make them comfortable, & well of [off] in the world.*

Please tell me all the news you can, wont you. I think I get all your letters now. I have got Nos. 1 & 2. You did not say anything about the allotment in your last letter. I guess you have got discouraged about it aint you. It is no wonder if you are. What in the world is the reason you dont get it. We were paid again last tuesday the 3rd. If they would do as well by you as they have by us I would find no fault. I see that [the Union] government is doing something about [increasing] the pay of soldiers. There is one thing, you will have more when you do get it wont you. Eliza, how is it about our debts now. Please tell me about the last you got in Oct. I hope you used it for yourself if you needed it. Oh that I could see you all to-day. It would be worth the world to me.

Well here we are where Mr. Field left us but I don't sleep on the bricks though. I have got a bedstead that I built myself, so I lay on the soft side of a pine board. It is rather hard sometimes but I sleep pretty sound however. There is nothing like getting used to a thing you know.

Willard has not got his discharge yet. I saw him Saturday. He looks pretty slim. His face was swelled up again & he was bloated considerable. Mr. Comerford was a little better I think. I am afraid they will not see Willard home very soon, but you need not say any-

---

* The deathbed watch, death, and burial of Mr. Morey are recorded by Eliza in diary entries for January 22, 25, and 28, 1863. Henry mentioned Mr. Morey's performing carpentry work for Eliza in a letter of November 27, 1862.

thing. I tell you it almost takes a mans life to get discharged from the Army. They will keep a man as long as they can if there is the slightest hope of his getting well. Mr. Fields can tell you all about that, I presume.* I pray that I may have my health continue as good as it has been thus far. I shall try to be careful of it as I can.

I shall not write much more this time. I don't [know] what to write hardly, but I will say Eliza be of good cheer. I long for the time to come when I can be with my family but this world is ful [full] of trouble & we must all expect our share, but it will not seem so hard if we are only contented, & bare [bear] up cheerfully. There is a great many things that I see every day & hear that I think as little as possible of & it is no use to mention them at all, but if I should give up to my feelings [of homesickness and loneliness] I should be miserable, & should give up in despair, but I hope my courage will not fail me. I will do as well as I can.

Please write often as you can. The dear little children. What would I give to see them, full of mischief no doubt. Kiss them & love them as I do. I little know how to appreciate the comforts of home until I was seperated from them.

Your ever true & loving husband

H. C. Foster

Eliza's Diary:

Tuesday, February 10: *How tiard and languied I am just now Its hard But how happy I am to know that Henry is well*

Wednesday, February 11: *All well today Quite plesant. I am glad to get a letter from (No. 2) Henry today He is well   4 cts [post-*

---

* David C. G. Fields was mustered into Company A with Henry. He seems to have been discharged for ill health. Perhaps he intends to call upon Eliza when he returns home.

age due]* Mrs. Camerford get her letter with the $20 dolars in it. I go out Mrs. Fox cales [calls] leaves aples, meet & etc.

The enormous bulk of Civil War mail challenged the U.S. Postal Service. In the 1850s the postmaster general consistently reported an annual deficit ranging from $1 million to $7 million. On a single day during the war, the Army of the Potomac sent to the Washington Post Office more than 800,000 letters. By the final year of the war, the Postal Service reported a surplus due to the flood of mail to and from combatants.[338]

Agents of the Sanitary Commission helped effect changes in the postal service that ensured letters to and from the field received special treatment. One change allowed letters to be forwarded without additional postage.[339]

Eliza's Diary:

Thursday, February 12*: At home All well at present & who can tell what another week will bring fourth Time flies Time wates for no one*

Friday, February 13*: We are quite well but lonley at home Then againe how thankful I am to know that we are spard from day to day with the blessings of this world to be well*

Saturday, February 14*: All well All at home & home is the plase for me*

Sunday, February 15*: Quite plesant today I stay at home all day Lybra [?] comes up her Mrs. [Agnes?] Cornerford [Camerford] and Lybra and I go to church I leve Charly Camerford with the children and they brake the Looking glas [mirror] I had betr staied at home***

---

* General postage was three cents per 3,000 miles. Stamps were scarce, and soldiers sometimes requested that they be sent from home.

** Mirrors were expensive, prized household possessions, and Eliza castigates herself for going out—thus giving the children (supervised by another child) the opportunity to roughhouse unchecked. Perhaps she fears a streak of bad luck—the old superstition—as well.

Under Marching Orders

Henry is reluctant to tell Eliza that his company may undertake a mission outside New Orleans, but decides to relay the news before she hears it from another:

(#6) Custom House New Orleans Feb. 15th/63

Dear Eliza:

I again undertake to say a few kind words to you this sabbath day hoping that by so doing I may help to cheer you on in the long interval that we are deprived of each others company but I still live in hope that the time [is] growing shorter & shorter every day & that the time will soon come when we can all enjoy the blessings & comforts of home & contentment & that I can be with my family.

I have been hesitating for 2 or 3 days about writing as we have been on the point of going somewhere. 2 Cos A & C have been under marching orders for 3 days to go on some kind of an expedition but it is all kept a secret so that I cannot tell you any thing about it but I would do so if I could. I thought I would not write at first untill we came back but we have waited so long I will write now and I hope you will not have any uneasiness about me on that account, will you dear one. I think most probable that we are going after sugar or cotton up the river somewhere, or we may not go at all, but we have not had any guard details out of our Co for 3 days as we expected to every minute to go.* I will write as soon as we return. We expects to be gone 10 days. I see that all the rest were writing so you would find out that we were going so I might as well tell you myself. Do not worry, please. The only reason I did not write before was on that account. I am well & feel first rate & I hope this will find you all well to. I feel as though I could not wait from one mail to another to hear from you but I am so used to waiting now I dont mind it

---

* Union forces burned sugar and cotton, to deprive the rebel treasury of funds.

so much. There are all manner of conjectures about where we are going but I presume none of them are right. Most every one has a different opinion some one thing some another. Some have it that we are going to Fort Warren in Boston with prisoners, but I guess the one that guessed that got wide of the mark but I don't pretend to know so I will not undertake to say but I wish we would either go or give it up & not keep us in suspense so long.

I saw Mr. Comerford yesterday & W. also. They were both doing well. Mr. C. is gaining quite fast. I could not stop long to see him for I had to run away, for I could not get a pass. Tell Varmann that I saw old Read yesterday. He has a store here right opposite the Custom House & I see Fisher Hildreth & Milton Parker most every day.[*] Parker is Post Master here. The Post Office is in this building.

I will close now hoping this soon go [goes] to you & hoping all may be for the best &c. I wish you all well. I bid you good bye. Yours truly your true & affectionate husband.

H. C. Foster

About the same time Henry composed this letter, U.S. Marine Henry Gusley realized how his notion of the war had changed since enlistment: "Feb. 17, 1863: The news from the North, like everything we have heard this year, was far from cheering. Of four expeditions (against Vicksburg, Richmond, Kinston, and Murfreesboro) but one was successful, and that success was dearly bought. Legislation on N [Negroes] and Generals is not doing the cause much good. We had an idea when we enlisted that the war was for the preservation of the Union and that McClellan was our most able General; now we have an idea that the war is for the abolition of slavery and that [William S.] Rosecrans is a better General than Burnside,

---

* This is likely the "Fisher A. Hildreth" nominated in the U.S. Senate by Franklin Pierce on March 16, 1853, to be deputy postmaster at Lowell. (memory.loc.gov/cgi-bin/query/r?ammem/hlaw) Fisher Hildreth was Ben Butler's brother-in-law, formerly sheriff in Middlesex County. Milton Parker is not listed in CWSS.

An engagement in the field. "Charge of First Massachusetts Regiment on a Rebel rifle pit near Yorktown." Engraving in *Harper's Weekly* from drawing by Winslow Homer.

McClellan, and Pope, combined. Strange how circumstances will alter opinions!"[340]

Eliza's Diary:

    Monday, February 16: *All at home and well I wash and bring my water How tiard I am I will ian to*

    Tuesday, February 17: *Not very well but so to be about is [it] is bery colde*

    I maile a letter to Henry today No. 5 first thing in the morning

    Wednesday, February 18: *Very plesant today All well Mrs. Fox came her [here] today he [Mr. Fox] came after her*

    Cash Account, February 18: *Mr. Fox bring one half bushel* *apples, 20 cents.*

Thursday, February 19: *Quite well today and at home Time pases but I don't accomplish much but I will do all I can*

Friday, February 20: *I will stay at home*

I have been cuting a dress for Mrs. Fitzp [Fitzpatrick?; probably the Mrs. Gilpadrick referred to below on Feb. 23]

Eliza's contemporary Harriet Robinson notes that if a seamstress "went from house to house by the day to spin and weave, or do tailoress work, she could get but 75 cents a week and her meals."[341]

Much of what Eliza did for customers is "plain sewing." However, the fashions of the day could be quite ornate, from layered sleeves to lace inserts, from festoons to flounces, with handmade fabric buds sewn to accent a neckline. In the late 1850s, the fashionable pagoda sleeve reigned, but by the early 1860s, a princess dress with a plain, fitted sleeve was more popular.[342] Striking decoration such as black lace over grass-green ribbon wound around sleeves, and ornaments borrowed from military applications, such as epaulets, perched on shoulders.[343] A dress for a grown woman used at least seventeen yards of fabric, and required thousands of tiny stitches.

I Like to Get a Letter Every Mail

(No. 7) Custom House New Orleans Feb. 20th/63

Dear Eliza:

I received your letter No 3 last Tuesday the 17th. They are ever welcome & joyous to me. I like to get a letter every mail from you. I was very glad to learn that you & the children were well. I trust this will find you all well. I am well to day. We have not gone on that expedition yet that I told you about in my last letter, and it is not likely that we shall go.

Yesterday we had a general inspection by acting Maj Gen [W. T.] Sherman & acting Brig Gen [A. B.] Farr, three Regts 26ᵗʰ, 47ᵗʰ, 42th [sic] or portions of each. None of them were full, several Cos [companies] of each being on detached duty. Well it was the hardest day the Regt has had since we have been in the service. We had to march 3 miles & back, heavy marching order & while we were on the field we had to stand over shoe in water. We were gone 6 hours & we only had our knap sacks of 20 minutes during the time. I tell you mine was some heavy by the time I got back to the Custom House again but I stood it pretty well. I feel much better this morning than I expected to. I felt a little lame that is all. Sergt Dick [Dickerman?] has got his appointment as 2d Lt. He is detailed into our Co. now but he belongs to Co. I. Corp. Foster is acting Sergt whether it will be anything more or not remains to be seen.***

Well it is pleasant here to day as a may day. I want to know if you hear anything from Andrew. Poor fellow he has seen hard service in the war. I hope his life has been spared, to his family. Eliza let us hope & pray that our lives may be spared & our healths also. Oh I pray for the close of this war, but we must not despair. I trust all will be well. God's will be done, & may we all receive his blessings and mercy & strive to do his will.

There is considerable excitement here to day on account of some secesh prisoners to being exchanged. Hurrah! Hurrah! The order has just come for Co A to be ready to march at one oclock with 3 days rations, & the boys are all crazy with excitement. I guess we are going with prisoners under a flag of truce. . . .

I heard from Willard & Comerford 2 days ago. They were doing well. Ed Sayer [Sawyer] is doing duty now. Willard has not got his

---

* Three men with the surname Dickerman enlisted in Henry's company: Alphonso, George, and Ormando. George Dickerman was Captain of Company A, Henry's company, when Henry reenlisted on January 1, 1864.

** Here Henry refers to himself in the third person.

discharge yet. I don't know whether he will or not. I will say good bye till my next. Write often as you can. I think if there is anything in dreams I shall get home for I dream of being to home most every night. I thought last night I saw you all as natural as could be except Etta & George had grown some. What a pleasant time I had. Oh kiss them & love them. Be good children & remember Father. A husbands and Fathers best wishes & love.

Henry C. Foster

Eliza's Diary:

Saturday, February 21: *Quite plesant but verry colde at home Sick so get a girle to get me water Mrs. Fitzpatrick up her this P.M. Sewing on her dress & etc.*

Sunday, February 22: *This is Gen Washington birthday* This is a day of rest All well today Frank and her Mother came up her today A.M. a few moments P.M. Mandana comes up and take tea have soupe good to I carey Mrs. Barnes paper home and go in to Mrs. Hayes [same as Hayez?] a few minits*

Monday, February 23: *I get up at six oclock Get ready & wash get thrugh before noon puter around and knit the rest of the time I am same in the evening not much to hard [to hand?] Finish Mrs. Gilpadrick dres & Mrs. Hasan came in to night***

---

* George Washington's birthday was first celebrated publicly during his administration as the first president of the United States, though it would not become official until 1885, when President Chester Arthur signed into law a bill making it a federal holiday. The day was sometimes celebrated with a parade, a reenactment of the Boston Tea Party, the preparing of Washington's favorite breakfast (corn cakes swimming in butter), or a cherry pie eating contest.

** If this dressmaking customer is the wife of Pvt. John Gilpatrick of Co. A, perhaps the dress is a black one for mourning. The 1853 Lowell City Directory lists four men with the surname of Gilpatrick: David, Joseph, Moses G., and Nathan. The 1861 Lowell city directory lists a John Gilpatrick, hairdresser with Woodsum & Gilpatrick, doing business at 130 Central Street.

Tuesday, February 24: *All is well that ends well I am lasy I wish I could see Henry darling I am same Sew & knit same and no letter yet what shall I do Who can tell I will go over to Rose shop and take tea with Lucy*

Cash Account, February 24: *Eliza purchases seven skeins of yarn and one hank of linen thread.*

Pleased at having returned safely, Henry reports on his mission upriver:

(No. 8) Custom House N. Orleans Feb. 24ᵗʰ 1863

Dear Eliza.

I received your letter (No 4) this day, with much joy to learn that you were all well. I am glad you write so often. We have just returned from our trip up river with prisoners. We are back all safe & well. We took up 327 secesh soldiers & sent them over to rebeldom. We went about 1 mile above Baton Rouge just across the rebel lines. Well I will give you some of the details of the trip. First we left the Custom House at one oclock Friday & went aboard the flag of truce boat Empire Parish to guard the prisoners & such a crowd as there was on the levee beat all 4ᵗʰ of Julys you ever saw swinging handkerchiefs & hooting and holering & some of the prisoners on the boat displayed a few rebel flags but we soon dried them up, by arresting 1 or 2 & sent them back to the provost Marshal & keeping them. The crowd kept increasing & the 26ᵗʰ Regt was called out at the long roll, to drive the crowd from [the] levee. * The most of the crowd was pretty little secesh females! Mind you. Soldiers were a little delicate [reluctant] about charging on women you see so it was almost impossible to drive them back. They would get the ladies (if I can call them such) in front & those back in the rear would not budge a peg.*

---

* The "long roll" is a military term for an alarm—a prolonged beating of the drum (especially the snare drum) as the signal of an enemy attack. The drum is beat with strokes so rapid as to be scarcely distinguished from one another as separate sounds.

Well in a few minutes the artillery came down on them. ha! ha! You ought to seen them scatter. Then the horses want afraid [were not afraid] to run over women or anything else that came in their way. Misses Secesh kept back at a proper distance after that.* *Talk about N Orleans being a Union City eh! I began to think there want [was not] a union soul in it, but I guess the whole population was not out that day. One pretty sure thing all the secesh sympathizers were out, and I have a little different opinion of N. Orleans now than before.*

Well we got under way at 3 oclock Saturday morning. The Pilot went ashore & got drunk. We had to wait for him. He did not come. They took another one, & through carelessness or ignorance, or willfulness he run into a gun boat and stove one of the wheels all to pieces. Here was a go [a situation not to be tolerated]. Well we made out to get up the river about 1/4 of a mile on to the opposite side & tied up. The [there] we lay until Sunday about 10 oclock. The New Brunswick came to our relief & we transferred prisoners & every thing on board of her. At 12 oclock salutes were fired for the aniversary of Washington['s] birthday. We got under way again about 2 oclock. There was a goodeal of hooting & swinging handkerchiefs all the time until we got out of the limits of the city, & now & then we would see a small crowd on the levee all the way up. I never saw

---

* Early in Butler's reign in New Orleans, the women of the city mounted a campaign of insolence, dubbed the Handkerchief War, against Union occupation. Dignified ladies ostentatiously gathered up their skirts if they crossed paths with Union soldiers—as if to protect the hems from being sullied. A sextet on a balcony lifted their skirts and revealed their bottoms to Butler on May 10, 1862. He observed loudly to his aide, "Those women evidently know which end of them looks the best." The incidents continued and seemed to be harbingers of violence. A few days later, as Farragut strolled through town, a chamber pot was emptied from a balcony, showering him. On May 15, Butler drafted the infamous General Order No. 28, known as the Woman Order: "It is ordered that hereafter when any female shall, by word, gesture, or movement, insult or show contempt for any officer of the United States, she shall be regarded and held liable to be treated as a woman of the town plying her avocation."

so much enthusiasm shown on any occasion as there was shown to-
wards those rebel soldiers, by the secessionists of N.O. They seemed
to be perfectly crazy. It is a singular infatuation those people have
got into their heads which amounts almost to insanity.

Baton Rouge is 120 miles from N.O.* We arrived at Donald-
sonville about 12 at night & took on a few more prisoners Lay there
until 3 oclock Monday arrived at B.R. at 10 oclock. The rebel flag
of truce boat Frolic was here waiting for the prisoners but they had
none of our soldiers for us to bring back [in exchange]. When we
came along side the rebel boat they had one Co of rebel soldiers
for guard & they were sorry looking fellows I assure you. I was a
little astonished. I assure you they looked more like convicts than
soldiers. Their cloths [clothes] looked worse than any old farmer
that had been shoveling manure, some with their knees out some
without shoes. All their cloths were thread bear & the men them-
selves looked so they might be hungry. What a contrast between
them and our own soldiers. We have no reason to grumble about
our fare, and we are clothed like princes compared to them. Those
that have been in the city here [i.e., the prisoners] their friends have
fitted them all out new with penty [plenty] of clothes. Oh! Eliza if I
was rebel soldiers I think I should despair at once to be treated as
they are. It is strange how deluded people will get & what lengths
they will go to carry out a blind polacy [policy].

I have told you about all, in regard to the expedition. We left
Baton Rouge yesterday at 3 oclock and arrived here this morning
at 7. There was one rather singular incident happened on board
the rebel boat, just as we were leaving. The rebs have to burn wood

---

* The Union Navy easily seized control of Baton Rouge on May 9, 1862.
However, an army of 2,600 rebels attacked the 2,500 federals at Baton Rouge on
Aug. 5, 1862. The rebels lost three generals, but superior forces led Farragut and
the Union land forces to abandon the city on August 21. However, Army and Navy
returned with a larger force on December 17, 1862, and regained and occupied the
city for the rest of the war.

*on their boats.' They had [a] pile of old wood & roots some 8 feet
high. Some of the rebel officers sung out three cheers for Col. Clark
(our provost Marshal Gen) who accompanied us up." Just as they
were cheering or trying to (for they dont know how to cheer) down
came the wood piles & knocked 7 or 8 of the rebels over board."* They
picked up 5 or 6 but some of them must have been lost I think. I was
glad they were out of our charge. We saw them safe into their own
promised land, but they met with a sad mishap pretty quick after
they got there.*

Yours Dear Eliza & the little ones.

Your loving husband

H.C.F.

Food was becoming scarce for Johnny Reb. Shortages were reported in a
February 28 article in one of the newspapers available to Henry, the *New-
Orleans Era*. According to the *Era*, twenty people (including former members of the Louisiana Guard) returned to New Orleans on the afternoon of
February 27, although they had been paroled into Confederate territory
months before. "They were all registered enemies, but got enough of secession, and came back ready to take the oath of allegiance [to the Union],
which every one of them did. Every one of them was suffering from actual
hunger, and the children were crying for food."[344]

In Richmond, prices soared, and hunger licked every plate. In April
1863 saw a food riot in the market, and President Davis himself was com-
pelled to exhort desperate civilians to disperse on April 2. "By the end of
the war, food had become so scarce that the sign of a pigeon on the wing

---

* Farragut stockpiled coal on Ship Island for his fleet.

** This may refer to Col. Franklin H. Clark, commander of the 12th Battalion.

*** Henry refers here to the infamous, blood-curdling rebel yell. Philip Katcher
calls that yell a "morale-builder," a "unique Confederate weapon that boosted the
charge . . . a high, piercing scream, a series of yips, constantly changing in volume
and pitch, which both scared Union defenders and reassured Confederate attackers"
(Katcher, p. 76).

[in Richmond] was a rarity, and clothing and shelter could be had only at great cost."[345]

A New Hampshire soldier stationed north of New Orleans at the time mentioned waiting for the blackberries to ripen and eating alligator for breakfast. "It tastied like A squirel," he wrote of the alligator meal.[346]

Eliza's Diary:

> **Wednesday, February 25**: *Quite well today Berrey plesant to-day How glad I am to get a letter from Henry today & he is well Get a letter (No. 5) and Mrs. Husey & [her son] Charles spend the day with me and evening callers* Mrs. Camerford and Mrs. Gilpatrick*

> **Thursday, February 26**: *All well today Not verey plesant Mr. Fox cals to see if we hear from H I do and he is well How plesant it is to know that the one that I love so well is truly well*

> **Saturday, February 28**: *Quite smart [that is, feeling well, alert, healthy] today but not do much only a horse around a little I wish Mother was with me I get a letter from Andrew with $2.00 in it*

During this month, Eliza's brother Andrew encamped near White Oak Church, Virginia, in winter quarters. In his letter of May 9, he mentions sending another $2. Eliza receives that letter but neglects to mention receiving it (or the enclosed cash) in her diary.

The money he sends is to repay a note of $17 (mentioned in his letter of December 24, 1863). He later adds $3 interest to the sum.

Eliza's Diary:

> **Tuesday, March 3**: *Quite well so I go out and get [?] spend the day with Sylvia*

> **Wednesday, March 4**: *Not well but so I do my work & I get two letters from Henry/ 8 cts [postage due], Ns. 6, 7 He is well*

---

* By using the genteel phrase "evening callers," Eliza seems to mean that the women are paying social visits—rather than visits to her as a seamstress.

House-to-house mail delivery did not yet exist in the United States. Eliza made trips on foot to the post office to inquire for mail or to post her own correspondence. Private key boxes were scarce. For "call box" mail, one stood in line to inquire about mail waiting.[347]

As he closes the March 7 addendum to the following letter, Henry confesses to having been under arrest for two days:

> *(No. 9) Custom House New Orleans March 6ᵗʰ/63*
>
> *Dear Eliza:*
>
> *As I am again permitted to write you, I will improve a little time [i.e., make good use of leisure time] by so doing. Although I do not feel quite as well to day as usual, I call myself well. I have a slight headache, & I have been troubled for 2 or 3 days past with my old complaint the colic brought on by eating to many beans. I came of [off] guard duty yesterday rather used up but am better to day. I have been a little costive. I am in hopes to get regulated in a day or so. I have been as regular as a clock ever since I left home & that is the reason my health has been so good.*
>
> *I received your letter last Monday of Feb. 17ᵗʰ marked No 4 though I think you made a mistake for I have received 2 No 4, so I shall call it No 5.*
>
> *I am sorry the mirror is broken, but children are full of mischief you know, & I presume there is as much in ours as any bodys but don't let that keep you to home if you can go. It might not happen again. Tell Sis for papa that she must not be naughty when Mother goes away. Father don't like to have his little girl do mischief. Etta must be a good girl when Mother goes out. She must be Mothers little house keeper & take good care of George. Father will come home as soon as he can to see you all.*
>
> *Seems as though you had a curious dream about my watch. I have not broke it yet but it wants cleaning & regulating very bad & what do you think they charge here. I carried [it] to a jewelry shop.*

They took it & looked at it & said he would put it in good order for 3 dollars. It runs pretty well now. The watch is not so much to blame as I am for I have let it run down every day most. I had rather send it home than to pay 3 dollars here on it. If W. [Willard?] goes home, I guess I will send it. He left the St James hospital & has gone to the Marine hospital. Our Dr. told him he would get his discharge before he had been there 3 weeks so I expect he will be home soon. He is about the same. I saw Mr. Comerford last Sunday. He is getting well. He told me he had not felt so well for a year as he does now but he was a very sick man. No one thought he would live, but he said all the time that he should get well. He was [of] good courage & that was more than I can say by many others. Mr. Arnold is not very tough. His lungs trouble him but he has not gone to the Hospital yet. Ed Sawyer is pretty well though he has the shakes [typhoid?] some. There are 2 Cos [companies] going away from here, so we shall have but 3 left. Day before yesterday, Capt Dick [Dickerman?] was officer of the day Armando [Ormando Dickerman] was Lieut of the guard I was Sergt of the guard & we had one Corp & 15 Privates besides on guard, so you can see it come pretty hard on us for guard now. I hope they will take of [off] some of the posts but I dont suppose they will. Lieut Dick told me he expected to have to go on again to day. Crackey [crickey] this is coming down on Co A.

It is a rainy day here to day. The river is very high, clear up even with the top of levee. If it keeps on rising N. Orleans will be all afloat. I have no war news to write as I know of. I received 4 letters the last mail, yours [,] one from Mabelia & one from Mother & one from Chancy & Clara. I hope they will keep coming. Please write as often as you can. I don't see but you are as hard up in Lowell for money as they are in N. Orleans. You did not tell me what to do with that 5 cts.* That was nothing new for we have been

---

* Henry mentions a coin he mailed home, probably intending to write "You did not tell me what you did with that 5 cts." The 3 cts. refers to the picayune.

paid with those the 3 last times we have been paid. That is Uncle Sam's money, you know, but the 3 Cts is quite a curiosity. We have signed the pay rolls again. We expect to be paid soon. Do you get any more from government. Oh I hope you will have enough to get along comfortable.

I pray this may find you all well. Be careful of your health as you can. I hope the children will be well. I do not see anything of your miniatures yet. I am waiting anxiously for them. You wont forget them will you. Tell Jim [Eliza's landlord?] to take good care of his boy & be lenient with his tenents [sic]. Ask him if he will give me a job if I come home. Tell him I aint out of one yet. I guess I shant be this week.

March 7th.

Good Morning dear Ones at home. I will say a few words more to you this morning. My ink you see is very poor. It is the last of that you sent me & I have reduced it [diluted] so much that it is very pale. How do you like your gold pen. Do you use it. Oh to morrow is your birth day isnt it. I wish I could send you something but I have nothing but my love & best wishes & lots of kisses.

You wanted I should tell you if they could keep me longer than 3 years. They can keep me only 30 days at the outside after my term of enlistment is up & I am in hopes the government will not need me so long but who can tell. It looks now as though they meant to continue this war for some time to come, & I suppose it will be as long as the rebels continue to hold out, so we must make the best of it, we can, though it is very hard. Do keep up good courage dear wife, & I will try to. We must make up our minds to surmount all difficulties, and look ahead with firm resolution. Your lot is hard I know, but dear one you must know that mine is no easy one. You don't know how easy it is to get into trouble in the army. A soldier has to be vigelent, & no excuses will be taken by officers on duty, *so you see that a man has to keep his eyes opened.* I have been very fortunate so far. I was put under arrest once by the inspector Gen. when we were at Lake end. I have never been put in the guard house. That is the advantage a non. commissioned officer has over a private, but still a Corp & Sergt has to bear all the responsibility. There was a charge sent in against me for neglect of duty, but Col Farr took no notice of [the charge] or at least I was kept under arrest only 2 days & then released to duty again.** I will tell you more about it if we live. I hope and pray that our lives may be spared, & that I may always do my duty.*

Good bye dear Eliza. Your loving husband

H.C. Foster

Eliza's Diary:

Monday, March 9: *Quite well to day Cold and a good deal of snow I shovel snow and get water to wash I get a letter from Henry He is well letter No. 8. 8 cts.*

Tuesday, March 10: *Quite well to day I wash or try to Mrs. Fox comes Hath her to diner I get a paper to day from Henry***

---

* Pickets might be posted five or six miles from camp with shells from both sides flying over them. It was lonely work, but it required considerable vigilance, as Henry notes. Occasionally the enemy would come from behind the pickets, and as they approached, the pickets would think they were their relief—until it was too late to defend themselves properly.

** Bell Irvin Wiley found that Billy Yank often fell asleep on post "especially during the early part of the war. While theoretically this was one of the most serious military offenses, punishable under articles of war by death, in practice it was treated with shocking leniency. In September 1861 a general court-martial of McClellan's command found six soldiers guilty of this offense. The severest sentence handed down was a month at hard labor and forfeiture of three months' pay."

*** On March 2, 1863, Union troops in the Western Theater set out on a three-week reconnaissance mission, beginning in New Orleans, and headed for the Rio Grande in Texas. News reports might have worried Eliza that Henry was participating in the mission.

Thursday, March 12: *Quite plesant but colde*

I will [?] mend for Mrs. Camerford

[She] Gets a letter from Mr. Camerford [another Union soldier; see note at Feb. 11] We are all well to day

Friday, March 13: *Quite plesant but colde We are all well George called Thurs A.M. Mrs.Leavejoy called this P.M. I go out to get pictures but get none see George [Hussey or Huszey?] and go in to day*

Saturday, March 14: *I stay at home and work It is verey plesant but colde Bake and cleane and sew some*

Your Husband's Thoughts Are Ever with You

(No. 10) Custom House New Orleans March 14th '63

Dear Eliza:

I will write you a few lines as a mail goes to morrow so that you may know that I am well &c. I trust you may all be well also. How well I should like to see you all to day & talk to you, but I hope we can be reconciled to our fate of being seperated so long, for it may be a long time yet ere we shall be able to see each other, but dear ones bare [bear] up. Be sure your husband's thoughts are ever with you, and the same though far away from you as he would be at home. The time is wearing away, though it seems slowly. The same time at home would seem very short. There is not much signs of this war ending now but who can tell. I think the conscription law is agoing to have a good effect in ending the war. One thing some of those stay at home men may get a chance to go to war yet. I dont think the rebels can possibly hold out a year longer, but they are very determined & they will fight to the last. One thing is certain. They cant always hold out.

Sergt Norton has just come down from the hospital.* He sends his best respects to you. He has been in the hospital 3 ½ months. He is a goodeal better now than he has been, but his knees are stiff & the chords of his legs a [are] drawn up so that he cannot straighten them, but I don't know, he thinks they will come all right, but it is a hard case anyway. He says Mr. Connerford [Comerford] is most well. We buried one of our Sergts a few days ago Sergt Chandler.** The rest of the boys are well as usual, I believe.

Great preparations are being made up the river for an attack on Port Hudson.*** Things remain about the same here in the city except troops are leaving every day for up river. I guess the 26ᵗʰ is destined to stay in N. Orleans for a while to come & it is pretty well scattered to. Only 4 Co's are left in the Custom House now. The rest are all on provost duty about the city. They seem bound to keep the 26ᵗʰ on guard duty & we have enough of it too.

I would write to Andrew if I knew where he is. I don't know why he does not write to me. I have answered all his letters but I have not received one from him since Sept. Tell me if you hear from him, how he is &c.

It is very healthy weather here now. Everything begins to wear the appearance of spring. It seems here now like the Middle of May at home. Trees began to leave [leaf] out the middle of Feb. and the sun is getting pretty warm. It will soon be hot weather and mosquitoes again. Well if my health is as good this summer as it was last

---

* Bradford S. Norton's ailment sounds like poliomyelitis. In this disease, paralysis of muscle groups can be followed by atrophy and permanent disfigurement. Henry also mentions Norton in his letters of Feb. 1 and April 23ʳᵈ of this year.

** This would have been Joseph Chandler, Jr.

*** In August 1862 General Butler requested more troops to capture Port Hudson, where the enemy had expanded and fortified an earthwork overlooking the Mississippi. His request was not answered in time for him to act. However, in May 1863 General Banks has sufficient troops to battle with the Confederates under Gardner from May 27 to July 9. Banks was the victor.

I shall be thankful. I hope I may have my health & that you & the children may be well also. I am in hopes we shall be paid soon. They owe us from the 1ˢᵗ [of] Jan.

Well Dear ones my love is all to you. I pray that our lives may all be spared to meet again & we will hope that the time will soon come, & may this war soon be at an end, but we must not look back but just forward with the same firm purpose to sustain the government that we started with. Oh please send the miniatures. Your loving husband.

Ever true

H. C. Foster

No Justice in Being Denied My Pay

Civil War soldiers often had to resort to extreme measures to collect their pay—though few went to the extent of one Joseph W. Wilber of No Name Pond, who had enlisted in the 19th Maine. Disabled at the Battle of Rapidan in Virginia, Wilber then enlisted in Hancock's Veteran Reserve Corps. He was assigned to guard duty near Washington, D.C. When a paymaster "abused him for his pains," Wilber went directly to Lincoln for redress on Feb. 18, 1865.[348]

"It was a matter of several weeks and . . . I could see no justice in being denied my pay," Wilbert recalled. ". . . On reaching the White House I was shown into the waiting room . . . and I sat in a chair made from the bones of animals with the seat of the tanned leather."

When Lincoln noticed Wilber, he exclaimed, "Let my son in." Upon hearing Wilber's complaint, the president said, "That paymaster is a servant, not an autocrat. . . . You are just as good as I am and he will find that out."

Taking advantage of his audience, Wilbert, six foot two and a half inches, measured himself against Old Abe, who was six feet seven and a half inches. The Rail Splitter wrote out a note for Wilber to give to his paymaster. Wilber claimed his money and sent it home to his mother.[349]

Eliza's Diary:

>   **Sunday, March 15**: *Quite plesant today I am at home all day Mrs. Southampson [Samuel Thompson? Glenn Thompson of Henry's letter of April 23, 1863?] in her Mrs. Bailey in her [here] Mr. Bailey comes in here * All well at present.*

>   **Monday, March 16**: *Quite plesant but no wash. I fix a dress for Mrs. Laines girl*

Eliza's skills as a seamstress would have been continually in demand, for herself and her own family as well as for others, for pin money. Nineteenth-century wardrobes of the working class were minimal. A woman might have only one new dress a year, and take her shoes for repair rather than replacing them. Infants of both sexes were dressed alike in shirts, slips, gowns, and petticoats. Boys were not dressed in jackets and trousers until they were toilet trained. Mothers stitched most of their children's clothing, including stockings and mittens and even lightweight shoes. Both women's and children's clothing was cut generously, and could be adjusted with tapes, drawstrings, tucks, and deep hems. Adult clothing might be cut down for children—taken apart, cleaned, and the pieces turned inside out to hide wear or fading.[350]

Eliza's diary:

>   **Friday, March 20**: *Quite plesant but [indecipherable; smudged] George called A.M. Mrs. Leavejoy called P.M. but I go*

---

* In the 26th Massachusetts Infantry, Co., A—Henry's company—there were two men named Bailey: Private George A. Bailey and Corporal George E. Bailey.

out to get pictures but get none so I go in to Sylvies a moment.[*]

Saturday, March 21: *This is a plesant day her and I stay at home all day I bake and mend and etc.*

Mrs. Chase and Mrs. Drinam [Drinan?] and girl caled a few moments

You Seem More Dear to Me Every Day

(No. 11) Custom House　New Orleans　Mar 21ˢᵗ '63

Dear & Beloved Wife & Children:

You seem more dear to me every day, & may God's blessing rest on & ever be with you. I hope & pray that your lives & healths may be spared you during my absence from you, & that I may be permited [sic] to return safe to you, but dear Eliza I am afraid this country never will be the free & happy land of Liberty that it once was. This is a ruinous war, but Oh! I am glad to see the firmness of the government in prosecuting this war. It looks now as though they meant to do something what [that] they had ought to have done in the first place. Oh I glory in our country's name. Every foot of it is dear to a true American, & when I see & hear of the base actions of the traitors in our own blessed land, it makes me more true, more attached to our country's cause, & I think our chance of success looks brighter at the present time than it has before since the rebellion.

I thought by what you wrote in your last letter (No. 6) that you thought of sending a box. If you don't start it before you get this I want you to send me a bottle of ink & some paper & envelopes. That

---

* Eliza kept a receipt from March 20, 1863. She may have postponed having photos taken, but she did feel flush enough to buy silverware: a set of tablespoons and a set of teaspoons, totaling $12.70. The receipt is from Amos Sanborn, "the only Jewelry Store in Lowell where Silver Ware is Manufactured," located at No. 25 Central Street. Was this Sylvie's place of employment? Or did she drop in on Sylvie to show off her purchase?

is all that I need & if we get paid soon I can get along very well. A box from you or anything else, dear one, would be received with much gratitude & joy, at any time, but I have never said anything about you sending much for I knew you needed the money that such things would cost. I care more about yours & the children's miniatures than anything else.

You spoke about a tick [a form of homemade mattress, or a ticking cover to contain mattress filling such as corn husks]. I have one already but it is useless for I cannot get anything to put in it. Hay nor straw dont grow in this part of the country except what is brought from the north. On ship island we used to get rushes to fill our ticks. I have a mattress now so I get along very comfortable.* There is no need of our laying on the bricks for every man can rig up a rude bunk of some kind if he has a mind to. I will tell you what I think about the blankets. When we landed at the Quarantine [sic] a year ago, the rebel prisoners had three or four blankets & bars [bolsters? bars of soap?] apiece.** Sergt [David C. G.] Field bought a pair of them. Those are the ones that he sent home. We could by [buy] anything they had for any price we was a mind to give but I did not have any money so I did not by anything except a bar for 50 cts worth 1.50. It seems to me Fields told you a curious story, for it is my opinion that woolen goods or any other cost as much here as at home. I dont know any reason why they should not.

There is another mail in with dates [postmarks] up to the 12th

---

* Bedding of the period resembled large pillows—ticks, or simple sacks of coarse fabric, containing a loose filling of corn husks, straw, feathers, or raw wool. Feather beds were used chiefly during cold weather. Turning and shaking up the bed ticks—and occasionally replacing the stuffing—was the duty of the housewife. About 1870, the mattress became The box-shaped, tufted mattress filled with coconut fiber, cotton, wool, or horsehair did not make its appearance until about 1870, and the spring mattress did not come on the market until the 1920s.

** There was a quarantine station on Ship's Island and a second, on the Mississippi below New Orleans, called Quarantine. Both were used to incubate and then isolate cases of yellow fever.

from N.Y. I hope I shall get some letters dont you. I guess I will wait & see before I finish this. It is dinner time now so I will stop.

[Letter continues.]

March 23rd.

I will finish writing this letter now, as I received no letter since the 28th Feb. The steamer Bio Bio arrived at this Port Saturday evening at 11 oclock with dates [carrying letters mailed up to March 10] to the 10th via Havanna [sic]. Sunday morning about 8 ½ oclock a fire broke out from the cooks galley & the ship was totally destroyed while lying at her wharf. The paper stated that her mail & books & money were saved. All the passengers baggage together with her cargo was lost. One person was killed by the falling of her masts.

It is rainy to day & our quarters look rather dark & gloomy. I cannot write you much news of importance. I am well to day & eat my regular baked beans &c.

Oh what would I give to see you all to day. Those dear little ones. I pray God to bless my family & protect them in my absence. Do the best you can dear Eliza. Use what money you get to make your [life] comfortable if you need it. Love our Children as I love you all, & may our lives all be spared to again meet happily together. Good bye for this time.

Your husband.

H. C. Foster

Eliza's Diary:

Sunday, March 22: *All well to day and it is very plesant to day, The snow is goin I have been writing to Henry No. 8 Frank has ben in to see me to day*

Monday, March 23: *Verry plesant to day and all well I wash*

Mrs. Barnes comes in A.M. Mrs. Camerford And Mrs. Gilpatrick P.M. but no letter from Henry yet and so goes the day Eve Frank comes in

Thursday, March 26: *Fast day*

Sunday, March 29: *Quite plesant but I am sick ... not able to sit up all day Mrs. Thompson comes in and Mrs. Gilpatrick comes in and gets some Tea and goes and gets whiskey for me. George comes in*

Thursday, April 2: *(Fast day)*

Friday, April 3: *Very plesant and I am at home and I get a letter from H. to day No. 11 & its all well & etc.*

Saturday, April 4: *It is bery plesant today I bake and cleane up and wash out my white close [clothes; "white clothes" often indicates lingerie, underthings]*

Mrs. Camerford comes in and Mrs. Gilpatrick comes in

Eliza complains of all this up-and-down stairs, because Henry's letter of April 23, 1863, encourages her to find an apartment at street level. His letter of July 22, 1863, reveals that she has taken his advice—although the move is not mentioned in this diary.

Sunday, April 5 [1863]: *I am at home all day and I thank my heavenly Father that we are well and have a home to stay at.*

I write to Henry to day.

There Seems to Be a Stand Still with the Mails

(#12) or (#13) Custom House New Orleans Apr 5th '63

My Dear Family.

How do you do today. Oh that I could see you to day & be with you or know if you are all well. It is a long time since I heard from you. The last letter was dated March 8th. There seems to be a stand still with the mails. I hope I shall get some soon.

My health is pretty good, though I got excused from duty to day. The second time that I have been excused by the Dr. since I enlisted. One side of my face is swelled. The Dr said it might be the mumps & it might not. A number in the Regt. were having them. My jaws are pretty sore any how, but I guess it is nothing serious however.

Mr. H. Stickney was here to day. He is well, & looks rugged [physically fit]. His Regt [is] just across the river on Algiers side. Most of the troops have come down from Baton Rouge. What it is for no one knows. Gen Banks has left enough there to hold the place however. I hope he knows what he is about & I think he does.

April 12th

You will [see] it has been a week since I began this letter. I am ashamed of it, but I have not felt like writing but nothing but laziness has prevented me. I received a letter from Mabelia last week dated March 15th but none from you. It seems strange, but I hope you are all well. I was excused 4 or 5 days but am on duty now. The tonsils of my throat are swelled some. I am well otherwise. One reason I have not written more is I have no ink & no envelopes & no money to get any & I cant tell when we shall get paid but I hope pretty soon. We had [religious] services to day the first time since last July.

I received the letter with the little book in it from Etta. Tell her papa thanks her & will send it back to her. I would send something else if I could, I and all my love to my wife & children. Oh I hope & pray God that I may soon be with you & I pray that you may all have health & comfort in my absence. Be of good cheer. I almost despair sometimes I get so tired & sick of the army, but I am thankful that my health has been spared me thus far, & I will try not to complain of my lot, for when I think how much better of [off] I am than many others that have gone forth in their countrys cause, I have reason to be thankful. Yes dear Eliza I have been fortunate so far, & I hope this war may be settled without much more blood shed, but it is hard to be away from my family, but I hope it is for the best. I am still hopful [hopeful] that this war will not last much longer.

Liut Dickerman has got his commission. I have not got my Sergts warrant yet but I expect I shall in a few days. It will date from the 12ᵗʰ of Feb. You see I have to wait for Capt Dickerman & he is never in a hurry about anything. When I get it I will tell you but I consider it all the same as though I had it.

I had a letter from Chancy & Clara last week but they never mentioned Mothers name at all whether she was well or not. I hope I shall get a letter from you soon. I hear from Willard every day or two. He remains about the same. Mr. C [Camerford] is most well. The health of the Co. is good now &c. Please write often. This from your true & loving husband

H. C. Foster

Eliza's Diary:

Cash Account, April 6: *Eliza purchases 10 yards delane [a lightweight fabric combining linen and wool] for $2.50, linen for 25 cents and canbrick [cambric] for thirty cents.*

Tuesday, April 7: *We are all well Verey stormey but I go out and get Lb. [indecipherable] and go in to Sylvies Have cup of tea with her Leave Elen [indecipherable; Goodwin?] with Etta*

Wednesday, April 8: *Quite plesant today so I go out & get pictures etc. Sylvie goes with me. I go down then and stop to Tea Get six pictures taken. 84 ct.*

Cash Account, April 8: *Eliza buys photographs as well as items for a care package for Henry:*

one reine [ream, or 480 sheets] paper, $1.

2 packs envelopes, 24 and 16 cents

paper wrappers, 12 cents

blacking box [polish kit for shoes?], 5 cents

one [indeciperherable] camphirs, 14 cents*

one bottle Ink, 15 cents

one pound tobacco, $1.

one box cigars, $1

one hankerchife, 30 cents

*cames [combs?],** 24 cents*

tape [woven material used for reinforcing seams and as draw-strings], 11 cents

pens & pens holders, 16 cents

shave things, 8 cents

boxes [probably tin cans] & saderin [soldering], 54 cents

The total expense is $5.95

Sunday, April 12: *This is a beautiful day to day her [here] Mrs. Barns came in Lucy, Rose, Frank, Mrs. Husey & [her son] Charles, Mrs. Gilpatrick came in and so pases the day Now I will write to Henry and etc. No. 11*

Monday, April 13: *Well, I send Henry box this morning pay one dolar/lbs. sixty-three by Express. Get one half [peck?] apples, Parker. I wash and cleane same [some?] and move my stove out*

---

* Camphirs could be camphor balls (mothballs to protect woolen clothing from moths) or camphor ice, an ointment blended of white wax, camphor, spermaceti, and castor oil, used for dry, chapped skin.

** Cames may refer to a "camise" or chemise—a loose-fitting shirt—but it is most probably "combs," much sought after by soldiers who often mislaid or lost theirs.

Frank comes in the evening. I send A paper to Henry

Eliza entrusted her precious cargo to Harnden Express, the Army and Soldiers Package Express. She kept the receipt, imprinted with the company logo: a man in a billed cap carrying under his arm a grain sack labeled "Boston" on one end and "New Orleans" on the other.

Tuesday, April 14: *Quite plesant today All well I cleane windows Mr. Fox comes I get a letter from Ephiran [her brother, Ephraim] Carey my stove up stairs & Mrs. Gilmore & Mrs. Barnard called to see me**

Frank come in with a ark [?]**

Wednesday, April 15: *Plesant today and we ar well Cleaning up and cleane stairs & etc. The children play out [outdoors] most all day*

Mr. Parker brought me peck apples

Sunday, April 19: *All well and all at home Quite plesant Mrs. Barnes is in [to visit]*

Sylvia comes in and Agnes [mentioned January 8 in diary], Charley

Monday, April 20: *All well and verey well I wash and get water in evening I ian and how tiard I am Frank comes in a moment Mrs. Gilpatrick comes in*

Tuesday, April 21: *All well to day & Mr. Parker came over Eggs Mr. Fox came with meet [meat]*

P.M. I go down to Mrs. Husey. Mrs. Gilpatrick comes in today

Bills Receivable, April 21: *Mr. Parker, eggs, 1 ½ [dozen?], 30 cents*

* One Isaac E. Gilmore was a private in Henry's company.
** Ark could refer to a popular wooden children's toy, reserved for Sunday play—a model of the biblical vessel Noah built to carry his family and menagerie during the Great Flood. Perhaps Frank carved the pieces himself.

Mr. Fox, meat, 40 cents

The following disheartened letter was sent by Andrew to his wife. Mary must have passed the letter on to Eliza, who saved it. "Expecting to move" means that the regiment is soon to leave winter camp and resume combat.

In camp near White Oak Church [Va.] April 21ˢᵗ, 1863

My Dear Wife & Children

I have not much news to write you of course but I know you must feel anxious about me as we have been expecting to move every day for some time but here we are as yet.

I am well but dear me I am so tired of this life.

Often it does seem as though I could not stay away from you another year if I live but then how could I see you to then come back to this miserable life. Nearly all the officers of this Regt. have been home on furlough & many of the noncommissioned officers & privates have been home too & all say it was hard to leave their friends for this life in the tented fields.

Mary, Dear Mary. Love me. Will you. Do you love me truly.

I long to see you once more. How I wish I could embrace you & dear children too.

I wrote you last Sunday so you will get it Sat. I suppose & this next Tuesday.

You will be glad to get my poor old letters this often Will you not.

If I thought otherwise I could not write or be happy. Indeed I have not enjoyed my self lately as well as I have heretofore for I have been so homesick & have not put my trust in God as I should have done though I have done no bad thing yet I am wicked every day I fear.

Mary I was in hospital tent Sunday eve & last eve to prayer meeting & as I heared several speak & pray of their pious parents &

wives praying for them I could but hope that you were pressing your suit at the throne of grace for your loving & true husband.

Mary Do you pray for me. Do not forget me in prayer to God & teach those dear children to pray too God every day.

We have not been paid off yet & what is the reason I do not see for the rest of our Division has been paid all except our Brigade.

Yesterday was rainy & to day cloudy.

I hear that it is very sickly in Oxford County. Do be careful of self & children.

Ebenezer I want to see you so I can take you up & hug you & play with you. Dear little man. Do you remmember [sic] dear father.

Mary Frances I want to see you too. I want you to kiss me on nose & cheek.

Mary Dear Wife I am sad. I want to see you much. I want to clasp your dear old form to my self once more. I want to see you because I love you dearly truly Do I not

O Mary I do wish I was honorably out of this so we could go somewhere. So we could live together for ourselves & children.

Write me just as often as you can for it seems so long to wait a week & then to wait 2 weeks. It is too bad Mary. I got but 3 letters from you in March.

I will give you a kiss for each letter when I get home.

If in times of peace before this wicked war with Northern Society I would much [like to?] live in <u>Va</u>. ev [even more?] than Maine.

Peach trees in bloom here a week ago. Dear Wife except [accept] my love & love me.

God bless you & children.

---

* This letter seems to show that Andrew and Mary are on good terms. There is no sign of impending divorce.

Yours Truly

A. J. Beane

These pictures for children.

Six days after the above, the Battle of Chancellorsville commenced. Lee suffered 20 percent casualties but defeated the Union forces through superior tactics.

Henry urges Eliza to find housing reached by fewer stairs. But he also moves gradually from practical, military, and money matters into more intimate territory. "Jennie" and "Jackie" are Henry's code for female and male sexual organs—allowing him to commit to paper thoughts he has no opportunity to convey in person.

Henry's use of code may surprise some readers, given that Victorian women were told that sex was to be endured, not enjoyed. Victorian attitudes about reproduction, sexual intimacy, and excretion were repressive, so that even piano legs were sometimes "dressed" in pantaloons. On the other hand, pornography flourished and mistresses were in vogue with the upper classes. Somewhere in between these extremes lay the attitudes of men and women bred on farms, who were not unaccustomed to witnessing the birthing and mating activities of animals.

Henry Foster was thus not alone in his time for his matter-of-fact, affectionate, and jocular take on sex, or to share such with his spouse. Andrew Bean's superior officer, Clark Edwards, writes to his wife, Maria, in an even more direct vein, referring to his "hard on" more than once as well as to "a good screw." Edwards discusses frankly topics ranging from the carnal appetites of the women around him, to the allusion that he has gotten Maria pregnant on this last furlough home.[*]

In closing this letter, Henry pledges his love to Eliza's initials.

(No. 14) Custom House N. Orleans Apr 23d 1863

(I should like very much to have you get out of the tennement

---

[*] Edwards Papers, various letters 1861–6.

you are in and move down stairs if you could. HCF)

Dear & Beloved Wife & Children.

I am thankful that I am able to sit down and address a few lines to you this morning & inform you that I am well. I hope to [too] that my dear ones at home are well also. I received your good letter of Apr 5ᵗʰ night before last. I was on guard. Yes dear one I was Sergt of the guard, & have been Sergt for over 2 month although I have not got my warrant yet for the reason that Dick has been reported as Sergt and is now & I as Corp. because I went to take his place instead of Sergt Chandlers [i.e., Joseph Chandler] who died the 10ᵗʰ of March. I have not said anything about it before as I wanted [to] get it [in writing] before I said to much about it, & I thought to [too] that you would hear all about it if I did not tell you for there is plenty [who] write all that takes place. We have no Orderly. The Capt. has been waiting to give it to [Bradford S.] Norton but I guess he will never be able to do any more duty in the Co. [Charles] Emerson is Acting Orderly & he probably will have it but I cant tell for certainty. We are detached from the Regt again or the Regt is from us rather. The Headquarters of the Regt are in Algiers just accross the river & Co's A & G are left in the Custom House. The duty is very hard since the prisoners have been brought in. The [there] is 9 hundred come in. There is two thousand in all so you see that Gen Banks is doing something.

Oh I hope there will be a goodeal done this spring to end this war. The rebels most of them are very much disheartened & it seems as though if our armies could press forward & attack them on all sides it would soon wind them up, but we must not be impatient. I hope & pray that all will be well yet. We are becoming used to War now & we can carry it on to their (the rebels) satisfaction. We are continually hearing of the suffering among the rebel community but I presume you hear as much of it as we do. Every day is reducing them to destitution. It is sad to think of, for many innocent people have to suffer, but the innocent always have to suffer with the guilty but Oh may Gods will be done on earth as it is in heaven & the just Laws of our land triumph. God will defend the right; Eliza you may think I am over patriotic, but I feel it, & I hope I may have fortitude enough to carry it through. God granting I will try to do my duty as well as I can. I am glad to know that you & the children are so well. I know it is very trying for you, Eliza, & I have had many a sad hour thinking of you & how you are situated, but it does me good to get such good & cheering letters from you & I hope to be able to recompense you for it if I live.

When I asked you if you got any more from the government I meant if you had received my pay as far as I had received it. It seems you have now, by your last letter. My getting more pay [through promotion] will make no difference with the allotment roll, but I hope I shall be able to send you a little of mine now and then. I shall receive 7 dollars here. We are expecting to get paid in a few days for 2 months up to March 1st.

Mabelia wrote me something about that little place [a farm] over in Dracut. She said it was for saile [sale], & wished you had it for she wanted to have you get out of the city where the children could have a chance to go out of doors. She said it was for sale for $300, and she thought that Dana would by [buy] it for us if we wanted it. Has she said anything to you about it. I have not made any reply to her yet. What do you say. Tell me wont you. I should like for you to have the place, but I should not want to be beholden to her [in her debt], though I think she means to do right, & is not half so bad as she seems to be. Still you know her disposition. Perhaps Dana would not be so willing to buy it. If you see him perhaps you can find out what he thinks about it.

Mabelia wrote me that they were going to have an addition

built on to their house this spring. Well I think they need it. I think
you have a nice man for Landlord now. Mr. Hubard is a fine man.
I think he will do the best he can for you in regard to getting a tenement [on the ground level]. Please to give him my kind regards,
& give my respects to all the people around there especially Mrs.
Morey if she is living & Mr. Genn Thompson's folks &c. [see letter of March 23, 1863]. Tell Rose to have her boy grow up fast so
to be ready for the war, but tell [her] to [too] that I hope he never
will have to go to war, nor any of the coming generation. Does she
hear from her Brother. Does Warmum talk secesh any now. Don't
he think the war ought to be stopped & give the south their independence. He used to hink [sic] so. Don't let him know that I wrote this.
How is May's folks getting along. Give my respects to him.*

    *Eliza I was a little surprised when you told me about that trea-
sury note.** That you had kept it so long. I have been sorry a good
many times that I signed the allotment roll for I could have sent you
my pay and you would have got [it] much quicker than you now do.
I wish I could send you a hundred such notes as I never realized the
difference before in those notes.*

    *I hope you will excuse me for not writing oftener of late, but I
have been a little short of materials &c. I have had the mumps but
am well of them. My health is first rate. I wish dear wife that your
health was as good. I fear you have many sick days as you used to
have but you dont tell much about it [in letters to me]. Tell me all
particulars wont you. (How is Jay [Jennie]. I don't let Jay [Jackie]
think much about such things I have to keep him pretty quiet or else
I could not do anything with him. He puts all trust in his dear J-y.
She must in him) Dear Eliza there is a true & loving husbands love*

---

* The two-story addition, called the "ell," enabled the family to purchase a
large cook stove and add soapstone washtubs at the other end of the room. The
small upstairs bedrooms of the ell, reached by a back staircase, were used for hired
hands.

** There are no explanations of this treasury note in other existing letters.

for his wife & children. Yours ever E.H.F.

Henry C. Foster

Eliza's Diary:

> **Saturday, April 25**: *I send A letter to Henry No. 12*

Much Joy Mingled with Sorrow

Henry finally receives the miniatures he has so long awaited.

(No. 15) Custom House New Orleans May 2d 1863

Dear & Beloved ones at home.

It is with feelings of much joy mingled with sorrow also, that I seat myself at this moment to commune with you. Joy that I have such a dear family at home, & a wife too that is dearer than all else, & the tokens of remembrance that I have received to day from you, but it makes me feel sad too, that I am so far from you but Oh! I hope and trust in God, who is kind and good to all that love Him, that we may all be spared to meet again soon. Though it seems a long time to wait the time will come, if ones lives are spared, but Oh how much I want to see you all.

I received my box you sent me this day; it all came safe. Eliza I can hardly express my thanks to you. Such a splendid box and such a lot of good things in it as I never thought of scarcely, but the miniatures is what I think the most of. But how poor [ill] you look dear one. I am afraid you worry to much but it is not strange that you should but I wish you would not, but it is a trial to be left with those children. Oh this war I wish it was over, but if the union is saved, and freedom & Liberty is left to us, I feel that we shall all be richly rewarded. This gives me hope, & I hope it will you too, for what is life without Liberty. But excuse me for wandering. My mind is crowded so full that I hardly know what I write. I think their [they

•

are] very nice pictures indeed. I should have known Henrietta's [face] but Georges should not. Etta looks as roguish as ever. My stars what a forehead georg has. I think he is a fine looking boy so they all think here. How he has grown. Etta has grown to but she has not changed so much [as] George has.

I am very glad of all those things you sent me. I shall have no trouble in disposing of them I guess, but I must say it was quite a supprise [sic]. Please tell me how much it all cost &c. I should thought you would sent the paper and ink this time however I guess I shall get along with what you sent me this time. I have sold 4 quires [24 to 25 sheets each] already. Willard gave me 30 cts for one quire & 6 envelopes. The rest I have not got pay [paid for] but shall as soon as we are paid which will be in a few days. I don't know whether that is enough for it or not. Please tell me when you write how much it cost &c. I shall not sell any more at present.

I have opened the honey & the tomato [preserves] but the two small boxes I have not opened yet but I spect there is something good in them.* As long as I stay here I can keep those things a long time but if I had to march I don't know hardly what I should do with some of them, but I see no prospect of leaving here at present. That tomato is so nice. Did you make it. I know you could make as good but being sealed up so nice** I cannot say. I shall endeavor to comply with your request, & keep my shoes tied up and my nose clean and try to keep a stiff upper lip to. How did you happen to think of the emory [emery, a grinding and polishing medium], but then you always did think of every thing. It will be nice to clean my gun with. Everything came safe but the box was broke open or burst open. The nails did not hold.

I received the papers yesterday. That was the first I knew of the

---

* Tomato marmalade was a Victorian sweet, as were tomato "figs"—candied tomatoes.

** Eliza had taken the precaution of having some containers soldered shut.

box & this morning I went and got my box. You ought to seen the crowd around me when I opend [opened] it. My segars are most all gone now but I delight in giving things to my comrades & so do all soldiers.

I am having any quantity of applications for paper. It is so nice they all want some of it but I shall see if I get pay for what I have let go first. I told you I got 30 cents for a quire but come to think it over after W [Willard] was gone it was but 12 sheets & 6 enve-lopes. However I will make it right with him next time I see him. I don't expect to see him but once or twice more before he goes home. He expects to go next Thursday. He has got his [medical] discharge papers. All he is waiting for now is his money. It seems rather hard to me to see men that enlisted with me going home, but I am glad I have my health for I should rather stay 3 years or 5 even than loose my health. I shall try to preserve my health to & it is [with] a sort of joy and mingled pride that I look forward to that time when I shall have served my country honestly & faithfully and can return home to my family again God permiting I will.

I received my warrent [warrant; certificate of appointment] as Sergt a few days since. It is dated only back to the time [of] Sergt [Joseph] Chandlers death, the 10th of March, and I will explain the reasons why it was not to the time Dick [Dickerman] was promot-ed. Lt. [Abel H.?] Stone is 2d Lt in this Co., & Capt has been trying to get rid of him for the last 3 or 2 months but has not succeeded yet so Dick has to [be] reported as sergt or go into some other Co which he dont want to do nor we dont want to have him [transfer] either. The boys all like him for Lt so the vacancy of Chandler was the only one. I guess I shall send it home and have you keep it for me. Also my Corporal's warrant though it is much soild [soiled] by carrying it in my knapsack and it got some oil on it to. I am sorry I did not send it home at first. I am going to see the Capt to see if I cant get a new one in place of it.

Well I will say to you dear Eliza be of good spirits, & I will try to be patient till the time comes. I hope you will all be comfortable and be well. What comfort those dear children must be to you, though they are [a] great deal of trouble. I will send you all my love & kisses &c. Give my respects to all. This from your true & loving husband with a thousand thanks & blessings. God be with & protect you all forever. Good bye for this time.

Sergt. H. C. Foster

In early May, Grant's forces in the Eastern Theater pushed inland toward Vicksburg. There was fighting at Bayou Pierre, Mississippi. Meanwhile, in the Western Theater, Union Col. Benjamin Grierson and 1,700 men completed their six-hundred-mile raid, riding hard into Baton Rouge, Louisiana. Grierson's raid, which began at La Grange, Tennessee, on April 17, was intended to lure Confederates away from Vicksburg.[351]

With plenty of stationery on hand, Henry waits only two days before writing again to Eliza:

(No 16) Custom House N. Orleans May 4ᵗʰ 1863

Dear Eliza.

*Having a few words I want to say to you I will do so by writing. I have just maild [mailed] 2 letters 1 to you & one to Mabelia & also a papers or papers [newspapers] to you. We have got some glorious news to day which you will find in those papers should you be fortunate enough to get them.**

* In the previous month, many events occurred which might strike Henry as "glorious news." On April 8, the Senate passed the Thirteenth Amendment to the Constitution, abolishing slavery in the United States. On April 17, Grant announced that he would exchange no more prisoners with the South until such releases were balanced equally—and would make no distinction between white and African-American prisoners. At this time, the North held 146,000 Southern prisoners. In one of the most imaginative engineering feats in military history, dams were being built to float the federal fleet (stranded by low water) over the rapids above Alexandria on the Red River. The work was completed in only ten days.

I have received all your letters up to No 12 except one No 11 between Ap 5th & Ap 12th. We had a mail last night but I did not get a letter. Another mail has come in to day which has not been delivered yet. I ant you to tell me how many letters you have received without being No [numbered]. I shall call this No 16 but I am not certain as it is right. I am always in such a hurry when I commence to write a letter that I forget to No them but I shall try to do better in future.

I have just been up top of the Custom House viewing the lines & witnessed some buisy scenes there. A steamboat is unloading cotton & sugar. Gen Banks has captured over two thousand prisoners. More than half of them have taken the oath of allegiance to the U.S. Gen Banks has issued an order for all registered enemies to leave the lines or else take the oath of allegiance. You will see the order in the papers I have sent you. *

I want to get something to send you when W. [Willard] goes if I get paid before that time. My segars are all gone. I treated the boys with them as far as they would go. They were splendid ones. The honey & tomato is so nice but the pesky ants are bound to have a share in [it] to, but if they get more of it than I do they will be smart thats all. The 2 little cans I have not opened yet. I used some of the emory [emery] this forenoon to clean my gun with. It is nice I tell you.

I went to meeting yesterday & heard a very good sermon at the Methodist Church on Carondolet St. Capt. Warren of Lowell, was

---

* The oath of allegiance required every captured Confederate soldier to lay down his arms and swear allegiance to the Union within sixty days. The New Orleans city council attempted to function for a while under military rule, but the councilors were eventually dismissed for refusing to take the oath. Their departure cleared the way for Butler to rule as he saw fit. Banks was simply enforcing what Butler put into practice—although Butler and his unscrupulous brother, Andrew, apparently used the oath as a method of enriching themselves with the goods of those who refused to take the oath.

there with his wife. It is a very warm day here to day but there is not so many mosquitoes here as there was at the Quarantine last year, and I am glad of it. Well I shall not write much more to day for I have got to go out on dress parade. We have 2 a day now but no drill. Oh! If I could but see you to day I would squeeze you a little, all of you. I live in hopes yes we will hope for that time [of reunion] to come soon. I will bid you good bye for to night.

Wednesday May 6th

How do you all do to day sweet ones. I hope you are well & may this find you so as it leaves me at present. Wilard [Willard] is going to morrow I suppose. He has got his [medical discharge] papers & money. I want to send you something & the children to. I have bought Georgy a little knife. I hardly know what to get for you & Etta. I have not been paid yet but W. let me have 3.00 dollars & I am going to send it to him when I get paid. Wilard is looking pretty well, but he complains a goodeal. If he goes to morrow he will get there as soon as this letter does so I don't know which you will get first. I suppose you will see him so he will tell you all the particulars about N. Orleans & the 26th [Regiment] & c., so I will not write any more now. This from your true loving husband,

[to] E. H. F.

[signed] H. C. Foster

A thousand kisses & blessings to you all & I hope [I] shall soon be with you. Be of good spirrits, & c.

Andrew does not write about the Battle of Fredericksburg because he feels Eliza will have seen reports in the newspapers:

In camp near White Oak Church Va. May Saturday 9th 1863

My Dear Sister

I am alive & pretty well but I am sick of such a life as this.

I was very glad to receive your letter mailed Apr. 18th & thought I would see Sergt. Barns & answer it immediately but we were about moving &c &c so I did not.

I suppose you have seen by the papers all about the battle at Fredericksburg &c.

Our Regt. was in the fight & lost 97 killed wounded & missing.*

I was not in the fight Thank God. I was with our Quarter Master.

I heared from Sergt. Barnes by one of their teamsters.

He is safe & well I hear. The 1st Mass. Battery [artillery company] belongs to our Brigade & is called a very smart & lucky one.

I have not received your pictures yet. I received a letter from Henry mailed Apr. 16th.

I think I did know Wm. H. Lovejoy & his brother Aaron. Tell Frank that I was up to Falmouth & inquired for 29th Regt. to see her [his?] brother but the Regt. had moved so I could not find him.

Sumner G. Holt [Eliza's cousin] is dead.

Dear Sister Eliza I wish I could see you. I am so tired of this life. We have had a big fight & back on our old ground. I wish I was with my wife & children.

I will send you 2 dollars this time & more soon.

Do write me often for I am sad. My respects to Sylvia Rose & Frank.**

From your loving

A. J. Beane

---

* Washington F. Brown, a Sergeant in Company I, was killed in battle, May 3, 1863. James C. Bartlett was wounded on the same day. Edwin Farrarr, serving with the 16th Maine Volunteers, died December 26, 1862, from wounds received at Fredericksburg.

** These friends often visited Eliza in Lowell.

Put Your Trust in the God of Battles

If Andrew stood picketing duty during this winter camp, he might have found it a relatively safe assignment. William Snackenberg, a Louisiana "Pelican" stationed below Fredericksburg in March 1863, was assigned to picket the Rappahannock River. He wrote: "While we were not doing active campaign duty [we] did not fire on each other. This seemed to be a general rule in winter when in quarters and the pickets used to have long talks with each other and always in good spirits. We used to [ex]change tobacco, which was scarce with them, for coffee, which was very scarce with us. [I]f either side got orders to fire on the pickets, we generally gave each other notice to go in their holes."[352]

Andrew reported being sick in October and being assigned to the quartermaster the following May. In July, two months later, he is still attached to the quartermaster. The U.S. Army Quartermaster Corps, born in 1775 during the Revolutionary War, was the Army's logistics arm, tasked with feeding, clothing, and equipping troops. The term originated in the sixteenth century to designate the person who went ahead of troops to prepare or acquire shelter or quarters for them.[353] During the Civil War, the Quartermaster Corps was assigned the additional duty of burying the dead—although that assignment did not extend to notifying next of kin. The Corps did not shoulder this duty themselves, but picked troops for the burial detail.

Henry writes again from Louisiana, sending his letter and some gifts by the hand of comrade Willard:

> *(No. 17) Custom House N. Orleans May 12th/63*
>
> *Dear Eliza.*
>
> *I take the great pleasure & consolation of having the opportunity of writing a few words to you this evening. Would that I could be so to talk to you, but that greatest pleasure must be defered a time longer. I hope it may be a short time, but we will be faithful &*

true and patient until that time comes. I pray it may be Gods will & pleasure, to preserve all our lives & our health & to prosper us through life's journey.

Willard has been here to see us this evening. He has gone aboard of the steamer that is to convey him to N.Y. He will sail to morrow morning at 8 oclock, so I embraced the opportunity of sending this letter by him. I have news to tell you. We were paid to day for 4 months up to May 1ˢᵗ. My pay was $18.00 this time. I am owing some little bills. After those are paid I [shall] send you a small sum, which you must consider your present this time for I could find nothing in N. Orleans that suited me to send you. I send Etta a little pin [item of jewelry] & George a little knife by W., and thanking you again for the generous gifts you have sent me in the box. I tender to you my grattitude & all my love, and dear one it is my aim to do the best I can, always.

I have great reason to be thankful for my good luck in the past and I will be hopeful of the future. I feel that it is no use to be down hearted, but it does make me a little homesick when I see others going home but I hope to see my companions in arms through & do my duty to the best of my ability. No dear Eliza I never have for a moment allowed myself to get discouraged, for if I did I should be miserable indeed. Rather I have tried to be as cheerful as possible, but being a soldier in war is no easy task & it is not exactly in accordance with my nature, but every one has to conform themselves to the kind of duty we have to perform & do as well as we can.

Hoping this will find you & the children well & happy as you can be under the circumstances, I will bid you all goodnight, from your true & loving husband

H. C. Foster

As a memento, Henry enclosed with this letter a ticket to the Grand Union Ball at the St. Charles Hotel, April 24, 1863. It is signed with the name

Miss Val. E. Jones. The card is decorated with pale pink angels and a garland. Henry writes in a postscript: "This card is one I begged of Dick [Heath]. He boasts that the bearer of the name on the card was the belle of the evening & so forth."

Soon Henry takes up his pen again:

(No. 18)   Custom House   N. Orleans   May 16, 1863

Dear Eliza.

I write you a few lines today so you may know I am well & I hope this may find you all well also. I received two letters from you two days since. How glad I was to hear from you & to learn that you ere all well. Those were Nos 12 & 13. I have had two No 12 so now I think I have received them all. I sent a letter by Mr. Wilmot. I hope you get it & I hope he will get home safe.

I am very sorry to hear that Mrs. Morey is so low, but we must all meet death sooner or later. I wish that we might all be prepared for it.

Mr. Connerford [Comerford] is here now from the Hospital. He is nearly well & is coming back to the Co. soon. We have but two men in the Hosp now. One of those is on duty there, so we have not actually any one sick in the Co now. The Co numbers 83 men aggregate. Good many men are on detached duty. Col. Farr has come back to the Regt and taken command. There has been some talk of our going up the River as soon as we were paid, but I have understood from good authority that we shall remain here at present. There are men from this Regt on duty in every part of the city. There are 2 Cos here, which is the most there is in any one place I believe. The Headquarters of the Regt. are here in the Custom House.

I am having my watch cleaned for $2.50. I thought to have my miniature taken, but I think I will wait till next pay day, & I guess to [too] the one I sent you last summer looked so bad you wont want to see another one. We have news here from the North up to the 7*th*. [Gen. Joseph] Hooker had recrossed the river, back to his old camp. I would like to know how matters stand now in Virginia. Oh if there could be some decisive victory gaind, I think the rebbellion [sic] would soon be over with but it seems rather discouraging that the army in Virginia does not accomplish more, but I try to think all will be well & for the best. I pray that it may be so, & still keep hoping that God will give us victory & peace in good time, if we are deserving of it, & I can but feel that we are justified in our cause of Liberty & the Nation's integrity.

I have not had a letter from Mabelia for some time. She wrote in her last that she had been quite sick but did not say what aild [ailed] her. It seems Mr. Morey was not so well of as was supposed. Well there always seemd [seemed] to be a mystery in his affairs as well as [the affairs of a] good many others. As his neighbors I had rather appear poor than to be called rich & be poor at the same time, but I will not say any more now.

Tell me all the particulars &c. I will close now wishing you well & the children also. May[be] we all be prospered & be permitted to meet again soon. Tell the children to remember Father & be good to Mother. Kiss them for me. This from your true & loving husband.

To E. H. Foster

Sergt H. C. Foster

I send you $5.00 dollars in this letter as a present.

Eliza's Diary:

Saturday, May 23: *I get a letter from Henry today All well*

Willard comes*

---

* Willard was stationed in New Orleans with Henry, and secured a medical discharge at the beginning of May. He would have brought Eliza first-hand news of Henry.

In the Battle of Chancellorsville in May 1863, General Hooker was too cautious and his reconnaissance was poor. The battle was a stunning victory for the Confederates—although they lost one of their best generals, Stonewall Jackson, as a result of it. Still searching for a commander with initiative and insight, Lincoln replaced Hooker in his turn with George Meade three days before the battle of Gettysburg.

On May 21, Union general Nathaniel Banks moved his troops into position near Port Hudson, Louisiana. He was setting the stage for the siege of that port. Banks' troops crossed the Mississippi on May 23 and fighting began. On May 24, the Union siege of Vicksburg took its final shape.[354] Henry comments on these maneuvers in the following letter.

(No. 19) Custom House   N. Orleans   May 27ᵗʰ/63

My Dear Ones at home.

I feel as though I must write a few words to you to day so you may know I am well, & I hope & pray you are all well also but as it is such a long time since I have heard from you that I feel very anxious about you & the children for fear that some of you are sick. The last letter I received from you was date [sic] April 26ᵗʰ. I suppose W. [Willard] is at home by this time. I hope he had a safe journey home. I would have given considerable if I could have gone with him, but I try to make the best I can of it until I can come home to you, & dear Eliza it gives me much pleasure that you bare [bear] up so cheerfully as is indicated by the tone of your letters. Such good letters too they are ever welcome to me, but I guess you have all stoped [stopped] writing of late. I have not had a letter from Mabelia for 6 weeks nor Clara either. Well perhaps they will all come in a bunch so I will wait patiently.

We are having cheering news here now, from up river Port Hudson [after a siege of 6 weeks] is surrounded by Gen Banks forces & Vicksburg [after a siege of 48 days] by Gen Grant's so that both places must soon fall, without doubt, but it is not best perhaps to be to [too] sure for we are not sure of anything only as it transpires, but such is the hopeful prospect now that the river will soon be open. When that is accomplished the rebels have got a hard blow.

I should like to send you some of the beautiful boquets I see here, if I could. There is some of the most beautiful smelling flowers here I ever saw. The Magnolia is splendid. It seems so odd to have all kinds of fruit at this time of year plums blackberries all kinds of garden sauce, & so forth.*

Well Eliza dear, things remain about the same with this Regt. No signs of moving at present. I do not think of much more this time. I cannot express my feelings. Oh how I should like to hold you to my bossom [sic] once more, & receive a tender kiss from you, & the dear little ones also. Be true to your "hus"band [sic] and re-member he is ever so to his wife and children, & I pray that the time will soon come that we can be in each others embrace, but we must be prepared to meet the events that may come during that time & bare up & be as cheerful as we can. I will do the best I can & help you all in my power, & may the best of heavens blessings rest upon you & our dear children. Good bye, from your loving husband ever,

To E.H. F.

H. C. Foster

Eliza's Diary:

Saturday, May 30: *Willard and Frank is in her [here] and spend the evening*

---

* Although applesauce is the chief "garden sauce" of the 21st century, from the Renaissance through the early 20th century, almost any fresh fruit or vegetable might be stewed into a "sauce." The term can indicate anything from cucumbers to cabbage. Beets and carrots were sometimes termed "long sauce," while onions and potatoes constituted "short sauce."

Cooking the fruit or vegetable helped preserve it for a few days without the use of refrigeration or canning.

Monday, June 1: *All well to day and at home*

Mrs. Willson called to see me *

I Am Well To Night

(No. 20)   Custom House   N. Orleans   June 1ˢᵗ 1863

My Dear Eliza.

Your letter of the No 14 was received to day & I hasten to answer it. I was very glad to get it as it had been so long since I had heard from you. It seems that Mr. Wilmot [Henry seems to confuse Wilmot and Willard] had not got home when you wrote though I see by N. York papers that the boat he went on had arrived in that Port. I am well to night & I hope you & the children are well also. We are having pretty hot weather here now. I was very sorry to hear of Mrs. Morey's death, though it was not unexpected after what you had writen in previous letters. I received a letter from Sister M. also she wrote that she had been quite sick & that Sylvester [probably Chauncy Lynch's brother] had gone home &c. It seems Mr. May has not gone on to a farm yet. How is Rose [Heasey] & her baby getting along. Did they ever receive a letter from me that you know of. I wrote once to them last fall but they have not answered it, so I shall not troble [trouble] myself to write them again. You need not say anything about it unless they tell you. Please give them my kind regards &c. Also all the neighbors, especially Mr. Thomsons folks. Tell them they are remembered by me, always & I am ever thankful to them all for past kindnesses & present to me & my family & shall feell gratful for their sympathy with [i.e., demonstrated to] my dear wife & children in the circumstances which you are placed.

You did not tell me what Mrs [no name given] had said or done about you but I hope you will not let it trouble you although it is

---

* There are three men with the surname Wilson in Company A: Franklin Wilson, Joseph Wilson, and Justus Wilson.

very disagreeable to have such persons in the neighbor hood. I had heard what a character she was before I left home, but dear one pass her by as best you can.

Everything remains about the same here in the city, except that most of the troops are goin up the river to Port Hudson. There has been many rumors that the 26th [Regiment] were a going but we have not started yet. There has been some hard fighting there with considrable [sic] loss on both sides but no particulars given. But our army is in good position and the place must soon fall. Gen Banks has them completely surrounded and all communication cut off, and he is only waiting for reinforcements. The news at Vicksburg is most cheering and the prospect is very good that the [river] will soon be open. Let us be hopful [sic] still.

I will close for to night. Please accept this with a husband's love, & a Father's for his children. Ever true, yours with all that I can bestow upon you. Kiss the dear little ones & tell them to remember papa for he never forgets any of you. My best wishes & hope Oh that I could but see you to night, but do not despair I will try to keep a stiff upper lip as I can so good bye dear

To E.H. F.

H. C. Foster

A few days after he penned the above letter, Henry moved by rail to Bayou Lafourche, in the heart of Louisiana sugar country. Plantations were sacked and ungathered crops of cane rotted in the fields.[355] Meanwhile, on Saturday afternoon, June 27, Joseph Mayo, Mayor of Richmond, issued a warning to the citizens of his city directing them to arms: "I have just received a message direct from the highest authority in the Confederacy, to call upon the Militia Organizations to come forth, and upon all other Citizens to organize Companies for the defence [sic] of this City against immediate attack of the enemy. They are approaching, and you may have to meet them before Monday morning . . . Remember New Orleans . . . Let [Richmond] not fall under the rule of another BUTLER."[356]

Eliza's Diary:

> **Wednesday, June** 3: *All well and at home*
>
> *I get A letter from Mother Lynch and one from Henry and two papers letter No. 18*
>
> **Thursday, June 4**: *All well this morning*
>
> *Sylvester [Chauncy Lynch's brother] goes to Vermont today*
>
> **Friday, June 5**: *All well and at home*
>
> *I get a letter from Henry and how glad to hear that he is well letter No. 19*

I Fear You Suffer a Goodeal

Henry expresses concern about Eliza's health:

> *(No 21)   Custom House N. Orleans   June 5th 1863*
>
> *My Dear Ones:*
>
> *I feell thankful to a kind providence that I am again permited to commune with my loved ones at home, and also that I am well, and I hope & trust you are all well and may these few lines find you all enjoying one of the best of heavens blessings[,] good health. But Eliza I fear you suffer a goodeal that you don't tell me of, for I know how many sick spells you used to have. Oh if I had known that I should have had to stay away so long, I should never [have] left home and all that was so dear to me, but perhaps it is well that I did not know it, for our country needs all her true sons of Liberty, and I only regret the long separation from my family and the sorrow and anxiety it causes you dear wife, to say nothing of my own feelings, but I feel that I have a good & true companion, that can bare up & be faithful to me, and you can have the same faith in me but it is useless to dwell on this for can we for a moment doubt each other. No! it seems foolish perhaps to write or even think*

about, but I hope it can do no harm to us. I trust we can think of other & better things, but Eliza I am glad you have confidence in me to speak of that, for I know you never could deceive me, just for a moment think where our happiness would be. Oh how miserable should we be. It almost makes me horror stricken to see how some men degrade themselves and no doubt women to [too] at home, but that is not for me to say. Perhaps it is by mutual consent. If so I suppose it [adultery] is all right. I should judge this to be the case from what I hear some married men say. (If you and I can agree to it why then its nobody's business, eh! I must joke you [jest with you] a little. I feel a little might [mite] roguish! Well please tell me what your opinion is [,] do. Perhaps we can agree on terms [for sexual matters] that will be satisfactory. Well I guess this will do for this time, on that score.)

I received another letter since I last wrote you, of May 4th No 14 so it seems you No [have numbered] two alike. This mail was 27 days coming but we got it [at] last. I have eat up the contents of my box what I did not give away. Those preserves were nice indeed. I thank you again.

I suppose you have seen W. [Willard] before this time & he has told you all the news. At least I hope so. I got a letter from Mother the last mail. Well good bye dear dear wife & children, from your true & loving husband,

H. C. Foster

To E.H.F.

Eliza's Diary:
Monday, June 8*: I send letter No. 18.*

In Louisiana, Henry continues in good spirits:

(No. 22)   Custom House   New Orleans   June 17th/63

Dear Wife & Children.

I take the great pleasure this morning of communing with you by letter. Oh what pleasure would it be could I be near you so that I could talk to you. Well we must be patient & wait the time to come, and we should ever be thankful that our lives are spared us thus far. I do feel thankful, and I will ever trust in God for my preservation and my family. I received a letter from you 2 days since. How glad was I to get it and learn that you were well. It was the date of May 24ᵗʰ. You said W. [Willard] had got home. I was glad to hear it, and glad you received the things I sent by him. I hope his health is improving, and that he will soon be well.

I was very glad that you had heard from Andrew much more so that he was safe and well, for we little known what he has been through. I hope his life and health may be spared him. I have not received any answer to the last letter I wrote him some months ago. I think [I] shall write to him again.

Well Dear Eliza I cannot write much this morning. My heart and my mind is so full when I think of home and my dear ones there, that I scarcely know what I say or do, but I assure you dear Eliza I am in as good spirits as possible, for me to be, although I cannot help feeling great anxiety. I know it is best to keep up good courage & bright hopes if possible. I try to take good care of my health, and hope to live through my time out in the army if necessary, and save my health to [too]. And you know a cheerful mind goes far towards keeping our health. I dont know but my letters seem void of affection to you but dear one I never can find words to express my emotions when writing or thinking of the dear ones at home. I am ever thinking of you all, and hoping for your good, and ours. Eliza dear may I ask you to be prudent and careful of yourself and the dear little ones, and make things as comfortable and joyous for yourselves as you can. I send you a thousand kisses and my best wishes. Kiss the dear little ones for me. Good bye [from] your

true and loving husband, and rest assured dear Eliza you have my
confidence ever in you, a good and loving wife, and may time or
seperation [sic] never change our fidelity in each other. Yours with
affection,

> *from*

> *Henry C. Foster*

Eliza's Diary:

> **Saturday, June 27**: *All well to day and at home but not settled*
> *yet**

> *I get a letter from Henry [June 17?] and he is well*

Encounter with a Contraband

> *Camp at Jefferson Station, La. June 29th 1863*

> *(direct as before)*

> *Dear & beloved ones at home*

> *I suppose you would like to know how & where I am &c. I take*
> *the opportunity to inform you I am well and I hope this may find*
> *you all well and [indecipherable] now. Left Custom House N.O. one*
> *week ago last Saturday. Got aboard cars at Algiers. Went up the*
> *Opelousas R.R. to Bayou des Allemands, 32 miles, 3 Cos. [of the*
> *26th Massachusetts Regiment] A, G & F. Stopped here & 5 went on*
> *(2 being left in the City) to Bayou Lafourche Sunday night they had*
> *a battle at this latter [?] place. The 26th made a good fight what*
> *there was of it. You see it was not my fortune to be in it. The 26th*
> *lost 4 killed & 4 wounded. There was 5 Co's 26th & 3 Co's 23 Conn.*
> *engaged on our side and 3 or 4 pieces of artillery. The loss was very*
> *slight on our side 9 killed in all & 18 or 20 wounded. The rebels*

---

* "Not settled yet" may refer to Eliza's move to another apartment, located on a lower floor of the tenement. See Henry's letters of April 23 and July 22, 1863.

lost over a hundred killed and a very large number wounded. All agree that the 26ᵗʰ made the handsomest fight that has been made in these parts. The reb's got a sound whiping, but their force being much larger than ours we have retreated down here on to the river 16 miles from N.O.

When our forces retreated our Co. was left alone at the place where we first stopped to cover the retreat. We remained there up to last Saturday night when orders came for us to burn the bridge and join the Regt. which we done, 8 miles this side whence we all came to this place. I can inform you no further for we are not liable to stay in any place long now. Gen. Banks has occupied all of that country once but has withdrawn his forces to Port Hudson, so the rebels have rallied again, quite a large force having come out of Texas, and they are threatening N.O. with the hope of raising the siege of Port Hudson, but they will not succeed. It is reported as true this morning that Port Hudson is taken by Gen. Banks. If it is so we shall soon clean them out on the R.R. The 26ᵗʰ & 7ᵗʰ Conn. Regt. is about all there is to protect N.O. but the reb's will not come very near the river for they are to much afraid of our gunboats.

The 15ᵗʰ Maine Regt. has come from Pensacola. They are camped 4 miles below us. I have not had a chance to see any of them yet although I have heard from Dr. Holt, so I think it must be a mistake that he is dead. His Regt. went up past us on the cars, to Bayou Lafourche the day after the fight and came back 2 days after. I was on picket when a contraband came along. He said he*

---

* The term "contraband" was used for a slave who had fled his master, been captured by the Union, and been pressed into informal military service. It comes from a statement of Benjamin Butler early in the Civil War about his intention to seize runaway slaves in Virginia as "contraband of war." The term caught the imagination of the public and overnight became a name for any runaway slave. On August 6, 1861, Lincoln allowed an act to be passed legalizing Butler's "contraband" order. Initially contrabands were given jobs to do behind the lines, but ultimately Army regiments were formed consisting of African-Americans.

was waiting for Dr. Holt [of the] 15ᵗʰ Maine. That when the Regt.
retreated he was left behind and he was going on down to find the
Dr. Well I was surprised but it looked so reasonable I could not
doubt but what Cousin [Summer] Holt was still alive & well which
the negroe declared was the fact, though there may be another Dr.
Holt in the Regt. for he could not tell me what his first name was.
However I addressed a note to him but have not heard from it yet.

Eliza I will now close & I assure you I am in good spirits & enjoy
the trip very much for a change. I hope this will [find] you in good
spirits & good health also. I am ever your true & loving husband.
With my tenderest feelings for you all.

H. C. Foster

I received your letter the day before we left the City but have
not had a chance to answer it before. I got one from W. also. He
spoke cheering to me of you my dear wife, and said you were in good
spirits. Oh I was glad.

After months of dress parade, picket duty, and guard duty in New Orleans, Henry was again assigned to the backwaters of Louisiana. Bayou des Allemandes was a marshy area near New Orleans, known for its waterfowl, catfish, alligators, and snakes. Bayou Lafourche, originally settled by Acadians fleeing religious oppression in eastern Canada, was located near Thibodaux and Larose, Louisiana.

Dr. Sumner Holt, Eliza's cousin, is mentioned again by Henry in his letter of July 31, 1863, when he reports that Holt died in April. In truth, Holt had died in Florida on March 25, 1863.[357] Since he was already long dead when Henry had the report that he was alive, it is likely the black contraband was not officially attached to an officer at the time—but feared what would happen to him if he revealed his true status to Henry.

Ten Thousand Kisses

There is neither a location nor a date on the following letter. However, Eliza was numbering Henry's letters as she stored them away, and the original is numbered No. 35—with the previous letter labeled as No. 34. Henry confesses he is relieved to have avoided combat.

[No salutation]

This is written in a hurry.

Our Army is making a pretty clean sweep of it this time. I guess Gen. Banks don't intend to have this country to fight over the third time for this is the second, but Eliza I wish you could see this country. So far as we have come, it [i.e., Louisiana] is a fine country, but it has not been cultivated much for 2 years past. Our Army moves slow but sure. I suppose we shall move on as fast as our supplies get along. The last news we had from the North the report was that Charleston was taken and Rosecram [Maj. Gen. William Rosecrans] had totally defeated [Gen. Braxton] Bragg. I hope it is true.

We have passed through the towns of Pattersonville, Centerville, Franklin, New Iberia & Vermillionville. The next is Opelousas. Perhaps you can trace our course out on the map We have had plenty of water so far. I think I have fated [fatted, fattened] up since I started on the march, but I don't suppose we have got started fairly yet.*

Charley [Richardson] is dressing a chicking now, and we will have it for supper. I think the rebels very kind to leave us so much

---

* The route Henry details is generally west of New Orleans to Patterson, then arcing north toward Lafayette and Opelousas—through marshy, swampy areas. It is approximately the route of Highways 90 and 182 today. Henry will return to the Vermillion and New Iberia area in the fall of 1863; see his letter of November 25, 1863.

poultry and fresh beef, but then they had a reason for it cause they did not have time to take it away.

Well dear ones I will close for this time. I have expected to see a fight before this time, but the kind hand of providence has ordered it otherwise, and I hope we shall meet with the same success in future. We have not been paid yet only to the first of July, and dont know when we shall be. I am pretty hard up for tobacco just now. I got the 25 cent bill you sent me long ago. I had thought I told you, but dont know as I did. Give my [love?] to Mabelias folks and tell them I shall write to them again for I have not forgotten them. Give my respects to all. I have not forgotten any of my old friends & neighbors.

Dear Eliza here is all a husbands love to his wife, and children and ten thousand kisses. Kiss the dear little ones for me, and tell them to remember Father for he never forgets little Henrietta & Georgy. May God bless and protect you all in my absence & forever, from your true and loving husband.

Henry C. Foster

Eliza's Diary:

Thursday, July 2: *[Sends] No. 19*

Sunday, July 5: *I send a letter to H. No. 20.*

Monday, July 6: *I carey Henry letter to the [post] Office this morning and get a box of [?] 1 ct.*

Saturday, July 11: *Quite well to day and at home I wash and ian some*

Sunday, July 12: *All well to day but I am tiard and I will sleep as I can't go to Dracut [to visit the Fox family] Mrs. Barnes is in*

---

* In Henry's Company A there are two privates with the surname Barnes: James E. and Timothy P.

Union dead west of the Seminary at Gettysburg. Dover Civil War Illustrations.

*Henry gives me some liles**

*Mrs. Hessey and Charly came in and then George comes****

July 1–3, 1863, saw the Battle of Gettysburg, but Andrew Bean does not mention it by name in his subsequent letter, and sources differ about Andrew's service at Gettysburg. If he fought there, he was fortunate to escape unharmed. Abner Small of Maine, among the troops there, described the chaos and carnage:

> [F]rom all the rebel line there was one vast roar, and a storm of screaming metal swept across the valley. Our guns blazed and thundered in reply. The earth groaned and trembled. The air, thick with smoke and

* Eliza may mean that Henry sent her some pressed lilies in a letter. He enclosed white clover blossoms in a letter in February 1864.

** George is probably the "George Huzsey" that Andrew mentions in a letter penned to Eliza on this same date. This surname is spelled Huse, Hussey and Hussy in *Clan MacBean*.

sulphurous vapor, almost suffocated the troops in support of the batteries. . . . [About 2 p.m., his brigade moved.] The air was all murderous
iron; it seemed as if there couldn't be room for any soldier upright and
in motion.[358]

Gettysburg's casualties were enormous: The Confederates reported
3,903 dead, 18,735 injured and 5,425 missing out of a force of 75,000. The
North went into the battle with 88,289 troops, and reported 3,155 dead,
14,529 wounded, and 5,365 missing.[359] An officer from Maine, Joshua L.
Chamberlain, was given credit for turning the tide for the Union. As a
Bowdoin undergraduate, Chamberlain attended discussions and teas given
at the home of Harriet Beecher Stowe and her professor husband.[360]

Good Water to Drink

The Fifth Maine was now in Maryland, where Andrew took a moment to
write and reassure Eliza:

South Mountain Md. July 12th 1863

My Dear Sister

*I was so glad to get a letter from you for I had lood [looked] very
anxiously for a long time & thought it very strange that you did not
write. You did not tell me whether you received the 2 dollars or not.
I wish you would tell me in your next letter.*

*I am quite well at present for we can get good water to drink
here in Maryland. I was glad when we got out of Va. on that account. You have seen by papers that our Army has had awful battles of late.*

*Our Regt. has been lucky for once—we have not lost a man yet
but other Maine Regts. have lost heavily. Several that I knew in
17th Me. were killed & wounded but the 3 from our town are Safe
I think. Gould was sick in hospital. Foster is safe & George H. Holt*

*was in charge of Gen. Birney's horses I think.**

Eliza I too wish very much that I could see you.

Keep up good courage & put your trust in the God of battles. He can keep us from harm & Henry. Dr. Sumner G. Holt died of a fever.

Eliza Dear Sister Do not worry too much. I know you must feel very bad for your dear husband. I too feel very anxious for him but if he is only alive we will Thank God. If he is only a prisoner he will get away some time.

I had a letter from Mother not long since. They were well.

I had one from my wife [Mary Frost Brown Bean] dated June 30ᵗʰ & expected one last night but I got only one from you.

I have been with Quarter Master all the time. Our Regt. is some eight or ten miles beyond us at present. I have expected a fight for 2 days but I am afraid that Gen. Lee will get away over the river again as he did last fall.

Tell me if George Huzsey [Husey?] has got home.

Now Sister do not neglect to answer this immediately so I can learn of you & Henry.

[part of letter missing]

I am very home sick at times but I hope for the best.

I want to see my wife & children so much I dare not think of the length of the future months I am holden in [beholden to; indebted to] my Country's Service.

Cheer up dear Sister. Good Cheer. Put your trust in God. Plead with Him for you & yours. He is so true. So good.

Do not forget to pray to Him every Single day & while at the throne of grace forget not this loving brother in our humble supplications.

* The CWSS website lists four men with the surname Gould in the 17th Maine (Charles, Thomas, Tobias and William P.).

From your loving brother

A. J. Beane

P.S. Please write soon. . . .

Eliza's Diary:

Monday, July 13: *All well to day I get a letter from Henry &*
he is well

Mrs Fox was her [here] to day and Mr Fox I pay him for seven
lb. of butter 1.54

I Would Give Worlds If I Had Them

Back from bayou country, Henry lodges once again at the Custom House:

Custom House   N. Orleans   July 14ᵗʰ 1863

Dear & Beloved Ones at home.

It is with pleasure that I to pen [sic] a few lines to you this eve-
ning in answer to yours which I received to day, and Oh! How glad
was I to get it for it seemed a long time since I heard from you, it
pains me to learn that your health is so poor, and I fear it is much
more so than your letters represent but dear one I hope you will tell
me just as it is. Tell me if anything new has taken place that makes
you unwell. Oh Eliza I would give worlds if I had them to give could
I see you to night, but I hope the time will come ere long that we
may see each other, that I can be with my dear ones at home once
more. Though I am still deprived of that privlege [sic], I am thank-
ful and it is with gratitude to God, the giver of all good, that my
life & health are preserved so long, and I trust that I may always
be greatful to my heavenly father for His goodness to me & I pray
heavenly blessings to rest upon my dear wife & children in my ab-
sence. Sometimes I venture to think that this war will be over soon. I
do sincerely & devoutly hope it will, but I am almost afraid to hope

for we have had so many reverses, that I almost tremble for fear the great victories that are now given to our union arms may turn into defeat, and this dreadful & destructive war still be prolonged, but I pray that our cause (believing it to be right & just & holy) may triumph & that speedily, but we must not be impatient.

You have doubtless heard of the fall of Vicksburg and P [Port] Hudson or you will ere you receive this. Those are great victories and the latest northern news up to July 4th were very encouraging to our arms. I hope it is true & may victory after victory follow the sons of freedom untill there is not an armed traitor in our land.

Well I will tell you where I am to night &c. I [am] here in my old room in the Custom House, but I cant tell you where I shall be likely to be to morrow night. We arrived here about 4 oclock to day. We remained where last I wrote you [near Opelousas—unless there is a letter missing], up to this day. You have doubtless heard some bugbear stories about this Regt. and things in this Department generally; but I hope you have got better news long before this time.* The Capt. seems to think we shall stay in the city now, until the war is over, but there is no surety of that, but I don't think there will be much more fighting nearer than Mobile or Galveston.

I have much that I want to tell you to night. I enjoyed the trip we have had out in county [country?] very much & I for one did not want [to] come back to the city, and that was the case with the majority of the boys. We had plenty green stuff such as figs watermelons and green corn and peaches to [too] but I did not [eat] much of any except figs. I did punish [in the sense of "consume or use up"] my share of those. I wish you could have some.

Well I will bid you good night hoping this will find you all well as it leaves me, my 29th birthday. I shall write again in a day or two,

---

* A bugbear is a bogeyman—anything causing excessive fear or anxiety. Henry uses the term here in the sense of "alarming."

*and tell you some particulars about our sojourn out of town, & I
will also send you some papers. We were gone 24 days. My sweetest
& best love to you & the little ones from your loving husband.*

H. C. Foster

Control of Vicksburg bestowed two advantages on the Confederacy. First,
because the port overlooked a bend in the Mississippi River, its guns could
control water traffic both north and south. Second, substantial Confederate
supplies originated west of this point, were ferried across here, and then
transported east by rail. The surrender of this bastion to General Grant on
July 4, 1863, robbed the South of both these advantages.

Henry rightly links the fall of Vicksburg with the fall of Port Hudson
because the battles were undertaken in concert, and the surrenders were
entwined. The Confederate stronghold on the Mississippi at Port Hudson
was besieged for forty-eight days (May 21 through July 9, 1863) by the
Union army under Maj. Gen. Nathaniel Banks. Southern forces surrendered on July 9 after learning of the fall of Vicksburg. During the six
weeks' siege, one Port Hudson resident noted that he and his friends consumed "all the beef, all the dogs, and all the rats that were attainable."[361]

Eliza's Diary:

Wednesday, July 15: *All well I cut and bast [baste] a wast
[waist; shirt or blouse] for Mrs. Cachers boy and apare of shirts to
make for him**

Cash Account, July: *"One pare shirts" for Mrs. Cackle
[Cacher], $1, paid*

Thursday, July 16: *We are all well to day*

I am sewing on the shirts & waste & etc

Friday, July 17: *All is well that ends well I finish a waste [waist]*

* In terms of boys' and men's clothing of the day, a blouse could be a tunic-
length shirt, worn on the outside of pants, and belted. A girl's or woman's waist
would be tucked in, or secured with buttons to pants.

for Mrs. Cachers little Joy

Saturday, July 18: *At home and all well*

Nothing of importance going on

I go down to the storehouse &

Mrs. Galergins childe berred today

Nely Thompson [see John McIver's letter of May 1864] pases me the mony she borrowed some time ago

Sunday, July 19: *All well and at home I write to Henry letter No. 21.*

I Have Much to Be Thankful For

Custom House   N.O. July 22nd 1863

Dear Dear Wife.

I am glad to have the opportunity of writing to you to day though how much more glad would I be could I see you and be with you, and the dear little ones. It makes me feel a little homesick when I sit down to write to my loved ones at home. I can not help it, but I try to make the best of it for if I should give up to [yield to] my feelings, I dont know what would become of me. But dear one I feel as though I have nothing to complain of, but I have much to be thankful for, that we are spared our lives and health thus far.

Dear E I am well to day & I trust this may find you all well. Col Farr & Sgt Davis arrived back here day before yesterday. I was on guard and had the honor of first turning out and presenting arms to him. The boys were all tickled to death amost [almost] to see him and he was quite as well pleased to see them. He stopped and talked with us a few minutes, asked about the fight and so forth and told us we were all looking in fine health &c. He took command

---

* "Little joy" could simply refer to a young child. A private Henry Joy was a member of Henry's company.

last night. He looks as though his northern trip had done him good, but it is not every one that can get that chance. I wish I could, but I fear it would be worse leaving home the 2d time than it was the first, but you better believe I should risk it if I could get a furlow [furlough] and free passage home and back. Oh I hope it will not be long before I can come home and stay. May God grant it & let us be patient till that time, but dear E. I must tell you frankly how I feel about it, so to meet the worst. I have made up my mind to stay my time out so if I should get home any sooner it will be a happy disappointment indeed.

I hope dear E that you & the children are very comfortable. I was very glad to learn that you have moved down stairs and I have wished many times that you were in a more convenient tennement [sic]. Please tell me how you like your new tennement[,] wont you. I thought by what you wrote in your last letter that you had got your allotment although you did not say. I hope you had however.

In regard to Mr. C's drawing his pay twice I can only say it was a blunder of the pay department. Whose fault it is I cannot say. Several others received their pay twice in the same way. They were payed in the hospital, and the Capt drew their pay also. Where they were payed in hospital the allotment [amount to be sent home to wives] was not taken out so they got their ful [full] pay. I know in some cases, and I thought all were rectified at the next pay. If his was not I dont know the reason why. He has been paid in the hospital all the time so I don't know how it is any farther than I have stated. Mr. C. [Comerford] is still in the hospital as nurse, he not being able to do duty in the ranks. Mr. [Isaac E.] Gilmore has got his discharge and is going home. I some doubt if he will live to get home, he is very slim in fact he is nothing but a skeleton but if home he will be better as no doubt he will if he gets his papers for home-sickness seems to be the most that ails him, but I may be mistaken so do not let any one know I said this.

The sick report of the 26th Regt is only 53 at the present time so you see we are all pretty healthy & our Regt Nos [numbers] the most men of any Regt in this Dept. I should like very much to get some news from the 8th N.H. but I cannot [say] only that it suffered greatly at P. [Port] Hudson and other places, so I know not if Mr. Stickney is alive but I hope he has been spared. Co. A & 4 other Cos of our Regt are on provost duty now guarding prisoners mostly, and we are subject to almost any call. Our duty is pretty hard now as we have the P. Hudson prisoners.***

Well dearest one I will close for this time. I send you many kisses. Kiss the dear little ones. Oh how I wish I could see you all. I did not get any letter the last mail. I hope you did not have to wait long for better news than you had when you wrote the last letter was date [dated] July 5th.

I can not write more this time so good bye dearest one from your loving husband.

H. C. Foster

Eliza's Diary:

    Thursday, July 23: *Sick a bed all day.*

    Friday, July 24: *I am sick and have the Dr. Pay 25 cts for a bottle of Medsson.****

    Sunday, July 26: *I write to Henry letter 22 and [to] Mother & Andrew & I send them By Mr. Bradley*

* No man by the surname of Stickney occurs in the existing records of the 8th New Hampshire Regiment (www.usgennet.org/usa/wh/topic/civilwar/nh8threg). However, according to CWSS, there were three men with the surname Stickney in the 8th New Hampshire Infantry: Charles H. and David in Company D., and Clesson R. in Company B. Mr. Stickney is mentioned again in Henry's letter of Aug. 30, 1863.

** The surrender of Port Hudson left the Union over 6,000 Confederate prisoners as well as large quantities of arms and ammunition

*** The doctor here is Daniel P. Gage, whose office was at 43½ Merrimac Street.

In late 1862, Mathew Brady's New York gallery exhibited photographs of "The Dead of Antietam." Writer and physician Oliver Wendell Holmes, Sr., viewed the exhibit after he had searched for his son at Antietam, and set down his horrified reactions in an article published in the July 1863 *Atlantic Monthly*. If Eliza read Holmes' article, she would have seen these words: "Let him who wishes to know what war is like look at this series of illustrations. . . . The honest sunshine . . . gives us . . . some conception of what a repulsive, sickening, hideous thing it is, this dashing together of two frantic mobs to which we give the name of armies."[362]

Thursday, July 30*: Take Mrs Page away**[*]

The "draft" referred to in Henry's July 31 letter (below) was the National Conscription Act (or Federal Enrollment Act) passed on March 3. The Union act made all single men age 20 through 45 and all married men to age 35 subject to a draft lottery. In the lottery, 292,441 names were drawn. About 190,000 were excused for physical disability or other reasonable cause. The thought of 300,000 more young men being sent from home to fight a war that seemed to have no end in sight terrified many families. The terror inspired a four-day draft riot in New York City in July, targeting chiefly African-Americans. Violence was so extreme that federal troops just back from Gettysburg were called in to quell the mob. More than 1,000 were left dead or wounded.[363]

It is interesting that Henry seldom mentions the Confederate "graybacks." Many of his contemporaries larded their letters with derogatory remarks—or complimentary remarks about the upright posture, gentility, and horsemanship of Confederate officers. As a guard of prisoners of war, he certainly had the opportunity to observe rebels and perhaps to converse with them. But he seldom comments (his letter of Feb. 24, 1863, is an exception).

He also rarely has anything to say about African-Americans. In the

---

* This laconic entry may be the record of a woman's being committed to an asylum. Perhaps Mrs. Page—never before mentioned—is a fellow resident of the tenement block.

following letter, however, he does make a reference—classifying them as body servants. (His regiment mustered in a "colored cook," Osborne Dean, but Henry never mentions him.)

Custom House N. Orleans July 31st 1863

(Please accept this small faveor [refers to enclosure] dear Eliza)

Dear beloved Wife & Children.

I can not wait no longer, without writing to you though it is a long time since [I] got a letter from you and I have written one or two since, but I hope you are all well.

I am well except a bad cold the first cold I have had since I enlisted of any account. This cold is in my head. My head aches some and I need a nigger to tend my nose, but it is some better.

We were paid again last friday for 2 months. I went to Mobile [143 miles northeast of New Orleans] with sick & wounded paroled prisoners from Vicksburg, under a flag of truce. Was gone 4 days. Had a very pleasant trip but did not go inside of the harbor. There has 5 steamers been with them and there is many more to come. Things begin to look a little more lively here though trade is not opend [opened] much yet from up river.

I suppose you are having exciting times at home now on account of the draft, though I see by the papers that every thing passed of well in Lowell, some of the boys had papers with a list of the drafted men, quite a number of the Belvidere folks that I know were in the List Well government acts as though they were going to do something now, but it give to [gives too] many a chance to get out of it by paying 300 dollars.***

I dont know but you think hard of me because I dont send you

---

* Belvidere is a section of Lowell around Andover Street.

** The ability to pay $300 to buy one's way out of service was obviously limited to the wealthy.

more papers, but I have had no money to by them. I shall send you more now, and papers are so full of lies that I sometimes think I never want to see another one, there is nothing in them but war news and everything is so wide of the truth that there is no consolation in reading them. Mr. Gilmore [Pvt. Isaac E. Gilmore] is dead. He died last week. He had his discharge papers when he died.

Eliza, I am very anxious to hear from you. I saw a Sergt from the 15th Maine Regt. He told me that Dr. Holt died in Apr he spoke very highly of him and said he was beloved by all in the Regt. The Regt [15th Maine] is at Camp Parapet 8 miles above the City [New Orleans].*

Eliza I beg of you to keep up good courage and let not passing events worry you to much, for I feel as though all will be well in the end. I hope & pray for our good and the good of our glorious Union that was and will be again and trust in God to the end for he will defend the right. May heavenly blessings rest upon you and the dear little ones in my absence, dearest one be confiding in one that is always so to the dear ones he has left at home, this from your true & loving husband ever

H.B. Foster

To E.H.F.

P.S. I send you $5 dollars in this letter. [This is the "faveor" referred to above.]

---

* Camp Parapet was a small Confederate fortification built at Shrewsbury to defend New Orleans from Union attacking forces headed down the Mississippi. (There were other camps by this name in Missouri and elsewhere, but the one cited here was in Louisiana.) It fulfilled a function similar to that of Forts St. Philip and Jackson. Obviously, at the time Henry writes, it was in Union hands. Various Union regiments were stationed here during the war, including the 42nd and the 50th Massachusetts Infantry and the 26th Connecticut. Slaves fled here, and Butler wanted to arm them.

On the lower portion of this sheet of paper, Henry has drawn a map of the camp location between the Mississippi River and Lake Pontchartrain.

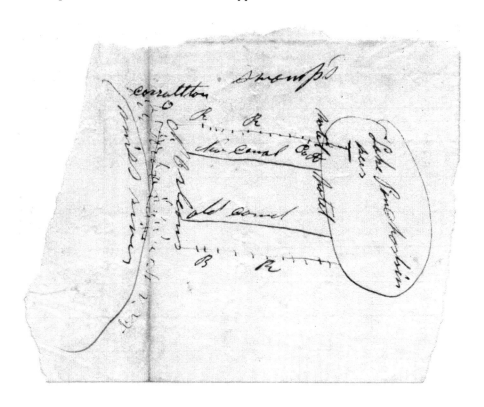

Thursday, August 6: *One pt jin 20 cts*

Cash Account, August 9: *Mrs. Cackle [Campbell?] paid 17 cents each for aprons, 17 cents and 20 cents for draws [drawers], 17 cents for a waist and drawers, and 17 cents to "finish a dres."*

Cash Account, August, no day given: *Mrs. Cackle owed 25 cents for a waist and paid in eggs. Eliza also fixed the waistband of a pair of pants. She records making a waist for Leines [Linus?] for 25 cents. Young boys wore waists that buttoned to trousers.*

* Like many of her contemporaries, Eliza doses herself with alcohol, whiskey, or gin when she is not feeling well. Patent medicines of the day frequently had a substantial alcohol content.

Henry's next letter is one of his most sexually explicit.

Custom House   New Orleans   Aug 12ᵗʰ 1863

Dear beloved Wife.

As I have neglected answering your letter of July 26ᵗʰ which I received some weeks ago, I will hasten to do so at this time and also one that I received to day of an earlier date. It has been laying in the P.O. all this time as it was over weight and I had to pay 6 cts on it but I was very glad to get it and it was such a good long letter to and was just what I like to have you write about, all about yourself and the dear little ones and about Jeny* to [too].

Oh Jackie is most to much for me sometimes when he is thinking about old times even now when the moment I began to write about J. he begins sticking up his head the naughty boy but thank God I have controled such passions thus far, and I shall endeavor to as long as we both live.** Yes dear Eliza it gives me great comfort to know that I am true to you my dearest and lovliest of all beings on earth, and also to feel that I have one that is true to me. Although there be many temptations here, I pray God I may avoid such temptations, and I trust the happiness we can enjoy in future will more than recompense us for the little we suffer from seperation for dear one those that cannot be faithful when seperated cannot expect to be happy together. Eliza dear it is very hard to be away from you but hoping & trusting in God the giver of all good gifts we will be ever patient, and hopeful that the time will soon come though should the time by any unforeseen event be prolond [prolonged] may we ever try to be prepared to face up against adversity & disappointment.

* Jeny/Jennie: Henry's pet name for Eliza's sexual organs; see letter of April 23, 1863.
** Henry writes here of controlling his sexual passions, stimulated by memories of past experiences and opportunities in New Orleans.

Eliza my health is as good as I could wish though I am awful lazy, and I guess it would come pretty hard for me to do a days work now though soldiering is hard enough it is very different from [manual] labor or anything else I ever undertook [to] do and much more difficult and disagreeable.

I assure you I am very glad you have heard from A. [Andrew]. It seems almost a miricle [sic] that he has escaped unhurt after all the perils and hardships he has gone through. May God bless him and spare him from all harm, and his family also, for I know he loves his wife and children as much as man can love, though there are difficulties to alloy their happiness we to well know. I have not had a letter from him for a long time, and I have not had an answer to the last one I wrote him but I think I will write to him and direct as before. No doubt he will get it as he is in the vicinity of Washington.[*]

I hear that the drafted men of L. [Lowell] have not got to come out by this draft on account of the surplus that was furnished from there last year. Please tell if it is so. There are three commissioned Officers and six enlisted men going to start soon from this Regt & from each of the other 3 years Regts here for Mass. to bring out the drafted men to fill up the old Regts but there is no one going from this Co. I believe all the boys are quite well that you know except Mr. [Calvin F.] Dearborn who went to the Hospital night before last quite sick with diarrhea.^{**}

Our duty is the same as when last I wrote you—guarding prisoners. If anything new takes place, I will try and keep you informed. I hope you will get the last present I sent you, in my last letter. Eliza please tell me just how you get along, if you have money enough to make yourself and the children comfortable. I shall be glad of it if

* Andrew wrote from Maryland in July 1863. His company at the time was attached to the Army of the Potomac.

** Dearborn's death is mentioned in Henry's letter of Dec. 6, 1863.

it takes it all. I dont want you to suffer for anything if I can help it. You have not said anything about our debts for a long time. Has Parker got over his fret yet, or not. I was in hopes he would be one of the fortunate ones to be drafted but I dont see his name on the list.[*]

I dont suppose he would come if he was [drafted] but it would take 300 dollars out of him. Is Messes going to stand the draft or will Parker and some of the rest of his friends by [buy] him of [off]. I see quite a number [of] familiar names in the list and some I should like very much to see out here.

Well dear E. I will close for this time for supper is ready, and we must eat supper and then go out on dress parade. The 26th draws quite a crowd every night on dress parade on Canal St [the Custom House was located at 400 Canal] but it is a nuisance and I never could see the benifit of dress parade, but I suppose it is all essential to military but I hate it, going out on line and standing an hour for nothing, and I am not the only one that despises dress parade.[**] No soldier likes [parade] any to well and that is the reason we have them I suppose. Well dear one good bye, ever your true and loving husband.

H. C. Foster

To EHF

Eliza's Diary:

Wednesday, August 19: *I get sewing Ma sheen and pay ten dollars towards it*

---

* Theodore E. Parker was a Lowell grocer with whom Eliza had run up a substantial bill. With a payment of $300, men could buy freedom from the draft. This was a provision of the National Conscription Act.

** Preparing their gear for dress parade and parade itself kept idle troops from getting bored. As Daniel Chisholm of the Army of the Potomac writes in his diary, "Drill, Inspection and Dress parade fills up the time and keeps us busy."

Buying a sewing machine changed Eliza's life, making it possible for her to multitask in the comfort of home while still earning. But it was not an ideal arrangement, as one scholar notes:

> "Many women were paid by the piece to sew garments in their apartments. That allowed them to stay with their children, but the working conditions could be even less pleasant than a factory because the tenements were so dark. Lighting was particularly important for garment workers who were expected to sew with a tiny backstitch; it took even an experienced needlewoman twelve hours to finish one shirt. And although the women were in the same place as their children, they were far from able to really mother them. 'I used to cry because I could not spend time with the baby,' said a Manhattan piece worker. 'I worked in the house but I had no time for the baby. I put the baby in the rocker by my feet and I worked and rocked the baby with my feet.'"[364]

The cost of Eliza's sewing machine would have ranged from a moderate $20 to a kingly $200, say antiques experts Carole and Larry Meeker: "This is very early and before mass production when treadles like those from the 1890s or 1900s could be had for $20–50 as the prices came down."[365]

Friday, August 21: *Get a letter from Henry*

These Come Out of a liquor shop

Custom House   New Orleans   Aug 22d 1863

Dear & ever loved ones at home.

I hope & trust you are all well to day, and hope this will find you all well as it leaves me. We have not had a mail in a long time but I understand there is one to day but not distributed yet. Well shall get it to morrow. I have just put a box into the express office for you, and paid charges $2.00 so you will have to pay nothing on it. It contain[s] some little things that I think will please you, which did not cost me anything, as it was confiscated property where I was *on guard and would be sold for little or nothing, an I don't know as I have done anything very bad, though I should not like to have it known so you can keep it to you[r] own self a little. Those crosses I dont mean for you I should not have you think but I hardly knew what to do with them. Those cigars I put in because it needed just that [volume for the] box to fill up and I had nothing else to put in the little box. You will know that box. I guess you can treat some of your neighbors if you dont smoke. Those are ladies cigars however. Those come out of a liquor shop. The place was confiscated for selling liquor to soldiers and keeping a disordely [disorderly] house. I hope you will get this befor[e] you get the box. I should have put it in but forgot it.*

I expect we shall soon be out of N. Orleans, and I am not sorry. We are going to P. Hudson. How long we shall remain there I cannot say and it is useless to conjecture, but where ever I am you will hear from me often, as long as I live, if it is possible for me to write. The 4ᵗʰ Regt native guards, in which Capt D.s brother is 1ˢᵗ Lt. is goin [sic] down to Ft. Jackson to relieve the 13ᵗʰ Maine and they are coming to relieve us. I expect we shall get [there] by Monday next.*

The boys are all well. I cannot write more now. If any one ask[s] [where] you got those things tell them they were presents to me. I am feeling quite delighted to get out of this city but we may get a worse place it is true, but there are to many temptations here for soldiers and the 26ᵗʰ has been here quite long enough and so hoping for the best & trusting in God for all, that He will guide us in our erring ways, and spare our lives to meet again. I remain your true and loving husband

* Forts Jackson and St. Philip guarded a strategic bend in the Lower Mississippi, 35 nautical miles from the Gulf of Mexico and 65 miles below New Orleans. The twin forts were crucial to controlling the southern approach to New Orleans. One of the weapons employed by the Confederates was the fire raft—a floating platform piled with dry brush, doused with turpentine, and cut loose to drift ablaze down river.

H.C. Foster

to E.H.F.

Considering Henry's condemnation of sexual promiscuity, it is wonderfully incongruous that he sends Eliza cigars meant for prostitutes. It seems that his delight in having something valuable to send her unbalances his judgment. The poles of Henry's moral world shift when he breaks the commandments against stealing and covetousness, and helps himself to plunder.

Henry's confiscating property from a house he was assigned to guard cannot be excused—even on the grounds that he kept nothing for himself and sent all to his wife.

In general, officers on both sides instructed their troops to treat civilians fairly, to eschew capricious pillage and wholesale destruction of property. Officers could face court-martial for encouraging their men to plunder, rape, rob, or murder civilians. The *Arkansas True Democrat* (Little Rock) had this to say on January 30, 1862, "As an evidence of the ferocity of the federal officers in Missouri, and the sanguinary character of the war waged by them, we note a wholesale massacre at Palmyra, Mo. A bridge was burnt and no clue could be obtained as to the persons who burnt it. The federal commander picked out forty suspected secessionists, all of them wealthy and worthy persons. Ten of them paid out, and were declared innocent of complicity in the burning. Thirty were tried by court martial, twenty-one of whom were found guilty and shot."

The *Democrat* continued: "At no point on the war frontier have the federal troops committed so many outrages, or waged so cruel, relentless a war, as in Missouri and on the Indian line. Property has been stolen or wantonly destroyed, women outraged, towns burnt and men murdered in cold blood. The Kansas jayhawkers boasted, some months ago, that they took no prisoners. . . . The most reckless and abandoned of all Lincoln's troops have got together in Kansas and north-west Missouri, for the openly avowed objects of murder and plunder."[366]

Accusations of pillage and plunder—every thing from bank robbery to rape—were heaped on both sides and were effective propaganda, whether based on fact or not. Native American regiments as well as Franz Sigel's German regiments had a reputation for relentless foraging. When soldiers lost touch with their own supply trains, they plundered farms and homesteads for food. Homes were ransacked, barns and mills burned, and crops trampled by cavalry horses. Brig. Gen. Samuel R. Curtis, driving the enemy before him through Missouri and Arkansas, wrote to his brother in February 1862 that the ravaged countryside was "a sickening sight."[367]

A week after Henry wrote his August 22 letter, *Harper's Weekly* published a wood engraving titled "Funeral of the Late Captain Cailloux, 1st LA Volunteers, Rebel prisoners in N.O. Custom House." The J. R. Hamilton illustration showed the interior of the Custom House. However, Henry was not there to witness the funeral—as his next letter explains.

In Camp at Baton Rouge   Aug 30ᵗʰ 1863

Dear Wife.

I will improve a few moments in writing to you to inform you where I am to day &c. I am well and hope this will find you all enjoying the same great blessing.

We left the Custom House [in New Orleans] one week ago to day. The 13ᵗʰ Maine Regt relieved us. We moved into another building and stayed until Friday morning when we formed into line at 6 oclock and marched aboard the steamboat Kennett and arrived here yesterday about 8 oclock, landed and marched a mile to our camping ground. Our knapsacks were pretty heavy and I was glad when we halted and had the [order] to unsling knapsacks [i.e., set them down on the ground]. I have a good many things in mine that I should have to throw away if I had [to] carry it any great distance. Well I was detailed with ten men to go to the boat and get of [off] the Quartermasters stores before I had hardly got my knapsack of. Well we went and worked all day in the sun and I was pretty tired

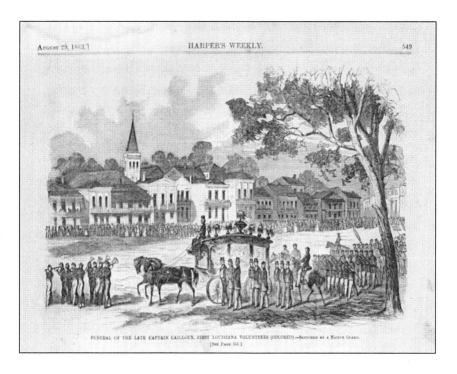

FUNERAL OF THE LATE CAPTAIN CAILLOUX, FIRST LOUISIANA VOLUNTEERS (COLORED)—Sketched by a Native Guard.
[See Page 552.]

A Confederate military procession in New Orleans. "Funeral of the Late Captain Cailloux, 1st LA Volunteers," J. R. Hamilton, wood engraving, *Harper's Weekly,* August 29, 1863. Collections of the Louisiana State Museum; used by permission.

last night, but I got well rested last night so I am feeling first rate to day.

We have shelter tents, two men to each tent, and on the march each man has to carry half a tent. Sergt Richardson and I are to-gether.** We are under marching orders now, and shall probably not stay here a week at the longest. Where we shall go next I cannot tell. We are ordered to leave everything except our blankets, why we did not leave them in New Orleans is more than I can tell but military*

* These half tents were designed to button together.
** Henry still shares quarters with Charles Richardson in November, as detailed in his letter of November 25. See also his letters of December 6, 1863, and January 21, 1864.

movements are beyond all comprehension. All a soldier has to do is to hear orders and obey them at the penalty of his life. Well dear one where we shall be when I write you again I cannot say but I shall write as often as I can. I am not any sorry we have got out of New Orleans, though we may have a little harder times, it will not be so disagreeable for the men cant get quite so much whiskey.

This Regt Nos about 800 men now. It is the generall [sic] opinion that we shall go to Mobile, but it is mere conjecture amoung [sic] the soldiers. There is any quantity of camp news [i.e., rumors] afloat all the time, but I dont pay much attention to camp stories. The latest, however, is that we are going to stay here all winter but I guess it is not reliable. The 8th N.H. Regt is in our brigade now but I have not seen Mr. Stickney yet. I heard from him before we left N.O. and he was well then, but their Regt is very small. There is very buisy movements of troops in this Department [i.e., the Department of the Gulf] at present and you may hear some interesting news soon. A great many of Grants men are between here and N.O. camped all along the river. Most likely Mobile will feel the effects of some of this force soon, and perhaps Texas to[o].

*Well dearest I believe I have written you about all the news I can think of this time. I saw Major Grover.** He was in command of the 13th [Maine] when they came to N.O. He is a fine looking man and looks as though there was nothing troubled him much. I should not have known him, with his uniform on. I did not speak to him as he appeared to be very buisy when ever I saw him, and furthermore I was sure he would not know me, and I should have to make myself known to him and I did not hardly dare to venture, but if I could*

---

* During the nineteenth century, many Christians took a pledge not to drink alcohol. Henry seems to be among them, and critical of his fellow infantrymen who imbibe. Clark Edwards was repeatedly frustrated by the alcohol consumption of his superiors.

** This may be Cuvier Grover, who commanded Union troops at Second Bull Run and later at Baton Rouge, Louisiana.

see him alone I think I should [have] spoken to him. I could not find any men in the Regt that I knew. The 13th is a fine looking Regt, and no doubt will give themselves credit in filling our place. This makes twice they have relieved our Regt.

The 26th aquited [sic] themselves with honor, and the good feeling of the citizens of N.O. as you will see by the papers, as I think no doubt it will get into the Lowell papers. There were two puffs [inflated compliments] put into the Era, by a citizen, wishing us to be presented with a new stand of colors by the people of N.O. owing to our good behavior gentlemenly [sic] conduct towards both friend and foe, and that aught [sic] could not be said against us as a body of men, by any one.* I for one as a member of the 26th feel a little proud of it. I wanted to send you the papers that had it in very much, but I must confess I was very hard up about that time and could not raise a pic [picayune; a three-cent piece], but some of the Lowell boys sent them home so I think you will see it.

Well Eliza my dear beloved one wishing you happiness and comforts of a home for you and the dear little ones, and hoping we may be all spared to meet again, that I can cherish and protect my dear family. I will bid you an affectionate adieu for this time and may God bless and protect you all in my absence. Yours ever true your husband

Sergt. H. C. Foster

To E.H.F.

P.S. Direct your letters as before as I think under the present signs it would be the safest. I shall get them if they come into this department. I received your letter of Aug 10th before I left the City, and one from M. also. I must hurry and get this into the box for it

---

* Camp colors were flags, eighteen inches square, used to mark the color line or points of wheeling. In the Union Army white camp colors signified infantry; they bore the regimental number and were mounted on eight-foot poles.

is about to close. Yours dearest

    H. C. Foster

Eliza's Diary:

    Thursday, Sept. 3: *Get a letter from Andrew with five dollars He is well*

    [Andrew is in Virginia at this time; this letter did not survive.]

    Friday, Sept. 4: *Get a letter from Henry [probably the letter written August 22.]*

    Wednesday, Sept. 9: *Go and & Pay Dr Gage [$] 2.25. Very plesant*

The Worst Night I Ever Passed in My Life

In the following letter, Henry describes real action—although he never fired a gun. He witnessed the Second Battle of Sabine Pass (September 8, 1863), part of a Union expedition into Confederate-controlled Texas. The federal navy had blockaded the Texas coast beginning in the summer of 1861, and the first battle of Sabine Pass took place on September 25, 1861. Two years later, with Lincoln anxious to sever a Confederate supply route through Mexico to the Western Theater, a new expedition was organized. This 1863 expedition consisted of four Union gunboats followed by transports carrying several thousand Union soldiers. Its aim was to gain a foothold at Sabine Pass, near the Louisiana border where the Sabine River flows into the Gulf of Mexico, and then to invade and occupy part of Texas.

Henry was one of 4,000 infantrymen sent from New Orleans by Gen. Nathaniel P. Banks under the command of Gen. William B. Franklin. At Sabine Pass, the Confederates had recently constructed fortifications known as Fort Griffin; the fort was an earthwork mounting six cannon, two twenty-four pounders and four thirty-two pounders.[368] Only a few dozen artillerists manned the cannon.

In the river channels, the First Texas Heavy Artillery Regiment had placed stakes as range markers; ground-shaking artillery practice continued until the fort's gunners achieved deadly accuracy. After losing two gunboats and 200 to 300 men to enemy capture, Franklin made the decision to turn back to New Orleans, although federal troops were able to occupy the Texas coast from Brownsville to Matagorda Bay later that fall.[369]

Henry sends Eliza an excellent play-by-play:

> *In Camp at Algiers La.   Sept 12th 1863*
>
> *My Dear Wife.*
>
> *I am thankful once more to be permited to commune with you, and to inform you that I am well, though somewhat fatigued, as our Regt has just returned from a long expedition and I am compelled to say an unsuccessful one. We gained nothing but lost two gunboats together with the expense of the expedition. The expedition was under the command of Maj Gen Franklin, from the army of the Potomac. He has command of the 19th Army Corps now under Gen Banks. I wrote you when at Baton Rouge, and I hope you have got the letter [of August 30] ere this.*
>
> *Well we started the next day, the 2d. Embarked just at night on board the steamer Crescent and have not been on shore since until this morning. We stored all our knapsacks in B.R. with everything [in] them. Whether I shall ever see mine again or not I don't know but hope so, for there are things in it that I think a great deal of especially yours and the childrens miniatures but I was compelled to leave them behind and if we had marched any distance I should had [have had] to dispose of some more things that I did take but I will try to give you some of the details of the past ten days.*
>
> *We started from B.R. Wednesday the 2nd and arrived in front of the city of N.O. at 2 oclock the next day, and lay at the wharf till the next evening when the boat run out into the stream and anchored*

but during the night started down river with a large ship in tow. Arrived at the passes Saturday just at dark and anchored inside the bar. *There were some twelve transports and two small gunboats in all. No one knew except the commanders where we were going, but everybody said in N.O. that [we] were bound for Mobile, and no one could contradict it though many thought we were bound for Texas, which proved to be true when Sunday morning the fleet all weighed anchor and headed for the west. Then we did not know what point we were going to strike, but we anchored Monday abut sunset of Sabine Pass the mouth of Sabine River. This river is the boundary between La. & Texas for a considerable distance.*

Well the fleet all lay at anchor until the next morning [September 8] about 7 oclock. We all got under way and started in over the bar to enter the river. All the light draft boats were soon over the bar. All went over that attempted it except the steamer that our Regt was on and she stuck fast in the mud. There was one gunboat and 5 or 6 transports that did not attempt to cross the bar as they drew to much water. There was 3 gunboats here blockading which made 5 in all. They all seemed to be waiting for our boat to get over the bar. Nothing was done, except one of the gunboats shelld the shore a little but did not receive any response from the rebels. They were laying a trap which proved in a measure successful to them. Well we [were] trying all this time to get over the bar up to 2 oclock in the afternoon when one of the river steamers came out and tried to tow us of but could not. We then got aboard of the river steamer and started in. About this time the rebels begun to open [fire] on our gunboats from a battery on shore and the engagement was very sharp while it lasted, but soon resulted in the surender [sic] of 2 of our gunboats the Clifton and the Sachem. Both got shots through their boilers [leaving them without locomotion]. Part of the crew escaped from the Clifton. They said that when the

* The Head of Passes was a location in the Mississippi River Delta.

boiler exploded a great many were scalded to death and caused them to surrender. There was thus only 2 gunboats left that could reach the battery and they soon hauled of. The rebel battery was much stronger than was anticipated by our commanders and they held their fire until they had coyed [decoyed] our boats within easy range and then opened a severe fire on them which no wooden vessell [sic] could stand long.

It did not take Gen Franklin long to decide what to do.* There was no possible chance for troops to land as the ground is all a marsh, and what gunboats we had were insufficient to compete with the rebel guns on shore [at Fort Griffin], and we had orders immediately to put back to the mouth of the Miss river. Our Regt was on the old river boat which was not safe a moment out to sea, and the steamer that took us out was hard aground and did not get of till about 12 oclock that night, and we had to stay on the old shell until morning. There was quite a swell on the sea and every one expected every minute she would go to pieces. It was the worst night I ever passed in my life. I would have much rather faced the rebel battery on shore, and I think all were of the same mind. I did not express my feelings to any one until I got of [off] from her, for there were plenty that did and I don't know what prevented one half of us from jumping over board. Any quantity [of enlisted men] were singing out for the officers to run us ashore and we would take the rebel battery, but we all lived through the night, and got safely aboard of the Crescent the next morning and started for the Mississippi where we safely arrived yesterday morning and lay until about three oclock waiting for orders, which came for us to proceed to Algiers.

We got here at 3 oclock this morning and came ashore about 9 oclock. We are encamped now about 2 miles from N.O. opposite

* William B. Franklin graduated at the head of his West Point class of 1843. He was in charge of the first brigade of the third division of McDowell's Army at Bull Run and in the summer of 1863 was assigned to the Department of the Gulf.

the city. Here I shall have to come to a halt, and a right about face. I dont know anything concerning movements any farther. We shall either go up the B.R. to Broshuar [Brashear] City and go to Texas by land (wither a part of the Army has already gone) or we shall wait until they get gunboats sufficient to silence those rebel batteries at Sabine Pass, and go that way again. I dont think we shall remain here long.*

*I received 2 papers to day. I hope George is better by this time. Is it the whooping cough. You said Sis had it. You can guess I was a little astonished when I got that letter before I opened it, for I knew it was not your writing and I could not imagine who it was from, but I soon found out to my great joy it was from my dear and beloved one, whome [sic] I love and adore above all and upon whome all my hopes and joys are centered is my dear ones at home.** Oh what would I give to see you, Eliza. I mean to keep up good spirits and do the best I can, and trust in God, to spare my life to my dear family, though these are trying times, we will not despair and you will feel that I am living for you & our dear children.*

Yours ever true, H. C. Foster

The following day, Henry pens a brief letter:

Sunday Sept. 13th/63   [probably Algiers, La.]

Dear Eliza.

How do you do this fine morning. I hope you and the children are well. I am feeling much better than I expected to. I had a good nights sleep last night the first for ten days. We could not rest on the boat night or day it was so crowded. I hope you have got your box [mentioned in Henry's letter of August 22]. Have you got your [federal] allotment. You don't have any trouble in getting [state and

---

* Brashear is today Morgan City, Louisiana.

** Perhaps Eliza dictated this letter to someone while she nursed George and Henrietta; perhaps someone else addressed the envelope for her.

city] aid money do you. I saw D Barnard yesterday. He looks well. I heard from Hazen when at B.R. He was at Port Hudson Clerk for the Q.M. [Quarter Master]. Dearborn is rather slim.* He has a diarhea, most all summer. I believe all the rest are well. Mr. C. is still in Hospital as nurse. He looks well.

This is about all the time. Write as often as you can and all the news. Good bye from your ever true and loving husband.

H.C.F.

Eliza's Diary:

Monday, Sept. 14: *Get a letter from Henry*

Friday, Sept. 18: *I go out and go in to Sylvie All well*

Saturday, Sept. 19: *Quite plesant I go out and go and pay Dr. Gage*

I Live in Hopes to Be with You

In Camp at Brashear City   Sept. 19th 63

My Dear Wife

I take this opportunity to write you a few words to let you know I am well and tell you where I am at this time &c. I hope you are well today, and the children also. We left Algiers on the 16th. Took the cars and came to this place. Arrived at 10 oclock, at night, all safe. Next day crossed over on to the west side of Berwicks Bay [80 miles from New Orleans] and are now encamped here. We have not seen the enemy yet, but I suppose as soon as the Army is over this side, we shall advance. It is said the enemy is some 12 miles from here, when we expect to have a fight but dont be alarmed dear Eliza. God is our helper and I trust in Him. I shall try to do the best I can, and take care of myself as well as I can. I don't know how

* Calvin F. Dearborn enlisted as a private in Henry's Company.

many men we have here in our Army but we have got a pretty large Army. Enough to do the work before us I think. I dont know when we shall get our mail now. We shall probably not get it very regular. The last from you was dated the 16th Aug and I have received two papers since. I must hurry this up for it is my only chance to send to the City and there is no Post Office any nearer.

Mr. [Calvin F.] Dearborn was left at N.O. in the Hospital. Mr. C is with us. He and the rest are well. It is quite cool here and it seems a relief from the hot weather we have had all summer.

Give my love to Mabelia's folks. Tell her I have not time to write her, but she must take the will for the deed. Oh E. I am ever thinking of you and the dear little ones but I live in hopes to be with you ere long if our lives are spared us. The time will soon roll around. I will bid you good bye for this time. I dont know when I shall have a chance to write you, but [will] do so every chance I have, and I remain your true and loving husband.

H. C. Foster

Eliza's Diary:

Sunday, September 20: *What a dark and lonsom day this is At home all day frank came in A.M. & Mandans's came in the after noon.*

Thursday, September 24: *Cut and make a apan [apron] for Chris & girl   17 [cents earned?]*

Friday, Sept. 25: *Finish a dres for Mrs. Cack [Cook?]* 17*

Saturday, September 26: *Willard and Frank in to see me He is well*

---

* One J. S. Cooke served as first sergeant and acting adjutant of Henry's regiment when Henry was promoted to sergeant in April 1863.

We Must Trust in His Kind Providence

On April 12 and 13, 1863, the Battle of Bisland took place at Fort Bisland, Louisiana, between Union forces under Gen. Nathaniel Banks and Confederates under Major Gen. Richard Taylor.* Banks was leading 17,000 troops on an expedition toward the Red River.

Months later, when Henry camps at Bisland, things are quiet:

Camp in the Field   Bisland [La.]   Sept. 27ᵗʰ '63

Dear Eliza.

I again have the opportunity of writing a few lines to you, so I will improve it, that you may know I am well and I hope and pray that you and the children are well also. I have not heard a word from you since I received those papers at Algiers, two weeks ago. Oh I hope you are all well but I am very anxious about you. I hear there is a mail at N.O. for us. I hope I shall get a letter from you. I wrote you when at Broshuar [Brashear City] a week ago last Saturday. We started from that place last Wednesday the 23d at 7 oclock and arrived at this place at 5 oclock the same day, marching 18 miles. A pretty good march for the first day, but I stood it first rate and we have had plenty of time to rest since.   We have seen no rebels yet but they only left here the day before we came. And our army is giving them plenty of time to keep out of the way to [too], and I am inclined to think they will improve their chance. I don't know why it is our army moves so slow, and it is no business of mine either. I suppose our Generals know what they are about. At least they should know. I suppose we shall start again in a day or two.

* The Battle of Irish Bend and Fort Bisland was part of a series of running battles between Banks and Taylor and the Army of Western Louisiana. It figured in the Lower Seaboard Theater of the war, which included Fort Sumter, Santa Rosa Island, Fort Pulaski, Forts Jackson and St. Philip, New Orleans, Secessionville, Simmon's Bluff, Tampa, Baton Rouge, Donaldsonville, Fort McAllister, Bisland, Irish Bend, Vermillion Bayou, Fort Wagner, Port Hudson, Gainesville, Olustee (near Jacksonville, Florida), and Natural Bridge.

This is a fine country, but the water is awful and we cant get no good water. We have to drink Bayou water and it is worse than any mud hole you ever saw. I drink as sparing as possible, but all our coffee has to be made of it. But it is not so bad after it is boiled. I hope we shall find better water as we advance.

I felt pretty lame and tired that night after marching all day, and then I had to go on guard that same night. Well I guess I was as well able to go on as any of them, for most all were complaining of something. Although our Regt stood the march better than some of the others, and we had less fall out on the road. We have the right of the Division and it is the easiest place to march. I have not been on guard but once since we left N.O. almost 4 weeks. I find some difference from the duty in the City. I like it much better so far, but I expect we have got a great deal of marching to do before we get through this campaign. But all I can ask is to have my health, and I will be thankful, and I shall be as careful as I can of myself and I tell you if a person don't look out for him self in the army no one will look out for him, and I don't see how any one can expect to be looked out for, for it is as much as one wants to do to look out for No 1 and all have an equal chance too.

Well as I said before 18 miles is a pretty good march. It is more than an army will average. Well I have not throwed away anything yet [from his knapsack] nor did not think of such a thing and I guess I shall not have to. I hope not for I have none to [too] much to keep me warm the chilly nights. We had to leave our overcoats and I am afraid we shall miss them when it comes winter but we could not carry them and we shall have to make our blankets do in place of them. Well I cannot think of much more to write this time.

Yours Affectionately.

I will say a few more words dear and beloved ones. Oh that I could see you or even know if you are all alive & well. I hope and pray so at least. Do write as often as you can. I suppose M. [Mabelia] feels hard because I have not written to her, but I hope she can excuse me. I shall try to do better in future, but I think like this she is so near you, that she can hear by your letters so it dont make so much difference. However I like to answer all letters I receive, and I think I have done pretty well since I have been in the Army for me.

I hope you have got your box &c. Please tell me the ladys [sic] name that lives up stairs for I have forgotten. I hope she is a friend to you, and you to her in return, for it is much more pleasant to be neighborly, & friendly, than otherwise, though there are some people that it is an impossibility to be so, dear Eliza do tell me all about yourself and the children wont you. You can judge how much I want to see you all. We can only hope that the time will come, and I pray that we may be spared the time. God is good and we must trust in his kind providence to protect us, and feel that all is for the best. Hoping this will find you all well, and enjoying the comforts and blessings of this life as best you can under the circumstances, and I regret that you are not better provided for, but dear one, you and I joined our hearts & hands to travel this life's journey together and God willing we will and I will always do the best I can to make the burdens of life easy to you. I have acted as my sense of duty lead me, and I have only repented for your sake, and I know it is very hard for you to be thus left as you were, but I could feel that you would be provided for, and I am thankful that I have not been disappointed thus far though nothing will compensate for our being seperated so long. We must bare [bear] that as one of the sorrows of this world, for it is full of such trials, tribulations.

Well I have written quite a long letter, and I will close for this time hoping to hear from you soon, good bye my dear wife & children. From your loving husband & father.

Sergt H. C. Foster

Co. A, 26th Regt Mass Vols

2d Brigade 3d Division

19th Army Corps

Department of the Gulf

N. Orleans

La.

(Direct thus if you can find room)

Men on both sides complained about the water they were forced to drink. Theophilus Perry of the 28th Texas Cavalry wrote to his wife from the West Side of Bayou Tensas in July 1863, "We are drinking Bayou water. It is intolerable but hard necessity forces us to drink. It preserves life but does not quench thirst. . . . Oh for a Carolina spring."[370]

Eliza's Diary:

> **Monday, September 28:** *Make an a pon [apron] for Mrs. Cack.*

After the Battle of Gettysburg in July, forces in the Eastern Theater had drifted south and skirmished ineffectually on the plains of northern Virginia. Bicknell described the attitude of Virginians toward Union troops in his account of October 10, 1863: "What few inhabitants there were left in such places as Culpepper, Warrenton, etc., manifested the most insolent disposition toward us, as we passed through their 'sacred' streets. Those who were once styled as ladies, hesitated not to heap the most opprobrious epithets upon the soldiery, frequently using language which would put almost a Five Point rough to shame."[371]

> **Bills Receivable, October** *(no day given): one peck potatoes, one dozen eggs. The price of the eggs is 22 cents. The price of the potatoes is not recorded.*

Stationed in Vermillion, many soldiers contracted fevers because of the nearby swamp.[372]

> *Encampment at Vermilion [Vermillion] Bayou between New Iberia & Opelousas [La.]*
>
> *Oct 10ᵗʰ 1863*
>
> *Dear Eliza*
>
> *I will now write you a few lines so you may know I am well &c. and I hope you and the children are well too. I have marched a good many miles since last I wrote you but I have stood it first rate as have all the boys. I received your letter when I was at Camp Bisland, the next day after I sent my last and have not had an opportunity to answer till now. There was a mail come to the Rgt. Yesterday but no letter for me and I was somewhat disappointed I assure you but however, I must wait for my turn, I suppose. You said you had a tooth broke of [off]. Well I have been served the same way only I have not had mine got out yet.* It does not trouble me now.*
>
> *Well dearest I have not got a sight of a rebel yet [on this particular campaign] but we got pretty near them yesterday, so that we could see the smoke of the gun and hear them skirmishing in advance of us. Our Cavalry took one piece of artillery from the rebs yesterday. There has been only one man killed on our side, and 10 wounded so far. The rebs keep out of our way as fast as their legs will carry them and it is wild goose chase, and I expect we will have [to] chase them out of Louisiana and all over Texas to [too]. I expect any minute we shall have to pack up and start on the march, so I don't know when I shall have a chance to send this but will do so the first opportunity.*

---

* Neither the Union nor the Confederate side had a dental corps. The Confederates conscripted dentists, giving them the grade of hospital steward. These stewards filled and extracted teeth and removed tartar. They also treated facial wounds that included the setting of broken bones.

We have camped at 6 different places since we left camp Bislad [sic]. We have marched from ten to twelve miles a day. We are now to pack up immediately and be ready to move so good bye dear ones, till I can get another chance to write.

Oct. 12

I will now try to finish this letter as there is a chance to send it to day. When I left of writing we started and only crossed the Bayou & camped over night and then started yesterday at 6 oclock [am] and marched until 1 o clock in the afternoon and camped where we now are, some 12 miles from Opelousas. We were in sight of the enemy some of the time yesterday. The Cavalry were skirmishing all day.

When we got [here?] we found some of their hominy cake on the fire just as the rebs left it so I think they must have left in a hurry.

I dont know how long we shall stop here, but we shall probably leave tomorrow. The boys are all well, here. Mr. C [Camerford] came as far as Franklin and was taken sick and sent back to N.O. I have not heard from him since. We are all in fine spirits and we have some curious [in the sense of "attracting attention because it is unusual or strange"] times. You ought to see the fresh meat come in the camp soon after we make a halt, all sorts, hogs, beef, sheep, hens & geese, turkeys &c. It is against the rules and the [they, i.e., the officers] make some attempts to stop it [i.e., foraging] but at the same time they don't care how much the men get.

Henry

Gen. Ulysses Grant planned to wage a war of attrition—to lay waste to both the enemy and the enemy's homeland. Foraging for provisions was one method of keeping food out of the mouths of the enemy, as Henry writes in his letter of November 3. Fresh grub also helped to prevent scurvy and added welcome variety to the soldiers' diet—benefiting morale.

Union private Elisha Stockwell, Jr., described foraging in Alabama in 1861:

We halted one day in front of a large house. The man [the homeowner] was leaning on the fence talking with the boys when a long-legged rooster came between the house and road with two soldiers after him. If ever a rooster ran, that one was doing it. The man seemed to enjoy the race as well as the rest of us . . . .

I said to the man, "It is tough to have men chase your chicks in your dooryard."

He said, "I expected that when the war broke out. You fellows have got to have something to eat. That rooster is the last living thing on this place, and if they can catch him they are welcome to it."[373]

In 1863 in Pennsylvania, just after Gettysburg, the shoe was on the other foot, as Northern women pleaded for their livestock. "During supper . . . women came rushing in at intervals, saying—'Oh, good heavens, now they're killing our fat hogs. Which is the General? Which is the Great Officer? Our milch cows are now going.' To all which expressions [Lt. Gen. James] Longstreet replied, shaking his head in a melancholy manner—'Yes, madam, it's very sad—very sad; and this sort of thing has been going on in Virginia more than two years—very sad.'"[374]

Eliza's Diary:

Bills Receivable, October 13: *Five yards delane at 62 cents a yard, $3.10.*

Bills Receivable, Oct. 14: *One yard of lining at 25 cents, and nine yards of poplin at 75 cents each ($6.90).* Sylvia apparently gives Eliza 30 cents worth of cambric.*

Thursday, October 15: *Mr. Fox lb. butter [indecipherable figures in margin; could be 75 cents for 5 pounds] It is verey plesant I go out and get some things*

---

* Poplin was a fabric of cotton or silk in plain weave with fine cross ribbing, used for raincoats and everyday wear. The name comes from Poperinge, a textile center in Flanders. Nine yards of the material would have been sufficient to create a dress coat for Henrietta.

Bills Receivable: *Fox, butter, total of 7 pounds apparently purchased on different dates, totaling $1.75. Eliza also purchased sewing materials: 20 cents worth of cambric, 8 cents worth of silk, 2 spools of thread (16 cents), and 44 cents worth of calico.*

Saturday, October 17: *George called her [here] He takes my sheers [sewing shears] and sharpens them for me*

Sunday, Oct. 18: *I am sick*

Monday, October 19: *Sick all day and able to sit. G brings my sheers back.*

Friday, Oct. 23: *Quite well and at home.*

How glad I am to see my Brother Andrew who comes at half past seven

Saturday, October 24: *All well I go to the depot with Andrew [to see him off to his home in Maine] Call at Sylvie's*

Wednesday, October 28: *Mrs Fox comes over They are her [here] to diner*

October 28: Bills Receivable: *I pay Mr. Bailey potatoes, $2.50*

Sunday, November 1: *At home all day and well Sylvia and George [Husey?] at home up her [here] I write to Henry*

Monday, November 2: *All well and all at home*

Wash and clean

Get a letter From Henry

Hear that Mr. Cornerford [probably Camerford] is dead

Tuesday, November 3: *Tuesday at home but how it smokes*

I go out and get my TA [Town Allotment?]

---

* Mr. Bailey is probably Anson Bailey of Rice & Bailey, provisions, located at 131 Central Street. He could also have been Alvah W. Bailey, a farmer at 67 Bridge Street.

Oh How Uncertain Is Life

Camp at Vermilion Bayou [La.] Nov 3rd 1863

Dear Wife. I don't know what you may think. I have neglected writing so long, but I hope you will not worry about it and I hope you can forgive me for I did not mean to neglect you so long. I have received two letters from you since I have written. I received your last letter two days since dated Oct 12th, and I was greatly rejoiced to learn that you and the children were well, and this leaves me well also. My health has been good all the time. How sad it will be to Andrew to learn [of] the loss of his dear little boy [Ebenezer, who died September 27, 1863, at age 6], but such are the vicisitudes [sic] of life, and we must all be prepared to meet the loss of dear ones on earth, for oh how uncertain is life.

You will see by the date of my letter [i.e., the place] that we are on the retreat. We have been no farther than Opelousas. We left that place on the 1st to fall back. The first days march brought us to Carencro Bayou and yesterday to this place. It is 28 miles from Opelousas here. How far we shall fall back or for what purpose I cannot imagine, for we certainly were not drove back. We found no enemy to make a stand as far as we advanced except a few cavalry who skedadled [sic] as our cavalry advanced. I suppose this to be a feint to attract the attention of the enemy this way while another has gone into Texas to get in rear of them, but it is not for me to say. I can only say that we are moving back towards N.O. The talk is now we shall stop here 3 days and then start again. We are scouring the country pretty thoroughly so that rebels will have a slim chance to follow us. We have got all our meat and a good many horses of the country.

The health of our army is first rate. You have doubtless heard of the death of Mr. Comerford, and I have also to report the death of Mr. Dearborn. I did not hear of his death until yesterday and I don't know when he died. He died in the marine hospital at N.O.

We were paid at Opelousas the night before we started for two months. They say they have lost the allotment rolls. This was a new paymaster. He said he knew nothing about any allotment and we were paid the full amount for July & August. I want to send the money to you but dont dare to trust it in a letter now until we can get where there is an express agent as there is none here. There is three mail carriers for the Army out of Co H and Jim Winn is one of them, so [you] may guess why I dont want to send it by letter. I think I shall have a chance in a few days to send it by express. I received a letter from Chancy & Clara in the last mail. They were all well. I don't think of much more to write now so good bye dearest one,

> *from Henry.*

The Far Western Theater saw little action at this time. Confederate forces under Downling battled federal forces under Franklin at Sabine Pass, Texas, on September 8. On the same day, Gen. Braxton Bragg's 65,000 troops marched out of Chattanooga and withdrew toward Lafayette, Georgia.[375] Banks's federal forces battled Gen. Kirby Smith's rebels at Fort Esperanza on November 27–29.[376]

In Louisiana, Henry takes up his pen:

Vermilion Bayou   Nov 4th 1863

Dear Eliza.

I am well to day & I hope this will find you all well. I am somewhat undecided what to do about sending this money. I don't want to trust it by letter so I will close this and send it along and I hope you may get it soon. I shall send the money the first chance I have by express.

The prospect is now that we shall remain at this place some time. There has been some fighting reported in Opelousas since we left with our advance guard but I cant learn any particulars.

We have some good news here to day that we are going home in 9 months from the 18 of Oct. last. I hope it is so. Do you hear anything about it.

Oh my dear ones. I hope you are all well to day. I shall try to keep up good courage & want you to & we will hope for the best & I trust all will be well. How do you get along with your sewing machine. Do not work to [too] hard but govern yourself according to your strength. I think it a good thing, though I suppose you have to work pretty cheap. I think you can handle one as well as the next one [i.e., seamstress]. This [sheet of paper] is full so good bye.

Your ever true & well wishing husband

H.C. Foster

Henry was correct in assuming Eliza would have to "work pretty cheap" with her new sewing machine: "Among the most exploited workers of the day were women who labored as seamstresses. Employed by both the government and private contractors, seamstresses were paid only pennies for making articles of clothing that took several hours to sew—and had to supply their own thread. A woman in New York earned 17 cents for making four pairs of drawers in a 14-hour day; the average week's wage for a seamstress was a pathetic $1.54."[377]

Eliza's Diary:

Wednesday, November 4: *At home and all well and at home*

Thursday, Nov. 5: *All well and at home*

Bills Receivable, November 5: *Pay Mr. Fox $3.50 for pork, butter, apples.*

In the following Henry expresses a continuing faith in the cause for which he serves:

Camp at Vermillion Bayou   Nov 12th 1863

Dear & Beloved ones at home.

I will improve a few moments in writing to you to day to inform you that I am well. I hope that you are all enjoying the same blessing to [to]. It is a month to day since your last letter was dated and I am quite anxious to hear from you. It is eleven days since we arrived at this place. There has been two battles between here and Opelousas since we left there but our Brigade was not engaged in either, but I don't worry but what we shall get into one soon enough. But we have been so near having a fight so many times that it seems as though the hand of kind providence was with me to protect me be it so or otherwise. I am ever willing to trust in God that His goodness will protect me from all danger so He will protect us all. Though we shall fall in battle or meet death in any other form if we but put our trust in Him all will be well.

It seems hard dear Eliza to think of the sorrow & suffering this war has caused, but we must not be selfish. Each man should feel that he ought to give his life and all if necessary for the good of his country & his fellow man. I hope the loyalty of the people if there is any left will be poured forth in a manner to show the world that Liberty Freedom & a Republican Government are worth saving though it costs blood & treasure. But we can begin to see the light breaking and I feel & hope the worst is over. The State Elections are telling well for the Union, and we will stick to it and it shall be saved yet but it takes time to accomplish any great work, and we must not get impatient. My enlistment is wearing away. It seems short to look ahead now to what it did a year ago. What is the talk now about our being discharged in June. It is talked of pretty strong here but we can learn nothing definite.

Well I have concluded to send this money $25.00 to you and run the risk in this letter for I have no other way to spend it and if I keep it here I am afraid I shall loose it or spend it all for nothing. So it might as well be risked one way as another and if [it] is lost

so be it but I hope you will get [the money] safe at any rate. Well I
will close hoping this will find you all well. & may God bless you all

  good bye, from Henry.

Settled in winter camp, Henry yearns for letters from home:

  Camp at New Iberia [Louisiana]   No. [November] 25ᵗʰ 1863

  Dear & beloved ones

  It is a week yesterday since I come to this place. I did not think I
  should write you before this but I have waited hoping to get a letter
  from you, but none has come since Oct 12ᵗʰ and I am quite anxious
  about you. I hope I shall get a letter soon. We left Vermillion on the
  16ᵗʰ and got to this place the 17ᵗʰ. We are 50 miles from Brashear
  and 150 from N.O. We expect to stay here some time. I wrote you
  on the 12ᵗʰ and sent you the money $25.00. I hope you will get it.

  The whole of the 15ᵗʰ army corps is here and most of the 13ᵗʰ
  and we have fortified this place some. There are two meting [meet-
  ing] houses a court house & a market in the place. It is about as
  large as Dracut side of Lowell. Steamers run up to this place from
  Brashear. I was delaited [delegated?] this morning to go to Brashear
  but missed going as we were to [too] late for the boat. I don't know
  as I shall go at all now. Our overcoats have been sent for and we
  expect them here in a day or two, and it will come very handy for it
  is getting quite cool nights.

  We have got a very poor camping ground here. It has rained for
  two days past and the mud is knee deep and lumber is very scarce
  to fix up our tents with. Charley [Richardson] and I found an old
  bridge about a mile from camp yesterday and we tore up the planks
  and made a floor to our tent. We have got one end laid up with
  poles log house fashion and the cracks stoped up with moss, so we
  have quite a comfortable house now although when it rain [rains]

*it leaks some.**

I know but little about the movements of our army or the rebels either. One thing certain we can handle them but the great trouble is to find them. They have followed us up, but they cant drive us. Gen Banks has gone into Texas with a force and we hear that he has met with perfect success but how much he has accomplished I dont know.

I should like to know how enlisting gets on in the north. I hope they will get men enough to take our places. Some of the men in our Regt received the Boston Journal in which it stated that our time would be out Feb 5th 1865. That's a big lie. I dont care who says it. Probaly [probably] some body put that in that had nothing else to do. Tell me if you hear any thing about it at home.

I expect to stay my three years out but I don't expect to stay any longer. I hope you will write as often as you can. Tell me all the news &c. Tell me all about the children to [too]. Oh how I do want to see you all, but it is impossible at present. We must keep up good spirits and the time will soon come if we live, and I pray God that our lives may all be spared to meet again. Hoping this will find you all well as it leaves me, I bid you adieu my dear wife & children. May God bless and protect you all in my absence

from your true and loving husband

H. C. Foster

Henry relates a dream of Eliza:

N. Orleans   Dec 1st 1863

---

* The structure Henry describes typifies winter quarters for enlisted men. The tent halves of the men sharing the house were joined for the roof and upper walls. Solid walls of logs or poles were erected beneath the tent to a height of three or four feet. The floor was dirt, spread with straw, or laid with boards—if available. Sometimes bunks were built along the walls. A wattle-and-daub fireplace and chimney were often constructed at one end of the house.

Dear Eliza,

As I have a chance to send a few lines to you by a discharged soldier from the 30*th* Mass Regt., I will improve it by so doing. I came down to N.O. with prisoners, left camp on Thursday last arrived here on Saturday. We return to day. I received two letters from you last Wednesday and the tobacco also. I had just mailed a letter a few hours before I received them. I am well and hope this will find you all the same. I dreamed of seeing you all last night and well and I was very happy but I wish it were a reality. How glad you must have been to see Andrew. I end [send] this by Mr. Brion. I have not time to write more. I don't know as you can read this. I start for N. Iberia to day.

Good bye,

from Henry

Eliza's Diary:

Friday, December 4: *Willard came in to see how I get along &. All well*

We Shall Meet in Each Other's Embrace

*Camp in the Field   New Iberia   Dec 6*th* 1863*

My Dear Wife & Children.

Its [sic] with feelings of thankfulness that I am permitted by the kind hand of providence to communicate a few words to you by letter but much more happiness would it afford us could we meet together to sympathise and talk with each other. But as I have always said and hoped I still hope the time will come and it is still nearer that if our lives are spared we shall meet in each others embrace. Oh with what pleasure & joy mingled with fear & doubt I look forward to that happy meeting. I have always tried to keep up the best

spirits possible, but I have many sorrowful moments when thinking
of my dear ones at home it makes me feel more sad knowing your
tender nature dear wife. And the many hours of loneliness you have
to endure. I know full well that as a natural consequence you must
have more sorrowful hours and days than I for you have less to take
up your attention. Though I assure you the monotony of camp life
is very dull.

It gives me great pleasure to get your good letters, and if you
do not try to deceive me by the tone of them, you seem to be in the
best of spirits. Yes dear Eliza we will hope hope on & put our trust
in Him who is ruler over all things and that is the best we can do. I
have tried to do thus far and I shall endeavor to do so in future, and
I feel that all will be well. But we must do our duty to ourselves as
well as to God. This is a world of sorrow, but we must not give up to
sorrowing but look on the bright side as much as we can.

I wrote a few lines to you last Tuesday when in N.O. and sent
it by a discharged [Brion] soldier from the 30th Mass Regt. When I
wrote it he expected to go right home, but I saw him again and he
told me he had got to wait for transportation some days, so I gave
him a postage stamp and requested him to put the letter in the
office at N.O. He said he would do so. I hardly know what I wrote
in that letter as I was in a hurry at time. I know I did not write
much however. I received two letters from you and the tobacco also.
Wednesday the 25th the day before I started for N.O. I did not ex-
pect to go any farther than Brasker [Brashear] when I started but
as good luck would have it myself with 14 men under command
of Capt [John?] Frost got a chance to go to N.O. with the prison-
ers.* We took down 75 rebs of all sorts and [captured] colors. We

---

* The official roster for Company A, 26th Massachusetts Infantry, lists a
Private John Frost. It seems unlikely a private would have been promoted to cap-
tain in two years. This man may be the Capt. E. R. Frost mentioned on p., 359 of
Oliver Ayer Roberts's *History of the Ancient and Honorable Artillery Company of
Massachusetts, 1637–1888* (1901).

were gone just a week and had a pleasant little trip of it. It being a change from camp life. We travelled the whole distance by steam, to Breasheas by steamboat from there to N.O. by rail. We stopped in N.O. 3 days. Capt Frost gave us a good time and all were ready to come back having no desire to stay in N.O. any longer.

Business seems to be quite brisk in N.O. The levee is pretty well crowded with sugar & cotton. I for one dont see where so much comes from, but it shows that the rebs have not burnt it all up yet. You have doubtless heard of the success of Gen Banks expedition into Texas. There has been some talk that we should go there but I hardly think we shall though I cannot tell. Gen Banks arrived in N.O. the morning I left.

Camp in the Field   New Iberia   Dec. 6th 1863 [second letter bearing this date]

Dear Eliza

I have a few more words to write you. I must tell you that I received my overcoat the night before I started for N.O. as did the whole Regt. and it was very fortunate to [too] for it was very cold while I was in the City, so cold that ice formed in many places and when I got back to camp the boys told me their canteens froze up solid so they had to thaw them out by the fire. Charley [Richardson] is in the hospital. I found him there when I got back. He got cold being on picket without any overcoat and was threatened with a fever but he is better to day, so he thinks he has got his fever broke up. He lost his overcoat last July when we were at Jefferson, and I lost mine*

---

* Fevers were often caused by malaria, which accounted for the deaths of 14,379 Union soldiers. The relationship of malaria to the bite of mosquitoes was then unknown; fevers were thought to be caused by "miasmas."

at the same time. *He never has drawn one since but he sees the need of it now. I drew one in August but never wore it. I afterwards had a chance to by one for a dollar just as good as new. The Capt was kind enough to take back the one I had drawn and I think he ought to for it was through his carlessness [carelessness] that they were lost, so I got another coat quite lucky. I sent for my housewife [sewing kit] you made me, which was left in my knapsack. It come with my overcoat, with all the miniatures safe and sound.*

What a joy it must have been for you to see Andrew. I am very glad he called to see you. Sisy [Sissy, Sister: i.e., Henrietta] made herself quite familiar. I should think dear child she had a right to. Did she think it was Father. I guess she would sit in Fathers lap if she could get a chance. I guess he would like to hold her a little while dont you, and baby to [too]. Well dear I will close for this time. I believe I told you that Mr. [Calvin F.] Dearborn was dead. It is strange you do not get my letters sooner. I have written 7 [9?] letters since the 27 [29?] Sept. That is not many I confess but I was on the move all the time so I did [not] feel so much like writing.

I hope you have got most of them by this time. Above all I hope you have got the money I sent you. Dearborn did receive the money but I knew nothing about it until I got you [your] letter and I spoke to Charley [Richardson] about it. He said he knew when he got it. Ed Sawyer is well, and all the rest of the boys. I hope this will find you all well, as it leaves me [well]. Give my respects to all & please accept a true husbands love. Remember the dear children to me

From your husband

---

* Troops were ordered to take only the most necessary gear when on the march. Thus were many separated from heavier items such as framed miniatures, cooking pots, overcoats and blankets—because they never returned to fetch them, or the articles were pilfered by others.

I Have Seemingly Done But Little

Henry now became aware of the "veteran act" which provided that all who reenlisted for the rest of the war would receive a month's furlough, transportation home, and a bounty.[378] In his next letter, therefore, he broaches the prickly subject of reenlisting. He may have felt this was a propitious moment to introduce this subject because of the good mood pervading Eliza's latest letters—a mood mentioned in the first half of his December 6 missive to her.

Bounties were offered by the Union, state governments, and many local governments. The result could be a lump payment amounting to many times the $156 annual pay an infantry private received in 1862. For example, the 7th Indiana Cavalry, raised in the fall of 1863 for three years' service, advertised that a $400 bounty would be paid to men who had had nine months' prior military experience in the U.S. Army. To keep men from deserting as soon as the bounty was in their pockets, the 7th paid $25 in advance, the balance on discharge. Men joining the 23rd Michigan Infantry received a $300 U.S. bounty, a $200 state bounty, and a $100 town bounty.[379]

During the winter camps of 1863–64, reenlistment was a topic throughout the Union army. Men smoked, played cards, wrote letters, listened to lectures, joined temperance societies, and discussed "pops" (slang for rumors). Much of their conversation hashed over the offer of a thirty-day furlough by the government and bounties by the states, offered to veterans in three-year regiments who would reenlist as Veteran Volunteers. "Units held meetings, heard patriotic speeches, and debated the topic among themselves. Bounties ranged from three dollars for Vermonters to one thousand dollars for men from New Jersey. . . . The temptation of a furlough—'an Oasis in the Life of a Soldier,' in the words of Sergeant Isaac Plumb—induced many."[380]

Near Culpeper, Virginia, on the evening of December 5, 1863, Albert Balcom of the 8th New York Cavalry made the decision to reenlist. He

Recruitment posters such as this one for Baker's Brigade of Philadelphia urged men to reenlist: "No compromise with traitors, and no argument but a knock-down argument." Courtesy Winchester Courthouse Museum.

wrote in his diary: "To day dawns a new history of mine. I am trying to make out [in] my own mind whether [I] have done right or wrong in enlisting over. My heart answers all right, and that I have done my dear one at home no miss-service [?] in doing so. May God in mercy nerve [strengthen] my arm in the cause of my country and humanity and restore peace and prosperity to this once happy land but now torn by cruel discord and may I be one of the [men] instrumental in serving more strong the branch of union. And when this my duty is done may I have a reunion of hearts with those dear ones at home whom I hold dear [dearer] than my own life."[381]

In Massachusetts, Eliza was startled to hear of enemy action quite close to home. On December 8, a Northern Copperhead seized the Union merchant ship *Chesapeake* near Cape Cod. This event must have given a start to Massachusetts residents, who thought the war was being fought far, far away. Federal ships pursued the captured vessel and retook it off the coast of Canada on December 17.[382]

The reenlistment offer for the 26th Massachusetts contained a twist that would definitely have figured into Henry's final decision: For a regiment to qualify for a furlough, the government required that three-fourths of the men reenlist.[383]

Camp in the Field   New Iberia [La.]   Dec 19th 1863

My Dear Wife & Children.

I hope you are all well this morning and I am thankful to be able to tell you that I am well. It is pretty cold here for two nights past the ground has frozen quite hard which is an unusual thing for this part of the globe and I tell you it takes hold of me. I never felt the cold any more in New England than I do here and I think a person needs more clothing here than in the north. It is because the blood gets so thin here. I dont know but I shall freeze up when I get home but if I had the chance to go I should run the risk don't you think I would dear.

I received your letter of the 2nd in which you said you had got the money I sent you. I am very glad you have for I felt a little uneasiness about it. I will send you a little in this letter. Ten dollars. We were paid the 10th for two months up to Nov 1st and our clothing settled up for last year. I had $10.00 coming to me for undrawn clothing but the allotments rolls were all right for those two months but the paymaster gave the Capts of Cos a roll for the men to sign to have the allotment broke up entirely and every man in our Co signed it. So I suppose I shall receive my pay in full hereafter. I thought it best to sign it as they were all doing so and there would be no more trouble about it and I can send you the money so that you will get it much quicker than you would by the allotment and if the government or the pay master has to pay it over again it wont be my fault. You will get those two months at the Bank   Oct & Nov or should get it at least.

Charley [Richardson] has just come back from the Hospital

and I am glad for I had to go away from home to sleep to keep from freezing. Some of the men are on duty every night so it leaves their chums to sleep alone and they are glad to get some body to sleep with them. Charley was pretty sick for a few days but he got his fever broke up so he is pretty well now.

You said you guess you forgot to put in the pieces [fabric samples] of your & Ettas dress. I thought so for when I read the letter I looked in vain to find them. But you can send them now and they will be acceptable for I should like to see them so I can see how you look. Oh how I should like to be with you this cold winter. You cannot imagine how I want to see you & the dear children. I got a letter from M. a few days since. She said she did not think I should know my children they have grown so, but I guess I would know them pretty quick if I could see them. I hope we shall get home in June as you wrote we should, but I don't depend upon it however I reckon on the whole time [i.e., the entire three years of his enlistment] but hope to get home sooner.

[No date given for the following addition]

There is some excitement here about the Regt reenlisting. There is an order from the Adjt Gen. of Mass. and we circulated yesterday to this effect that is two thirds of the Regt will reenlist for 3 years more. They will receive a furlough of 30 days in the state after they get ther [their] exclusion of going & coming. This furlough is to be before the expiration of the present term of enlistment. I must say that inducements for re enlisting are great, but I have not enlisted yet, and think I shall not unless you want me to. Now I am going to show you how much money I could make by reenlisting if you have not thought of it. Perhaps you have figured it up. Regular monthly pay $17.00   State bounty $20.00. Government bounty $11.16 per month. State aid $12.00 which amounts to $66.16 sixty dollars and sixteen cts per month. Pretty good pay is it not, besides clothing and board. I am satisfied it is better than I can do anywhere else *as far as pay is concerned, but money is no inducement for me to reenlist but if you think best I will do so. Please let me know. Now dear Eliza do not take this to heart at all for you may be sure I have not the slightest idea of such a thing. I guess we can make a living some way if I am fortunate enough to get home, if I do not get quite so much money and I am satisfied with risking my life and health for 3 years without trying it again, before I get out of this. Let some of those that have had their comfort at home try it. However I have never seen anything yet but what I felt as safe as I would at home, but I consider that I have been very fortunate and so has the whole 26th Regt so far and I am thankful for it but we do not know what we may see yet, but I think it best not to borrow any trouble about the future for sufficient unto the day is the evil thereof.*

There is another thing vis [regarding] that order for reenlisting that I should dislike very much, that in case that two thirds of the Regt reenlist the rest will be assigned to duty in other Regts. But I think there is no danger of getting two thirds of the Regt as they talk at present, and the Officers say nothing about it either.

Well dear hoping this will find you all well as it leaves me, I bid you good bye. Be of good cheer and trust God, for he is the giver of all good, from your true & loving husband & Father

Henry C. Foster

Later he writes another letter in which he comments on the state of rescued Union soldiers:

Camp in the Field   New Iberia [La.]   Dec 29th 1863

My Dear Wife & Children.

I will now write a few lines in answer to your last letter of the 6th which I received and was very glad to learn that you were all well and I hope comfortable and I hope this may find all well to [too] as it leaves me. My health never was better and the health of all the troops in this Dept is first rate.

There is no movements here of any consequence. The enemy has all seemed to vanish before us. It is said they have gone back in to Texas. One man of our Co [Company A] and a Lieut of Co I of this Regt together with 600 other prisoners that have been captured by the enemy since we started on this campaign were exchanged last week. They say the rebels have no force between here and Alexandria on Red River and not more than 1500 there and they are in a wretched condition. I never saw such looking sights as our men were when they came in to our lines [as prisoners of war]. They were treated more like hogs than human beings.

Matters have the appearance of our leaving here soon. Our siege hospital was moved to day and I suppose we shall go soon but where I cannot tell. Christmas has passed and New Years is close at hand   the third one since I have been in the Army. It passed much the same as all other days   hard bread [i.e., hardtack or pilot bread, sometimes called hard crackers] and coffee. I bought me a pair of boots to day. Paid six dollars for them.*

Just before our Regt left N.O. I had the good fortune to swop [swap] a pair of army shoes for a pair of boots and they have lasted until now and I know I should have worn out two pairs of shoes in the time. Boots are much better where there is so much mud and water to wade through as there is in this country, and I thought I might as [well] spend a little money for something that would do me some good as to spend it all for nic nac [knick knacks; that is,

---

* Much of the Union's hardtack was baked in Milton, Massachusetts. In 1801, Josiah Bent founded a bakery that produced hardtack. His grandson, G. H. Bent, took over in 1891, and the firm became known as G. H. Bent Company. Today it is known as Bent's Cookie Factory. It produces hardtack as well as a wooden box labeled "Army Bread" for use in reenactments.

in this context, extra food] at the sutlers. Many a man spends his whole wages at the sutlers for butter   cheese and other little things. It is just like throwing money away   he charges such high prices for everything.*

I sent you ten dollars in the last letter. I hope you will get it. I received the papers you sent me. I hope they are getting along well enlisting at home. It seems as though there is a prospect of this war ending the coming year. I hope and pray it will and soon to. I don't know of any in our Regt reenlisting yet but I presume there will [be] a good many. If the Regt should all reenlist, I should not like to have to serve out the rest of my time in such other Regt   but I think I should before I should reenlist. I want to serve my country as much as any other man and I want to see this rebellion put down in the shortest time possible, but I know it to be my duty to be with my family and let others do as well as I have done that have been staying at home and I will be satisfied. Although I have seemingly done but little   I have tried to do the best I could and all that has been required of me.

Hoping this will find you all well   I close this with a husband

---

* Sutlers followed an army to sell food and/or liquor to the soldiers. The sutler was a civilian retailer attached to a specific regiment. Traveling in a covered wagon, he sold tobacco, newspapers, and even clothing. Sutlers were more common in the Union armies than among the Confederates (Katcher, p. 311). A member of the Union's Irish brigade noted the high prices sutlers charged while he was in camp near Brandy Station, Virginia, in April 1864: "butter at 50 cents, Eggs 60 cents pr doz, Cheese 40 cents per tb [?pound?]"(Menge, ed., *The Civil War Notebook*, p. 109).

Sutlers who haunted the halls of hospitals also charged high rates. When Daniel Chisholm of Pennsylvania was hospitalized with a leg wound at City Point Landing, Virginia, he noted in a June 28, 1864, letter to his father, "Sutlers sell awful high, $1.25 for a can of Peaches, 50 and 75 cents for a very small can of jelly, so the less money a fellow has the better it is for him for he is mighty apt to be tempted. I have seen some of the boys pay a Dollar for a six cent loaf of bread and a quarter for a hardtack" (*Civil War Notebook*, p. 122).

& fathers love.

   H.C.F.

Eliza's Diary:

   Tuesday, December 22: *Get a letter from Henry*

   Thursday, December 24: *Not very well but so to keep around*

In the following letter, Andrew Beane mentions the Second Battle of Rappahannock Station (November 7, 1863)—a Union victory. As New Year approached, the weary infantryman anticipated his discharge from service. He also seems to recall the delights of Christmas Eve back on the farm:

   In camp on left bank   of Hazle [Hazel] River not far from Brandy Station, Va.

   Dec. 24ᵗʰ 63

   My Dear Sister Mrs. Eliza H. Foster

   I was very glad to receive your kind but short letter this P.M.

   It found me quite well for a soldier for several reasons viz. I am looking forward to May or June when I shall be free from the Army.

   We are in good winter quarters & I have a chance to make a little money now & then but not by gambling dear Sister but by hard work as I will tell you some time.

   Eliza I had thought very strange at not having a letter from you.

   How I wish I were with you this night.

   I have not seen Sergt. Barns yet but saw one of the men who said that he was well &c.

   Do you mean when our Regt fought at Rappahannock station for it did suffer there but it did the biggest thing of the war or do you mean the last move over the Rapidan & back to our old grounds. Our Regt. was not in the fight or rather lost no men killed except a Corp. of the Brigade cattle guard who was shot not far from where I was sleeping [indecipherable] the guerrillas that night that they took the mules & burned 14 waggons near Brandy Station.

My wife was homesick [lonely] & has gone to Bethel Hill & is to Uncle Jacob Heaths.

She went to Maine about 25th of Nov. Eliza I had forgotten but not I guess I owed you 3$ beside the note of 17. Did I not. I will send you 5$ in this with many thanks for interest &c & more if you say so & more dear Sister if you are out of money at any time now or hereafter.

Let me know & I will send you some as I am nearer you than Henry at present. You had better see some good [trustworthy] person about your allotment for you should have it.

Now Eliza Please answer this just as soon as you get it so I shall know if you got the money.

Yours

A. J. Beane

Eliza Please send me some three cent postage stamps for the 30 cts.

Eliza's Diary:

Friday, December 25: *I go down to Mrs. Heuyzes to tea*

Saturday, December 26: *Quite well Have a lode of wood of Mr. Parker 6.00 [indecipherable]*

I get my check [her allotment?] Pay her 9.00 cash down

Sunday, December 27: *Willard comes in to see how I get along*

Tuesday, December 29: *Get a letter from Andrew. He sends me five dollars*

At this time, Andrew was in winter camp with his regiment in Orange County, Virginia. The regiment would remain there until May 3, 1864. Since his previous letter to Eliza, the 5th Maine had participated in the Mine Run Campaign, which included clashes at Payne's Farm and New Hope Church and continued from November 27 to Dec. 2. Mine Run was Gen. George Meade's final opportunity to plot a strategic offensive, but the results were inconclusive.

> **Wednesday, December 30:** *Mr. Parker brings me some pork Comes to one dollar sixty-five.** *Get a letter from Henry mailed Dec. 11*

On one of the final pages of her diary, Eliza kept a summary of cash account in which she recorded her federal allotments from the government and her aid from the state and city. Eliza was scheduled to receive twenty dollars a month from Henry's service with the Union Army, but these payments were often in arrears. The diary entries seem to show that she takes in more sewing when the allotment has not arrived and she is short of cash:

> *January [1863]: received allotment to November first [1862], $40.***
>
> *Received of city, $12.*
>
> *February: Received of city, $12.*
>
> *March: Received of city, $12.*
>
> *April: Received allotment, $20*
>
> *Received of city, $12.*
>
> *May: Received allotment to April 1, $40.*
>
> *Received of city, $12.*
>
> *June: Received of city, $12.*

---

* Perhaps Eliza purchased a large roast—to ring in the New Year with guests.
** In her diary entry for January 30, Eliza says this allotment covers the period from July first to September first.

July: Received of city, $12.

August: Received of city, $12.

September: Received of city, $12.

"Up to July first," no sum given. (The amount would have been $40 for May and June. If she did receive this, her total Union payment for 1863 was $160—not $240. That is, the Union government was in arrears by 30 percent, or $80.)

October: Allotment, $20

    Received of city, $12

November: Received of city, $12

December: Received of city, $12.

The Red River Campaign

By the end of 1863, Northern textile mills were facing a severe shortage of cotton because of the diminished flow from the American South and England's monopoly on cotton from India. Control of the Red River region would allow Union forces and government-authorized traders to acquire cotton and perhaps win the loyalty of Louisiana planters.[384]

The Red River Campaign (March 1 to May 13, 1864) was the Union's attempt to establish total control of northern Louisiana, to capture Shreveport (headquarters of the Trans-Mississippi Department) and occupy Texas. Gen. Ulysses S. Grant did not see the point of any major effort in the area, but his opinion was overruled by President Lincoln and Gen. Henry Halleck.

Lincoln and Halleck had compelling reasons to undertake the campaign. First, the Federal government was concerned that the French, having invaded Mexico in the summer of 1863, might also harbor plans to invade Texas. Federal officials had learned that the Confederates were exploring the possibility of collaboration with the French in Texas. Second, a demonstration by federal forces through Louisiana into Texas could bring

Union control of both states. Third, a strong show of Union force could disrupt Confederate military resistance. Fourth, two million bales of cotton (worth more than $600 million in 1864 dollars) awaited seizure along the Red River.[385]

As Andrew penned the following letter, Henry was, at long last, enjoying a month's furlough at home. Encamped with his regiment at Wellsford's Ford, Andrew remained there until the evening of May 3, 1864. Wellsford's Ford is located on the Hazel River, just north of Brandy Station, where one of the largest cavalry battles of the war was fought a year earlier, on June 9, 1863.

The Fifth Maine Infantry would subsequently participate in the battles of the Wilderness, Spotsylvania, North Anna River, and Pamunkey before their term of enlistment expired on June 22.

> *Camp of 5th Maine [Wellsford's Ford] Va. April 28th [1864]*
>
> *Dear Brother & Sister*
>
> *I was very glad after waiting so long to receive your letter this P.M. I am quite well but it is time I was in bed & I am tired for I have been very busy all day but I will pencil a few lines to you to tell you how glad I am that my time is so near out. Just eight weeks from tonight it [his term of enlistment] will be out.*
>
> *We expect to start for Maine about the middle of June but God only knows [if that expectation will come to pass] yet I am looking forward to the time to come.**
>
> *Henry I know too well the wrong and opposition at home & the awful sin in the Army yet we must Stand by the right, our dear country, and our God.*
>
> *I am wicked indeed but dear brother I am so glad that I have stood as well as I have for the last three years or since the day I left*

* According to a 1903 record from the Soldiers and Sailors Historical and Benevolent Society, Andrew was honorably discharged at Portland on July 27, 1864.

my wife & three little children I have not sworn a word I have not played a card Since I have been in the Army. I have drank no liquor [only?] to tast of whisky.*

I am so glad for myself & I think all my friends are for me. Henry Do not forget me in prayer to God.

We are expecting a move here from & a big fight of course. We expected to have moved today but did not & may not for several days.

Henry I did not expect that you would reenlist at all but you thought it right to do so and now God bless you for it. I hope & pray for the est [best] for your safty &c. I wish I could see you before you go back but I cannot do it. I am so glad that you are a good Christian man. It is so much better for yourself, your dear family, your friends, & everybody.

Eliza Dear Sister May God bless & strengthen you for the coming trial [that is, Henry's returning to duty]. Do not make yourself sick but cast your all into the hands of the Lord. As you take leave of Henry [in Massachusetts on furlough] commit him into the care of God Who is able to save. Be a Christian. Be a Christian wife & mother & all will be well.

I have not heard from Albany [Maine] lately. Mrs. Frank Cummings has swaped her farm there [indecipherable] town house [locals' term for Albany Town Hall] for a stand on Bethel Hill. Sam [?] Sloan was very sick last I heard & Mary Lovjoy was sick. Mr. Newell [Howell?] some sick. Be sure to write me soon both of you.

Your Brother

A. J. Beane

---

* Whiskey was part of the soldiers' ration. Andrew is saying he has not overindulged in alcohol, but may have used it as a tonic—or could not refuse it when the ration was distributed to the company.

Andrew's regiment broke camp at Hazel River on May 3, 1864, and crossed the Rapidan at Germanna Ford. Clark Edwards notes that the Fifth Maine had been reduced to "about 275 effective men," including himself, Lt. Col. Millett, Maj. Daggett,* and Adjutant Parsons as well as captains Robinson, Small, Harris, Sanborn, Ladd, Clark, and Lemont.[386] A few days later, on May 13, 1864, Edwards wrote home, again mentioning Andrew. His phrasing makes it obvious that he considered Andrew valuable—even when he was not on the front lines: "Bryce [Clark's brother] Sunday Russell Littlehall Wormell are all right. Andy Bean is with the team in the rear."[387]

I Am Better

In letters from Maine, Andrew mentions being in poor physical health when mustered out. He probably shared the feelings of Maine paymaster J. D. Pulsifer about the prospect of home. Pulsifer wrote to his wife, Helen, from Norfolk, Virginia, in 1864, "It will not be much pleasure to you I fear to have a sick man come home to nurse. It will be a sad pleasure to me but home is home. I feel it possible that I will jump right up [be restored to health] as I go north, get the northern air, northern water, northern food, & above all the warm sympathy of northern hearts—enclosed in my home circle."[388]

> *Albany [Maine] Oct. 1864 Sunday One P.M.*
>
> *Dear Sister*
>
> *Eliza I was glad to get your letter last eve after looking anxiously for it a whole week &c.*
>
> *I am better. I have been gaining for a week & am quite smart for me though I am weak & poor yet.*

---

* Aaron S. Daggett enlisted as a private in the Fifth Maine and was promoted to major in 1863. After the Civil War, he went on to fight in the Indian wars, in the Spanish-American War, and in China and the Philippines. When he died in 1938 at the age of 100, he was the last surviving Union general.

Mother is pretty well but She is working very hard indeed. She has got out one web [of cloth woven at home] for Mrs. Hunt [?] of 16 yds. I road [rode] out with Geo. French yesterday P.M. & carried it home &c So I waited & got mail, the paper & letter & came home afoot. It was coldest night last night we have had but nice & pleasant to day.

Uncle Abbott has been here this A.M. & has gone to Uncle Uriah's [Uriah Holt of Albany, born 1812] to see Sarah Pitts & the rest of them. Geo. [George Holt *] Has come home from the West. Is to be married to day or tomorrow. He & wife John, Sarah her children & husband & his father & mother are all going to leave Albany for the West to morrow.

Eliza A week ago yesterday I had dear little Jacky & Ebenezer's bodies taken up & buried in an other place.

They have got the yard [that is, Songo Pond Cemetery] fenced out to the road in nice shape & I loted [lotted, measured] it off & I took a lot by my self. I had Jacky's coffin put into the box that was made for that purpose & has been in the house ever since. Now I feel better than I did to see it standing round the house &c.

Mrs. Dea. Wheeler died that day. It has been quite sickly here but I think it will be more healthy now the rains have come.

[no signature **]

Andrew re-buried his two sons at Songo Pond Cemetery in Albany, where their tombstones can still be seen.

* George Henry Holt served with the 17th Maine Volunteers and was badly wounded just before the end of the war. Discharged with the rank of corporal, Holt moved to Wisconsin, and in 1879 homesteaded near Crookston, Minnesota. He served as a municipal judge in Crookston.

** The lack of signature could indicate that there was a second page to the letter—a lost page.

When This Cruel War Is Over

Three and a half years into the war, Andrew was recovering at home, while Henry continued to suffer the privations of the field. The Union's efforts in 1864 focused on demoralizing the Confederates and destroying the South's ability to support its troops. At the end of April, Gen. Ulysses S. Grant roused the Army of the Potomac from winter camp, and during May and June put it through its paces in his Overland Campaign. Grant's ambitious campaign began at the battle of the Wilderness and forged ahead through Spotsylvania, Cold Harbor, and Petersburg. Other Union forces operated in the Shenandoah Valley, and below Richmond on the Bermuda Hundred peninsula. Meanwhile, Gen. William Tecumseh Sherman carried out campaigns in Georgia, with battles at Resaca, New Hope Church, and Kennesaw Mountain. A series of battles paved the way for the Union's capture of Atlanta in early September.* These combined pressures on weary and undernourished Confederate forces ultimately succeeded in stretching Southern military resources to the breaking point.[389]

After three years of bloodshed and chaos, both sides longed for peace. The best-selling sheet music of 1864 was "When This Cruel War Is Over," with its refrain of "Weeping, sad and lonely." Other song titles reinforced the general sentiments of weariness, grief, and sadness: "Bear This Gently to My Mother" and "Tell Me, Is My Father Coming Back?"[390]

Henry's first letter of the New Year was written from the Louisiana coast, 120 miles southwest of New Orleans. The letter lobs a ticking bomb into Eliza's lap:

---

* In July, Sherman struggled to cut Atlanta's last rail link with the upper South. He lost James McPherson in the attempt, and then gave command of the Army of the Tennessee to Oliver O. Hoard, a one-armed general from Maine. Civilians were fleeing Atlanta in August, but the Confederate newspapers still thought the city could not be taken. Soldiers made "Sherman neckties" out of the last railroad by heating the rails over bonfires and twisting the metal around trees. To avoid being trapped in the city, John Bell Hood destroyed everything of military value and evacuated Atlanta on September 1. Expressing gloom and doom, Mary Boykin Chesnut wrote in her diary, "We are going to be wiped off the earth."

Camp in the Field   Franklin [La.]   Jan 11ᵗʰ 1864   [No. 55]

Dear Eliza,

It is with some feelings of reluctance that I commence this epis-
tle to you, for I am almost afraid to tell you that I have reenlisted
for 3 years more, but the same spirit induced me, as did to enlist the
first time, and the bounties were a great auxillery [sic] to [too] but
dear Eliza if you were here you would not blame me I am sure you
would not. I am not one to forsake my country in its time of need.
I will tell you just the situation I was in before I re-enlisted. I had
no more idea of doing so than I had of cutting my head of [off], and
I thought there was not money enough in the world to induce me
to. Well Col. Farr called the Regt. out New Years day. We formed*
a square, and he made [a] little speech to us. He said it was not for
him to advise the men to reenlist or not to reenlist and there is not
an Officer in the Regt that has urged any one to reenlist. The men
have done it all themselves. Their own feelings have prompted them
to do it. Well I waited until the 4ᵗʰ. The Col told us that all who re-
enlisted must do so before the 5ᵗʰ as the bounties would be stop[p]
ed then, but he said if two thirds of the Regt reenlisted we should
go home as a Regt and have a furlough of 30 days in the state, and
those that did not reenlist would be transferred into other Regts to
serve the rest of their time which would expire on the 18ᵗʰ of Oct,
next. Such was the order from the war department.

Well, I [could] see that all the men were reenlisting, and I could
not bear the idea of being left here to serve out the remainder of
my time in some other Regt. I knew not what it would be or where,
and have the Regt go home. I never have regretted enlisting the first
time when I did and where I did, for I think I have been very fortu-
nate and have been prospered far beyond my expectations, and I
hope and pray that I may be in future. I always try to look on the

* This is Alpha B. Farr of the 26th Regiment, Companies F and S. He enlisted
with the rank of Lt. Colonel and was promoted to Colonel.

best side and hope for the best, for sufficient unto the day is the evil thereof. Well I thought it all over and saw other men of sound minds go up and put their names down. No one was urged at all, but here was the sticker. We have got to serve the most of this year any how, so it will be for only two years more if we reenlist and again we stand a chance of getting out of it about as soon as those that do not reenlist, for the Presidential election will no doubt have a goodeal to do with ending the war, and that takes place next fall, and then again the old troops reenlisting will do more than many great battles would do, towards sustaining the government, and puting [sic] down the rebellion, and again if we have to serve our time out, on the new enlistment we are getting great pay for it, such pay as no other soldiers ever got in the world.

Now dear one I pray of you not to let this over come [sic] you. Do be candid. Think of it candidly. I shall probably be at home if I live, in two or three months, from this time. The time is not appointed yet for this Regt.   Col Farr tells us, as we are the oldest Regt in this department we shall be the first to go home and he said we shold [should] probably go home sooner than we wanted to on account of the cold weather. We are agoing to be veteran cavalry, when we come out again so we shall not have to hoof it through the mud and over dusty roads, and carry a heavy load on our backs. I think I shall like it much better. All have reenlisted in our Co but 14. The total of our Co is 69, making 55 veterans, about 500 in the Regt all together so we shall go home as a Regt and take the colors with us.

I suppose dear one you will think me a heartless man, that I do not think of my family. Perhaps you will think I do not love them, but Oh Dear Wife: do not I pray of you let such a thought enter your mind for God knows that no man ever loved his Wife and Children more than I do and duty only keeps me away from you and there is many others here that have families and doubtless think as much of them as I do of mine that have reenlisted, but that is nothing to do with me for I went independently, and voluntarily, as I felt it so strongly a sense of duty, in every way both for my country and my own interest, for there is no other way that I could earn so much money, in the same space of time. I believe I told you in one letter [see letter of Dec. 19, 1863] how much my pay would amount to, and the pay has been raised since to [so] it will be 3 dollars a month more. Our new term commences the first day of Jan 1864. I hardly know what to say to you dear one, but I hope & pray that you can pardon & forgive me in my extremety [sic]. I know that I sacrificed the comforts of home for that of hardships and danger and I have also sacrificed your comfort, which I regret the most for It is for my family I wish to be spared to [too]. I think but little of my own hard-ship, but I hope the honor and the money to [too] will compensate, in part for our deprivations.

It is useless to deny that the money was a great temptation, for $2000 two thousand dollars is not gained easily, and I was afraid I should be sorry for it if I did not avail myself of this opportunity to secure it, for if the war should end next fall, or within eighteen months as there is a great chance that it will, I should feel very cheap then if I had not reenlisted. I know that I am runing [sic] some risk in the Army, but as I told Capt Dickerman when I put my name on the roll, I and my family also have been prospered so far in this cause. There is no reason why they will not be in future. It is true some must fall in this struggle. It may be me, but I feel that my life could not be given in a better cause.

Well I will close hoping you dear one will bear this with forti-tude & a true and patriotic spirit. I shall never neglect my family. Though duty calls me away I love them none the less true.

I received your letter of the 21ˢᵗ Dec [1863] yesterday, and the the [sic] paper and envelopes all safe. How glad I [was] to hear from you and to learn that you were well.

John Woods has reenlisted.* So has Ed Sayer [Sawyer]. We started from New Iberia the 7ᵗʰ and got here the 9ᵗʰ and it was awful marching, mud knee deep freezing and thawing. We have had severe cold weather since this year come in. On the night of the 4ᵗʰ we had snow and it is not all gone yet. We are 28 miles nearer N.O. The talk is that we shall stay here 4 weeks. I don't know where we shall go then. There is no enemy on our front.

I shall write again in a day or two, so I will close this hoping it will find you all well as it leaves me. From your true and loving husband, to his dear wife and Children

from H. C. Foster

At the top of page one of the preceding letter and continuing along the right-hand margin is a note in Eliza's handwriting. She forwarded Henry's letter to someone (unnamed, but likely Andrew Beane) to elicit that person's opinion of her husband's reenlistment. These are her words:

I got your letter. I am well. Please do write me. I cant write now. Tell me what you think. From Eliza.

Send this back. Frank has gone to V.I. [Vermont?] now.

Both Andrew and Eliza immediately wrote their reactions to Henry. Ten days later he replied to Eliza from Franklin. Situated on Bayou Teche, Franklin was home to large sugar cane plantations and thrived as a sugar port after steamboats began to ply local waterways.

Camp in the Field   Franklin   La.   Jan 21ˢᵗ 1864   No. 56

My Dear Ones: At home.

I am continuallly [sic] thinking of you, & hoping that you are all well, and hoping this will find you well, as it leaves me to day. Oh dear Eliza I wish your health could be as good as mine is and

---

* There were two men by the name of John Woods, Junior and Senior, in Henry's Company A. Henry refers to a John Woods again in his letter of June 26.

has been ever since I have been in the Army. How thankful I should be, but I trust you are usually well, and the children also, and with these wishes, I will endeavor to answer your two good letters of the 3d & 6th which I received yesterday, and how glad I was to learn that you were well and I hope you and the little ones are comfortable this cold winter, for from all accounts it is a very severe winter all over the country. People here say it is the coldest in 20 years. This is the first real warm day since Christmas, and it seems quite comfortable to get in the shade to day.

It made me feel bad when I read your letters, in regard to re-enlisting, but dear E. I hope you will not denounce me as being to [too] cruel, and I hope you will bare [bear] it with a true womanly spirit and be calm, and reasonable about it, for believe me dear one I acted according to the dictates of my conscience and to the best of my judgment. No one urged to [me] to re-enlist, and I think you would not find a man in this Regt that was induced by anything more than the promptings of their own feelings. There is but 13 men in our Co. not re-enlisted and 2 of those wuld [sic] have gone but were rejected by the surgeon. I suppose you will say I might have been one of that No. So I might, but there is only one regret that I am a veteran volunteer, Eliza, and that is for the sorrow and loneliness it will cause you, but I beg you will be reconciled. One idea I had in my mind was this, perhaps and it is very probable to [too] that I shall not have to serve much longer, by re-enlisting. This you will say is a vain idea for the same thing was said 2 years ago, but I think different for the rebellion is not so strong by half, as it was then, and the union is twice as strong   yes   I might say three times as strong   as it was then and is growing stronger every day, and the rebellion growing weaker. Who can doubt the result. I may be deceived as to the time [i.e., timing of the end of the war] but not as to the final result. By re-enlisting [we] will strengthen the government and forward our cause.

I feel very anxious about you and shall until I get a letter in answer to the one I last wrote you telling you I had re-enlisted, and I am sorry I did re-enlist on account of my family, but it is to [too] late now, to look back, and I pray you will agree with me, and think it is for the best. It is very hard I know. It is hard for me as well as you, to venture such an undertaking, but you know the old adage nothing ventured nothing had, and we have to venture much in this life. Perhaps we venture to [too] much sometimes, and you think I had no need of doing what I have done but I hope to get a little start in the world, and I hope to do what I feel is my duty to do for we cannot end this war to [too] soon and there is but one way that it will be done, and that is by the power of our Armies, and thus when this cruel war is over, we can hope for peace and properity [prosperity] and feel that we are worthy of it, as one of Gods blessings.

I received a letter from Andrew a week since and have answered the same. I was very glad to get one from him, and to learn that he was well. He said he should not re-enlist as his time was so near out in May or June. If my [time] was so near out I dont think I should have done so. As it is I can but think there will be a great deal done in the next nine months towards ending this terrible war and bringing about an everlasting peace I hope. He said 73 men had re-enlisted in his Regt. Some Regts all had re-enlisted but he said he thought he should have soldiering enough when his time should be out. I presume he has seen harder times than I.

There has [been] severl Regts gone home from this Dept [i.e., Department of the Missouri] on furloughs and I am longing for the time to come when it will be our turn to go though I some dread the cold weather in going north this winter. It is said now that we shall start the 15ᵗʰ of February though I am not certain but such is the talk now. We are to be fitted out as cavalry very soon. The 14ᵗʰ Main [Maine?] Regt started for home on the 16ᵗʰ of this month.

It is Charles Richardson, that I chum with. He has gone on picket to night so I have got to sleep alone but it is not cold to night. I received Willards good letter the same day I did Andrews but have not answerd [sic] it yet but shall so soon. W. said May was at work for Jim. Where does he live. I thought he had gone up country. Mr. [Royal] Nason in our Co had a letter from L [Lowell] of the 8th stating that her quota was full. I am very glad of it. I hope there will not have to be a draft for it seems to be a long a [and] tedious way of raising troops. It seems as though the people are getting awakened to the perilous situation of the country, but if men would not enlist under the present circumstances   they must be selfish and stupid indeed and not worthy of having a government to protect them. I see by the papers that all those re-enlisting will be admited [sic] into the quota. I do not think this is right, and it seems it has not done them much good for they have straind [strained] to the utmost to fill it up before being aware of the fact, and I hope they have done as well everywhere as in Lowell.

I am very sorry that Varnum could not go, but he probably thought he was safe enough or else he would [have] enlisted. I expect this army will winter here at this place. It is [a] very pleasant place. Our Regt has been mustered out and musterd in to the service again for three years more unless sooner discharged. We have not been paid again but expect to be soon, when we shall receive our $100. dollars bounty on the first enlistment and two months pay up to Jan 1st 1864, when our new term commences. Then we shall receive 60 dollars advance on the U.S. bounty and 50 on the State bounty. I think I shall take that and the 20 dollars a month instead of the 325 down.

I expect Liut. Dick [Dickerman] will be Capt of our Co. and the Capt will be Major. They are well as are all the rest of the Co. There is scarcely a sick man in our Regt now. Be comforted dear Eliza. My prayers and best wishes are with you daily and for you, and I trust we shall be prospered in the future as in the past, and that we shall

yet be a free and happy people as of yore. Thus hoping I trust you
will not blame me but forgive, if you can your ever true and loving
husband & Father, who is trying to do all he can in good faith for his
lovely Wife & Children.

> *Ever Truly yours Eliza*

> *from Henry.*

The best-laid plans of infantrymen oft go astray. Henry counted on receiving his bounty as he laid it out above, but no less an official than the
adjutant-general of the Commonwealth of Massachusetts confessed that
difficulties could arise: "A great many men who had enlisted during the
year [1864], elected to take the State bounty of fifty dollars in advance,
and twenty dollars a month. The monthly bounty was to be paid by the
State Treasurer every two months; and the pay-rolls were to be made out
by the Adjutant-General [William Schouler, who refers to himself in the
third person throughout his history] from certified rolls made by the regimental or company officers at the front. . . . Many of the officers neglected
to forward the rolls as required, which prevented the Adjutant-General
from making the pay-rolls; and, as many of the men had arranged, before
leaving the State, to have their families draw their monthly pay, considerable disappointment and suffering ensued."[391]

White Clover Blooms

> *Camp in the field, Franklin [La.], February 16, 1864   No. 57*

> *Dear Wife & Children:*

> *I hope you are all well to day, and I trust these few lines may*
> *find you so. My health is first-rate, but I am very anxious about you*
> *as it is a long time since I received a letter from you, the 6ᵗʰ of Jan.*

> *I suppose you blame me a goodeal for re enlisting but I thought*
> *it for the best. I am getting rather impatient for our furlough to*
> *come. Col. Farr says we shall be at home by the 15ᵗʰ of March. I am*

very anxious to get home as you may well suppose but I suppose it would be better for our healths to wait until warmer weather. Dr. Ward the Dentist is here. He leaves to night for Lowell. I spoke with him yesterday. He took my name and the <u>No</u>. [street number] where you live and said if he has time, before the Regt got home, he would call and see you but he had a great many places to go, as he had taken messages from all the Lowell men in this Regt and the 30ᵗʰ Regt also. There are over 200 men in the 30ᵗʰ from the City of Lowell who have re-enlisted and a 150 in this Regt. I saw D. Barnard the other day. He has re-enlisted. Quite a number have re-enlisted in this Regt lately and I think more will do so as they have until the 1ˢᵗ of March. I am sick enough of the war but I want to see it over, and it is the opinion of almost every one that it will be over this year. Col. Farr and finally most all Officers advise the men to take the $325 [bounty] down in preference to the $20 per month, as it is their opinion that we shall not serve long enough to make up that amount but I think I shall prefer to take the 20 per month, for if I serve 14 months it will amount to $5.00 more than the 325 down, and if I don't have to serve that length of time I will be satisfied if I don't get quite so much, and thankful too, when this war shall be over. We had 25 recruits come to our Regt last night from Mass. None of them were from Lowell. All the Lowell men that came out went into Capt Pearsons Battery.

It is said there is a mail at N.O. for us and it will be up to night. I hope I shall get a letter from the loved ones at home. If I do I will answer it imediatly. I will send you some white clover bloms that I picked to day.

What is the trouble with John Woods wife. He showed me a letter from his sister, that give her an awful runing [ruining? Harsh criticism?]. Said she was drunk half of the time and had been arrested. Then he showed me a letter from his Wife that showed it to be true. He got me to write a letter to her last night for him. He can-

not write himself. I am thankful I can write for I should not want
other people to know my bussiness. Well dear Eliza I will close, hop-
ing this will find you all well and I pray that God may bless you
and the dear Children, and that he may spare us all yet to enjoy
the blessings & comforts of life. I sometimes feel that I have done
wrong, by re-enlisting, but I pray you will not judge me to harshly,
for I try to do that which is for the best. I remain your true and lov-
ing husband.

To E.H.F.

[from] Henry C. Foster

The 26th Regiment departed Franklin on February 24 and returned to New
Orleans, where it remained on duty until March 22.

Angry over Henry's re-enlistment, Eliza seems to punish Henry by
ceasing to write to him. Henry remains in the dark about his lack of mail
from her.

New Orleans, March 13th, 1864   *(No. 58)*

Dear & Beloved Wife & Children.

I will write you a few lines this evening so that you may know I
am well, and hope you are all enjoying the same great earthly bless-
ing, but it is so long since I have received a letter from you, it seems
as though I should go crazy sometimes. Why think it is almost three
months since your last letter was written that I received, and the
only way I can account for it is that you are expecting me home,
soon, and fear I should not get the letter, and I compose myself the
best I can by thinking so. I trust there is no other reason for your not
writing. I have no doubt you feel very bad about my re-enlisting,
and I feel myself sometimes a brute, almost and that I have done
very wrong, and would give almost anything had I not done so, for
your sake. If I thought I had got [to] be away from home 3 years
longer, I should almost despair myself, but I looked at things in a

different light and I came to the conclusion that it would be for my advantage and that of my dear family to do as I have done, and let us dear Wife trust that so it may prove.

I don't know but you have heard that our Regt is in N.O. once more. We left Franklin on the 24ᵗʰ Feb. and arrived here the next morning, and took up our quarters in the Alabama Cotton Press (buildings for storeing Cotton). Yesterday, we had a parade arround town for the first time since we arrived here. We went up in front of Gen Banks's residence and had a parrade. I have sent you the Era [newspaper] containing an account of the parade, and the Gen's speech to us. The paper also states that we shall leave here for Boston about the 20ᵗʰ. Whether that is any authority or not I cannot say but if so we shall arrive about the first of April. We have received our cavalry uniform, and shall wear it home. I don't know whether we shall get our equipment or not. We have received 2 months pay since we came here but the allotment was taken out up to the first of January. The Paymaster said we should not receive our bounty until we got to Mass, and it is a good thing for a great many men and their families, especially. Hoping soon to be at home with you my dear dear ones. I remain your true and loving husband and Father.*

Yours Affectionately

Henry C. Foster

The Red River Campaign took place more or less between these two letters written by Henry. Banks's 30,000 troops were supported in their march by Navy rear admiral David Dixon Porter's fleet of gunboats.

An unsigned letter sent from Baton Rouge on April 26, 1864, tells something of the campaign: "Solgars [soldiers] going up the river [Mississippi] every day there was fore [regiments?] went up this morning.

---

* Henry implies here that most of the men would spend—or be feloniously relieved of—their bounties before they reached home.

They are bound for read [Red] river I think for they are fighting up there pretty harde."[392]

As a whole, the Red River campaign was not a triumph for the Union. A small but significant victory was that Maine lumbermen from the 29th and 30th regiments successfully built dams to save the Union fleet. The dams raised the river's water level and provided sufficient depth for Union vessels to escape downriver.[393]

By early April, Henry was on leave.

Camp Meigs, Readville [Mass.], May 6, 1864 (No. 59)

Dear Wife:

I hope you are all well to day. I feel quite lame. My cold hangs on yet. We left Boston yesterday at 3-1/2 oclock. This [Camp Meigs] is 8 miles from Boston. I don't know as I can get leave to come home. The Capt told me yesterday if there was any passes given to anybody I should have one. There is no chance to get any yet, and if I don't come to day I want you to come down to morrow in the first train if you can. When you get in to Boston you take the Horse Cars for Providence Depot and from there you take the cars for Readville. Our camp is on the left hand side as you get out. I will meet you at the Depot if I can.

I presume there will be some [other Lowell residents] coming down. The first Train leaves Lowell at 7-1/4 oclock in the morning. Our Sergt Major told me this morning that an order was published in the Journal for us to start for New York Sunday or Monday. If so there will be little chance of getting leave. This is a pleasant place. Much better than the Island, by all accounts. I shall come to day if I can. Bring those peces [pieces] for my Jacket if you have them ready.* If not don't stop to make them. Major Clark thinks we shall get paid here before we leave. I hope Mother has not gone, so you can leave

---

* Civil War uniforms were generally ill-fitting. Eliza must be making alterations to Henry's new cavalry jacket.

Henry C. Foster, in a photograph taken while he was on leave in Lowell, Mass., in late spring 1864. Courtesy Bethel Historical Society.

the children with her, for it would be to [too] tiresome to take them. You will have no trouble in finding the way. Be sure and come if you can, if I don't come to day. I shall come if possible. I am afraid you wont get this in time to come to morrow. If not come Monday. If you don't come before noon to morrow I shall try to come home to morrow night. McIver has not come yet. I sent you the money yesterday. I write this so you will be sure to come, if I dont come home. From your loving husband ever true yours.*

* Henry's friend John McIver, who reenlisted with him as a Veteran Volunteer, seems to have construed their friendship as reason to temporarily join the family.

Henry C. Foster

Bring some stamps.

Camp Meigs was a 139-acre training facility in Boston, located south of the modern Neponset Valley Parkway. Thousands of Union soldiers trained here before departing for the front. The camp was perhaps best known for training the African-American members of the 54th Volunteer Militia Regiment, which was memorialized in the 1989 motion picture *Glory*. Prominent black leaders such as Frederick Douglass acted as recruiting agents for the 54th; two of Douglass' sons served in the regiment. Only about 4,500 African-Americans resided in Massachusetts in 1860, so men were recruited from as far away as Ohio.[394] Twenty-five percent of the men were former slaves, but the majority had been common laborers.

Camp Meigs, Readville, May 10, 1864. (No. 60)

Dear Wife:

I arrived here at 7 oclock this P.M. Sent word by Mrs. Howard to that effect but I have heard some news since—that I want to tell you.* Lieut Dickerman come through the quarters this afternoon and told us to be ready to move to morrow forenoon but whether we go or not is another thing. Hy Barnard arrested Charley Packard [for not returning to camp on time] last night soon after I left him but Charley gave him the slip and run in to Dan Eastmans.** Got under the Counter and 5 or 6 Policemen after him. He said he heard them say they had got 9 in the station house then, and told some of their names. Mc's name [McIver] was mentioned among the rest,

---

* There were two men in Henry's Company A with the surname Howard: Frank and James.

** Daniel Davis Eastman, born in New Hampshire in 1828, married Eliza Nichols in 1848 in Lowell and died 1875 in Lawrence. He was a house painter whose brother Ezekiel was a first lieutenant in Company A of the 26th Reg. Mass. Volunteers—that is, the same regiment as Henry and McIver. They probably visited the shop earlier in their furlough to deliver news of Ezekiel, and McIver now trades on that slight acquaintance.

so I suppose they have got him fast enough. Charley laid under the counter until they went away. Then he borrowed Dans Coat [i.e., civilian garb to cover his military coat] and went down on to the Boatt and staid over night. He said he want [wasn't] more than out of doors this morning than they were after him again. He run over on to Church street and found Bailey with a team and got in with him and rode to Brighton and hired another team and rode here, so I guess I had rather a narrow chance by his story, but poor Mc is up a spout this time I guess.

I don't know when you will get this letter but I shall send it to Boston if [I] can. If I had known this soon enough, I should have written and sent it by Susan [Howard?]. I feel pretty well except a slight headache. I hope you and the children are all well. I don't know what to say about your coming down, but if we should leave to morrow forenoon it would hardly be worth while. I will wright [write] again in the morning, so good bye for this time with a true husband's love.

Yours Truly

H. C. Foster

I Hope for the Best

On Board Steamer Comodore [sic], Stonington [Conn.] May, 11, 1864*

Dear Wife,

I will pencil a few lines to let you know that [I] am well & etc. I [feel] very bad that you was not down to see me start. I did not think

---

* The *Commodore*, a 944-ton wooden screw steamship newly launched in 1864, was purchased by the Union Navy in March—two months before Henry's voyage. Recommissioned as the USS *Iuka* during May 1864, for the rest of the war she sailed with the East Gulf Blockading Squadron, operating in the Gulf of Mexico off Western Florida.

*we should go so soon. Mc got he [here] just in time to get aboard.
If [I] was sure last night that we should [have] started [so soon], I
should [have] come home last night sure but perhaps it is as well. I
hope so. I feel sad indeed that I could not see you again before starting, and that Mc should come from my home last, made me more
so, but it [is] nothing after all. I hope for the best. I hope you will get
word so not to come to morrow.* I hope you are all well. I don't know
that I can send this yet but shall if possible. I will keep up good
spirits if I can. Nothing said about pay. I will write again in N Y if
I can. Good bye for this time. Be of good cheer and think of Henry.*

Yours

H. C. Foster

As Henry returns to the Western Theater, lack of pay becomes a problem
once more:

New York, May 12, 1864

Dear Wife,

*I will pencil you a few lines again. I wrote you last night before
leaving for this place. I made a mistake in the name of the place. It
was Groton Connecticut where we took the boat [the Commodore].
I am well this morning and I hope you are all the same. What I said
about Mc. was foolish on [of] me but I felt so bad I did not know
what I was writing. I felt as though I wanted to see you last of any
body, but I hope you are well. Do not think that I have any thing
against you. No, it was because I felt so bad about leaving. We are
now a going aboard of the Cahawba, the same steamer that we*

---

* Henry does not reveal until some while later that McIver is a drinker, or
that he was indeed intoxicated when he went to a studio with Henry's family to be
photographed. Henry might have suspected that Mc was intoxicated when bidding
Eliza good by and perhaps compromised her.

came on. We are going to N.O. No Pay. I don't know what to think,*
but I hope it will all come out right. Do not worry about it. If you
can make what money you have got last you until you get some
more I shall be glad. I think we shall get it as soon as we get to N.O.
I will write as soon as I get there so good bye now Dearest one from
your loving husband.

H. C. Foster

Several days after his departure, Henry's words to his wife take on a sour and jealous tone. In one of his longest and most soul-searching letters to Eliza, he chides her for behavior unbecoming a married woman. Henry wrote in his first letter of 1863, "I hope there never will be any jealousy between us." But here he is consumed with jealousy, baffled by actions that strike him as wanton and unpredictable—although all Eliza has done during their sojourn together was to show generosity to his friend McIver.

His new vocabulary word is *ignominy*.

On board transport steamer Cahawba, May 16th, 1864

Dear Eliza:

I will try to write you a few lines, hoping that you and the
Children are well. I have not felt very well since I started on this
voyage but am feelling a good deal better now. It is mostly home-
sickness that ails me I guess. I never felt so before and hope I never
shall again. I was not sea sick but for four days I [had] no appetite
to eat anything, and I felt blue enough. I never knew how to appre-
ciate home before, but I assure you I do now. There is no place like
home, dearest one. Oh! What would I not give if I was only clear
of the army, that I might enjoy my home with the dear ones there,
but Eliza this may make you feel bad. I know you feel bad enough
without anything to make you feel worse, but I cant help telling you

* During the 1850s, the U.S.M. steamship *Cahawba* regularly sailed as a luxury liner between the ports of New Orleans, Havana, and New York City. It served as a troop carrier and transport during the Civil War.

how I feel. I wanted to tell you, and many times when at home. I was prevented from speaking as I felt for fear you could not bear it, and I did not want to say anything to make you feel bad for I wanted to have you enjoy the little time I was at home as much as you could, and I think we both enjoyed ourselves much better than we should if we had kept thinking of being seperated [sic] again, for I can say that I never felt any more miserable than I have since I started from Readville.

I hope you have written to me before now. If not I hope you will soon, for I should be glad to get a letter from you soon as I get ashore but that can hardly be, but do write often and tell me everything, wont you. Oh wouldent I squeeze you if I could see you now. I have written you twice once at Groton and once at N.Y. but don't know as you will get them, but I don't know what I wrote I was so blue. Perhaps it will be as well if you don't get them. I was almost tempted to jump off the train several times and go back.

Oh if I only had known as much then as I do now I should [have] stayed at home another night you better believe. I just as much expected to see you again before I came away as I ever expected anything in the world, but I hope all is for the best. I have heard that the Capt told some one that if I was gone much longer I should lose my stripes, but that would not [have] hindered me from staying, though. He has said nothing to me however, and he better not. Dick [Dickerman] boards with the Co. He said he was not going to pay twenty dollars for his board, when he could get just as good in the Co. but I guess there is a good reason for it but don't say anything. Dick may do me a good turn some time. He always used me tip top. His Wife is with him.

We are of [off] the coast of Florida to day. We run in sight [of] Charleston harbor yesterday and Communicated with the fleet and left them some papers. I should like very much to know what the news is from Gen Grant to this time. I hope and pray he has been successful. Oh hope this war will be over this summer and I think it will be to [too], but we must wait.

[Letter continues on a separate sheet:]

I am well. So are all the boys. J. F. Upham has got his warrant as hospital steward. A good thing for him and he is worthy of it. Brad [Bradford S. Norton] has not got his commission yet but expects to soon.

I am going to No. each letter to you here after and I want you to do the same then we shall know whether we get them all or not. Commence from the beginning since I left home.

You asked me how much I thought you ought to live of [off] from. I don't wish to stint you but I think you ought to live on the State Bounty and State Aid which amounts to $32.00 Thirty two dollars and pay some bills to [too] don't you. I know prices are so high it cost a goodeal. Money dont go so far as it used to but you are having a considerable sum of money altogether, about sixty dollars a month. It would be a good plan for you to keep an account book and keep an account of every cent received and all you pay out. This is what every one should do, and if [I] had always done so I should be better of [off] to day no doubt. I intend to do so here after.

It is understood now that all the men that were enlisted into our Regt in La. and re-enlisted will be discharged this fall when the first term of the Regt expires, as they did not receive their government bounty with the rest of us, but they may keep them 2 years from their first enlistment and then give them their new bounty and keep them 3 years from that time. I dont know how it will be yet, but most likely they will be discharged next fall when the rest are that did not re-enlist. I would like to be one of them but then I don't worry much for it is no use.

I am of strong opinion that this war will be closed next spring, *at the longest. I now think it rather doubtful about Lincoln's being elected again, but whether he is I think the result will be about the same as far as stopping the war, if our Armies do not gain any very decided advantage before next fall election, I hope Lincoln will be defeated, as I have no doubt he will be, for it is useless to continue the contest if we cant whip them this summer we never can.* Every one sees it in the same light I think.** Well it matters little to me now which way the thing goes so the war is ended. I don't know but I am getting to be something of a Copperhead [Southern sympathizer] myself, but I cant help it for the war is carried on so foolishly and with so much selfishness, by men in high authority that I have lost most all my patriotism, and I find that a good many others are taken the same way. The fact is there is a good deal of wrong on both sides about as much on our side as the other, but I never can give up the Union, although I think it may be saved as well without fighting, for this is nothing more nor less than a Political War.*

We had another review yesterday, and it come pretty near using me up it was awful hot.

I will tell you more how my mind is changed, and as we grow older we grow wiser. When a man becomes convicted [convinced?] it is no harm to acknowledge it. I only wish I had known as much before I re-enlisted as I do now, but it was not so to be. I shall write to Mabelia to day. You said you got a letter from Mother, I suppose it was Mother Bean [his mother-in-law, Mary A. Holt Bean]. Is she coming to Lowell. You said nothing about Mother Foster [Lynch].

* The electoral college met on February 12, 1865, and Lincoln was declared elected as president for a second term. However, his election had been uncertain for nearly nine months.

** In May 1864, editor Horace Greeley, reflecting on the feelings of many voters who were dissatisfied with Lincoln, wrote in the New York *Tribune*, "Our own conviction is . . . that it is advisable for the Union Party to nominate for President some other among its able and true men than Mr. Lincoln."

Has she gone home. Kiss the children for me and accept a thousand for yourself.

> *Henry*

[Still on board the *Cahawba*.]
[no salutation]

I have had some very disagreeable thoughts in my mind for the last 12 hours but I have striven to drive all unhappy thoughts from my mind and I hope you dear will do the same, for if indulged in no knowing what they might lead to. You know I never was very bad, but always tried to do the best I could. I am going to tell you all, for I have a right to. I woke up this morning at 3 oclock dreaming about you. You know we had some talk about some things, that we ought not to though I hope no harm will result from it. You of course will know what I mean (in regard to other men and women). I know it is a foolish thing to mention, but we want to understand each other perfectly. If we do not there can be no happiness. Although we are seperated for a time, we can be just as true to each other and love each other as much, and enjoy ourselves in proportion. I have never had the slightest reason to doubt your constancy to me since I have known you, and I am sure you can have no other opinion of me, but you know this world is so deceitful and sinful, and you have had passions aroused within you, no doubt for I know I have myself, that are hard to overcome, for the more anyone indulges in such passions the more they want to, but Oh dear One think of the course the [of] conduct that many others have pursued, placed under the same circumstances that you are, and see the disgrace the ignominy it has brought upon them just for a few moments of enjoyment. God forbid that you or I either should ever for a moment harbor the first thought of inconstancy, unfaithfulness to each other. Oh think of our dear Children. What disgrace it would bring on them, and always be on your guard, for all willy [wily] tempters.

Temptation is great sometimes for me as well as you, but a woman is placed in a different position I know but I know there is no man can get around a woman unless it is with her consent, and no one need to tell me any different, and you know it as well as I. Oh! Have fortitude at all times, and be true to yourself and your husband whom you know is ever true to you and I am sure you never had reason to think otherwise. I do not say all this because I doubt your fidelity to your husband, nor that I have any feelings of Jealousy for that is the most unhappy feeling that any person can have. No dear Eliza hope there never never will be cause for such feelings between us.

Oh I cannot think of what might be and of what we have seen with others. No I merely have written the thoughts that have come to my mind, as I was sitting upon the wheelhouse of the boat all morning all alone until day light. It was so warm I could not stay below [i.e., below decks], and the dreams I had during the night brought such thoughts to my mind. This is from Henry as good advice and I trust will do you no harm, at least. I trust dear one you will have no hardness towards me for it, and forgive me. Now I have resolved to make the best of my misfortune because I know I cannot get out of it until Uncle Sam is ready to let me go, and we must both be prudent and save every cent we can for it [is] high time we should begin to save something for our Children if we can. I am going to save every cent I can and I know you will help me. I feel better about my State bounty now than if I had taken it down for most of those that did have nothing to show for it now.

Oh it is hard to be seperated, but may God grant that we be spared to meet again to live together and comfort each other.

Henry

But until then remember it is for each other we live, so ever may it be. Write often.

John McIver also wrote to Eliza from the *Cahawba*, underlining and capitalizing for emphasis, and using a familiar, slightly flirtatious tone. His lighthearted version of events is a distinct contrast with Henry's:

> *On Board the steamship Cahawaba   May 19, 1864*
>
> *U. S. Forces in the field*
>
> *Franklin La.*
>
> *Mrs. Foster*
>
> *My worthy friend I am not going to forget your kindness to me when I was a stranger in a strange country. I hope soon to reward you, unless I will die very soon, I am very sorry for taking that money from you fore I might heave [have] known that you would need it. –I was in such a hurry that day, I run all the [way] to the <u>cars</u>, and got their just when the <u>Train</u> was in Motion, all the <u>Peoples</u> that met me thought that I was <u>crasey</u>, or going <u>mad</u> or something or another fore they Stared me In the Face like as I would...be a Runaway <u>thief</u> or a <u>Covict</u> [convict],*
>
> *As Mr. Foster will give you all the News, I heave [have] but little to Interest you, only If I could say Something that would make you Laugh, Sayer [Sawyer?] is down on me, for [courting] Nelle Thompson, he wont believe anything but that I cut him out, Now this is <u>Leap Year</u> and If any of the young <u>Ladies</u> will write to me I will be glad to answer them, I mean Miss Thompson or Miss Merill. I Promised Miss Merill one of my <u>Pictures</u>, and I suppose you will heave to give one to Miss Thompson. You will have to send me one of Mr. Fosters fore he wont give me any,**
>
> *My Love to <u>adda</u> [Etta] and <u>george</u> My respects to Miss Thomson and to Miss Merill, and to all who May Kindly ask for me.*
>
> *Excuse mistake[s] and oblige give Miss Merill one of my pic-*

* McIver refers here to photographs taken in Lowell when he and Henry were on furlough. One shows Henry and his family.

tures and one to Miss Thompson Send the Rest of them to my ad-
*dress**

> *Respectfully your[s]*
>
> *J. A. McIver*

Not long after the 26th Massachusetts returned to Louisiana soil, McIver went AWOL. One imagines Eliza muttering, "Good riddance to bad rubbish!"

Emotionally dependent on letters from home, soldiers in all wars entertain thoughts of being forgotten—even being betrayed. Albert Balcom who served with the 8th Cavalry from Rochester, New York, was wracked with doubts. Balcom wrote on November 20, 1863: "Been expecting a letter and cannot get one. Rather hard for a poor fellow down here [in Virginia] to be forgot by ones folk. Had no letter from my wife since Oct. 4. God forgive her for coming back on me as freely as I do, but I will not blame her nor believe her anything but true to me."[395]

I Feel I Shall Come Home Again

In his next letter, Henry continues to pursue the theme of marital fidelity, delivering a regular sermon. Because of the casual talk he hears around him, he cannot shrug off his suspicions. (He will return to the theme on June 3.)

Henry is wrestling with an angel. Eliza cannot answer these suspicions, this paranoid harangue; she can only endure the attack.

Henry adopts an elevated tone as he lectures Eliza in such phrases as *hymen's altar,* but then, speaking of friends, he uses slang uncharacteristic of his custom, such as *duds* and *chum.*

---

* Upon receiving a veritable flood of Henry's doubts about her relationship with McIver and her faithfulness in general, Eliza chooses not to follow McIver's directions about delivering photographs to young ladies; she sends them all to McIver.

No 4 Camp in the field

Carrollton [north of New Orleans]

May 22, 1864

Dear Wife

Eliza I am well this morning, in bodily health, though the pleasant memories of my dear home are so fresh in my mind, it gives me much sadness to think I am not there with my loved ones, and when I look at the realities and the long time that in all probability I am to be deprived of those comforts and endearments, it seems almost to much to endure. Oh that I could have known ere it was to [too] late what my feelings would be, known what I now realize, but then it is almost useless to regret the past. Whats [sic] done cant be helped so we must all live and learn and make [the] best of it but I feel sometimes as though I would sacrifice almost anything to be out of the army, but I dont want this to worry you in the least, for I shall put the best face possible on my lot and trust kind providence in good time to restore me safe home to my loved ones, and I also pray that the same kind hand may protect you all, and keep you safe from all harm and temptation, that everywhere beset[s] this wicked world.

You cannot be to [too] careful of your character and reputation. I know to [too] well the situation you are placed in. The eyes of a frowning world are ever cast upon us, and [at] the slightest improper act they are ready to dart their arrows to wound you, or injure you. Therefore my light[,] my love, my dearer than all else, ever remember the cherished vows we have made, and be true to one that is ever true to the one that he at the hymens [Hymeneal] altar swore as long as life should last to love and cherish, and may it be Gods will that in His good time, we meet again to enjoy each others company, and Oh; let there be nothing to mar our happiness should be both be spared that happy boon. You have vowed to me that you would die before you would try to deceive your husband. Do not forget that vow, for I should much rather see you dead than know you had been faithless to your husband. Eliza I never can distrust you. No God forbid that I should!

But Oh I have seen so much and heard so much of the faith-lessness of woman and man to [too]. I can but feel that I should give you a loving husband's kind admonitions that you may not depart from the paths of honor and rectitude. You know I talked, lightly to you of things that perhaps it would have been better not to have said but I feel that I have that confidence in you that such joking would not affect you in the least. Talking is a quite different thing from acting. Oh I have a thousand things I want to say to you could I see you, and had I know [known] I was coming away [from his furlough] without seeing you again, I should have said much more than I did, but Oh what disgusting talk have I heard ever since leaving home. There is nothing talked of but whores and soldiers wives and even some that their husband's are at home. Oh how should I feel did I have the least thought that you was not true to me. I know I have no reason to doubt your constancy and I am thankful that I have not. I was talking with Brad [Bradford Norton] one day coming out and got to speaking of Mrs. Sawyer. He said she has been burnt, and was about as tough as they make 'em. One man by the name of Moore in Acton, got home and his wife had a youg [young] one the night before he got there. He did not go near her but took his duds and left and has not been seen since and I don't blame him. What wont some folks do, if I may call them folks. They are not, they are inhuman.

Dear Eliza. Now that I have written one sheet to you about things that are nearest my heart, and hoping you will answer me in true confidence—and I pray I have given you no offence—I will now try to tell you how we arrived here and how we are situated. When I wrote the letter that I sent you, I intended to write another that would go in the same mail, that was written and sealed up some days before we arrived here. I did not have time to write another so I sent that the same night we got here as I heard there was a mail going the next morning so I suppose you will get it some time before you do this. You may think stranger of it that I did not write more, but this will explain it and make it all right I hope.

We had a very pleasant passage out. We entered the mouth of the Miss. River at 3 oclock Friday morning. We did not stop at N. Orleans but a few minutes and arrived here at 3 oclock Friday afternoon, a little more than eight days from N.Y. We remained aboard the boat that night and landed yesterday afternoon. Received new shelter tents and here we are fairly encamped in the field again. Charley [Richardson] and I chum together again as we have done ever since we first came out and we get along pretty well. I guess there is no other 2 men stuck together as we in the Co. and as I got my tent pitched and laid down in it, it did really seem like a dream to look back 2 months past, and it would be a happy dream were it not that I am now to be deprived of that happiness I have experienced for 30 days now past, but we must nerve ourselves up eaqual [sic] to the occasion, as much as possible and hope that time will soon again come when I shall be home and not have our happiness alloyed with the idea that I have got to go away again. I have no reason to complain yet however, for I had got all this time to serve had I not re-enlisted and I should undoubtedly been in several hard battles and we know not who would have fell. Surely there seems to be a kind and over ruling power to guide us, and let us pray that it is all for the best, and that the same good fortunes may ever attend us all that has ever seemd [seemed] to thus far. No knowing what great event may take place before the time would have been up that I should had to serve on my first term. I hope this war may be at an end before that time, but none save One can tell.

The news in this Department seems to be bad enough but [not] so bad as represented. Banks whole Army has fell back to the mouth of Red river on the Miss.*And had almost continual fighting all the way back but whipped the rebels in every battle. I think there will be no more forward movements in this Army at present, but I dont know.

We expect to get paid in a day or two.

We have good news from Grant, that he had captured 9,400 prisoners up to the 12th inst. and Lee was retreating.** It is desperately hot here. Boys are pedling black berys, and every [thing] looks like July at home. Well I will close hoping you are all well, &c. Write often and tell me all, in confidence and love. This from your ever true and loving husband. Kiss the children for me.

Henry.

Mc has written a note to you about his pictures. Send them in my letter and send a few of mine. Perhaps you will like to write to him however but it might make talk: you know.

I did not have quite room to write all I wanted to in my other sheet so I will finish out in this one. I have taked [talked] [to] Mc about what you wrote in regard to the album. He sends his respects [and] says he guesses he will have to send you one so you can look for one. He said he would write to a friend of his in Boston and have him send you one. He sends this picture and says you can give it to the one [eligible miss] that wants it most or burn it up. He says tell

---

* Henry's information about the Red River Campaign seems out of date. On May 13, the last federal gunboats were able to move past dams erected on the river and head toward the Mississippi, while Banks's troops marched out of Alexandria toward Simsport. As a whole, the campaign was a failure, but there were moments of triumph.

** Grant had been engaged in the Battle of the Wilderness—a move against Lee's Army of Northern Virginia. The Army of the Potomac crossed the Rapidan the morning of May 4, hoping to cut Lee off from Richmond and perhaps capture his whole army. The battle continued through May 6, with staggering casualties: 17,666 Union killed, wounded, or missing.

Simpson [the photographer] he don't want no more pictures unless they are better than these, says Mc. Says he, they look as though I was drunk. Well says I you was pretty near it. Well he said he did not know whether he was or not.

Well dear one be of good spirits as you can and we will hope for the best. At any rate, hope is the light of life, though we hope some times in vain, but, Eliza I feel that I shall come home again, and have always felt the same. Thus hoping let us still hope and pray God may spare us all to meet again soon safe at home, dear sweet home. Tell Etta and George Father thinks of them every day and wishes he could see you all. Kiss them for Father and tell them to be good little children and please Mother.

This is from your ever true and loving husband.

Henry C. Foster

to E. H. F.

I have received paper [newspapers] twice from you. Did you get a N.O. paper. Mc said he sent you one. Perhaps you had better wait until you hear from me again before you answer this. I shall write again as soon as I find out where we are going.

Henry

Henry continues to wait for his pay:

(No. 5) In Camp near Carrollton La.

May 27th 1864

Dear Eliza:

I will write you a few lines this morning. I am quite well, and I hope you are all enjoying the same blessing. I have not received any letter from you, yet but there is a mail due to day and I hope to get some letters. We have not been paid yet, nor mustered in and I dont know when we shall be. I am afraid you will be short of money, but you must be careful and saving of your money. Mac says you gave him ten dollars that morning he left. I should not [have] thought you would, but if you can get along it will [be] so much less we owe him. I do want to save some thing if we can. We can not enjoy each others compy [company] now except by happy recollections of the past and hoping for the best in future, so we cannot enjoy spending money, except what is actualy necessary but I want you to have enough and if I only get what is due me you will have enough.

Oh how much I do want to see you all, but dear one keep thinking that this war will be over this year. Let it go which way it will. We have no news from Grant since the 18ᵗʰ but we have had rumors through rebel sources that he has captured Richmond with a 100,000 prisoners, but it is not confirmed. I wish it might be.*

There is no chance at all now for us to be Cavalry, for there is no horses and even if there was I dont think we should be. The 2ⁿᵈ Maine Cavalry is here. There is no prospect of any forward movement here this summer, but still there may be. As near as I can find out Gen Banks is removed but things [changes in officers] are kept very still [quiet].

Oh I never was so homesick in my life. It completely upset me to leave home this time, but I will stick it out the best I can. Write often and tell me everything. (How is Jen. J . . k dont hold his head up hardly. We must forget such things now, till we meet again. I hope she is all right. You probably know by this time. I feel somewhat worried about it. Tell me wont you.)**

Has Mother gone home yet. I wrote to Clara yesterday. Well I

* Sheridan destroyed vital supplies near Richmond on May 24, 1864. On May 30, Union forces were within ten miles of Richmond. It is not until eleven months after Henry hears this rumor, that, on the morning of April 3, 1865, Richmond, the Confederate capital, finally surrendered.

** Henry resorts to his private code, wondering if Eliza is pregnant.

will close for this time hoping you are all well, from your husband
in true love, yours ever. Kiss the dear Children for me.

Henry

Husband & Wife Should Never Tire of Loving

Henry's new word is *unsullied:*

> *No 6 Camp near Carrollton [La.] June 3d 1864*
>
> *Dear Eliza.*
>
> *As there is a meail [mail] going to morrow, I thought I could not let the opportunity pass without writing a few lines to you, for my mind is ever with you and the Children. Oh worlds would I give if I had them could I only be with you.*
>
> *I much expected to get a letter last mail. There was quite a large mail come for the Co. Mc got one from Nell [Thompson] as near as I can find out although he will not tell me. Eliza I am almost distracted when I think how long I am liable to be deprived of the comforts of my home, and to think of your loneliness, but Oh dear one be of good cheer, and I will do the best I can. Never forget to be true to yourself and your husband. Remember that we are bound together by the strongest ties that are in the power of God and man to give and never can be broken so long as we both live, though a cruel war has seperated [sic] us for a time as it has many thousands [of] others in this once happy land, and you know as well as I that to [too] many Alas! have given way to weakness and folly and degredation [sic], regardless of the consequencess. Oh it pains me beyond desciption [sic] that I am not and cannot be with you to protect and comfort you, but Eliza dear one, I trust in you. I hope I know you never could deceive the only one that is true to you. I have always had perfect confidence [in] you. Oh keep your character unsullied, above all things, and you and I will be the happier. I*

feel that there is no need of this admonition to you, but when I think of the sinfulness of the people of this world and the misery that follows, dear one I cannot help speaking my mind, to you, and I hope you will forgive me, for so doing, for it is in love and kindness I do so. Husband & Wife should never tire of loving, or rather their whole life should be one continued courtship, is it not so dear [Dear].

Well dear we are not paid yet but we expect to be every day. I dont know why they delay so long. I am afraid you will be short of money. I hope we shall get paid soon.

I don't think there will [be] much fighting in this Dept this summer, and Oh I hope this summer will end it everywhere. Those men that did not re-enlist have come back to the Regt and they don't like it very well. I asked [Charles C.] Horn if he knew Mark B. Horne. He said [he] did, but he was no relation of his. I asked him if he knew his wife. He said no but he had heard of her. Said I some think she is rather fast [promiscuous]. He said he did not doubt it for that used to be her style so I guess you have not judged her for nothing. Oh I am glad to see you shun such company and I hope you will always for the less any one has to do with such characters the better. Oh how can her husband feel but perhaps he is no better than she, but you know the feeling against a [sinful] woman is much more than a man, and I think justly to, for few men will force themselves into a womans company, unless favorably received.

Oh I hope to get a letter soon. Write me a good long letters and keep nothing from yours ever true. My health is very good, and I hope you are all well. Goodbye.

Henry

Kiss the dear children for me.

[He adds to his letter.]

Well Dear.

I will write a little more now. We have just had another inspec-

tion. It seems to be about all they can do in this Regt inspection inspection [sic] every 2 or 3 days. I suppose we are all such a good looking set of fellow that they want to keep looking at us. There is so much humbug in military [life] that I am perfectly sick of it and if I thought I had got to stay this [second enlistment of three years] out, I should be tempted to desert, and I am almost as it is, but I still think I shall get out of it almost as soon as those that did not re-enlist. This war cant last 3 years longer. Next spring must end it I think.

We have continued good news from Virginia. The last news we had, Grant had the rebels to within 10 miles of Richmond, and the news were good from all other quarters, except this. Though not so bad here as represented, though bad enough. I think from all accounts the rebels were whiped [whipped] full as bad as we were, and had it not been for the low water in Red River, all would have been well no doubt, but Gen. Banks made a great blunder as all Officers and soldiers testify, in sending so small a force to the front, without support. It seems he did not know the position of the enemy as well as he ought to, but I dont know the truth. Suffice it to say that the soldiers and most everybody else is very indignant against him. He is still in N.O. notwithstanding all the reports that he has been ordered to Washington, and Gen [Edward R. S.] Canby in Command of the Army in the Field, where our Regt soon expect to be. An order was read to us a week ago to the effect that the 1st Brigade composed of the 16th & 30th Mass. 110th N.Y. & 7th Vt. Vols. would proceed without delay to Morganza Bend [on the Mississippi above Baton Rouge] to report to Brig. Gen. T. W. [sic] Sherman in Command of the 3d Division 19th Army Corps, but we are not gone yet and I suppose we are waiting for our pay and everybody is so slow so much red tape, it is enough to try the patience of Job or any other man.

The place spoken of above is 10 miles above Port Hudson, near *the mouth of Red River. I forgot to tell you about the direction of my letters but all that is neccessary [sic] is to direct to 26ᵗʰ Mass Vet. Vols N.O. La and they will find the Regt from there.*

Mc just give me a box [tin?] of sardines. He is down to the City about half of the time. The boys are all well, & c here we are with plenty of mud. Mc sends his love to Etta & Georgy. Kiss them for me and tell them to remember papa and be good to mama. From your true and loving,

Henry

On the same day as Henry wrote the above, Chancy Lynch writes to Eliza of his concern for Henry's safety. Chancy recently visited Eliza in Lowell:

Castleton [Vt.] June 3 1864

Dear Elisa

. . . . I feell very anxious to hear from Henry for we hear that they are fighting near Richmond and it is expectdded [sic] that they are preparing to take it. People here are very anxiously wating to hear the result. If you have heard anything from Henry do write to me for I want to hear [about him] and I want to hear from you how you get along with your stomach ache and how the Chilldren get along. I suppose you see I left my dirty hanckief [handkerchief]. I had not got 3 rods from the door before I mist [missed] it but I had another in my Satchel. I dont know that I left anything else. Clara was pleased with her bed collar and so was Cara with her neck tie.ˣ I hope you wont worry to [too] much about H but I must say that I feell worse about him than I ever have before since he has ben [been] in the army but I hope and pray for the best and commend him to god who is able and willing to save all that put their trust in him. . . .

* The bed collar and necktie were gifts sent by Eliza—perhaps sewn by her. Clara is Chauncy's wife, Clarinda Foster Lynch. Cara is perhaps the child the couple obtained in a manner that Henry deemed mysterious.

C Lynch

When you write to H tell him to write direct to me [in Vermont].

C

Henry penned his next letter from Morganza in Pointe Coupe Parish on the lower Mississippi. About 3,000 Union soldiers camped there in intense heat during the summer of 1864. The town was surrounded by swamp and cane fields, which Confederate forces used to advantage in 1865. Sweating, marching, cooking, sleeping together, tent mates became close friends. Among Andrew's effects was a photo of his companion in the field, Tom Applebee. Around the edge Andrew wrote, "Tom Applebee who used to sleep with me and Sue Sawyer." (Tents held two; winter huts held four.)

Tom Applebee, friend of Andrew Jackson Bean. Andrew has written around the edge "Tom Applebee who used to sleep with me and Sue Sawyer." Courtesy Bethel Historical Society.

Camp in the Field
Morganza, La. June 19ᵗʰ, 1864 [No. 68]

Dear Wife,

Long have I waited for a letter from home, but Oh! I cannot tell the reason why I do not get one. I thought I would not write again until I got one, but we got our pay yesterday, so I must write and send you the money. We got two installments of bounty on the new enlistment our old hundred dollars, and four months pay up to May 1st, amounting in all, to $2.78 [$278]. I will send you 2.50 [$250]. I paid Mc 15.00, and that wont leave me but 13.00 I want you to put it in the Bank. I think the Rail Road Bank as good as any. You will have four months pay from the State probably as soon as you get this if you have not already, and you must get along with that and your State aid. You may think I am coming down rather hard but if we don't begin to save something we never shall have anything, and if they ask you where my pay is, tell them I sent it to the Bank. Mr. [Micah?] Howard Suke's Husband wants to send his with mine. He sends $2.00 [$200]. He thinks it will go cheaper. I suppose it will cost about $3.00 three dollars to send it. The [there] is an express agent here.* Those notes I send you are interest bearing notes. We can get 5 per cent interest on them, next Aprill, that is $5.00 five dollars on a hundred, if you think it would be safe to keep them, but I think it safer to put it in the Bank, but these times it is not safe to trust anybody.

I should rather let Dana Fox have it, than any one I know of, that is if he would take it. You might ask him and see what he says and if he dont [sic] want it, put it in the Bank.

Oh I hope you are all well to day. What would I not give to see you to day, but we will hope for the best.

I am well. We left Carrollton on the 8th for this place. Arrived here the 9th. This is on the river about 180 miles from N.O. and 20 above P. Hudson.

I have not seen Mr. Stickney, and dont expect to. There is strong talk of our going to Georgia to reenforce Sherman but I don't know how much truth there is in the report.** There is not much signs of any rebels in this vicinity. We have had two reviews since we came

* Henry prefers to entrust his money to an express agent rather than to the Postal Service.

** On June 15, 1864, Sherman's troops under Thomas, McPherson and Schofield were closing in on Confederate positions near Marietta, Georgia.

here. There is about 25,000 or 30,000 troops here. The 15ᵗʰ Army Corps alone under Command of Gen Emery [probably William H. Emory].

It is said there is two large mails down to N.O. for this Regt. but why we do not get it is more than I can imagine. I was in hopes to hear from you before I sent this, but I want to get this money of [off] as soon as possible. Oh it is awful hot here, and plenty of musquetoes. Charly is well and all the rest of the boys, &c.

I will send you 2, 20's and 2, 100's making 2.40. Howard sends 2, 100's. His are dated April and yours March so you will know the difference. I guess you may keep it in the house if you think it will be safe for five per cent is about as good as you can do if you put it in the Bank. Perhaps I will send the other 20, soon if I dont get a chance to speculate with it. I am going to send my dress coat and cavalry jacket if I can. Write as soon as you get this money and tell me what you conclude to do. Dont pay out these notes if you can get along without.

Your dearest, from Henry

A month and a half after leaving Lowell, Henry finally hears from his beloved Eliza.

(This is letter No. 9 to you) [since returning from furlough] [Eliza's No. 69]

Morganza [La.] June 26ᵗʰ 1864

Dear & beloved Wife and Children

I am glad to write you in answer to your letter which I received yesterday, dated the 4 & 7ᵗʰ and it is the only word I have had from you since I left home. I expected to get more than one letter after waiting so long, but it seems by your writing in this one that you have written some previous to this, but you did not say so. This is the ~~eighth~~ ninth letter I have written to you since I left home [May

11]. Please tell me if you have received them all. I wrote one at Readville, one at Groton where we took the steamboat for N.Y. one at N.Y. and one that I wrote on the passage one Sunday after we landed May 22d one May 27th one June 3d and one June 19th that I sent with my money.

This letter I received yesterday leaves me rather in the dark about news. You spoke of going to Boston, and that is all I know about it. When you went or what you went for I dont know. There seems to be a goodeal of irregularity about our mail. Perhaps I shall get your previous letters if you sent any. You said you sent Mc's pictures but he has not received them. I also expected some of mine. Please send some if you have not, for I have promised several. You said you merely wanted to treat him as you would like me to be under the same circumstances.* I suppose you refferred [sic] to Mc. but you mentioned no name.

As to the coat I have tried to send it and the Cavalry jacket. I went to the Provost Marshal's office to get a permit, for the express will not take anything without but his office was closed it being after hours. They were tied up and a news paper put around them. The express said they would not receive a package done up in that. I then asked what the charge would be on those two articles. He said $3.00. I thought [the charge] rather steep, but I shall get a box if I can and try it again. You said that coat would be worth five dollars to make over for F.** I must confess I don't know what you mean. You will have to explain. There is not going to be another in the family I hope. Keep nothing from me dear one. You need not fear Dear Eliza but what I shall try to do the best I can, as I have always endeavored to since you and I were one, and as I have told you before many times, I have the most perfect confidence in you,

---

* Eliza seems to refer here to giving McIver ten dollars—a parting gift which Henry objected to.

** Eliza is probably referring to Frank Wilson. Lightly worn quality fabric was often recycled into other garments rather than consigned to the rag bag.

and what I have written to you, I felt no more than my duty and right. Not however dearest reflecting the least upon your character, and I trust you will above all things sustain your pure character beyond all reflections. I merely spoke of such matters to keep your eyes open to the true state of things. There was so much talked of by all the men, after going home, how this one and that one carried on, it was enough to disgust Satan himself. You undoubtedly know, as well as I do, how such things are. Surely it is a disgrace to humanity, if a woman or a man cant live without giving way to such weakness and dishonor, they ought not to live among decent people, nor no where else on the fact [face] of the earth.

Do not have anything to do with that Irish bitch Woods. I hope they will put her out of the community. John [Woods] is pretty still. He dont have much to say to any body. He has not asked me to write any letters and I hope he wont. He got a letter yesterday but I dont know who it was from nor care. We got about a dozen letters. He got one from L [Lowell] he showed me the hand writing on the envelope, and asked me if I knew it. It was signed Nellie but it sticks him to know which one it is from. He would tell me nothing more. You can get their hand writing if you can and send me each, [if] you can without any suspicions from them. . . .*

Henry

Such a Confusion of Joy and Sorrow

Three letters, Henry's numbers 10, 11 and 13, go missing (he is not aware of this for some time). From the miserably hot, humid West Bank of the Mississippi River, Henry reflects on "wars and rumors of wars," invoking his knowledge of the Old and New Testaments—or perhaps a sermon or religious tract he has encountered—with allusions to Matthew 24 and Isaiah 40–55.

---

* McIver's letter of May 19, 1864, references a Nellie Thompson.

(No. 12) Algiers [La.] July 5ᵗʰ 1864   [Eliza's No. 70]

My Dear Wife:

I wrote a letter to you yesterday, and sent it by Lt. Dick, to the Office last night, but as I received another letter from you to day I thought I would write again in answer, as we have not moved yet, but momentarily expect to, and we dont know what moment we will have to fall in. I am trying to see how well I can write this letter. I know as a general thing I write in to [too] much of a hurry. It is not easy nor natural for me to write any way and I always rattle it of [off] the quickest way I can, and one reason is that makes me write so fast and take so little pains is because my hand trembles so after writing a few moments I cannot carry a steady hand to save my life, but I will try to improve some if I can.

I also received a letter from Chancy['s] folks. They were all well. Mother had [come] home to Uncle Oliver's but they had not seen her. I answered their letter and wrote to Mother also, and I have been looking for a letter from Mabelia but I dont know as she will write until I do although I dont know why she should wait.

I received your good letter to day of June 15ᵗʰ. You said you hoped you shold [should] get another letter to morrow when you closed this, but I did not write again until I sent my money, on the 19ᵗʰ. I [was] feeling pretty bad all that time as you can well guess, for up to that time I had not received a word from you [since May 11], and I knew not what to think, but I hope our letters will go more regular in future.

I hope you have got our money safe by this time. I shall write as often as I can. It may be some time before I can write again but I hope you will not worry. I thought at first I would not say anything about moving for fear you would worry about it but I [knew] there was plenty that would write all they knew and more to [too], so I thought I wuld [sic] tell you all I knew about it as I know you['d] rather know it. Yes Eliza Etta is a darling child and I should be glad to please our Children as much as any one but you know our means do not admit of it so much as many other people. I want them to have enough to make them comfortable and you to[o], but we must buy that that will be of the most benefit. Mc says he wants to send some pitcutres back so I suppose he will send them in this letter. I suppose he will send one to Nelie but which one. Perhaps he will send one to Delia [Merill?]. I think she is a curious woman. . don't you. I will just hint to Mc about the album. I think as you do many times about war, but you know law and order must be sustained and the government upheld. Authority must be submit[t]ed to by any people and war is carrying out authority on a large scale. This is all the way I can look at it and it seems right in that view. There always have been wars and rumors of wars and I suppose there always will be, says the Bible. The nature of humanity is naturally rebellious, and rebellion must be punished. It seems so ordained from a higher power than any human being can control, but I much wish it were otherwise, but it does seem as though this people have sacrificed enough and I pray the conflict may soon cease, and I do hope and pray I may be spared to my dear family. I know I talked some foolish things when at home and done many foolish things, that I have felt sorry for, but I was like a bird out of a cage. I felt such a confusion of joy and sorrow that I was not myself hardly, joy at getting home once more safe to my family and sorrow that I had so soon to go away again but I feel and trust that you will always remain firm and true to Henry as you may be assured he will to his highest and best gift of earth a true and loving wife   one whom he can always confide in. Well this is about full and I will stop to eat supper.

[no signature]

Now that the Union had the Western Theater firmly in its control, some forces were reassigned to the Eastern canvas of the war. In his book *Decision in the Heartland: The Civil War in the West*, Steven Woodworth argues that the war was won and lost in the West, that Union victories on that front deprived the Confederacy of resources, goods, and production centers and influenced the 1864 presidential election. Meanwhile, the East was bogged down in a bloody stalemate. As Rebel morale flagged, Union forces again concentrated in Virginia—Henry among them.

Headed for City Point (modern Hopewell), Henry wrote his next letter in such haste that he forgot to include a forwarding address. From June 1864 to April 1865, Gen. Ulysses S. Grant directed the Siege of Petersburg from the grounds of Appomattox Plantation at City Point, site of Fort Monroe and an important tobacco shipping port only eight miles northeast of his target. Grant stayed in a cabin on the grounds, where his wife and son joined him for the last three months of the grim, ten-month siege. The longest siege on American soil, the maneuver was an integral part of the campaign that led to Lee's surrender.

During Grant's occupation, City Point became a bustling Union supply depot. Warehouses bulged with food for 100,000 men as well as forage for 65,000 horses and mules. President Lincoln spent two of the last three weeks of his life there overseeing the final push to Petersburg and Richmond. Union forces continued to occupy the town after Lee's surrender at Appomattox Court House, remaining there through November 1867.

(No 14) On board transport steamer George Thomas July 19th, 1864 [No. 72]

Dear Wife:

I will improve a few moments in writing to you but I dont [know] as I can send it. Our Regt is here on board this steamer lying of [off] Fort. Monroe. We left N. Orleans one week ago yesterday, and arrived here this morning, and are ordered to City Point on the

James river. We shall leave here at 6 this eve. I cannot write but a few words. I hope this may find you all well. I am as well as can be expected after a long voyage huddled up top of one another on this small steamer. We had to bury two men at sea.

Send me 5.00 dollars if convenient and I will send you this 20.00 dollar bill as I have not used you [not used you well?] but it is all I have got. Write soon as you get [this]. Tell me if you have got your money.

Good bye.

Henry C. Foster

The majority of the Civil War's battles were fought on the soil of Virginia, where commanders learned that terrain was as crucial as tactics. Warren Lee Goss, a private in the Army of the Potomac, explains the lay of the land:

> The poverty of Virginia . . . was one of its strong defensive features. An army moving through its labyrinth of tangled woods must be fed, and its trains of supply protected. Its superior artillery could not be brought into the 'continuous hammering' in this wood-entangled region.
>
> On the other hand, the Confederates were familiar with all its by-paths, its intricate and confusing mazes. Its inhabitants were their spies and scouts.
>
> To the Union army it was like a voyage of discovery made in unknown lands, among warlike enemies lying in ambush."[396]

In 1611, the Bermuda Hundred settlement was established and named on the peninsula at the confluence of the Appomattox and the James. The following year, John Rolfe cultivated tobacco there.[397] Whatever crop grew there two hundred years later quickly vanished underfoot in early May 1864, as troops, horses, artillery, and stores were landed there for the use of Maj. Gen. Butler. The Army of the James, a force of more than 30,000 soldiers commanded by Butler, began the Bermuda Hundred Campaign on May 5.

The battle that determined the outcome of the campaign for Petersburg did not take place until April 2, 1865. Known as the Breakthrough, it pitted more than 14,000 Union troops against a section of Confederate fortifications on the Banks, Boisseau, and Hart farms—fortifications partially built by slaves.

(No. 15) In Camp on James River

Bermuda Hundreds [sic], Va.   [No. 73]

July 20th 1864

Dear & Beloved Wife & Children:

It is with feelings of gratitude to an ever kind and over ruling providence that I am spared to commune a few words to you after a very tedious voyage of 9 days from N. O. [New Orleans] to this place, and I am glad I am as well as I am, though I feel just about played out [exhausted], for the last two or three days & nights it has ben [been] more or less rainy, so as I had the good fortune to have an outside passage on deck, I could not sleep much nor rest either, but I consider myself better of [off] than those below after all for more were taken sick below than those that took passage on deck. The Regt left 20 men at Fort Monroe that were taken sick on the passage and two were buried at sea, William Warner of Co. D., & [James H.] Barton of Co. H.

I wrote or rather scribled [sic] you a few lines yesterday while we were laying at Fort Monroe, but I was in such a hurry that I dont know hardly what I wrote. I forgot to tell you how to direct your letters. You can direct to Fort Monroe Co A, 26th Regt Vt. Vols 19th Army Corps, so I hope you may get this before you send any money so there will be no mistake.

I suppose there is two mails lost that were sent to N.O. The Locust Point was sunk, and we herd [sic] yesterday that the Electric Spark was captured last Sunday of [off] Charleston by the Florida a rebel pirate, but I hardly credit the report.*

Well dear Eliza her [here] we are on Virginia soil at last. We are in hearing of the heavy guns at Petersburg, this about 70 [?] miles from Fort Monroe. We arived [sic] here about 11 oclock to day and come imediately [sic] ashore and pitched our camp a few rods from the river. James river is very wide. Much wider than the Miss and about as crooked. We shall probably stop here until the rest of our troops arrive from N.O. and how much longer or shorter I cannot say. I suppose there is some fighting for the 26th yet, but I will borough [borrow] no trouble. There will be time enough when it comes and I must say I am not very anxious to see it but I must make the best of it.

I want to hear from you very much and it seems as though I had got almost home now. Letters will go so much quicker. I hope I shall hear from you often. I wrote you the day we left N.O. It will be probably be some time before I get those letters that have gone to N.O. if I get them at all.

I would send you this 20.00 dollar[s] now but I dont want to be left entirely without money.

I hope this will find you all well. My health is very good after I get a little rest and sleep. Charly [Richardson] is well also and Mc. [John McIver] and so are all the boys in Co A. How good it will seem to get a letter in 2 or 3 days after it is written. It seems as though I could almost talk to you. Oh how I wish I could. Well dear one I will close for this time for I dont feel much like writing though I have not told you half I wish I could. I remain your ever true and loving husband.

Henry C. Foster

---

* There was a pirate indeed—and a busy one. The privateer *Florida* managed to burn five ships in the space of a few days, according to an article in the *New York Times*, July 13, 1864, p. 8.

To E. H. F.

P.S. Remember me to all enquiring friends and especialy [sic] to Etta & George. Kiss them for Father and tell them to remember me. Please send me some papers [newspapers] for I dont know as I can get any here.

Send a few stamps also

Bringing the Country to Ruin

Except for his bout of blues aboard the *Cahawba,* his initial misgivings about McIver and Eliza's relationship, and his mention of feeling "despondent" on July 11, Henry's spirit remained upbeat in the course of his re-enlistment. But in the following letter he admitted to being "sick of soldiering" and "getting quite indifferent." Some of his melancholy might have derived from the fact that Andrew was now home safe and sound, service completed.

(No 16) Tannally Town, Maryland⁎   [Eliza's No. 74]

Bivouaced [sic] in the woods

August 3d [1864]

Dear Wife:

I have just received two letters from you, making 5 only that I have received since I left home. How many you have written I dont know, but it seems rather strange. I am quite well, though very fatigued as we have had several marches and one skirmish, and las [last] Sunday morning we started at 1 oclock, and marched 8 miles and embarked on board of a transport for Washington. When we arrived on the 2d [2nd] after being pilled [piled] [on] top of one another where there was not room enough to sit down, then we marched through Washington & Georgetown to this place some

* Camp Tannally was named for a section of Georgetown.

8 or 9 miles. *We expected to march again last [night] after raiders and had orders to turn our knapsacks in and be ready at any time but for some reason it was defered [sic] and we were allowed a night's rest and we are still here, and this is all I can say about our movements.*

I am getting more and more sick of soldiering every day, and about all it amounts to is killing of men and bringing the country to ruin. We have not only got all the South against us but a good portion of the North who are bound Old Abe shall not win, and I am to [too] much afraid they will succeed. Well I am getting quite indifferent now so we must abide the result. We have turned in our knapsacks and are left with nothing but a rubber blanket and shelter tent. I received the ten dollars you sent me, but as there is no prospect of getting paid ever again I shall not send this [$20] now. I came the nearest being used up yesterday that I ever was marching, it was so hot, but I expect we have got a goodeal march to do yere [yet? here?]!

Well I will close for this time. Tell brother [brother-in-law] A I congratulate him and am glad for him that he has got home safe, and I wish I had been as wise as he was not to re-enlist but perhaps it is all for the best. Let us hope so at least.·

Give my kindest regards to Mother and all relatives & friends

Kiss the dear Children for me, and tell them to remember father. I trust you may enjoy your visit [to Maine] much and have a safe return &c. I hope you will write me a long letter and give me all the news and be true to your ever true and loving husband.

H. C. Foster

Direct the same as before.

---

* Here about an inch and a half has been torn from the bottom of the page. Perhaps Eliza wanted to show the letter to someone else—and the sexual code was a bit transparent.

(No. 17) Tannallytown   MD.   August 6, 1864

(This is the P Brigade 2d Division 15ᵗʰ Army Corps)

[No. 75]

Dearly loved Ones:

I again will commune a few words with you through the only channel [left open?] to me but I am thankful of the privilege to thus address you. I hope you will improve [take advantage of] every opportunity to write to me for you must know that I look with much anxiety for letters. It seems quite hard and very strange that I have received no more letters but I wait with as much patience as I can. I have not received any stamps if you have sent any. We got the mail from N.O. yesterday but I got no letters. I received brother A's letter yesterday dated July 17ᵗʰ and where it has been all this time is more than I can tell. Tell brother [Andrew] I was very glad to get his good letter and am glad my family has gone to visit you [him], and trust you may all enjoy yourselves much. How I wish I were with you all to day, but that cannot be, so you must substitute the wish for my presence. Tell brother A I trust this letter may answer for all of you for I [am] rather short of material, for I had to leave most all my paper in my knapsack but dear Brother do not forget to write often, and I will try to return the compliment.

Well dearest, I will tell you about the money. The bill you sent I could not pass so I got the $20.00 bill broke this morning so I will send you back the Lowell bill and ten of the other, and I hope you will get it safe. I dont know why you should not get your money from the Treasury. I hope you will get it soon. You did not tell me how big the bill was you let [unclear; Puffer?] have.* I hope I shall get that good lone [long] letter you spoke of, soon. Write as soon as you get this. I went to the surgeon's call this morning. The first time

---

* James F. Puffer was a dealer in furniture, carpets, feathers, mattresses, stoves, crockery, and house furnishings located at 9, 11, and 13 Market Street, Lowell.

for most ten years.* I have not felt well since I was on the boat from N.O. and they tell me I am looking poor, and I dont much wonder for I guess they mean to starve us to death. I have some diarhea but I guess I shall soon be better. I hope we shallnot [sic] have to march far until I feel better for I dont feel very stout [strong in body] but if they will keep us of from Transports I shall be thankful. I have had about enough of sea voyages of late. Deliver me from being packed like stowing away bricks. I have not left camp since I have been [unclear; here?].

Mr. Goodwin of the old 6th was in here. It seems Hussy did not go this time.** Couldn't Syl [Husey's wife] drive him of. Well I don't blame him but he must look out for the draft. The 6th is camped about 3 miles from here on Arlington heights. Charly is going over there to day & Howard. Mc has given us the slip.*** I guess he has not been seen since we marched through Washington. I have been almost tempted to start for home myself and I would if it were not for the name of the thing [i.e., desertion]. I believe a man is thought more of now a day for deserting, but you need not be surprised if you dont see Henry at home until he can come and hold his head up, I trust with honor.

This sheet is full and I must close, asking Gods [sic] blessing to rest upon us all through all these trying times of strife & contention, among a distracted [confused] people.

From your ever true & loving husband

H. C. Foster

* Henry has forgotten that he was excused for duty because of possible mumps on April 5, 1863. He mentions in his letter of that date that this was "the second time that I have been excused by the Dr. since I enlisted."

** From the context, it seems that Mr. Hussey did not return to his company after his furlough.

*** John McIver has gone AWOL.

Henry continued to be unwell and to lack sufficient food.* These circumstances did not bode well for his survival when he was wounded. For
Eliza's sake, he tries to put the best face on his condition. When he wrote
on August 25, the rations seem to have improved. When he wrote on
August 30—after partaking of plenty of fresh food— his mood had bright-
ened; perhaps his illness was scurvy, a condition ameliorated by fruits and
vegetables.

> *(No 18) Tannallytown within the defences of Washington D.C.*
> *[No. 76]*
>
> *Aug 18th 1864*
>
> *My dear Wife,*
>
> *I will write you a few lines in answer to your letter which I
> received two day[s] since but was unable to answer it sooner as I
> was on duty all day yesterday. I hope this will find you all well. I
> am pretty well though somewhat run down. I have not been so poor
> since I was sick 3 years ago. Our rations have been very bad and
> I have not had much appetite, though I have been on duty all the
> time. I am feeling first rate now since I have had a chance to buy
> something to fill up with but it takes a fortune to buy any thing of
> [off] pedlers [sic]. They are dearer here than in N.O. I could spend
> a dollar a day here and eat every cents worth of it and then be
> hungry.*
>
> *I see no sign of leaving here at present. We have been regulating
> our camp to day and got our Brigade properly formed for the first
> time, under Brig Gen. [H. W.] Birge. The following are the Regts [:]
> 9th Conn 14th N.H. 26th Mass 12 & 14th Maine & 75th N.Y.*

---

* Edward Davis, serving in the same division as Henry during Third Winchester,
writes about the lack of food several times. On Sept. 27, for instance, "The boys are
out of hard bread and if it were not for the apples corn beans &c that they go out and
get we would go hungry." On Sept. 30, he writes, "We stayed here [near Stanton]
for several days not much going on scarce of rations a good share of the times."

Gen. Grover commands the Div.* The rest of the 19th Corps are down in the vicinity of Harpers Ferry somewhere. I dont know exactly where. Our Regt had a 5 miles tramp yesterday to Fort Slocum and back.** Thats [sic] where the late fight was in July when the rebs took Washington!! We went to cut down brush in front of the fort. It was a very warm day and I was pretty well used up but I feel all right to day. No tidings have been herd [sic] from Mc yet. I have got 7 letters that belong to him. Among them I think I recognize your hand writing.

The boys are all pretty well in Co A. You said you thought you should not stop long down to A's [Andrew's].*** You keep worrying about things at home. Well it is perfectly natural, but I should like to have you visit as long as [you] want to and the folks in Vt [the Lynch family] would be very glad to have you come and stay a good long while with them. Cant you & Mabelia start up an excursion and go. I wrote to M but have got no answer yet. Tell me if you get all my letters. One of those No 11 I am not much surprised that you did not get it for I sent it to the [Post] Office by Dick, the day we arrived at Agiers [Algiers] from Morgan City. It was the answer to your first letter with the Photografs [sic] which were detained for postage. They would not recognize those [stamps?] on the back. I hope you may get it yet. No 10 was written June 29th and had two Photograps in it. I dont reccollect [sic] whether I put a stamp on it or not, but think I did. It may be detained for postage.

I told you in that letter that I had sold my Cavalry jacket for $3.00. My dress coat I packed with Charly's and his brother's in a box to send home when we were at Bermuda Hundreds [Hundred], but we had marching orders in a few minutes after, and the box

* Probably Gen. Cuvier Grover.

** Fort Slocum is today located within Rock Creek Park, in the District of Columbia. It was built by troopers from Rhode Island.

*** Eliza seems to be in Maine, visiting her brother Andrew. "Down Maine" is a New England idiom.

with its contents went with the rest of the extra baggage to Norfolk to be stored. Whether I shall ever see it again or not I dont know, but I got rid of lugging it or throwing it on to [the] ground which was the most likely.

As near as I can judge there must be 7 or 8 letter[s] of yours that I have not received. I got 3 in La. The first one was May 30ᵗʰ and the [second] one with the pictures and the 3d June 17ᵗʰ, then the next one I got at this place was No 11. Well this sheet is about full and I must close. Remember me to Mother & A. and all the friends. Kiss dear little Etta & George for me, and imagine as many as you can for yourself & accept this with a husband's true love.

H. C. Foster

I Am Bound to Make the Best I Can of It

The following letter reveals a deeply despondent Henry who has lost faith in President Lincoln and the strength of the Union. On the day Henry penned this letter, Gen. Jubal Early had cornered Sheridan on the Potomac and was able to resume roaming in West Virginia, threatening new incursions into Maryland and Pennsylvania. At sea, the Union also experienced defeats; Confederates had captured thirty-one Union vessels in the past three weeks.

(No 19) Camp behind breastworks [low defensive walls]
[No. 77]

Halltown Va.

Aug 25ᵗʰ 1864

Dear Wife: Eliza

I will write in answer to your good and thrice welcome letter. I received last eve No 19, of which I have received only 8. You mention nothing about receiving my letters, although you said you had received mine of the 6ᵗʰ but said nothing about the money 15.00 I sent in that letter, but I suppose of course if you got the letter you got the money to [too].

Our Div. started from Washington on the 14*th* for the Shenandoah valley and marched every day until the 18th, stoped [sic] 10 miles from Harpers Ferry. We marched nearly west from Washington across the Chain Bridge through Leesburg & Snickes gap. Our Corps has seen no engagement yet, though some portion of Sheridans Army is skirmishing every day and some of them [the skirmishes] amount to battles. I am expecting every day there will be some warm work here. It is said that one half of Lee's Army is in our front. We have got a very strong position here on the heights west of Harpers Ferry & pretty well fortified. I think there is no danger of the rebels attacking us here. They know the place to [too] well, but still I know but little what may take place at any hour.

I am bound to make the best I can of it, but I wish there was something done to stop this war. If the people of the U.S. are getting tired of it the soldiers are no less so and the sooner it is stoped the better for the longer it lasts now the worse it is for both sections of the Country, and the South is gaining strength every day, and more united or else I cannot see things in their true light, but so it seems to me, and I cannot help it although I am sorry to say it. However it has been brought about whether it is the fault of the administration or whether it was inevitable I am not responsible [i.e., qualified] to say, but such nevertheless appear to be facts and facts cannot be denied. I have little hopes of the Union now. One thing I am quite convinced it cannot be saved by fighting, but Oh I hope and pray that a change may be brought about by the ballot box this fall to stop this war for we have had enough of it, and who can tell where it will end if it goes on as it is going. As long as there was a chance I had hopes but the summer campaign has failed as all others have although it is not ended yet.

I fear there is little chance of success. How the draft will succeed *remains to be seen.* If that succeeds well and the men are brought promptly forward [i.e., trained and sent to the front] all may be well yet.

Well Eliza about the farm. Do you think you could be contented to live on it. If you could I think it the best thing for us, and the best way money can be laid out, at the present time. If it suits you, and you can buy it on reasonable terms, you have my consent to do so, for there is no knowing what the money will be worth in 6 months or a year from now and you can probably live much cheaper, than you can in Lowell & why not move this fall as soon as you can conveniently. I will say no more about it this time, but I hope this will be satisfactory to you. I expect to get paid again soon. My health is first rate and now [and] I can eat all I can get hold of. I have left of using tobacco.

Hoping this will find you all well. I will close with love to all, and may God bless you all.

Your ever true & loving husband

H.C.F.

The following letter is written on the stationery of the U. S. Christian Commission. Materials for correspondence were high on the Commission's list of things troops wanted.

Henry has not been receiving letters from his extended family. Nevertheless, he seems to have recovered some of his optimism about the future.

Charlestown Va.

August 30th 1864

Dear Eliza,

---

* On February 1, 1864, when the turmoil that followed the Enrollment Act of the previous year had somewhat subsided, President Lincoln called for 500,000 additional draftees for the Union.

This is the first chance I have had to answer your letter which I received last Saturday as we have been on the move ever since and we are only hanging on here, occupying the old breat [breast] works, which our Army fell back from a week ago. The enemy has now fell back probably on their way to Richmond, but I think it is not exactly certain where they are just now. Our Cavalry was skirmishing with a force of them yesterday in our front probably their rear guard. We shall soon be out of this [spot] I am thinking, but whither I know not.

I was very glad to get your good letter and I hope you will write often. I have not heard from any of my folks since I left La. I have written to Mabelia & Chancy's folks but have got no answer.

I suppose dear Eliza if you make up your mind to move down on to your farm you can draw your State [actually City of Lowell] Aid just the same or leave it with some one to draw for you, and send to you. Others have done so. I assure you I am very favorable to the plan of buying the place, and I want you to do the best you can. I know you can get along with a goodeal less in such a place than the city.

I am in hopes to be at home with you by next spring, but I may have to serve my 3 years out should I live but we will hope for the better, and I do pray this cruel war may soon be over. The next 6 or 7 months seems to me will be the greatest for great events for this country, of anything wittnessed [sic] yet. God grant the people may be wise and candid, and may he help them to do what is [best] for the greatest good of our country and its people.

I hope this may find you all well, as it leaves me. My health is good now and I am hungry as a bear, since I left of [off] using tobacco but I manage to get enough to fill up with of some kind[;] it is not the best. We get plenty of green corn and apples, and some fresh meat. I have eaten so much corn sometimes that I was almost fritened [frightened], for fear it would hurt me but it has not and I am fatting up. Charley & I swore of [off] using tobacco together but he could not stand it and has gone to chewing again but I am going to stick to it [my resolution].

I feel very bad for A. but it seems to me he is foolish to have any thing to do with that bedlam.* I would trust the child [Andrew's first wife? Andrew's surviving daughter?] to Gods mercy and put so much distance between her & me that she would not trouble me, or I her, but one cannot always tell what we will do.

Well dear write soon. Give my respects to all, from

Henry ever truly yours

This was the final letter from Henry. Having endured three years of marches, war rations, and worry for his family back home, Henry had escaped injury on the battlefield. But as the Union's fortunes soon took a turn for the better, Henry's own luck would run out in September, in the trenches of a key victory for the Union.

The March to the Sea

Although a candidate for reelection, Lincoln undertook no personal campaigning during 1864. In a draft memo written in September—a memo he never issued—he wrote, "Much is being said about peace, and no man desires peace more ardently than I. Still I am yet unprepared to give up the Union for peace which, so achieved, could not be of much duration."[398]

Throughout the fall of 1864, Lincoln's generals began to turn the tide. Sheridan, acting cautiously at first during the runup to the November 1864 presidential election, would eventually lead the Army of the Shenandoah to victory in Virginia. Sherman, after taking Atlanta on September 1 and

---

* The use of the word "bedlam" here suggests that Henry is commenting on Andrew's decision to commit his first wife to a sanitarium. Henry agrees with Andrew's plans.

remaining in the captured city through mid-November, would begin his infamous March to the Sea with nearly 50,000 men, wreaking near-total destruction across Georgia and capturing the port of Savannah as a "Christmas gift" to the president on December 21. Grant hoped to "eat out Virginia clear and clean"—to deprive the Confederacy of its breadbasket. By early October, Sheridan would devastate the fertile farms of the Shenandoah Valley, destroying more than 2,000 barns filled with wheat, hay and farm equipment, as well as 70 mills, driving off more than 4,000 head of stock, and killing or issuing to his men for food at least 3,000 sheep. Third Winchester, on September, 19 was part of Early's attempt to stop Sheridan's raiding.[399]

The Battle of Third Winchester

At Third Winchester, Henry's regiment was assigned to the 2nd Brigade, commanded by Gen. Henry Warner Birge, 2nd Division (Grover), 19th Corps. The troops had been camped near Berryville, and were roused about 2:00 a.m. to march the five miles to Winchester. Joshua L. Chamberlain describes a typical early morning march: "They are there—the men: shivering to their senses as if risen out of the earth, but something in them not of it. Now sounds the 'Forward'. . . . And they move—these men—sleepless, supperless, breakfastless, sore-footed, stiff-joined, sense-benumbed, but with flushed faces pressing for the front."[400]

Edward Heavey Davis of the 24th Iowa also marched with the 2nd Division. In his diary Davis recalls September 19:

> [We] halted at day break until the 6th corps passed while waiting here we could hear canonading at Opequan Creek some 2 mis. [sic] in the advance . . . took our position on the right of the 6th corps now—our infantry faced Earleys army fighting commended with us about noon advanced once more and were repulsed the whole line fell back a short distance then rallied and again advanced. And finally drove the enemy from the field. Our cavalry (with Crooks Command) came in on the

right and flanked the enemys left put them in confusion such a route [rout] was never known at Winchester[.] Early lost a [*sic*] least 7000 in all 5000 reported killed on both sides[.] the battle was a hard fought battle[.] when we fell back we suffered most Stoner Ira Miller Wood and John Johnson wounded all luck to us none killed we continue [continued] 1 ½ mile beyond Winchester when we went into camp tired and hungry having eaten nothing since morning and no water to be had.[401]

Another witness to this day was Henry Estabrooks of the 26th Massachusetts. Estabrooks, a native of Dorchester, was captured during the battle. As introduction to his tale of escaping from the Confederates and traveling overland for more than a month seeking Union forces, Estabrooks tells much the same story as Davis: "A little after sunrise [on September 19] we were again in motion, and pressing on at the double-quick towards Winchester. . . . At last we reached a muddy stream running over rocks and sand. It was the Opequan Creek; and there we saw our first wounded man, lying near the smoking ruins of a flouring-mill, which a body of our cavalry had destroyed the night before."[402]

On the far side of the creek, Estabrooks and his comrades passed wagons, ambulances, captured Rebels, and then took a field-hospital "with detached legs, arms, hands, feet, and every form of mangled humanity, scattered about on the green grass around it."[403] He continued on and managed to slip through a shallow ravine just before Rebel batteries begin to rake it. Looking back, he writes, "I saw our poor fellows dropping every here and there."[404]

The 26th Massachusetts dodged bullets under the autumn leaves of First Woods during the morning's combat.[405] The bullet that struck Henry's knee on September 19 missed a major blood vessel. Had an artery been severed, he would have bled to death in three to five minutes. He escaped that fate but was robbed while he waited for help. It took some time for him to be found and rescued; subsequently, his leg was amputated—the common medical approach to the quandary of badly mangled limbs. Instruments

Winchester graveyard, with marker commemorating the three battles of Winchester.
Photo by Fernand L. Chandonnet.

were not sterilized, and blood poisoning, tetanus, and gangrene frequently attacked stricken soldiers.[406] Henry Foster died on September 21, two days after being injured.

Writing on September 27, Edward Heavey Davis supplies a rare account of those wounded at Winchester: "[S]ome of the boys come up . . . Tinker from Winchester he reports the wounded getting along well and in good spirits says they are sending them to Baltimore and from there to their own states."[407] But the casualty numbers paint a grimmer picture: there were so many wounded at Third Winchester that on September 22, Sheridan's medical doctor, James Ghiselin, ordered the construction of the largest temporary field hospital of the war. Located on Opequon Avenue, it was called Sheridan's Field Hospital or Shawnee Springs Hospital. Warmed like a Roman bath with an unusual system of underground hot air, the hospital contained 4,000 beds. After Surgeon James Blaney assumed command on September 28, 4,000 casualties were quickly treated and released to make room for more. Of course, the hospital sprang into existence too late to help Henry.

At Third Winchester, 39,240 Union forces confronted 15,200 Confederates. Total casualties for three days of running conflict numbered 9,000 for both sides, with about 5,020 of those on the Union side.

During the war, the Union Army recorded almost 175,000 gunshot wounds to extremities, leading to 30,000 amputations. Three-quarters of the patients survived.[408] Location of the wound was a good indication of chance of survival; knee amputations carried a 58 percent fatality rate.

Henry was not there to join his comrades in huzzahs marking the turning of the tide. Nevertheless, with Sheridan's rout of Early's Confederates in the Battle of Cedar Creek on October 19, prospects for Lincoln's reelection improved. Victory was in the wind.

Chatting around campfires during these winter months, some Massachusetts men felt reinvigorated. Sergeant Walter Carter of the 22nd Massachusetts declared: "I would rather be as poor as Lazarus was, and die as he did, than have remained at home during these historical times. I glory in the word soldier, as applicable to myself even, and I'll never regret my army life."[409]

Although Lee surrendered to Grant at Appomattox Court House, Virginia on April 9, 1865, it was not until May 26, 1865, that Gen. Kirby Smith surrendered all Confederate territory west of the Mississippi to Gen. Edward R. S. Canby, ending organized resistance in the Western Theater.

The Weary Are at Rest

Henry's comrade in arms Charles Richardson, "Charly" in Henry's letters, assumed the responsibility of writing to Eliza concerning her husband's death. He and Henry, knowing that their families might not otherwise receive informed words about their ends, probably made an informal pact to notify each other's relatives should circumstances warrant it.[410]

Recuperating in the army hospital from his own injury, Richardson has time to choose his words diplomatically. Richardson's carefully crafted phrases let Eliza know that Henry was not shot in the back—indicating that Henry had fought honorably.

Richardson naturally wrote first to his own mother about the death at Third Winchester of his only brother, Luther. Then, with great delicacy, invoking scripture from Job 3:17, Richardson gently assures Eliza that Henry had a proper burial. As he writes, he believes that Lt. Dickerman has already written, enclosing a lock of hair. But perhaps before Richardson sealed this letter, he touched base with Dickerman and found out otherwise—as a lock wrapped in brown paper is enclosed with Richardson's letter.

> *McClellan U.S.A. Hospital*
>
> *Near Philadelphia Pa.*
>
> *October 7th 1864*
>
> *My dear Friend*
>
> *You will undouptedly [sic] think that I have been very negligent in not writing to you before but I assure you that my seeming neglect was not because I have not thought of you in your affliction and thought of you a great deal, but I could not bear to be the first to break to you the sad tidings of your dear husbands [sic] fate, which though glorious and Heroic is none the less hard to bear.*
>
> *He received his death blow in a good cause and like a true Soldier and a hero upon the battle field with his face to our countrys [sic] foes.*
>
> *Let us hope that his spirit freed from its earthly tenement will find that peace and rest in the Mansions above which was denied him here below. There "the wicked cease from troubling and the weary are at rest."*
>
> *Although he had as yet ascended but the first steps in the ladder*

*of fame he always thought that his position was an honorable one and he never by any wilfull act dishonored the uniform he wore.**

He was always prompt and strict in the discharge of his duty and was one in whom his superior officers reposed the utmost trust and confidence.

*His remains enclosed in a warriors shroud are interred in the Winchester Cemetery.*** He was badly wounded in the left leg and when our forces were repulsed after the first charge he with all the rest of our wounded was left in the hands of the enemy, —they took his watch and everything else that he had in his pockets. I searched our Hospitals over and over again, but could get no trace of him until after I went to Winchester when he was brought in from the 8ᵗʰ Corps Hospital where he had been carried through mistake. When at last I found him life was extinct.**** I cut a lock of his hair which I gave to Lieut Dickerman to send to you. I should have sent it to you imediatly [sic] but I knew that you had been away from Lowell and I did not know as you had returned.*

I cannot write half that I feel upon this subject which is painful to both you and Me and as it is getting late I will close. I shall be at home about the 15ᵗʰ of this month when of course I shall see you and will give you the ful [sic] particulars as far as I know.

Rest assured my dear Madam that you have my most heartfelt sympathy in this your great affliction—and if you ever stand in need of a friend I shall feel myself injured if you do not at once call upon me.

* The use of "willful" here suggests that Charles Richardson knew of Henry's two days spent under arrest, and that, whatever Henry's offense, it was not intentional.

** Coffins were unavailable for most Civil War dead; Richardson puts this as gently as possible.

*** In other words, Richardson has no last words to pass on to Eliza. Final words—especially those expressing devotion to God—were considered of great importance to convey to the bereaved.

Accept my most sincere wishes for the welfare of yourself and children.

I will close by signing myself with the greatest respect

Your Friend

Charles Henry Richardson

Eliza's overwhelming grief would have been tempered by the fact that Henry died for a cause greater than himself. Her grief may also have been assuaged by the fact that the victory at Winchester was greeted with jubilation throughout the North. Referring to the battle and its impact on the November elections, James Garfield used a rhetorical metaphor: "Phil Sheridan has made a speech in the Shenandoah Valley more powerful and valuable to the Union cause than all the stumpers of the Republic can make."[411]

Not until well into the twentieth century—during the Korean conflict—did the American military routinely ship bodies home for burial.[412] But Eliza was determined to bring Henry's remains to Lowell. On October 3, fueled by nervous energy or naiveté or a potent mixture of the two, she pinned on her dignified veil and ventured to the office of Hocum Hosford, mayor of Lowell from 1862 to 1864, to ask if he would use his influence to help retrieve Henry's body from Virginia.* From the context, it seems that there were two dozen other remains that could be brought home to Lowell or Massachusetts as well. This fact would have added weight to her personal request. Eliza may also have consulted a state agent, a representative who delivered messages and packages to picket lines, advocated for leave, assisted hometown visitors, and helped arrange transportation home for bodies.[413]

---

* Eliza probably buttonholed the mayor at what is called today the Old City Hall (1830), designed by Kirk Boott. It housed commercial establishments on the ground floor and city offices on the second. It stands at the corner of Shattuck and Merrimack Streets, across from St. Anne's Church. Just around the corner on Shattuck is the Lowell Institution for Savings (1829) where many early mill girls maintained accounts.

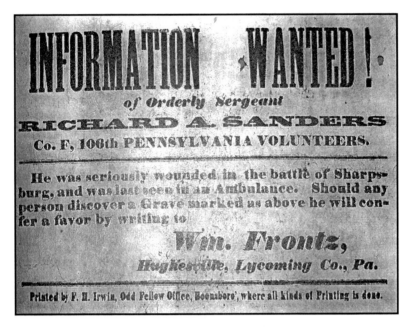

Public advertisement seeking information about grave of orderly sergeant missing at Sharpsburg illustrates the difficulty of obtaining details about missing, wounded, or dead soldiers. Courtesy Winchester Courthouse Museum.

The phrase "all of the 26" may be the clue to the method by which Eliza brought Henry home. The state agent, working in concert with Hosford, may have had the power and funds to disinter all twenty-six bodies and transfer them north.

For a widow to do it herself was very difficult, fraught with expenses and red tape. Pennsylvania began a program in the fall of 1865 to reimburse one family member to travel south to retrieve the body of a relative. Not all states followed suit. Getting railroad vouchers and passes was time-consuming, and travel vouchers were not always granted. Women with empty purses could not pay for bodies to be dug up or for coffins. Women with young children found it hard to travel at all.[414]

Because of the press of casualties at Third Winchester, it can safely be assumed that few of the bodies were embalmed. Airtight coffins were especially costly. Railroad officials were naturally reluctant to transport unembalmed bodies, and government transports did not allow them. Furthermore, many of the South's railroads had been destroyed, necessitating connecting travel by carriage, hearse, and boat or on foot.[415] With Eliza's limited means, retrieval by her own hand seems most unlikely. No documentation of the retrieval survives, neither in Eliza's papers, at Winchester Cemetery nor with the Quartermaster Corps.

Furthermore, no telegram or letter survives notifying Eliza of Henry's death. She could have heard it from a returning soldier or from Charles Richardson's mother. Obviously word arrived soon after September 22, because she wrote to Maine asking her mother to join her. And Mary Bean arrived on October 3.

Eliza writes to Andrew of her mother's safe arrival.

> *Lowell, Oct. 3, 1864*
>
> *My Dear brother*
>
> *Mother has just got [here] safe & how thankful I am to have a Mother to come to me in time of need, but I am so disapointed [sic] in not seeing you to night. I do wish you would come to night.*
>
> *Dear brother I cannot write it seames as though my heart would brake. I have not herd any thing more. I went to see the Mayor to day. He wanted I should keepe up goode curage & said he would see that my family was cared for.*
>
> *He has writen on to have the bodies sent home if it is posable [sic] to get them, all of the 26. I expect Charley (he was wonded & his only brother [Luther L. Richardson] killed at the saime time) to home[.]* *He wrote to his Mother that he should come & see me then*

---

* Several men enlisted in Henry's regiment bore the Christian name Charles and boasted a brother in the same regiment. They include Charles Johnson (his brother was William A. Johnson), Charles Richardson (Luther L. Richardson), and Charles Taylor (two brothers: James F. and Peter). This is probably Charles Henry Richardson, from whom Eliza has had a letter.

I shall know all [about Henry's final days]. Mother is very tiard &
it is quite late & dark as pitch but I will go with this to the [Post]
Office. I will write to Ephriam [sic] this week. If you come bring
your things. Your [uniform] pants you can have colord [that is,
dyed so they no longer resemble military trousers]. I wish you was
her [here]. Mother sayes bring all he [her?] thing [things]. I want the
carpet. It is most ten. I must go. The children are well.

    Your sister E. H. Foster

[Note at bottom of page, perhaps about a trinket or charm enclosed]
    Perhaps this will bring you to [EF; me?]. It is good. Put it in
you [your] hat in sight after you get in and you will be all right I
think. . . .

Full of Trouble

Just three letters survive in Eliza's small, regular hand, all of them written to her brother Andrew in Albany after Henry's death. In contrast to
the precision of her penmanship, Eliza's emotional state is sorrowful and
desperate—as she says, "full of trouble" and yearning to have immediate
family at her side.

    Three months after Henry's death, Chancy's outspoken wife, Clara,
dispatches a rather prickly missive:

    Poultney [Vt.]   *Jan 8ᵗʰ 1865*

    Dear Eliza

    We recved your letter two weeks ago yesterday & as it was di-

---

    * Records at Winchester were expunged when bodies were moved, according
to information gleaned during phone call, Ann Chandonnet to Winchester, Dec.
12, 2007. Cemetery officials did not know how common it was for remains to be
removed. The Quartermaster Museum, the surviving records of Lowell's Mayor
Hosford, and Edson Cemetery have no record of Henry's remains being moved.

rected to me I of course opened it & being anxious to know if it contained any thing about Henry I read it. I suppose from what you said in that letter that you consider me very hard hearted towards you because I said that I thought it was his duty to go if he felt it to be so, & that he showed more love for his wife and Children by going then he would have done by acting like a coward as some do & staying at home & as yet I have seen no reason to change that opinion though he was a dear Brother to me, & the thought that he is dead grievs me much, yet I believe he fell in a glorious cause, & from the tone of his letters I can but hope & believe that his tired spirit has found the haven of eternal repose, where wars will no more come.* I suppose you will not receve any thing from me as meant in kindness because I differ from you about his going, but   I think he had to suffer the most in his feelings for I know it was as hard for him to go as it was for you to have him go for he always said that was the only thing that troubled him about it   the fact of leaving his family   but he felt it to be his duty to go & I believe it was the means of saving his soul, & I do hope that the belief that he is gone home to heaven may serve to tare [tear] away your mind from the follies of the world & fix them on things Heavenly.

Now Eliza believe me when I tell you that I sympathize with you in your sorrow & that if there is an[y] thing I can do to lighten that sorrow I would most gladly do it. Do not as you have seemed to do try to keep yourself aloof from us, but let us know of your plans for the future. . . .

Sister Clarie

Next, Eliza received a letter of condolence from William H. Kendall, who had suffered a loss himself:

---

* This seems to be a paraphrase from a popular volume of funeral hymns by Charles Wesley, first published in London.

Greenwood [Maine] Feb 5th 1865

Dear Cousin Eliza H. Foster

I take this time to answer your kind letter which I recved and was glad to here [hear] from you to here that you was well. We are all well now and hope this will find you Enjoying the Same blessing. Cousin Eliza I feel to mourn with you for the [loss] of your Dear husban [sic], for I know how to Simphathise with you in the death of our little Ella which we have lost Since you was here which is a greate los [loss] to us, Something that no one knows until they have a trial of the Same los of a Child.

The death of Ellar [Ella] came very near killing my Mother. She was very near crazy for Some time but her health is good at present   very good. You Spoke of Uncle Jacob Holts death. He died very Suden. He was Sick but a few days. His disease was hermage [hemorrhage?] in the bowels. I Saw his wife the other day and she Said it Seamed that they was all gone Since Uncle died as they all looked up to him. Oh Eliza you have met with a greate los in the death of Henry but we must Say that it is the Leords [Lord's] will not mine but it Seames hard to have a Child Suffer as Ella did with the Croop [croup]. She was only Sick twenty foure hours. She was so presed for Breath she was not in one position five minuets to a time. You could here [hear] her breath all over the house. If your Children ever have the croop be sure and keep the Hive Syrup where you can put your hand on it any time. * *Doct Wiley Says that will cure it. I should [like] to see you and Talk with you to Comfort you in you [your] troubles but am deprived of it at pesent [present] but hope I Shall Some time. . . .*

* Cox's Hive Syrup was a popular expectorant and cough remedy. Also known as Syrup of Squill, it was distilled from the roots of a wildflower, bloodroot (*Sanguinaria canadensis*), a member of the poppy family, and mixed with honey. Later versions were made with corn syrup or sugar. Listed in *King's American Dispensary* of 1898, hive syrup continued to be marketed well into the 1950s.

I am Pedeling [peddling] this winter   Washing Fluid and writ-
ing ink and Jewerly & other things to [too] numerous to mention.
We are having a very cold winter and any quantity of Snow....

From your absent Cousin and Friend   Truly

Wm H. Kendall

On the same day that William Kendall took up his pen, a female relative, J. A. Hobbs, lends the weight of her words to the family's suggestions for Eliza's future:

Greenwood   Feb the 5 1865

Dear Cousin

I now seat myself to answer your letter which we received
and was happy to hear from you and hear that you was all well.
William [Kendall] was away and his wife was over here and she
opened the letter when it come and we was glad to hear from you[.]
we have looked for a letter from you this long time[.] I should have
wrote to you but I did not know where to direct but I shall write
often now. Oh how I wish you lived where I could come in and see
you and your Children and Mother. I should be glad and I hope it
will be so I can some time[.] [T]ell your Mother that Mother is real
smart [mentally acute and physically active; alert, efficient] she
sends her love to you all and says if you lived where she could come
with a team [of horses] she would come and see you sure. Uncle
Abbot [Holt, Mary Holt Bean's brother] is quite smart now he is to
Mr. Haskells now he has ben real slim, and Uncle Jacob [Holt] was
very sick[.] [H]e only lived 7 days after he was taken [sick] we have
not seen them since the Funeral and I don't know the particulars
about his sickness William has been there he knows better than I
do he is a going to write to you   he has met with a loss losing his
Ella[.] he bears it better than I thought he would[.] she was his Idol
and Mothers to [too] it seemed hard to us all to part with her but

I suppose it is all right – Gods will be done   but his loss is nothing compared with your but you must be thankfull that you are spared to take care of your Children, it is getting late and I will draw to a close we all send our love to you & your Mother, write often as you can[.] [S]isy [Hobbs' young daughter?] sends her love to your Children[.] [S]he is not so fat as she was   Frank [Hobbs] and Albert are in the woods this winter [i.e., working at a lumber camp] John is at home some of the time   good night   From your friend

J. A. Hobbs

A few days later, Clarinda Foster Lynch, Henry's mother, addresses Eliza:

Poultney   Febuary 16 [?] [1865]

Dear Daughter [daughter-in-law]: Elisa

I will try and write you as it is some time since I have heard any thing from you. . . . I think I can sympathize with you Henry being my youngest and left Fathless [fatherless] when but 11 years old. I his Mother of course had the greatest anxiety for his wellfare and he was allways [sic] in my mind more than the rest of the Children that was older and could take care of themselves. O he dont know how many tears I have shed for him that he might grow up to man hood and be respected in the world and be a follower of the loving Savior that gave himself a ransom for the sins of the world. . . .

I felt after I came home from Lowell last spring [during Henry's furlough] that I should never see him again in this world and I felt so bad to think I could not say more to him. . . .

He wrote [in a June 1 letter to Chancy and Clara] when he got where he knew where he was he would write again. That is the last we have any of us ever had. Oh I [would] have been so glad to [have] had a letter from him. It would be so much comfort to me to [have] had it to read. . . . I suppose you heard by some one that was with him or how did you hear. O do write how he felt when he died. Poor boy how much he must have sufered [sic]. I hope the Lord did have

*mercy on him and comfort him for I am sure if [I] was dying and
in distres without the presence of my god I should be miserable. . . .*

Give my love to your Mother. I [am] glad you have her with you.

From A Mother [Clarinda Foster Lynch]

Kiss the Children for me.

Eliza's birthday anniversary was March 8, and the party mentioned in the
following letter to Andrew must have been a surprise celebration of that
occasion. The money waiting in Boston could be her pension.

Lowell March 7, 1865

Dear brother

*I received your letter to day with the twenty dollars in all safe.
Andrew I was full of trouble when I sent to you for that (& I did not
know which way to turn but I can see a way out – I toulde you that
I setled with Mr. P [Parker] & then Mr. D sent in a bill ll. [$11?]. &
I went to see him. I give D [a] few words. He said he did not expect
me to pay untill I get his pay [Henry's pay?; or "this" meaning her
monthly wages from mill work] & c. . . . I get paid to day. I had 20
dollars for foure weeks in Mill. I also get word to day that there is
money for me in Boston but I don't want to go alone & there is a girl
by the side of me [in the mill] that wants to do & go out to Legion.*

*Cant we meet in B— & go to Le [American Legion?] March 9
A. I am sick to day. Miss Carter got me a surprised party last night.
Treacle trifle [a rich dessert layered with cake, pudding, jam and
sherry]. A good time.*

*But what I want to know this time is if you are out of money. I
have a good mind to send this right back, but if you want it say so
& I will send it to you. I can send it as far as Bethel any day. I shant
use it untill I hear from you. Write quick.*

I can get along now untill I get som [some]. I borrowed [from]

Mrs. C [Camerford?].

My love to all [and] Mothers to [too]. I will tell you all soon. I cant write more now sick headeache.

E. H. Foster

Sometime between February and June 1865, Eliza yielded to the wishes of her family and visited Maine. After Eliza's return to Massachusetts, J. A. Hobbs was heard from once more, voicing her opinion on Eliza's future. The letter strongly implies an offer of marriage from one Brice.* Was Brice too shy to write on his own behalf?

Greenwood [ME] June the 10 1865

Dear Cousin

*I will try [to] answer your letter I recved and was glad to hear from you and that you was well. We have been most sick with a cold but the rest are smart [i.e., alert and healthy] around here. I wish I could see you. I could tell you more news in one hour than I can write in a day. I have been out and see [seen] your Mother [Mary Holt Bean]. She was glad to hear from you. She has got moved down stairs. She has got the house all cleaned up ready for you to come and keep store [at Holt's Corner] and she wishes you to come and I wish you would come down here and live for I think it would be better for you. If you was down here [i.e., in Maine] now you could have some of Brices [sic] fresh pork.** He and Ephraim [Eliza's brother]*

---

* J. A. Hobbs is probably referring to a Greenwood neighbor, farmer Brice Edwards Kimball, born December 19, 1842, in Albany. Brice was the nephew of Clark Swett Edwards, and named for his uncle Bryce McLellan Edwards. Brice was a neighbor of the Holts and Beans. He died in 1915 in Albany.

** Fresh pork may seem slight culinary enticement to readers accustomed to refrigeration, freezers, and air freight. However, in the 1860s, butchering a hog would have permitted its owners to dine on fresh pork for only a day or two—depending on the ambient air temperature. To preserve most of the pork, it was salted down in barrels or crocks immediately. Pork aged in brine, a diet that persisted well into the twentieth century, was what farmers ate for most of the year.

went and killed a hog for Sam Haskell and he bought half of it and E and your Mother is a going to have a quarter of it. I have not seen Brice but your Mother has. She sees him often. He inquires after you and sayse he wishes to see you and the children and sends his best respects so she told me to write to you and tell you she was ready for you to come down and go to keeping store. She thinks bout you a good deal. She boards the Teacher this summer. . . . Your Mother felt sorry that you did not leave the children with her so you [could] get your things and come back and I am sorry to for I wish you was down here now. It is beautiful weather. Every thing looks so nice.

. . . I want you to write me next time that you will and next Sunday the [there] is a Meeting out to the T [Town?] House [i.e., the local name for Albany Town Hall] and I mean to go and I shall tell Brice that if he will buy the farm out here that you will come and live on it and I think you would like [it] out here. . . . I tell you we would have some good times sure. . . .

> *your cousin*

> *J. A. Hobbs*

In the following letter, Eliza's thoughts ramble apace—but she is able to derive satisfaction in the milestone of her son's first day of school. George is now just four and a half; perhaps he was exceptionally bright, or perhaps Eliza was enrolling him in school to allow her more uninterrupted time in which to sew for customers. She now had her mother in residence for companionship, so George could be spared. Her mother was taking over some of the household chores, which gave Eliza welcome leisure. Eliza may also have thought that the classroom routine would help George deal with his own grief.

> *Lowell, Feb. 27, 1865*

> *Dear brother*

> *I will write you to night but I have not time to write much. We*

are quite well to night. George commenced goin [going] to Scholl [school] Tuesday.

There was a great fire here last night. The Merrimack house was burned.[*]

Mother is quite well. She has washed to day.

I wish you was hear [here] to night. We want to see you very much Andrew. I donot know what I can do but stay here & work in hopes to get a living some way. If I ever get ketched up [caught up with her debts] I shall be glad. I cant get a sent [cent] only what I earn & wate [wait for her pension to begin?] and every thing is so high her [here] this winter.

I did not want to ask you for that money but Dear brother I donot know what to d [do]. I must have some some way.

If you can spare it send it just as soon as you can.

Are you to settle her [Mother's?] bills [run up in Maine?].

Mother wants you should write all about it.

I have settled with Parker [a local merchant]. He & I are dun [done]. I must pay Farington &c. I trade with Starbird now.[**]

Aint you coming up her as soon as you get through with you [your] busin [business?]. Write and tell me all the news. The folks are all well Mrs F [Mabelia Fox?] NE [?]& ec Mrs. Horn has ben sick.[***] How is Uncle Abbot [Holt] & Suell. Mother saias [says] she wants to see Mr. & Mrs. Hunt very much.[****]

* The Merrimack House was a luxury hotel built in 1832.

** The 1861 Lowell City Directory lists a DeWitt Farrington, dealer in furniture, stoves, and housekeepers' goods at 1 & 2 Prescott; and a Daniel Farrington, dealer in hats, clothing, and furnishing goods at 108 Central. It also lists a Charles D. Starbird, butcher.

*** Mrs. Horn may be the mother or wife of Charles Horn, a member of Company A.

**** This may be George Hunt (b. 1833) and his wife Louisa, who was the daughter of Lucinda Bean. The Hunts were married at Stoneham, Massachusetts.

Sylvia had a letter from Ann. They are well. Are you agoin to sell you [your] place or keep it.*

Mother wants to know. Write as soon as you get this.

From your Sister

E H Foster

Truly

This the last surviving word from Eliza.

Brice Edwards Kimball reappears in a July 2, 1866, letter from Andrew to Eliza, in which Andrew takes pains to recommend him to his sister as a religious man. Eliza was hardly alone in shunning Brice's proposals; thousands of Civil War widows chose not to remarry.[416] In the summer of 1866, Eliza was instead considering another stint of mill work—or had perhaps already returned to mill employment. But her mother attempted to convince her to return to her home state of Maine and continue custom sewing there.

In the following letter, Andrew is a changed personality, exulting in the companionship of his new wife, Elizabeth ("Lizzie") Temperance Hayes Piper Coburn, whom he married a month earlier in Dracut.

As his cup runs over, he employs the word *beautiful* three times.

Albany July 2ⁿᵈ 1866

My Dear Sister

Here we are at the west window in our house. It is a beautiful day and we are enjoying ourselves nicely. Mrs. A. J. is bound to be happy and (better still) to make me so too.

We came to Portland all right and stopped at her Uncle Capt. Morris. Had a very pleasant time indeed. He took me through the new City building then down to his office on Exchange St. & c—gave me an introduction to Mr. Sparrow the State Agt. We stopped at

* Eight Ann Beans and two Ann Fosters are listed in *The Clan MacBean in North America*.

Elizabeth Hayes Piper Coburn Bean, second wife of Andrew Jackson Bean. The date of this photograph is unknown, but her neckline is antebellum, and she wears what appear to be memorial bracelets on her wrists. Courtesy Bethel Historical Society.

Uncle Morris' all night. Saturday A.M. We called on cousin Harriet and then called on Mr. Eggington Superintendant of Glass Works.* He and his wife are very nice people. They took us all through the Glass works. P.M.[417] *we came home. Ephm [his brother Ephraim] met us at Depot. Yesterday was a beautiful day indeed. We went to meeting house to meeting [church service]. There was old Stacey [?]. We took tea at Sam Haskell's then came to Town house with them & Randall Cummings. Brice was to town house [Albany Town Hall] to Sabbath School.** David Haskells girl is sick.*

Mother says she thinks of you often & wishes that you were here with the rest of us.

---

* The Portland Glass Company (which used the mark "P.G.Co.") operated from 1864 to 1873, producing pressed glass tableware sets in both clear and colored glass. The factory would have been brand new when Andrew visited.

** Sam Haskell, Brice Kimball, and Ephraim Bean were neighbors at the Albany end of Songo Pond.

I have been out in town this A.M. Found them all well &c &c.

This is a beautiful P.M. Here we are at the window in the cool breeze quite happy.

Except [sic] Love from us all

Mr. & Mrs. A. J. Bean

Mother & Mary Frances

Lizzie says Tell Eliza that she had to pitch the tune for them in Town house &c. *Eliza Please carry Julia her letter as soon as you get it. A.J.B.*

Eliza's mother writes again a week later with much the same message:

Albany [ME] July 10ᵗʰ 66

My Dear Daughter

I have but a few moments in which to write but will improve what I have.

Andrew has been down with his wife. They were not here long enough so I got much acquainted with her. They started for home today. She gave me a dress and I am going over to Mrs. Kendalls and get her to fit it for me. It is pretty black & white.

Mary Francis [sic] says she likes her mother [i.e., stepmother] <u>tip top</u>.

I want to see you so much. It seems as if I never wanted to see you so much in the world. I am so lonely but should be more so if the teacher didn't board here. Why cant you come down and stay with me a while. . . .

Mary F is going to stay till Silvia comes down & if I go to Lowell she will stay til I go. I dont want to go. My home seems here and my things—Ephriam [her son, Eliza's brother] carried them [i.e., trans-

* Andrew seems to use indirection again, recommending his new wife to Eliza for her musical talents.

ported Andrew and Elizabeth in a horse-drawn vehicle] out to the Hill and got me some molasses & sugar.

The first Sunday Andrew came they went to the meeting house to meeting and the next to the town house.

Mary F sends a kiss to you [,] Georgie & Henrietta.

I send kisses to you all. Tell Georgie I sit up and most finished his mittens last night. Come & stay with me this winter. I cant stay here alone.

All Mr. Kendells folks [probably the family of William H. Kendall] were here last Saturday. It was dreadful warm. I wish you could be like her too. They are all teasing me to spin & weave for them but I dont think I shall. I am making that quilt I commenced when you were here.

Your loving Mother

Mary Beane

As late as 1866 Eliza's kin were still urging marriage to Brice Kimball, as this letter from SAH, an unidentified female relative or friend, indicates. She had recently been to visit Lowell and left a hat there; she wishes Eliza to fetch the hat and have it refurbished according to the latest fashion dictates. SAH demonstrates an idiosyncratic phonetic spelling.

[Albany, ME]   August the 2   [1866]

Dear Eliza

I hant [haven't] had time to Right yet But Eferem [Ephraim] has Come in and is goen Over to the hill So I thart [thought] I wood try and rite you a line. I Cant Right hafe wat I yont [want] to tell George. I arived to Albany Saft and Sound. Mother yonted me to tell you Mrs. [Andrew's second wife?] has Not Pad eney Bard [paid any board] for Marry Sence She Came heare Nor never Oferd to Buy eney [thing] Sence She has Ben ther. I thenk it is to Bard [too bad]. Mother don't Now wather [know wheather] She Can Come yet. I let you know when I do Com.

She [Eliza's mother] ses Brise [Brice] is well an [and] does well. Your Mother yonts to se you and wod lick [would like] to have the Children Com and Stay with her. [Mother] is quite smart for her. I picked you some risbares [raspberries] to dry and tha all Mald [they all molded]. She hant git the hay Moved Oute of the Baren. Thay yont Move it[.] . . . She yonts to know if Henderson has got home yet She Started last Fridiy to goe home. She yonts to know if you Sent a kis to Brise By hendersone. She younted to kis hen [him] for her [you?] Brise ant goen [ain't going with; isn't keeping company with] eney yone [anyone].

Elisa I yont you to goe into my House and git My hat and take the Riben of and Carey it oute [to a millinery shop]. I yont it Coleard and Prest[.] [I]t is in the Parler Closet and So God By.

Rite Sone.

Tell George I havt time to rite.

S A H

Another plea—this time for Eliza to help her Mother—is sent along in December. "Sarah" seems to be JAH's daughter, and the unnamed baby, a boy. This letter indicates that Andrew has relocated to Lowell, leaving Mary Frances behind.

Happy New Year

Greenwood [Maine] Dec the 30   1866

Dear Cousin

I now seat myself to write you a few lines to let you know that I have wrote 2 letters and have not received any answer but I was out to your Mother [Mary A. Holt Bean] the other day and she showed me a letter that she had from you and you thought [it] strange I *did not write and I suppose you did not get my letters and I will write again and see if you will get this. I hope you will and then I hope you will write to me as soon as you get this with out fail. Your Mother is very slim [i.e., wasted from sickness]. She was real sick last week but she is some better but she is not fit to live alone. I went and staid with her some and Mother come out and I come home and she wanted I should write to you and tell you that she wanted you to come down as soon as you could. She would soon let Mary Frances go if you would come and I think you ought to come. It is not fitting for her to live there unless some one [adult] lives with her. She has had two spells of the nose bleed in the night so that she nearly fainted away. You cannot think how poor your Mother looks. You would be supprised to see her [that is, surprised by her unhealthy appearance] and you tell Andrew from me to send his Mother some Sarsaparilla* to take. She has got to have some thing [i.e., a tonic] to take or she will not do much more work. She is very poor [in health] and she says she is weak and lame all over. She is very much pleased with her things you sent her. She has not got her skirt made yet nor her woolen dress. I cut and made Mary Frances dress and she has got enough [fabric left over] for your little girl one. She says she dont know what she shall do if you do not come and live with her. She says it is hard for her to live alone. She says she never can think of going to live with Andrew nor you at Leowell but if you would only come down here so that she could live with you she should be happy. I dont think she ought to work so hard. She has got a web [a length of cloth] in the loom to weave and if you was with her, folks would not bring her so much work. I don't know how*

---

* Sarsaparilla was an herbal tonic, sometimes confused with sassafras, the root and bark of which were used to flavor root beer. Sarsaparilla is flavored with the root of a vine (*Smilax regelii*). The bitter, tuberous root is used to flavor beverages and as a homeopathic remedy. The roots contain valuable plant steroids and saponins. Because of its reputation as a blood purifier, it was officially accepted by the American medical community from 1820 to 1910 as a treatment for syphilis.

she will get through with the winter unless you do come and I hope and pray you will come and let Andrew take his girl and bring her up. Your Mother is not fit to take care of her. She has got to be to [too] old to have the care of her.

Mother has got your blanket [quilt?] done for you and she wants to know how much you ask for the hair [wool? Quilt batting?]. She says she will pay you when she sees you. I suppose you have heard how Mrs. Noyes is dead and Albert Holt died last week [December 30, 1866]. The rest of the Relations are well except your Mother. We are all and all send their love to you. Your Mother worries about you a great deal. She said give her love to you and children. I guess I have wrote more than you can read. It is so dark I can hardly see. Tell Etta that Sarah is well and tell George that my baby is about as big as he is. Give my love to AJ [Andrew Jackson Bean] and wife and accept the same. Oh how I wish I could see you.

Good bye

J. A. H. [Hobbs]

to

E. H. F.

In the months after this spate of cajoling missives, Eliza surrendered to her relatives' pleas and takes her children to Maine on a visit. She remained there from February to April of 1867; Andrew wrote her there, urging that she stay until her health improved.

At the time, Eliza was corresponding with a Sam Wily or Wiley, a widower with children.* In two letters written in April 1867, Andrew let her know in no uncertain terms that he did not consider Wiley a good match.

Andrew had divorced his first wife on September 9, 1865. (The "sick sister" is probably a reference to Eliza's health.) The playful tone of the

---

* Among the Wileys and Willeys listed in *The Clan MacBean in North America*, there is no Sam. Eliza's correspondence with Wily has not survived.

following letter, written as winter's early dark settled on the snowy city, again seems inspired by Andrew's marriage to his second wife, Elizabeth. Eliza and her brood appear to have been visiting Maine when Andrew writes from his new residence. Because he does not append a street address, other letters must be missing.

> *Lowell [MA.] Feb. 3 1867*
>
> *My Dear Sister—*
>
> *Mother & Mary Frances*
>
> *George & Etta*
>
> *How do you all do this Sunday eve.*
>
> *We are quite well though I have been real stupid [dull-witted, slow to act] to day so I have not been to church this dull rainy day but we have been to John St. AM Preyer meeting this eve. Just get home & got kindling wood for the girl to build fire in morning for it is half past 4 now you know.*
>
> *All about same here in Lowell & more too since this big snow[.] So much you never saw in L.—I guess.*
>
> *Have I told you that Mr. Snell's boy was drowned. Judge Crosbey's wife is dead. Sam Wily is out round [getting around? Recovered from a past sickness?] So is Winchester I Suppose. Dea. [Deacon?] Whitney is very sick.*
>
> *Mother my footings are wearing out but I don't know how you can get any to me unless I go down there ofter [to Maine after] them. Elizabeth has been telling about knitting me some but she has more than she can do without knitting I can tell you.*
>
> *Mary Frances Father wants to see you very much to see how much you have learned this winter. I want to kiss my little bird on nose & cheek.*

Eliza   Marrianna* has closed up business with Horace and a Charly Stevens of Lawrence is the man now. He came up last eve. Is here now. I like him quite well.

Tell me all the news. Hussy [Hussey] says he guesses you have to ride often that gray mare & that you are better if you could go to Bethel. Tell me all the news all about Mr. Hunts [?] folks. If Parsons is fearful of not getting his pay of me or Mr. French or the town.

Did you get the ten dollars. I sent a paper with mail in it so you could get it last night.

They have cut down pay on some of Corp [mills] & stoped carpet [weaving carpet?] 3 days &c &c. Write often. Tell Mary Frances to Tell father a bit how she is a grand [proud?] Mama.** Is Gibson*** on B. Hill. Can Ephm. [Andrew's brother] Get Eggs or D. [dried?] Apples.

Here we are in our Chamber [bedroom]. The dearest place to me. Elizabeth so sleepy but she often remembers our dear sick sister by asking God to heal her if it be consistant with His will but if otherwise determined to fit & prepare you for the change [?]

My Dear Sister Eliza May God bless us all.

Truly yours,

A. J. Beane

A Cozy Scene

Andrew's next letter reveals that he is taking in boarders, a common method of increasing income. Historian Wendy Gamber estimates that "up to 30 percent of all 19th-century households took in boarders."[418]

---

* Perhaps the "Mandana" who visited Eliza on February 22, 1863.

** Mary Frances was nine years old at this time. Perhaps she was a grand "Mama" to a new doll.

*** S. F. Gibson was a Maine attorney.

Lowell [MA.] Feb. 24ᵗʰ 67

My Dear Sister Mother Mary Frances Etta & Geo.

I hope you are all well. We are pretty well. We received your letter yesterday. Got tired of waiting to hear from you all.

Eliza do not get homesick for if you do not content yourself you will not improve in health. Do make yourself as comfortable as possible for I want you to get well soon.

We had quite a Snow Thursday night but I used waggon. We went over to Richardsons Friday eve to circle. Had good time. Wife's father & mother are up here. Marrianna has given up Horace [as a husband or fiance] & taken a Stevens of Lawrence [Lawrence, Mass.]. She is working down in Dracut to David Richardson's. Came up yesterday P.M. & gone back on Stage.

Sam Wily is quite Smart [i.e., healthy, vigorous, alert]. Is selling Poultry, Eggs, Butter &c. He is not going to work at his trade.

Our trade [at Massachusetts Corporation] has been very dull for last month. The families [boarders?] have all moved out of the old house & I took my horse away & put it in Snell's Stable.

They have not found his boy yet. I had teeth ache last night so I did not get up early enough to go to Church to day.

*Was about full of boarders. I got footings [socks knitted by his mother, Mary Bean]. They are just right but have no yarn to run heels.**

I do not understand why Mr. Hunt's [?] folks do not call. Do they have meetings to town house or any thing now days. Who did Mr. Hunt sell Bog Meadow to.

How I wish I could see you all this eve.

---

* Knitting stockings was a complicated and time-consuming affair, and weaving extra yarn into the toes and heels of stockings was one way to prolong their wear.

I want to see my little bird. Did Mary Frances like her School &
did she learn a good lot.

Mary Frances cant you send some word to father.

Eliza tell me all the news.

Elizabeth says she will send a large pattern then you can cut
one smaller for Mary Frances.

Mother I wish I could see you to night & have some of your egg
toast [French toast?]. Geo the little boys want to know when Dorde
[George's nickname—perhaps his childish pronunciation of his own
name] is coming.

A. J. Beane

Elizabeth, Andrew's second wife, had been married twice before—and
widowed both times. During this period, a widow had virtually no legal
standing. Custom (and most wills) granted her use of only one-third of
her home—the standard "widow's third." Her nearest male relative would
receive title to all the property, while she could use either a third of the
physical property or a third of the interest resulting from its sale—which-
ever that relative decided. In other words, she would become a ward of the
son or son-in-law who received the other two-thirds. She would probably
be expected to help with chores and completely dependent on that male
for everything. Elizabeth may well have been glad to be relieved of that
fate—though Andrew has saddled her with a boardinghouse.

Nearly a month passes before Andrew again took up his pen. Eliza
remained in Maine, in poor health. Andrew reports driving his sleigh the
six miles to Dracut to visit the Fox family and other acquaintances. He
reminds his sister to write, and while nonchalantly informing her of the
disappointing status of funds she is seeking, brags about his new carpet:

Lowell [MA.] March 21ˢᵗ 67

My Dear Sister

Tell me if Gibson is at Bethel now or will be next week. I want *to send you $11.00 to pay to Gibson the first time you go to Bethel or have Ephm [his brother] take it to him.*

We are well. Are having good Sleighing.

We have been up to Mr. Sheet's one evening to Mr. Ephm Brown's on Chestnut St. He is Elizabeth's S.S. teach [Sunday school teacher] & Over to Sam. Richardsons to Circle Lizzie & I to Sleighride & called on Capt. Fox folkes.

I had a letter from Mr. Hunt [former owner of Bog Meadow; see Andrew's letter of Feb. 24] yesterday. I am glad that he is so smart [feeling well].

Mr. Frye [his Lowell attorney] Says that all that there is for you is the old Pension. That is all that any one can get yet.

I had a letter from Eunice E. Coffin. Her husband is unable to do any thing & they are poor.

Elizabeth has got a new carpet on the parlor floor.

No [now] get the money to [attorney] S. F. Gibson just the first chance So he can Send me the note.

Eliza Do be careful of yourself & get well this Spring or I fear it will be too late. Do not come back here too soon.

Business is very dull indeed here.

The other half of this sheet is for Gibson you See. I have been looking for a letter from you for a week.

J. Beane

Lowell March 21ˢᵗ 67

Mr. Gibson

I do not know where you are so I send this money to you by my Sister in Albany with interest I guess & many thanks.

Please send me the note & direct

J. Beane

Lowell Mass.

No. 35 Mass. Corp. [Andrew's business address]

While in previous correspondence Andrew has said nothing to indicate outright disapproval of Eliza's apparent suitor, the widower Sam Wily (Wiley), by April he feels he must deliver an unflattering report to his sister. Evidently Wily has expressed interest in marrying Eliza, but Andrew disapproves of her even corresponding with this man. Andrew returns to the subject of Wiley in his April 14 letter; this suggests that Wiley is a debtor and his sons undisciplined.

Lowell   Apr. 4th 1867

Eliza:

I was glad to receive your letter with the note in it [promissory note from Gibson mentioned above] but was sorry you could not write me more about things.

I cant see what you want to write to Sam Wily for and more than that I don't like it very well to think you do so.

I hope you are taking care of your self so to get well this Spring.

We are quite well only Elizabeth is getting tired for our girl [servant] has gone to work in Mill & we have not got one yet & 24 boarders.

Get well before you come back [from Maine]. Tell me how Mother is. Mary Frances too. I wish I could see you all.

This is fast day* here & I am home this P.M.

We had lots to do in Shop this A.M.

* April 4 was a Thursday in Lent of 1867, so the meaning of "fast day" is unclear.

Lovejoy has got a sore on one of his legs. It is quite bad.

It is a beautiful day here & it is getting quite dry. High St. is almost dry.

I have not got your letter that you was going to write Sunday.

Eliza I got your 16 dollars the first of this month but I will only send 10 & I want you to have Ephm send me 2 Bbls. Best [seed] Potatoes he can find white ones & you pay him for them. Tell him to put in a Bushel of early ones for I want to plant some if I can get a chance. Tell him to head them up strong & mark them

J. Beane

Lowell Mass.

Via. Lawrence**

Tell him to have them put it in the bill so then they will come all right.

I hope Ann will get well soon. It must make it very hard for them.

Mary Frances How is father's little bird. Can she kiss father on nose & cheek. Mother How do you done [do] & how is Eliza & how are Etta & George.

Yours A. J. Bean

I want all good Potatoes & have them sent the first of next week.

(Fire bell just struck)

Write me just as soon as you get this so I shall know that you got the money.

---

* This probably indicates "Lawrence Manufacturing Company," chartered in 1831 as one of Lowell's original ten large textile corporations. Portions of the mill yard at Perkins and Aiken streets still survive in the twenty-first century, converted into residential condominiums.

Andrew's next letter continues to issue orders to everyone. He also renews his criticism of Wiley and extends his opprobrium to the man's progeny. Simultaneously he seems to stress his own churchgoing.

Lowell Apr 14th 67

My Dear

Sister & Mother

And Little folks

How do you all do this beautiful Sabbath day. I hope there has been a meeting [worship service] in town House [Albany Town Hall] so you could go to meeting to day. Wife & I have been all day & to Sunday School.

Eliza I received your letter & glad to get it too. Do be careful of your self & get well this Spring.

All inquire for you. Never mind the potatoes if they are not plenty. I supposed they were plenty down there.

Next time you see Dr. Wily ask him to make out my bill & hand it to you so I can have it when I go to Albany for I shall not want to wait for him to make it out then. It is dry & dusty here.

If you ever want to get well do not go out & get your feet wet. How is Mr. Hunt going to get along this year.

Here is a dollar for Mary Frances to have a Sabbath School Paper [a subscription?] & use the rest to get her something that She needs. I want her to go to Sabbath School every Sunday & to meeting too So to be a good girl. O Eliza tell Ephm not to work & drive round So much Sundays. [If he attends church] He will feel So much better on Monday.

Sam Wiley is owing Lovejoy for meat &c & cannot pay. He has got to go to work in his trade. His boys were taken up with other boys for Sauce [saucy language to an official?] & breaking windows *on fast day.*[*]

Do not call Mary Frances Mary any more or let any one else for her name is Mary Frances.

Mother Do not worry now you are too old to fret. Though you may out live me you will soon have lived to a good old age and then must die. O Mother that we all may meet in heaven.

Mary Frances Father is glad his little girl is learning to read his letters. Be a good girl.

Etta & George How do you get along. Samy [Sarry? "Sairy" was short for Sara during this era] & Esther want to see you.

Eliza Lovejoy was not able to do a thing last week on account of the sore on his leg. His brother helped me. I had to work hard I tell you. Our girl has gone into the mill so wife & Marrianna did the [boardinghouse] work. It was too much but you know Elizabeth is one of the smartest [clever and fast-working]. We got a woman [hired servant] yesterday. I am afraid his [Lovejoy's, perhaps a hired man] leg will not get well so I can go to Albany as soon as I want to. Write as soon as you get this so I shall know if you get the dollar for Mary Frances.

Tell me when the snow gets off so I can tell when they begin to work on land.

A. J. B.

This is Andrew's last surviving letter to Eliza.

In addition to the 28 letters Andrew sent to Eliza between 1857 and 1867, a handful from his later years were saved, many of them dealing with his pension. In these last letters to Eliza, Andrew portrays himself as a man of affairs, a man with underlings. Issuing impatient directives by the

---

[*] The front page of the Nov. 8, 1895, *Lowell Daily Courier*, in a police court column headed "All Kinds of Offences," mentions this sort of mischief: "Two respectably dressed children, a boy and a girl, charged with stubbornness, promised reform and were placed on probation."

score, sending Eliza on errands, he seems to have lost the compassion he expressed for his little sister during his military service.

Riding the Gray Mare

Although Eliza has been ill during her sojourn in Maine, she has also experienced days when she was well enough to ride horseback and pay calls. Leaving her children with her mother, galloping through the fresh spring air, she perhaps has a respite from her travails, and perhaps her coughs and headaches fly away with the mare's tail. Her girlhood flashes through her mind, and her body settles into an easy rhythm. But this dream of freedom and health could not last. Sometime after April 14, Eliza returned to Lowell with her children and mother. Her condition deteriorated, and she died on the twentieth of August, a sultry month known to be fatal to mill girls.

Two of the most poignant family papers deal with Eliza's final illness, funeral, and interment. The first is a bill to "Mrs. Eliza H. Foster's Estate" dated July 8 to August 19, 1867, for seventeen medical visits, for a total of $21.25. The bill is from D. Packer & A. Thompson, "Homeopathic Physicians and Surgeons," of 16 Central Street. Packer and Thompson advertised their practice as paying special attention to women and children. Their fee for a basic home visit within city limits was $1.25. The second document is a bill from J. W. Brooks, dealer in coffins, caskets, and grave clothes. Dated August 22, the bill lists these goods and services: one casket ($34), one box ($3.25), "preserving remains in ice" ($3), posting death notices in two local newspapers (30 cents), and burial ($4.25). Eliza was buried beside her husband in Edson Cemetery on Gorham Street; they share a single marble marker.

The two inscriptions on the marker are in different styles, indicating that Eliza managed to retrieve Henry's body from Winchester before her own demise. This would have afforded her a sense of achievement as well as a shrine for shedding tears.

Like thousands of other Northern wives, Eliza experienced the end of

the terrible war and saw her husband's dream—the dream of a union pre-served—come to pass. Her brother was safe. Her children were thriving. When she was low, she had love letters to read again and again.

We come to the end of Eliza's story. It is not a tragedy, but the unvarnished story of an ordinary American, an American like millions of others who strove and did not yield. Lonely and impoverished in Lowell, she carried in wood and kept the home fires burning. She served her family in a variety of ways, perhaps to the detriment of her own health. Her courage and fortitude are an example to us all. Her devotion to family may not merit a Medal of Honor—but it deserves honor from those who read her story through the fragmentary record of history.

Sugar, sarsaparilla, and molasses were insufficient to save Eliza's mother, Mary A. Holt Bean; she died the following year of "paralysis of heart." Andrew had her remains interred close to Henry and Eliza. In time he, Lizzie, and Mary Frances would join them.

In the meantime, decades would pass away. In the role of guardian of his niece and nephew, Andrew received from the government eight

dollars each a month, a sum increased to ten dollars a month in March 1870. At his home, 212 Tenth Street, Andrew stored all Eliza's letters and memorabilia. The family paper trail continued to grow, fueled by Andrew's pension-seeking correspondence, a letter from the grown Henrietta to her Uncle Andrew, various deeds and gas bills, tax receipts and business cards. Wind stirs the leaves, and the generations pile up like dust.

Opposite: **Obviously ailing Eliza Bean Foster with daughter, Henrietta,** probably late 1866. Courtesy Bethel Historical Society. Above: **Grave marker of Henry C. and Eliza H. Foster,** Edson Cemetery, Lowell, Mass. Photo by Fernand L. Chandonnet.

·

Appendix 1.

Lewellyn D. Bean: Diary Excerpts

Lewellyn D. Bean was one of eight children born to prosperous farmer/cabinetmaker John Marean Bean of Gilead, Maine, and his wife, Mary C. Mason. John Marean Bean was a son of Ebenezer Shaw Bean and his first wife, making him a half brother, thirty years older, to Eliza Howard Bean.[419] "Aunt" Eliza was four years older than Lewellyn. They were probably members of the same household, growing up together until Eliza left home at age sixteen for employment in the textile mills.

Lewellyn was born on February 12, 1839. He began his diary in Gilead at the close of his twenty-third year. Penned in a ruled, bound notebook, his diary commences in his clear and precise penmanship on Monday, December 1, 1862, and ends abruptly in Ioka, Idaho, in May 1864. (Glued to the front cover of this notebook is a smaller diary for 1876, with entries only through July 16; the entries, made in pencil, are smudged.) A few days after starting the diary, Bean moved to nearby Newry to keep his first school. Bean often had severe colds. He suffered from asthma, and many of his entries show him "unwell," coughing, having difficulty breathing and/or unable to sleep at night.

In January 1863, he records the long weeks during which he and the family with which he boards go through smallpox in quarantine. "To be shut up here and have people act as though they were afraid of us is none too pleasant," he writes on January 31. "No one has been nearer the house than the road, except the doctor, for two weeks. They dare not take a thing from the house nor go into the barn. If we want any thing Mr. Riley gets it and sets it down by the side of the road and we go and get it."

When not in charge of a classroom, Bean labors as a woodworker, making butter churns and cheese presses (equipped with cranks) as well as window frames and gun stocks. He also repairs wagons and frames barns, tinkers with clocks, dabbles in patents, supplies local news to regional papers, and draws up warrants for town meetings. He helps his father with haying as well as with details related to his status as town treasurer, selectman, and justice of the peace. Among Lewellyn's correspondents are his brother Fon (Alphonso, living in Iowa), Albert W. Grover, Mell Wight (studying to be a physician), his sister Mary Almeda (known as Almeda), and his Holyoke-educated sister-in-law Lucretia. He regularly spends half of Sunday writing letters.

Although many Beans remained rooted in New England, some members of the family hankered for greater elbow room. For example, the Bean Wagon Train left New England for the West in 1855, with some members of that group settling in Iowa, Missouri, and Texas.[420] Alphonso and Lucretia moved to Iowa shortly after their 1857 marriage, and urged him to join them.

During the summer of 1863, Lewellyn makes up his mind to "go out West" with his friend Nat. They acquire new clothes and a trunk, take the momentous step of purchasing railroad tickets to Chicago, and set off on September 22, 1863. In Ioka, Iowa, Lewellyn teaches, turns out an occasional axe handle or coffin and intermittently tends the post office. Sometimes he holds special evening sessions called "arithmetic school" or "spelling school." The following March, he and Fon partner to manufacture two-horse cultivators.

In 1870, Lewellyn moved further west, to Denver, with his brother Rinoldo (or Rinaldo, b. 1842). Partners in carpentry, they executed the finish work on Denver's famous Teller House.[421]

Rarely in perfect health, Lewellyn never married. He died May 27, 1892, in Littleton, Colorado.[422]

Lewellyn's older brother, John, served the Union. His brother Rinoldo also served, mustering in as a sergeant with Company B of the 23rd Maine

Volunteer Infantry in September 1862.[423] Apparently too ill to enlist himself, Bean has an intense interest in the Civil War and records some incidents related to Maine's Copperheads (Northerners who sympathized with the South at the time of the Civil War).*

> **Gilead, March 2, 1863**: *Father and I started for town meeting pretty early in the forenoon, that we might be there in season. I was chosen moderator to the dissatisfaction of the Copperheads, and when I called them to order one of them appeared very much supresed [sic], said he "guessed," he should talk as long as he "was a mind to," he owned some of the house and thought it strange if he could not say what he pleased. As he did not seem inclined to come to order I called upon the constable to take charge of him. The constable read the law to him, in regard to making a disturbance in town meetings when he concluded to come to order. The rest of the day passed without disturbance. We elected our board of officers, of course. I was chosen chairman of the Superintendent's School Committee.*
>
> **March 3:** *Sent a list of the town officers to the Oxford Democrat. Read some.*
>
> **May 22:** *Worked in the shop [on churns] until nearly night, then went to the Conner [Bean's Corner?]. On my way met Parly Heath with whom I got into conversation about the war and in my remarks I gave him to understand that I thought he was a sympathiser [sic] with the Rebels, for which he threatened to give me an awful thrashing and even took off his coat to do so, but finely [finally] concluded he had better not.*
>
> **May 27:** *Worked in the shop in the forenoon in the afternoon had callers[.] S. S. Twitchell and J. W. Greely called in to see me.*

---

* "Copperhead" was also applied to members of the Democratic Party or "Peace Democrats," who criticized President Lincoln's war policies and hoped for an armistice with the Confederacy.

Greely has been a soldier in the Maine 19ᵗʰ, was taken prisoner in Banks' retreat [from Fort Royal?] and retained [i.e., imprisoned for] four months. E. Jane Beane* also came for a certificate. She is going to teach the school in our district.

June 13: *Went to W. B[ethel] in the evening; found Mell Wight there. He and I called out to Mr. G's a few minutes then went to a copperhead meeting at the W.B. school house. We were not very welcome guests.*

July 3: *Had five hands [helping frame a barn] again today; intended to raise but did not get ready. Learned at noon that the 23rd Maine Reg. had come to Portland and some of the boys had come home and among them was Nat. Started for home at night and on my way met Nat coming for me; he looks healthy.*

The 23rd Regiment of Maine Volunteer Infantry, organized in Portland, mustered in for nine months' service on September 29, 1862. National Park Service records that the infantrymen were officially mustered out on July 15, 1863—although Lewellyn's diary proves that certain individuals reached home before that date. Among the 1,235 men on the regimental roster, there are ten with the first name Nathaniel. Their surnames are: Courson, Cousins, Davis, Dean, Field, Hill, Lander, Ordway, Quincy, and Skelton.[424]

July 4: *Rained some in the morning, but toward noon broke away and Nat and I went down to L. Grovers for some of Nat's things. In the afternoon we went down to W. Bethel where they were having a copperhead meeting, but did not patronize it much.*

July 11: *I, with a number of others went to South Paris to a "Union Rally." Listened to patriotic remarks by John J. Perry***,

---

* This may be Jane Bean, sister of Eliza Bean, a long-time teacher.
** This is probably John J. Perry (1811–1897) of Maine, who delivered an anti-slavery speech in the U.S. House of Representatives on March 7, 1860.

Silvanus Cobb Jr.,* Rev. A. Southworth, J. T. Gilman, Enoch Woodbury and Mrs. Parker.**

August 4: *Wrote a warrant to call a town meeting, on the authority of Moses Mason and several others, to see what the town will do about paying something to keep the soldiers at home who have been drafted in this town. But they will not get any thing for <u>that</u> purpose in <u>this</u> town.*

August 11: *Went to town meeting in the afternoon. The copperheads tried to raise $300 for each of the drafted soldiers in this town that they might pay their commutation and stay at home, but we voted them down.*

August 12: *The C's [Copperheads] presented another petition for another town meeting; I wrote a warrant for them.*

September 5: *Wrote a warrant for town meeting. Went to caucus to help nominate a candidate for representative [to the State Legislature?]. Nominated George Burnham.*

Sept. 8: *In the evening, went to Bethel and listened to speeches by Wilson of Mass. and S. Cobb Jr.*

Sept. 9: *Staid with A. Grover last night. Went into school a few minutes in the after noon then went to a Copperhead gathering. Littlefield and Paris were the principal speakers. They talked every thing but union.*

Sept. 15: *Had some words with the C. heads at West Bethel.*

Sept. 22: [Heads West by train.]

Ioka, Iowa, September 26: *Pretty tired, found my brother*

---

* This is most probably Sylvanus Cobb, Jr., a prolific journalist and fiction writer who worked for temperance and against slavery. Lewellyn hears Cobb speak again on the evening of Sept. 8.

** Mrs. Parker could have been the wife of Rev. Theodore Parker of Boston, a controversial Unitarian minister called "Minister to the Fugitive Slave."

[Alphonso] and family well.[*]

Ioka, May 1, 1864: . . . *Went to Rock Creek to the Baptist meeting today; went into the burying ground near the meeting house. Among other graves that I noticed was one with a board placed at the head bearing this inscription: G. Cypress Talley Aged 29 yrs 1 mo and 28 days. Murdered by the Abolitionists, Aug. 1, 1863. I should have known that I stood by the grave of a traitor from that inscription if I had known nothing of the circumstances which brought about his death. He was, I am told, a Baptist preacher [by] profession, but for some time previous to his death, had been taking a very active part in the "peace meetings" of the copperheads and at the time of his death was known to be the Captain of a company organized to <u>resist</u> the draft. He was shot by Union men for treasonable language used in a speech that he made.*

---

* Alphonso F. Bean and his wife Lucretia had five children, all born at Hedrick, Iowa.

Appendix 2.

Fifth Maine Volunteer Infantry:
Activities and Service

The 5th Regiment Maine Volunteer Infantry was one of the first Maine regiments to be mustered in after Lincoln's call for volunteers in April 1861. The original regiment numbered 1,046 men from southern and central areas of the Pine Tree state. The 5th was nicknamed "the Forest City Regiment" because Portland (which filled up several companies) was known as the Forest City.[425]

The basic organization, attachment, and service record of the regiment are taken from a compendium by Civil War veteran Frederick H. Dyer available at www.civilwararchive.com/regim.* Dyer's record of Union regiments is generally considered reliable. However, Clark Edwards's 1889 address at Gettysburg supplies some rather different details regarding the 5th. In the following, whenever Edwards's testimony differs from Dyer's, Edwards has been cited.

The insider's report of the regiment is George Bicknell's *History of the Fifth Regiment Maine Volunteers* (Portland, 1871). This important source has been reproduced with illustrations by Ward House Books. *Civil War Books, A Critical Biography*, calls Adjutant Bicknell's work "a superior personal reminiscence of service in all major battles of the East save

---

* CWSS does not list Dyer as having served the Union. However, the website about his *Compendium* says he served with the 35th Massachusetts Infantry. A source about the *Compendium* states that Frederick H. Dyer served as a drummer boy and later a private with the 7th Connecticut Infantry. Because Edwards had personal knowledge of the movements of the 5th Maine, his recollections have been favored over Dyer's research.

Chancellorsville; written with objectivity and insight."[426]

In addition to Andrew Jackson Bean, *The Roster of Union Soldiers* lists 153 Beans who fought for Maine.[427]

For many, the unplanned three-day battle of Gettysburg marked the flood tide of the Rebellion. The first of 1,500 memorials were erected on this battlefield in the spring of 1879.[428] The memorial to the 5th Maine, Bartlett's Artillery Brigade, stands on South Sedgwick Avenue.[429] (Maj. Gen. "Uncle John" Sedgwick was the commander of the Sixth Army Corps, of which 5th Maine was part at the time.)[430] The memorial to the 5th Maine Infantry Regiment stands below (and to the north of) Little Round Top, where the men formed up in support of the Third Corps late on the evening of July 2, threw up a stone wall* early on July 3, and held their ground through the terrible cannonading of that afternoon.[431] The eleven-foot-tall monument was dedicated October 3, 1889, and bears the coat of arms of Maine—a Greek cross and war trophies including a rifle and a canteen. Among those who fought there were Franklin Bean of Company A, Biddeford's Aaron H. Bean of Company B, and Bethuel Sawyer, David A. Edwards, John E. Bean, and John S. Wormell of Company I.[432]

Organization and attachment

Organized at Portland, Maine. Mustered in June 24, 1861. Left Portland by train, stopping briefly in New York, where they were presented with a silk flag by Portlanders living in that city.[433] Upon arrival in Washington, D.C., they were attached to Howard's Brigade, Heintzelman's Division, McDowell's Army of Northeastern Virginia, until August 1861. Subsequent attachments: Heintzelman's Brigade, Division of the Potomac, to October 1862. Slocum's Brigade, Franklin's Division, Army of the Potomac, to March 1862. 2nd Brigade, 1st Division, 1st Army Corps, Army of the Potomac and Department of the Rappahannock to May 1863. 2nd Brigade, 1st Division, 6th Army Corps, Army of the Potomac, to June 1864.

---

* This stone wall could still be seen in 1898 but was no longer in evidence in 2009.

Service

1861

June 26: Transferred from Maine to Washington, D.C. Camp at Meridian Hill until July 9.

July 9–12: Crossed the Potomac, and went into camp near Fort Ellsworth. Picket duty.

July 12: Advanced to Claremont.

July 17: Ordered to move against the enemy at Bull Run (Manassas, Va.)

July 29: Battle of Bull Run (First Manassas).*

July 1861– March 1862: Duty in the defenses of Washington, D.C.

October 3: Expedition to Pohick Church, Va.

1862

March 10–15: Advanced on Manassas.

April 4–12: McDowell's advance on Fredericksburg, Va.

April 22: Ordered to the Peninsula.

April 24–May 4: On transports during Siege of Yorktown.

May 7–8: Battle of Eltham's Landing (West Point, Va.). Made first bayonet charge.

May 24: Transferred to Slocum's division of Franklin's (Sixth) Corps; skirmished and fought at Battle of Chickahominy River.

June 25–July 1: Seven Days' battles.

June 27: Battle of Gaines' Mill.

June 28: Battle of Garnett's & Golding's Farms.

June 29: Battle of Savage's Station.

June 30: Battles of White Oak Swamp and Glendale [Frayser's Farm]

July 1: Battle of Malvern Hill.

Until August 15: At Harrison's Landing.

August 15–27: Retreat from the Peninsula and movement to Centreville, Va.

---

* Sgt. Alonzo Stinson, aged nineteen, was the first soldier of the 5th Maine killed.

August 27–31: In works at Centreville.

Sept. 1: Assisted in checking Pope's rout at Second Battle of Bull Run (Second Manassas) and covered retreat to Fairfax Church House.

September–October: Maryland Campaign.

September 14: Battle of South Mountain, Crampton's Pass.

September 16–17: Battle of Antietam*, Md.

Sept. 26–Oct. 29: At Hagerstown, Md.

October 29–November 19: Moved to Falmouth, Va.

December 12–15: Battle of Fredericksburg

1863

January 20–24: "Mud March."

Winter 1862–63: In winter quarters on the north bank of the Rappahannock.

April 27–May 6: Chancellorsville Campaign.

April 29–May 2: Operations at Franklin's Crossing.

May 3: Second Battle of Fredericksburg (Second Battle of Marye's Heights).

May 3–4: Battle of Salem Church.

May 4: At Banks' Ford on the Rappahannock.

July 1: In camp near Manchester, Md. Began 36-mile march to Gettysburg at 9:30 p.m. Fifth moved to the front as far as Plum Run.[434]

July 2–4: Battle of Gettysburg.

July 5: In pursuit of Lee's army. Engagements at Fairfield and Williamsport.

July 10–13: Near Funkstown, Md.

July 13: Battle of Williamsport (Battle of Hagerstown).

August 15. In camp at Harrison's Landing. Transferred to Alexandria, Va.

August 26–29: At Fort Lyon, Alexandria.

August 23: Destroyed bridge at Cub Run. Marched into Maryland.

---

* Antietam is considered the bloodiest single day in American history. The battle cancelled the Confederacy's first attempt to invade the North. The 23,000 casualties shocked the civilian population.

November 7–8: Advance to line of the Rappahannock (VA.)

November 7: Second Battle of Rappahannock Station.[435]

November 26–December 2: Mine Run Campaign.

1864

December 2, 1863– May 3, 1864: In Culpeper County and Wellford's Ford, Va.

May 3– June 15: Campaign from the Rapidan to the James River, Va.

May 5-7: Battle of the Wilderness.

May 8: Battle of Laurel Hill.

May 10–12: Battle of Spotsylvania Court House.

May 23–26: Battle of North Anna.

May 26–28: On line of the Pamunkey River.

May 28–31: Battle of Totopotomy Creek.

June 1–12: Battle of Cold Harbor.

June 19–22: Before Petersburg, Va. Ordered to the rear for muster out.

July 27: Mustered out at Portland, Maine, upon expiration of three-year enlistment. Re-enlisting veterans and new recruits transferred to 6th Maine Infantry.

Losses

Regiment lost during service 8 officers and 99 enlisted men killed and mortally wounded; one officer and 76 enlisted men lost by disease. Total: 184.

Details of the day-to-day operations of the regiment are supplied by George W. Bicknell's *History*.

As the boys from Maine marched, they fantasized about the "ideal of lovely villas and gorgeous residences" that might become "their future residences" once confiscated from the defeated Secessionists.[436]

At Manassas on July 21, 1861, the Fifth Maine was the second-to-last in a long parade heading for the battle. They were obliged to run six to seven miles, at huge cost. Adjutant Bicknell described their travails:

"Our thinning ranks began to show the effects of overexertion. Men seemed to fall in squads by the roadside, some sunstruck, some bleeding at nose, mouth, ears; others were wind-broken, while others were exhausted to such a degree, that the threatening muzzle of the officers' pistol, failed to induce them a step further."

The Fifth Maine lost half its men to the march, but only one to actual combat.

Fifth Maine Infantry Monument below Little Round Top at Gettysburg. Photo by Fernand Chandonnet.

During the War Between the States, the Regiment served in 22 major engagements—the majority of them in the state of Virginia. These engagements included the First Battle of Bull Run, Gaines Mill, Antietam, Fredericksburg, Chancellorsville, Gettysburg, Rappahannock Station, Spotsylvania, and Cold Harbor. During this time, 107 were killed or died of their wounds; seventy-seven men died of disease. Despite their losses, many re-enlisted into the 1st Maine Veteran Infantry. (Andrew Bean did not re-enlist.)

The Fifth Maine left Portland for Washington, D.C., on June 25. Arriving in D.C. on the evening of June 27th, the regiment was brigaded with the 3rd and 4th Maine and the 2nd Vermont as part of the Third Brigade, Third Division of the Army of Northeastern Virginia. With less than a month's training, the soldiers were ordered on the "double quick" on July 16 to Manassas, VA. This two-day march in sweltering heat proved disastrous for many of the Fifth, who collapsed from exhaustion, sun stroke and dehydration. The Union army was allowed to rest while its commander, Brigadier General Irvin McDowell, searched for a way to outflank a force of 21,000 Confederates under Brig. Gen. P. G .T. Beauregard. McDowell led 28,450 men—the largest field army on the North American continent to that date.

In February 1862, passes were issued for some soldiers to visit the capital. Some boys of the Fifth Maine helped prepare the regimental payroll, and were then told they could play tourist until due back at camp. Corporal Rhodes of Rhode Island accompanied them and later described the scene:

> We turned first toward the White House, feeling that could we only get a glimpse of 'Uncle Abe,' we should be amply repaid for the labor we had already performed. Approaching the door to the public entrance, hat in hand, we were met at the threshold by some burly officer who wanted to know what we wanted. Conscious of our position—soldiers, only common soldiers, we hardly dared to explain that we came only out of curiosity, but yet ventured to remark that we were very desirous of seeing the White House. Immediately we were told that we had better leave; when, at that moment, who should appear but the president himself, passing out toward the street, perceiving us, humble as we were, a smile seemed to overspread his features, and slightly bowing, he said, 'How do you do, my boys?' Giving us each a shake of the hand, accompanied by a look which seemed to say that we might enter.... It was some such little acts of President Lincoln which endeared him to the hearts of the soldiery.[437]

After the war, Civil War veterans felt the need of a place to meet and share reminiscences. In 1888, former members of the Fifth Maine (including Andrew Bean) funded construction of a large Victorian cottage on the south shore of Peaks Island in Casco Bay. Stained glass windows etched with veterans' names ornament the walls. Wide covered porches made the cottage a favorite vacation retreat.

The Fifth Maine Regiment Memorial Building, placed on the National Register of Historic Buildings in 1978, currently operates as a Civil War Museum as well as a community center for Peaks Island.

Appendix 3.

Fifth Maine Volunteers, Company I: Roster

"Some Southerners have argued that if Maine had not taken part in the military campaign of the War, the South might have won." [438]

The following roster was extracted from the CWSS (Civil War Soldiers and Sailors System) database compiled by the National Park Service and unveiled at Ford's Theatre in 2004. The database holds the records of 6.3 million soldiers as well as regiments and battle histories. These names were selected from those available at http://www.itd.nps.gov/cwss on January 17, 2007.

For the purposes of this book, only members of Company I—Andrew Bean's company—are listed. Some of the names may be repeats/misspellings or the interpretation of unclear handwriting, such as James C. Ayer and James C. Ayers and Dennis Dailey and Dennis Daily, all privates. Note the variants of "Besee." However, because the enlistees came from a limited geographical area, families were large and families often reused names from relatives (or appropriated the names of celebrities), it is possible that Lowell B. Pratt and Lowell W. Pratt are cousins. An alternate source of regiment members, Bicknell's history, lists only one Pratt, Lowell W. of Bethel.[439] Fathers and sons, uncles and cousins sometimes enlisted together. Certainly these names were recorded under distracting, noisy, emotional circumstances, in haste, often by scribes with better penmanship than spelling.

It must be noted that the roster printed in the *Clark S. Edwards Fifth*

Maine Volunteer Regiment Compiled Letters, 1861-1903 (Pearce Civil War Collection, Navarro College, # 2002-310, no date) differs in many instances from the CWSS roster. Ayer is James C. Ayer. There is a single Besse, for instance: Caleb Besse. Peter Brahant, Peter Breahart, Horace K. Chace, Josiah Estese, musician Charles Freeman, Thomas Lamlet, Thomas Lawler, Thomas Lawlet, Jacop W. Martin, Thomas S. Maxwell, John F. Nesbit, Lowell B. Pratt and John H. Spalding do not appear in *Letters*. Dennis "Dailey" is "Daily." "Ase" Ellenwood is "Asa." Patrick Farran is "Farren." "Fessenden," "Glidden," "Goodenow," "Hamlin," "Lawrence," "Littlehalll" are preferred spellings. Four men carry the surname "Foye." "Augustus A. Granier" becomes "Joseph Augustus Grenier." CWSS's "Micah Howard" and "Michail Howard" are reduced to a single Michael Howard, as "Edward B. Sturges" and "Edward G. Sturgis" are reduced to "Edward G. Sturgis" while "Levi W. Toll" and "Levi W. Towle" become "Levi N. Towle." "Angie J. Mitchell" and "Auger J. Mitchell" are listed as "Anger J. Mitchell." CWSS's "Tessenden Swan" is listed as "Fessenden Swan." The five variants of Vailencourt are reduced to one man, "Henry Vaillancourt." The three variants of Whitmore become "Enoch Whittemore." Two Lot Wileys boil down to "Lot D. Wiley." Names appearing on the Edwards's list that CWSS does not mention include George Cook, Albert L. Deering, Bryce M. Edwards, Lewis H. Lunt, P. Jordan Mitchell, Spencer T. Peabody, Washington B. Robertson, Lorenzo Russell, Fred G. Sanborn, Daniel M. Stearns, William A. Tubbs and Adelbert B. Twitchell.

According to the website of the Fifth Maine Museum, 1046 men served in the original regiment; another 500 joined later. After three years of fighting, only 193 men mustered out in July 1864.[440]

The rank given below is the rank at initial enlistment. Note the many Beans.*

---

* The website "Some Civil War Soldiers of Northwest Maine" (www/geocities.com/barbour1048/CWsoldiers) lists Francis O. Bean (17th Maine Infantry), John H. Bean (29th Maine Infantry), Roscoe G. Bean and John S. Bean (8th Maine Infantry).

Abbott, John F. .... Private
Abbott, John T. .... Private
Adams, Charles .... Private
Adams, Thomas.. Private
Andrews, David E. .... Private
Ayer, James C.. Private
Ayers, James C. .... Private
Bean, Andrew J.. Private
Bean, Barzley K.* .... Private
Bean, Franklin ** .... Private
Bean, John E.*** .... Private
Beard, Lewis C... Private
Bennett, Joseph.. Private
Bent, John A. .... Private
Besee, Jr., Caleb .... Private
Bessee, Jr., Caleb... Private
Bessey, Jr., Caleb... Private
Bessy, Jr., Caleb... Private
Bowden, James H. .... Private
Boyd, James... Private
Brackett, Joel W.. Private
Brahant, Peter.. Private
Breahart, Peter... Private
Brown, Washington F. .... Sergeant****

* This is probably farmer Brazelia Kendall Bean, born in West Bethel in April 1837.

** There are six men with the name Franklin Bean listed in *The Clan MacBean in North America*, p. 123. This is probably the one born in 1830, cited as having died in the Civil War on July 2, 1863.

*** There are six men with the name John E. Bean listed in *The Clan MacBean* genealogy. John Edward Bean (b. 1833) was the older brother of Brazelia Kendall Bean. There are details of his life on p. 203 of that genealogy.

**** In his letter of April 9, 1864, Clark S. Edwards notes that "...at Salem Chapel fell the Brave & gallant Brown of Bethel...."

Brown, Washington I. .... Sergeant

Bryant, John F. .... Private

Burbank, Stephen .... Musician

Campbell, John .... Private

Chace, Horace K. .... Private

Chase, Horace K. .... Private

Cook, Dustin A. .... Private

Cross, Isaac C. .... Wagoner

Cross, Sidney T. .... Private

Dailey, Dennis .... Private

Daily, Dennis .... Private

Dolloff, Levi W. .... Corporal

Dunham, Charles .... Private

Edwards, Clark S. .... Captain*

Edwards, David A. .... Corporal

Edwards, Sidney D. .... Private

Ellenwood, Ase F. .... Private

Ellingwood, Asa F. .... Private

Estes, Isaac W. .... Private

Estes, Josiah. .... Private

Estes, Jr., Stephen .... Private

Estese, Josiah. .... Private

Evans, James M. .... Corporal

Fargo, George W. .... Private

Farran, Patrick .... Private

Fesenden, George W. .... Private

Fessenden, George W. .... Private

Fletcher, Oliver .... Private

Foley, Patrick .... Private

Foy, Edgar .... Private

* Edwards was promoted to colonel in January 1863. He was later breveted to brigadier general for bravery in battle.

Foy, John A.	Private
Foye, Edgar	Private
Foye, John A.	Private
Freeman, Charles	Musician
Glidden, John E. W.	Private
Gliddon, John E. W.	Private
Goodnow, Lafayette G.	Private
Goodwin, Lafayette G.	Private
Grady, Thomas O.	Private
Granier, Augustus A.	Corporal
Grant, Daniel	Private
Grenier, Augustus J.	Corporal
Grenier, Joseph A.	Corporal*
Hamblin, Joshua G.	Private
Hamlin, Joshua G.	Private
Hammond, James B.	Sergeant
Hammond, Joseph B.	Sergeant
Harper, William R.	Private
Heath, Clement S.	Private
Horn, Charles W.	Private
Horne, Chas. W.	Private
How, George	Private
Howard, Micah	Private
Howard, Michail	Private
Howe, Robert	Private
Hutchins, Sullivan R.	Sergeant
Jackson, Aaron F.	Private
Jackson, Aaron H.	no rank given
Jordan, Asa D.	`no rank given

* Grenier is listed as a 2nd Lieutenant in the state website www.maine.gov/sos/
arc/archives/military/civilwar/offpix.htm. This website contains about 600 carte-
de-visite photographs of Maine officers solicited by the Adjutant General during
and immediately after the War.

Jordon, Asa D. .... Private
Kelley, James... Private
Kelly, James... no rank given
Knapp, Peter G. .... Corporal
Lamlet, Thomas.. Private
Lapham, Richmond M................................. Private
Lawler, Thomas.. Private
Lawlet, Thomas .... Private
Lawrance, C.R.. Private
Lawrence, Cyrus R. .... Private
Lemont, Daniel.. Private
Littlefield, James A....................................... Private
Littlehale, Stillman N. .... Private
Lufkin, Samuel E.. Private
Martin, Jacop W... Private
Martin, Jerry .... Private
Martin, Royal T. .... Private
Maxwell, Thomas S....................................... Private
Maxwell, Thomas T. .... Private
McInnes, Hugh F. .... Private
McInnis, Hugh F... Private
Miller, James .... Private
Mitchell, Angie J. .... Corporal
Mitchell, Auger J. .... Corporal
Morgan, Charles F. .... Private
Morgan, Jacob W. .... Private
Morse, George A. .... Private
Nesbit, John F. .... Private
Nesbit, John F. .... Private
Nugent, Thomas .... Private
O'Grady, Thomas O. .... Private
Parker, Alonzo F. .... Private

Parker, Alonzo S. .... Private
Peabody, A. Samuel .... Private
Peabody, Samuel A. .... Private
Peabody, Thomas S.* .... Corporal
Penley, Ephraim C. .... Private
Penley, Rufus C. .... Private
Perry, Albert K. .... Private
Pingree, William H. .... Private
Poor, Lorenzo D. .... Private
Pratt, Lowell B. .... Private
Pratt, Lowell W. .... Private
Rice, Nelson .... Private
Ricker, George W. .... Private
Rolfe, Henry A. J. .... Private
Rundlet, Gardner F. .... Private
Sanborn, Simeon W. .... Sergeant
Sawyer, Betheul S.** .... Private
Sawyer, Joseph C. .... Private
Scott, Silas .... Private
Scribner, Daniel W. .... Sergeant
Shackley, John .... Private
Shaw, Samuel Y. .... Private
Shedd, Levi .... Private
Small, George E. .... Private
Smith, John .... Private
Smith, John H. F. .... Private
Spalding, John H. .... Artificer

* According to unpublished "The Civil War Diary of H. G. Otis Perkins" (p. 94), Thomas Peabody was captured by the Confederates while on a work detail with Lt. John Stevens of Company D on Dec. 14, 1863, by a band of guerillas. Stevens spent the rest of the war at Libby Prison. The fate of Peabody is unknown.

** According to the letters of Clark S. Edwards, Betheul Sawyer was known as "Su Sawyer."

Sprague, Thomas H. .... Private

Steward, Thomas .... Private

Sturges, Edward B. .... Private

Sturgis, Edward G. .... Private

Swan, Tessenden.. Private

Thompson, Josiah... Private

Thurlow, Cyrus S... Private

Thurlow, Cyrus T... Private

Toll, Levi W.. no rank given

Towle, Levi W.* .... Private

Vailencourt, Henry... Private

Vaillancourt, Henry .... Private

Vaillencourt, Henry .... Private

Valencourt, Henry.. Private

Valincourt, Henry .... Private

Walker, John B. .... Lieutenant

Walker, Milo C.** .... Private

Wentworth, Charles M....................................... Private

Whitman, Alanson M. *** .... no rank given

Whitman, Alonzo M. .... Private

Whitmore Jr., Enoch.. no rank given

Whittemore Jr., Enoch...................................... Private

Whittimore Jr., Enoch...................................... no rank given

Wiley, Lot D. .... Corporal

Willey, Lot D. **** .... no rank given

---

* Towle is listed on p. 336 of *Roster of Union Soldiers*.

** According to "Otis Perkins" (p. 94), Walker was an 28-year-old farmer from Bethel. He was captured with three other Maine men and sent to Andersonville Prison in December 1863. He died there on July 24, 1864.

*** Whitman is given the rank of Corporal by "Otis Perkins." He was captured with Walker and others and sent to Andersonville. He died there August 2, 1864.

**** Wiley is given the rank of Corporal on p. 358 of *The Roster of Union Soldiers, 1861–1865*, Maine and New Hampshire Volume.

Wormell, Cyrus M.*, ** .... Second Lieutenant

York, Cornelius M. .... Private

York, Willoughby R....................................... Wagoner

Two officers of the Fifth Maine. Col. Clark S. Edwards (left) and 2nd Lt. Joseph A. Grenier. Courtesy Maine State Archives.

* Edwards mentions a John Wormell in a letter fragment. In his letter of Oct. 5, 1863, he mentions "Wormell" without a Christian name.

** Both a Cyrus and a John Wormell are mentioned on p. 365 of *The Roster of Union Soldiers*. John S. Wormell was in Company I and re-enlisted in Company B of the 1st Maine Veterans Volunteers with diarist Otis Perkins. John Wormell was a stone worker by trade. Perkins mentions writing to him in his diary entry for April 19, 1865 (p. 118, "Perkins").

Appendix 4.

Twenty-Sixth Massachusetts Infantry: Activities and Service

Basic facts about the organization and assignments of the Twenty-Sixth Massachusetts Infantry Regiment are recorded in www.civilwar-archive.com/regm.htm. Specifics about Henry Foster have been added.

Organization and assignments

Organized at Camp Cameron, Cambridge, Mass., August 28, 1861. Moved to Camp Chase, Lowell, Mass., Sept. 23, for basic training. Moved to Boston, Nov. 19. Sailed on steamer *Constitution* to Ship Island, Miss., Nov. 21, arriving there Dec. 3. Attached to Ship Island Expedition with duty at Ship Island until April 15, 1862. Attached to 2nd Brigade, Department of the Gulf, to October 1862. Defenses of New Orleans, Dept. of the Gulf, to January 1863. 2nd Brigade, 2nd Division, 19th Army Corps, Dept. of the Gulf, to July 1863. 2nd Brigade, 3rd Division, 19th Army Corps, Dept. of the Gulf, to February 1864. 2nd Brigade, 2nd Division, 19th Army Corps, Dept of the Gulf, to June 1864. 1st Brigade, 2nd Division, 19th Army Corps, Dept. of the Gulf, to July 1864, and Army of the Shenandoah, Middle Military Division, to January 1865. 2nd Brigade, 1st Division, 19th Army Corps, Army of the Shenandoah, to April 1865. 2nd Brigade, 1st Provisional Division, Army of the Shenandoah, to April 1865. 2nd Brigade, 1st Division, Dept. of Washington, 22nd Army Corps to June 1865. Department of the South to August 1865.

Service

September 21, 1861: Henry Foster enlists in Company A.

Dec. 3, 1861–April 15, 1862: Occupation of Ship Island, Mississippi.

March 8, 1862: Skirmish at Mississippi City.

April 15–18: Movement to the passes of the Mississippi River.

April 18–28: Operations against Forts St. Phillip and Jackson.

April 28: The forts surrender. [441]

April 29: General Benjamin Butler details the 26th Massachusetts to garrison the forts.[442]

April 28 to July 1: Movement to New Orleans and duty there until June 20, 1863.

September 13–15: One Company makes an expedition to Pass Manchac and Ponchatoula.

December 24: Butler is recalled by President Lincoln. The 26th escorts Butler and his wife to the docks. Hundreds of supporters bid him goodbye, and he shakes every hand. [443]

June 20, 1863: Regiment moved to LaFourche Crossing

June 20–21: Action at LaFourche Crossing, Thibodeaux.

June 26: Moved to Bontee Station.

June 30: Moved to Jefferson Station.

July 15: Moved to New Orleans, and on provost duty there until August 28.

August 28–29: Moved to Baton Rouge.

Sept. 4–11: Sabine Pass Texas Expedition. At Algiers until Sept. 16.

Sept. 16: Moved to Brashear City and Berwick City.

Sept. 23: Moved to Camp Bisland.

Oct. 3–November 30: Western Louisiana "Teche" Campaign.

At New Iberia until Jan. 7, 1864.

Jan. 7–9, 1864, Moved to Franklin; duty there until February 24. Henry Foster reenlists.

Feb. 14–25: Moved to New Orleans, and duty there until March 22.

March 22 to May 20: Veterans on leave. Henry visits his family in Lowell.

Camp Carrollton until June 8. The steamer trip each way takes about 8 days, giving him a total of about 30 days of furlough.

June 8: Moved to Morganza and duty there until July 3.

July 3–4: Moved to New Orleans, thence to Fortress Monroe and Bermuda Hundred, VA.

July 22–28: On the Bermuda Hundred front.

July 28–29: Deep Bottom.

July 28-30: Demonstration on the north side of the James River.

July 30–August 1: Moved to Washington, D.C.; thence to Camp Tennally, August 1.

August to December: Sheridan's Shenandoah Valley Campaign.

Sept. 19: Battle of Third Winchester, VA. Henry is fatally wounded.

September 22: Fisher's Hill.*

Oct. 19: Battle of Cedar Creek, VA.

Oct. 19: Non-Veterans left front and mustered out Nov. 7.

October 1864 to May 1, 1865: Provost duty at Headquarters of Middle Military Division and Army of the Shenandoah at Winchester.

May 1–2: Moved to Washington, D.C.

May 2–June 3: Camp at Washington.

June 3–7: Moved to Savannah, GA.

June 7–August 2: Provost duty.

August 26, 1865: Mustered out.

---

* After its defeat at Third Winchester on Sept. 19, Early's army took up a defensive position at Fisher's Hill, outside Strasburg. On the morning of Sept. 21, the Union army, under the command of Sheridan, advanced and was able to capture high ground. On the following day, Brig. Gen. George Crook's Corps moved along Little North Mountain, outflanked Early and launched a surprise attack at about 4 p.m. The Confederate defense collapsed and other Union corps joined in the assault. Early's army retreated to Rockfish Gap, and the Union commenced its scorched-earth program. Mills and barns from Staunton to Strasburg went up in flames in what was called "The Burning" or "Red October."

Sept. 12–18: Transported to Boston and there discharged from service.

The Regiment lost during service 3 officers and 61 enlisted men killed and mortally wounded, and 3 officers and 182 enlisted men by disease. Total: 249.

Although histories of or diaries/letters related to Massachusetts infantry regiments are available for the 1st, 2nd, 3rd, 5th, 6th, 7th, 9th, 10th, 11th, 12th, 13th, 15th, 17th, 19th, 20th, 21st, 23rd, 24th, 25th, 27th, 29th, 30th, 32nd, 33rd, 34th, 35th, 36th, 37th, 38th, 39th, 42nd, 43rd, 44th, 45th, 48th, 49th, 50th, 52nd, 53rd, and 57th regiments, there is no history for Henry Foster's 26th. Some information regarding the 26th Infantry was gleaned from William Schouler's *Massachusetts in the Civil War* (1868).

Appendix 5.

Twenty-Sixth Massachusetts Infantry, Company A: Roster

Patriotic Lowell and surroundings contributed sixty-one infantry regiments to the Union cause. The men ranged in age from 18 to 54—the oldest a band member. Company A, Twenty-Sixth Regiment, Massachusetts Infantry was the company in which Henry Foster enlisted. The following roster of company members was selected from a National Park Service website, www.itd.nps.gov/cwss/Soldier_Results.cfm on January 16, 2007. The complete CWSS list includes 2058 names arranged alphabetically, followed by company, rank in and rank out. (About a dozen men lack a company designation.)

In numerous instances, some of these 2058 names could be repeats/ misspellings. For example, Walter Alward is probably the same man as Walter Alwert, Walter Alwood and Walter Alwort. William H. Comerford may be the same enlistee as William Cumerford. Furthermore, Henry's friend John A. McIver seems to be listed a second time, as "John A. McKiver." Corrections of these probable doublings have not been attempted, although they are indicated in the Index.

The names listed below are from Company A. The rank given is the entering rank. Ranks in this company ranged from undercook to teamster to surgeon, with the majority of the men ranked private. Examination of the list reveals that rarely did a man who enlisted as a private rise above that rank.

Men who shifted from Company A to another are not listed below.

Men who were in Co. F (or another) and later in A are not listed. At least one individual, Sgt. John L. Keyser, served in three companies: initially in Company F, next in A, and finally in C. (An exception has been made for Ezekiel Easman—actually Eastman—because he figures indirectly in one of Henry Foster's letters. Eastman originally enlisted in Company H of the Twenty-Sixth.)

Abbott, Amond C. .... Private
Aitchison, John S... Second Lieutenant
Alward, Walter... Private
Alwert, Walter .... Private
Alward, Walter... Private
Alwood, Walter.. Private
Alwort, Walter .... Private
Applby, Jacob .... Private
Arm, Adolph.. Private
Armstrong, George.. Private
Arnold, William W. .... Private
Atkinson, Thomas A... Private
Austin, Samuel G. .... Private
Austin, William H.. Private
Bailey, George A. .... Private
Bailey, George E.. Corporal
Bain, William... Private
Balcolm, Horace A. .... Private
Balcolm, Horace O. .... Private
Barnes, James E... Private
Barnes, Timothy P.. Private
Bassett, Martin L. .... Private
Bean, Henry... Private
Beeman, James .... Private
Bennett, Edward T. .... Private

Berry, Frank S..Private

Blackmer, Warren A. ....Private

Blake, John..Private

Blood, Leonard...Private

Bohonon, Joseph ....Private

Bowen, William..Undercook

Brogan, Charles H. ....Private

Brown, Roscairous * ....Private

Buchannan, James ....Private

Bulmer, John..Private

Burk, John ....Private

Burnes, Henry...Private

Burns, Henry ....Private

Butters, Edward...Private

Calahan, John ....Private

Canihe, Theodore W. ....Drummer**

Cannor, John...Private

Carson, Michael...Private

Cavanagh, James ....Private

Chamberlain, John R. ....Private

Chandler, Jr., Joseph......................................Sergeant

Clark, Charles W..Private

Classon, John B. ....Private

Closson, John B...Private

Comerford, William H....................................Private

Conihe, Theodore W......................................Drummer

Conihie, Theodore W.....................................Drummer

Conlan, Edward...Corporal

Conlin, Edward...Corporal

* On the CWSSS website, his first name is spelled "Roscavious."

** In CWSS, this is the proper spelling of the surname of this individual—not "Conihe" or "Conihie."

Connor, James ....Private
Connor, John...Private
Connors, James..Private
Connors, John...Private
Cook, Kames* ....Private
Cooke, James..Private
Cooke, James G..Private
Crafts, Henry C...Private
Crosby, Alonzo ....Private
Cross, William B. ....Corporal
Cruse, James..Private
Cumerford, William...Private
Dean, Osborne..Colored Cook
Dearborn, Calvin F. ....Private
Dickerman, Alphonso T......................................Private
Dickerman, George M. ....Captain
Dickerman, Ormondo W.......................................Second Sergeant**
Downing, Edward F..Private
Downing, Edward T..Private
Downing, John A..Private
Duhig, Daniel T. ....Private
Dwinnalls, Andrew H. ....Private
Dwinnals, Andrew H. ....Private
Dwinnells, Andrew H. ....Private
Eagan, Michael M. ....Private
Easman, Ezekiel W. ....Second Lieutenant
Elliott, Thomas C..Private
Emerson, Charles F...Corporal
Emerson, Charles H...Private
Farrell, James...Private

* In CWSSS, the first name is "James."
** According to CWSSS, Ormondo was later promoted to First Lieutenant.

Farrell, Michael J... Private

Field, David C. G. .... Private

Ford, Robert H... Private

Ford, William.. Private

Foss, George W.. Private

Foster, Henry C. .... Corporal

Frost, John .... Private

Garvin, James A. .... Private

Gilmore, Isaac E.. Private

Gilpatrick, John .... Private

Goodhue, John... Private

Goodwin, Thomas J... Private

Gower, William D... Private

Grout, Chauncey L. .... Drummer

Grout, Frank N. .... First Sergeant

Grout, Frank R.. First Sergeant

Halpin, Patrick... Private

Helpin, Patrick... Private

Hogan, James.. Private

Horn, Charles C... Corporal

Howard, Frank... Private

Howard, James .... Private

Huggins, Adoniron J.. Private

Huggins, Eri.. Private

Huggins, Judson A... Private

Huntington, James H. .... Private

Irving, William .... Private

Jackson, James.. Private

Jay, Henry.. Private

Johnson, Andrew J.. First Lieutenant

Johnson, Charles.. Private

Johnson, William A. .... Private

Jones, Edward F...Private
Joy, Henry...Private
Keatan, Daniel...Private
Keating, Daniel..Private
Keaton, Daniel..Private
Kelley, Hiram ....Private
Kelley, John ....Private
Kelly, John..Private
Kelly 1st, John..Private
Kent, Jr., Charles ....Private
Knapp, Charles M..Private
Laffam, Joseph ....Private
Laflin, Joseph...Private
Lynch, William ....Private
Mace, William H. ....Private
Marble, Charles H. ....Private
McDonald, John ....Private
McIver, John A. ....Private
McKiver, John A. ....Private
McManis, Philip ....Private
McManus, Philip ....Private
Morey, Lyman J...Private
Nasan, Royal T. ....Private
Nason, Royal F. ....Private
Nason, Royal T. ....Private
Norton, Bradford S. ....Sergeant
Nugent, Ruben...Undercook
O'Neil, John ....Private
Oaks, Alphonson ....Private
Osgood, Jesse C...Private
Packard, Joseph ....Private
Peabody, Isaac ....Private

Perry, Benjamin .... Private
Quimby, G. W. .... Private
Quinby, George W. .... Private
Resdin, Samuel .... Private
Reynolds, John .... Private
Richardson, Charles H. .... Corporal*
Richardson, Luther L. .... Private**
Richard, Luther L. .... Corporal
Riley, Patrick .... Private
Ripley, Joseph B. .... Private
Risden, Samuel .... Private
Russell, James .... Teamster
Sanborn, John .... Private
Sawyer, Barnard H. .... Private
Sawyer, Edward A. .... Private
Searles, Henry D. .... Private
Searles, William A. .... Private
Searles, William D. .... Private
Shaw, Chase S. .... Corporal
Slater, Joseph .... Corporal
Smith, Charles J. .... Private
Spencer, Robert .... Private
Sprague, Frederick E. .... Private
Sprague, Thomas .... Private
Stone, Abel H. .... Private
Stone, George H. .... Quartermaster Sergeant
Straw, Daniel .... Private
Sullivan, Daniel .... Private
Sullivan, John S. .... Private
Sweeney, Michael .... Private

* Tent mate of Henry Foster.
** Brother of Charles H. Richardson.

Taylor, Charles E. .... Drummer

Taylor, James F. .... Private

Taylor, Peter.. Private

Temple, Emery .... Private

Terrill, James L. .... Private

Thomas, Richard E. .... Private

Thompson, James G. .... Private

Turrell, James L. .... Private

Turrill, James .... Private

Veet, Charles.. Private

Veete, Charles.. Private

Wardsworth, Dura... Private

Ware, Nicholas N... Private

Wedgewood, Edwin S. .... Private

Wedgwood, Edward S. .... Private

Wedgwood, Edwin S. .... Private

Weeks, Henry A... Private

Welch, Patrick.. Private

Willey, William H... Second Lieutenant

Wilson, Franklin T. .... Private

Wilson, Joseph H... Private

Wilson, Justus B. .... Private

Wing, Julian A. .... Private

Withee, Thompason H....................................... Private

Withie, Thompson H. .... Private

Woodard, Alexander... Private

Woods Jr., John E. .... Private

Woods Sr., John E.. Private

Woodward, Alexander .... Private

Bibliography.

PROFESSOR JAY HOAR HAS COUNTED 260 NAMES for the war, among them the Irrepressible Conflict, the Tragic Years, and the Ruckus.[444] Whether one calls it the Rebellion, the War of Northern Aggression, the Lost Cause, the War Between the States, or the War for Southern Independence, the American Civil War is the subject of more than 108,000 books.[445]

More than forty titles treat Maine's role alone.[446] The *Memorial and Letters of Rev. John R. Adams, D.D.* (1890), written for friends and family and issued in a private printing, is typical. Adams served as chaplain of both the 5th Maine and the 121st New York. Among the most recently published personal records is *"Without a Scratch:" Diary of Corporal William Holmes Morse, Color Bearer of the Fifth Maine Infantry* (2007).

Unpublished Material

Letters by Eliza Howard Bean Foster, Henry Charles Foster, Andrew Jackson Bean, Mabelia Foster Fox, Mary Holt Bean, Amanda Wood Foster, Clarinda Patterson Foster Lynch, Henrietta Foster Hickford, and others in the archives of the Bethel Historical Society, Regional History Center, 10–14 Broad Street, Bethel, Maine 04217.

Diary for 1863 by Eliza Howard Bean Foster on file with Bethel Historical Society.

Various deeds, receipts, military documents, pension documents, textile mill rules, etc., on file with Bethel Historical Society.

Unsigned letter from Baton Rouge, Apr. 26, 1864. MSS 1990.16. Louisiana State Museum, Baton Rouge, La.

Diary of Albert Balcom of Sherburne, N.Y. Courtesy of Charles Stewart, Attic Treasures Antiques, Madison, Ga.

Diary of Lewellyn D. Bean. Archives of the Clan MacBean in North America, 441 Wadsworth Blvd., Suite 213, Denver, Colo., 80226.

Letter from Peter Costelloe. Mss1St124a24. Virginia Historical Society, Richmond, Va.

H. D. Cushing correspondence. Virginia Polytechnic Institute and State University.

Diary of Edward Heavey Davis. Handley Regional Library Archives, Winchester–Frederick County Historical Society, Winchester, Va. Accessed from U.S. Army Military History Institute Archives, Carlisle, Pa.

Letters by John R. Dunban. Woodson Research Center, Fondren Library, Rice University.

Papers of Clark S. Edwards, 1861–1903. Pearce Civil War Collection. Navarro College, Corsicana, Tex.

Diary of Walter H. Farwell. W. P. Palmer Regimental Papers. Western Reserve Historical Society. On file, Box B-47, library of Gettysburg National Military Park, Gettysburg, Pa.

Letter from Daniel P. Mason. 18630324. RG68. 1975.18. Louisiana State Museum, Baton Rouge, La.

The Roy Ancestors. http://freepages.genealogy.rootsweb.ancestry.com/~dianastar/CAMLEY/roy.html, accessed on Feb. 6, 2009.

Books, Lectures

Bean, Joseph S. *The Clan MacBean in North America, Inc.: A Genealogy and History*. 6th ed., revised from earlier edition in 3 vols. Denver, Colo.: The Clan MacBean in North America, Inc., 1992.

Beattie, Donald W., Rodney M. Cole, and Charles G. Waugh, eds. *A Distant War Comes Home: Maine in the Civil War Era*. Camden, Maine: Down East Books, 1996.

Bicknell, George W. *History of the Fifth Maine Regiment*. Portland, Maine: Hall L. Davis, 1871. Repr. Eustis, Me.: MacDonald's Military Memorabilia and Maine Mementoes, 1988.

Blight, David W. *Race and Reunion: The Civil War in American Memory.* Cambridge, Mass.: The Belknap Press of Harvard University Press, 2001.

Bowman, John S., ed. *The Civil War Almanac.* New York: Facts on File, 1983.

Bryant, Blanche Brown, and Gertrude Elaine Baker, eds. *The Diaries of Sally and Pamela Brown, 1832–1838; Hyde Leslie, 1887, Plymouth Notch, Vermont.* Springfield, Vt.: William L. Bryant Foundation, 1970.

Catton, Bruce. *Terrible Swift Sword.* Vol. 2 of *The Centennial History of the Civil War.* New York: Doubleday, 1963.

———. *Glory Road.* Vol. 2 of *The Army of the Potomac.* Garden City, N.Y.: Doubleday, 1952.

"Chamberlain's Last Review." Maine vol. 3 (vol. 18), *Papers of the Military Order of the Loyal Legion of the United States: Articles Relative to the Gettysburg Campaign.* Folder 20, Box B-68. Accessed at Gettysburg National Memorial Park, Gettysburg, Pa., May 2009.

Chambers, Henry A. *The Civil War Diary of Captain Henry A. Chambers,* ed. T. H. Pearce. Wendell, N.C.: Broadfoot's Bookmark, 1983.

Civil War Times. Leesburg, Va. Various issues.

Coco, Gregory A. *The Civil War Infantryman: In Camp, on the March, and in Battle.* Gettysburg, Pa.: Thomas Publications, 1996.

Collins, Gail. *America's Women: 400 Years of Dolls, Drudges, Helpmates, and Heroines.* New York: HarperCollins, 2003.

Commager, Henry Steele, ed. *Living History: The Civil War, The History of the War between the States in Documents, Essays, Letters, Songs and Poems.* 1950. Revised and expanded by Erik Bruun. New York: Tess Press, 2000.

Conklin, Eileen, ed. *The Journal of Women's Civil War History: From the Home Front to the Front Lines.* Gettysburg, Pa.: Thomas Publications, 2001.

Coombe, Jack D. *Thunder along the Mississippi: The River Battles That Split the Confederacy.* Edison, N.J.: Castle Books, 2005.

Denney, Robert E. *Civil War Medicine: Care and Comfort of the Wounded*. New York: Sterling, 1995.

Donald, David Herbert, ed. *Gone for a Soldier: The Civil War Memoirs of Private Alfred Bellard*. Boston, Mass.: Little, Brown, 1975.

Edwards, Abail Hall. *"Dear Friend Anna": The Civil War Letters of a Common Soldier from Maine,* ed. Beverly Hayes Kallgren and James L. Crouthamel. Orono: Univ. of Maine Press, 1992.

Eisenschiml, Otto. *The Hidden Face of the Civil War.* Indianapolis, Ind.: Bobbs-Merrill, 1961.

Estabrooks, Henry L. *Adrift in Dixie; or, A Yankee Officer among the Rebels*. New York: Carleton, 1866. Repr. South Boston, Va.: South Boston–Halifax County Museum of Fine Arts and History, 2007.

Fite, Emerson David. *Social and Industrial Conditions in the North during the Civil War*. New York: Macmillan, 1910. Repr. Williamstown, Mass.: Corner House Publishers, 1976.

Fox, Simeon Moses. *Descendants of Thomas Fox*. Manhattan, Kans: privately printed, c. 1910.

Goss, Warren Lee. *Recollections of a Private: A Story of the Army of the Potomac*. New York: Thomas Y. Crowell, 1890. Repr. Alexandra, Va.: Time-Life Books, 1981.

Gross, Laurence F. *The Course of Industrial Decline: The Boott Cotton Mills of Lowell, Mass., 1835–1955*. Baltimore, Md.: Johns Hopkins Univ. Press, 1993.

Hearn, Chester G. *When the Devil Came Down to Dixie: Ben Butler in New Orleans*. Baton Rouge: Louisiana State Univ. Press, 1997.

Hewett, Janet, ed. *The Roster of Union Soldiers 1861–1865*. Maine and New Hampshire volume. Wilmington, N.C.: Broadfoot, 1997.

Hewitt, Lawrence Lee, and Arthur W. Bergeron, Jr., eds. *Louisianians in the Civil War*. Columbia: Univ. of Missouri Press, 2002.

Jackson, Donald Dale, and the editors of Time-Life Books. *Twenty Million Yankees: The Northern Home Front*. Alexandria, Va.: Time-Life Books, 1985.

Lafavore, Paul. "Through Brady's Eyes: The Art of Civil War Photography," lecture delivered at the Hickory Museum of Art, Hickory, N.C., Dec. 10, 2006.

Maine. Gettysburg Commission. *Maine at Gettysburg: Report of Maine Commissioners.* Portland, Maine: Lakeside Press, 1898. Repr. Gettysburg, Pa.: Stan Clark Military Books, 1994.

Massey, Mary Elizabeth. *Bonnet Brigades: American Women and the Civil War.* New York: Knopf, 1966.

Mrozowski, Stephen, Grace Ziesing, and Mary Beaudry. *Living on the Boott: Historical Archaeology at the Boott Mills Boardinghouses, Lowell, Massachusetts.* Amherst: Univ. of Massachusetts Press, 1996.

Murray, Aaron R., ed. *Civil War Battles and Leaders.* New York: DK Publishing, 2004.

Rhodes, James Ford. *History of the Civil War, 1861–1865.* New York: Macmillan, 1917. Repr. New York: Dover Publications, 1999.

Robertson, James I., Jr. "Civil War Rations: A Test of Endurance." Lecture given in Blacksburg, Va., March 28, 2008, under the auspices of the Peacock-Harper Culinary History Friends Group.

Schouler, William. *A History of Massachusetts in the Civil War.* Boston: E. P. Dutton, 1868. Repr. Scituate, Mass.: Digital Scanning, 2007.

Shaara, Jeff. *Jeff Shaara's Civil War Battlefields: Discovering America's Hallowed Ground.* New York: Ballantine, 2006.

Shepley, Bulfinch, Richardson, and Abbott. *Lowell National Historical Park and Preservation District, Cultural Resources Inventory*, vol. 1. n.p.: National Park Service, 1980.

Wagner, Margaret E., ed. *The American Civil War: 365 Days.* New York: Harry N. Abrams, 2006.

Wiley, Bell Irvin. *The Life of Billy Yank: The Common Soldier of the Union.* Baton Rouge: Louisiana State Univ. Press, 1971.

Young, Robin. *For Love and Liberty: The Untold Civil War Story of Major Sullivan Ballou and His Famous Love Letter.* New York: Thunder's Mouth Press, 2006.

Secondary Sources

Angle, Paul M. *A Pictorial History of the Civil War Years.* New York: Doubleday, 1967.

Bean, Eva M. *East Bethel Road.* Bethel, Maine: Bethel Historical Society, 1959; repr. 1981.

Barrett, Alyson. "Nursing the 'Dragon': Activist and Crusader Dorothea Dix..." *Hallowed Ground,* fall 2008, p. 15.

Barry, John. "A Matter of Honor," *Newsweek,* Feb. 23, 2009, p. 32.

Bennett, Randall H. "Bethel Hill Village, Maine: A Walking Tour Presented by the Bethel Historical Society." Bethel Historical Society, Bethel, Maine, 1999.

Bennett, Randall H. *Bethel, Maine: An Illustrated History.* Bethel, Maine: Bethel Historical Society, 1991.

———. "Dr. True As Historian," *Bethel Courier* 1:2 (June 1977); no pages; accessed at www.bethelhistorical.org/True_as_Historian.html

——— ed.. *The History of Bethel, Maine, by Dr. Nathaniel True.* Westminster, Md.: Heritage Books, 1994. Originally printed in serial in the *Bethel Courier* between 1859 and 1861.

Bilger, Burkhard. "Mystery on Pearl Street," *New Yorker,* Jan. 7, 2008, p. 61.

Billings, John Davis. *Hardtack and Coffee, or, The Unwritten Story of Army Life.* Lincoln: Univ. of Nebraska Press, 1993.

Bolotin, Norman. *Civil War A to Z: A Young Person's Guide to Over 100 People, Places, and Points of Importance.* New York: Dutton Juvenile, 2002.

Boston & Maine Railroad Historical Society archives, www.trainweb.org/bmrrhs/history, accessed Dec. 1, 2007.

Bowers, Q. David. *The Waterford Water Cure: A Numismatic Inquiry.* Wolfeboro, N.H.: Bowers and Merena, 1992.

Broome, John. "My Own Account of the Fall of New Orleans." Ed. Michael J. Miller. *Civil War Times Illustrated,* May 1987, pp. 39–43.

Cannon, Florence. "Our Honored Dead." *Quartermaster Review,* May–June 1952, www.qmmuseum.lee.army.mil/mortuary/Honored_ Dead.htm, accessed Apr. 12, 2009.

Carmichael, Peter S. Review of *A Volunteer's Adventures: A Union Captain's Record of the Civil War* by John William DeForest. *Civil War Times,* Oct. 2008, pp. 60–66.

Chamberlain, Dick, and Judy Chamberlain. *Civil War Letters of an Ohio Soldier: S.O. Chamberlain and the 49th Ohio Volunteer Infantry.* Flournoy, Calif.: privately printed, 1990.

Chandonnet, Ann. "Salt Horse and Ham Fat: Union Soldiers Write Home about Civil War food." *Food History News* 17:4 (2007).

Chatelain, Margaret, Karen Green, et al., "Chateauguay: A Study of Social and Historical Patterns in a Nineteenth Century Vermont Settlement," paper for Sociology 63, Human Communities, by students of the Vermont Off-Campus Study Program, 1970.

Chisholm, Daniel. *The Civil War Notebook of Daniel Chisholm: A Chronicle of Daily Life in the Union Army 1864–1865,* ed. W. Springer Menge and J. August Shimrak. New York: Orion Books, 1989.

Christie, Jeanne. "'No Place for a Woman,' City Point, Virginia, 1864–1865." *The Journal of Women's Civil War History,* vol. 1, pp. 31–35.

Chrostek, Alina. "Occupational Health and Safety in Textile Mills." accessed at www.yale.edu/ynhti/curriculum/units/1996/2/96, Mar. 28, 2008.

Clarke, Ted. *Boston Curiosities: A History of Beantown Barons, Molasses Mayhem, Polemic Patriots, and the Fluff in Between.* Charleston, S.C.: History Press, 2008.

Coburn, Silas R. *History of Dracut, Massachusetts,* called by the Indians Augumtoocooke . . . . Lowell, Mass.: Press of the Courier-Citizen, 1922.

Cooling, B. F., and Wally Owen. "Washington's Civil War Defenses and the Battle of Fort Stevens." *Hallowed Ground,* fall 2008, pp. 24–28.

Coopersmith, Andrew S. *Fighting Words: An Illustrated History of Newspaper Accounts of the Civil War.* New York and London: New Press, 2004.

Cotham, Edward T., Jr., ed. *The Southern Journey of a Civil War Marine: The Illustrated Note-Book of Henry O. Gusley.* Austin: Univ. of Texas Press, 2006.

Cozzens, Peter. "General Grant's 'Living and Speaking Conscience.'" *Civil War Times*, Oct. 2009, p. 29.

Crain, Caleb. "Brother, Can You Spare a Room?" (Essay on Thomas Butler Gunn's *Physiology of New York.*) *New York Times Book Review*, Mar. 29, 2009, p. 23.

Croly, Jane Cunningham. *Jennie June's American Cookery Book.* New York: American News Company, 1870.

Crowe, Mike. "Confederate Ghost Ship." (Gouldsboro, Maine) *Fishermen's Voice Monthly Newspaper*, Apr. 2005.

Culpepper, Marilyn Mayer. *All Things Altered: Women in the Wake of Civil War and Reconstruction.* Jefferson, N.C.: McFarland, 2002.

Davis, William C., and the editors of Time-Life Books. *Brother Against Brother: The War Begins.* Alexandria, Va.: Time-Life Books, 1983.

"The Diary of Edgar Harvey Powers," *The (Bethel) Courier* 13:2 (summer 2007), pp. 1–4.

Donald, David Herbert, and Harold Holzer. *Lincoln in the Times: The Life of Abraham Lincoln, As Originally Reported in the New York Times.* New York: Macmillan, 2005.

Dublin, Thomas, ed. *Farm to Factory: Women's Letters, 1830–1860.* New York: Columbia Univ. Press, 1981.

Ecklison, Eric. "Samuel Slater: Father of the American Industrial Revolution." Accessed at www.woonsocket.org/slater.htm, Aug. 21, 2009

Engler, Harriet A. "Harriet's 2007 Catalog" [of period dress, patterns, costume supplies, etc.]. Danbury, Conn.: Harriet's TCS, 2006.

Faust, Drew Gilpin. "'This is My Last Letter to You.'" *Civil War Times*, Feb. 2008, pp. 32–40.

Federal Writers' Project. *Maine: A Guide "Down East."* Boston: Houghton Mifflin, 1937.

"Fifth Maine Infantry." www.state.me.us/sos/avc/archives/military/civil_war/5meint.htm. Accessed May 9, 2009.

Fifth Maine Museum website, www.fifthmainemuseum.org. Accessed various dates.

Fremantle, Col. James. *The Fremantle Diary; being the journal of Lieutenant Colonel Arthur James Lyon Fremantle, Coldstream Guards, on his three months in the southern states,* ed. Walter Lord. New York: Capricorn Books, 1960.

Fromberger, Albert R. "Memorial Brass: Civil War I.D. Tags." www.memorialbrass.com/history.htm. Accessed Sept. 26, 2008.

Fuller, Gary (Butch). *The Civil War Diary of H.G. Otis Perkins, Co. K, 5th Maine Infantry Regiment. A soldier from Oxford, Maine.* Privately printed, 2001.

Fuller, Margaret. "On Woman in the Nineteenth Century" [1845]. Accessed online at www.vcu.edu/engweb/transcendentalism/authors/fuller/sillahonfuller.html, Oct. 2, 2007.

Furry, William, ed. *The Preacher's Tale: The Civil War Journal of Rev. Francis Springer, Chaplain, U.S. Army of the Frontier.* Fayetteville: Univ. of Arkansas Press, 2001.

Geffert, Hannah. "West Virginia Women and the Civil War Military Pension System." *The Journal of Women's Civil War History,* vol. 1, p. 112.

Geer, Walter. *Campaigns of the Civil War.* New York: Brentano's, 1926. Repr. Old Saybrook, Conn.: Konecky & Konecky, 2001.

Geisburg, Judith. "Widows on the Battlefield: Platforms of Grief." Excerpted from "Army at Home: Women and the Civil War on the Northern Home Front," in *Hallowed Ground* 10:4 (Winter 2009), pp. 28–30.

Gibson, Marjorie, and Lynn Betlock, "Tuberculosis and our Ancestors." *New England Ancestors* 6:3 (summer 2005), pp. 6–20.

Giorgi, Valerie Dyer. *William Heath of Roxbury, Massachusetts, and Some of His Descendants*. Santa Maria, Calif.: privately printed, 1993.

Gould, William B., IV, ed. *Diary of a Contraband: The Civil War Passage of a Black Sailor*. Stanford, Calif.: Stanford Univ. Press, 2002.

Haines, Michael. "Fertility and Mortality in the U.S." 2008. www.eh.net/encyclopedia/article/haines.demography. Accessed Sept. 10, 2009.

Higginson Civil War Books, "Catalog No. 6," Salem, Mass.: Higginson Book Co., n.d., p. 13.

Hitching, F. K., and S. Hitching. *References to English Surnames in 1601 and 1602*. Baltimore, Md.: Genealogical Publishing Co., 1968.

Hoar, Jay S. *New England's Last Civil War Veterans*. Arlington, Tex.: Seacliff Press, 1976.

Hoehling, Adolph A. *Damn the Torpedoes! Naval Incidents of the Civil War*. Winston-Salem, N.C.: John F. Blair, 1989.

Hoogenboom, Ari. *Gustavus Vasa Fox of the Union Navy: A Biography*. Baltimore, Md.: Johns Hopkins Univ. Press, 2008.

Howe, Stanley Russell. "General Oliver Otis Howard Speaks at Bethel." *Bethel Courier* 29:2 (2005). Bethel Historical Society.

———. "William Berry Lapham: Local Historian and Genealogist." *Bethel Courier* 27:4 (winter 2003).

———. "Life on the Home Front: Bethel [Maine] during the Civil War." *Bethel Courier* 7:4 (winter 1983), accessed at www.bethelhistorical.org/Life_on_the_Home_Front_Bethel_During_the_Civil_War. Based on a paper originally presented to the Bethel Historical Society, Nov. 6, 1983.

Jacobsen, Joyce P. *The Economics of Gender*, 3rd ed. New York: Wiley-Blackwell, 2007.

Johnson, Dirk. "Coffins, Hearses, and Other End-Time Curios," *New Yotk Times*, Mar. 28, 2007, H-32.

Judd, Richard W., Edwin A. Churchill, and Joel W. Eastman, eds. *Maine: The Pine Tree State from Prehistory to the Present*. Orono: Univ. of Maine Press, 1995.

Katcher, Philip. *The Civil War Source Book*. New York: Facts on File, 1992.

Katz, William Loren. *Eyewitness: The Negro in American History*, rev. ed. New York: Pitman, 1971.

Kessler-Harris, Alice. *Women Have Always Worked: A Historical Overview.* New York: Feminist Press, 1981.

Lapham, William B. *History of Bethel, formerly Sudbury, Canada, Oxford County, Maine, 1768–1890*. Augusta, Maine: Press of the Maine Farmer, 1891. Accessed at www.oxfordcounty.blogspot.com/2008/05/bethel-civil-war-soldiers.html., Feb. 9, 2008, Feb. 11, 2008, Mar. 14, 2008.

———. *My Recollections of the War of the Rebellion*. Augusta, Maine: Burleigh & Flynt, 1892.

Larkin, Jack. *The Reshaping of Everyday Life, 1790–1840*. New York: Perennial Library, 1989.

Lawson, Russell M. *Passaconaway's Realm: Captain John Evans and the Exploration of Mount Washington*. Hanover, N.H.: Univ. Press of New England, 2004.

Leisch, Juanita. "Who Did What: Women's Roles in the Civil War." *The Journal of Women's Civil War History*, vol. 2, pp. 168–69.

Lepore, Jill. "Vast Designs: How America Came of Age." *New Yorker*, Oct. 29, 2007, p. 92.

Lewellen, Faye. "Limbs Made and Unmade by War." *America's Civil War*, Sept.1995, pp. 38–39.

Lillie, Chris Ballou. "Walt Whitman's Calling Card." *Civil War Times*, Oct. 2008, p. 42–44.

Longacre, Edward G. *A Regiment of Slaves: The 4th United States Colored Infantry, 1863–1866.* Mechanicsburg, Pa.: Stackpole Books, 2003.

Loubat, J. F. *Narrative of the Mission to Russia, in 1866, of the Hon. Gustavus Vasa Fox, Assistant-Secretary of the Navy*, ed. John D. Champlin, Jr. New York: D. Appleton, 1873.

Lowell (Mass.) Daily Courier. Various issues, 1850–1900.

"Lucy Larcom's Bethel," *Bethel Courier*, 30:2 (summer 2006). Bethel Historical Society.

Massachusetts Spy (Worcester, Mass.), Jan. 3, 1838.

Macaulay, David. *Mill*. Boston: Houghton Mifflin, 1983.

McGrath, Ben. "Muscle Memory: The Next Generation of Bionic Prostheses." *New Yorker*, July 30, 2007, p. 41.

McPherson, James M. *Battle Cry of Freedom: The Civil War Era*. New York: Oxford Univ. Press, 1988.

McSherry, Frank, Jr., Charles G. Waugh, and Martin Greenberg, eds. *Civil War Women: American Women Shaped by Conflict in Stories by Alcott, Chopin, Welty and Others*. Little Rock, Ark.: August House, 1988.

Meltzer, Milton, ed. *Voices from the Civil War: A Documentary History of the Great American Conflict*. New York: HarperTrophy, 1989.

Miles, Rev. Henry A. *Lowell, As It Was, and As It Is*. 2d ed. Lowell, Mass.: N. L. Dayton, 1846.

Miles, Rosalind. *Who Cooked the Last Supper? The Women's History of the World*. New York: Three Rivers Press, 2001.

Minnigh, L. W. *Gettysburg: "What They Did Here."* Gettysburg, Pa: N. A. Meligakes, 1924.

Morrow, Kevin. "The Birth of Photojournalism: How Pioneering Civil War Cameramen Such As Mathew Brady and Alexander Gardner Forever Changed the Way the World Views Warfare." *Civil War Times*, Sept. 2007, p. 42–45.

Noyes, Sybil, Charles Libby, and Walter G. Davis. *Genealogical Dictionary of Maine and New Hampshire*. Baltimore, Md.: Genealogical Pub. Co., 2002.

Nylander, Jane C. *Our Own Snug Fireside: Images of the New England Home, 1760–1860*. New Haven, Conn.: Yale Univ. Press, 1994.

Pendergast, John. *Dracut*. Images of America Series. Dover, N.H.: Arcadia Publishing, 1997.

Perret, Geoffrey. *Lincoln's War: The Untold Story of America's Greatest President as Commander in Chief*. New York: Random House, 2004.

Perry, Theolphilus. *Widows by the Thousand: The Civil War Letters of Theophilus and Harriet Perry, 1862–1864*, ed. M. Jane Johansson. Fayetteville: Univ. of Arkansas Press, 2000.

Pusiak, Rick. "Sudbury USA! Strange But True 300 Years Ago." *Northern Life*, Sept. 23, 2001, p. 3.

Rhodes, Elisha Hunt. *All for the Union A History of the 2nd Rhode Island Volunteer Infantry in the War of the Great Rebellion. . . .* Ed. Robert Hunt Rhodes. Lincoln, R.I.,: A. Mowbray, 1985.

Richmond, Katharine F. *John Hayes of Dover, New Hampshire: A Book of His Family*. 2 vols. Tyngsboro, Mass.: privately printed, 1936.

Rivard, Paul E. *A New Order of Things: How the Textile Industry Transformed New England*. Hanover, N.H.: : Univ. Press of New England, 2002.

Ross, Alice. "Boarding Houses." *Journal of Antiques and Collectibles*, March 2003. Accessed at www.journalofantiques.com/March03, Apr. 20, 2007.

Rosson, Joe, and Helaine Fendelman. "Sewing Machine is Circa 1879, but Condition Limits Value." "Treasures in Your Attic" column, *New Hampshire Union Leader*, Nov. 28, 2006, C–1.

Sheridan, Philip. *Civil War Memoirs*. Introduction by Paul Andrew Hutton. Eyewitness to the Civil War series. New York: Bantam Books, 1991. Originally published as *Personal Memoirs of P. H. Sheridan*, 1888.

Skelton, Kathryn. "Jay Hoar and the Civil War." (Lewiston, Maine) *Sun Journal*, May 24, 2009, A-1, A-5.

———. "Sumner Henry Needham: 'I sense there will be trouble to-day.'" (Lewiston, Maine) *Sun Journal*, May 24, 2009, A-5.

Sloane, Eric. *Diary of an Early American Boy, Noah Blake, 1805.* New York: Ballantine, 1974.

Springer, Marlene. "Angels and Other Women in Victorian Literature," in Springer, ed., *What Manner of Woman*.

Stahl, Joseph. "Identification Disks," *America's Civil War*, Sept. 2006, p. 48.

Stanford, Ann. "Images of Women in Early American Literature." In Marlene Springer, ed., *What Manner of Woman: Essays on English and American Life and Literature.* New York: New York Univ. Press, 1977.

Stearns, Lisa. "The World of Barilla Taylor: Bringing History to Life through Primary Sources." *OAH Magazine of History* 12 (fall 1997). Accessed at www.oah.org/pubs/magazine/women/stearns.htm, Apr. 18, 2007.

Stockwell, Elisha. *Private Elisha Stockwell, Jr., Sees the Civil War,* ed. Bryon R. Abernethy. Norman: Univ. of Oklahoma Press, 1958.

Stowe, Harriet Beecher, letter from Maine, originally printed in *The Portland Transcript* of Sept. 25, 1852; reprinted in the *Bethel Courier,* 29:1 (2005). Bethel Historical Society.

Symonds, Craig L. "Damn the Torpedoes! The Battle of Mobile Bay,*"* *Hallowed Ground,* winter 2008, pp. 19–24.

Taber, Thomas, ed. *Hard Breathing Days: The Civil War Letters of Cora Beach Benton, Albion, New York, 1862–1865.* New York: Almeron Press, 2003.

"Three of Josiah D. Pulsifer's Civil War Letters." *Androscoggin Historical Society Newsletter,* June 1995. Accessed at http://www.roots-web.com/~meandrhs/0695.html, Mar. 3, 2007.

Trudeau, Noah Andre. *Out of the Storm: The End of the Civil War, April–June 1865.* Baton Rouge: Louisiana State Univ. Press, 1994.

Ulrich, Laurel, and Lois K. Stabler. "'Girling It' in Eighteenth-century New Hampshire." In Peter Benes, ed., *Families and Children,* annual proceedings of the Dublin Seminar for New England Folklife, 1985, pp. 24–31.

Weisberger, Bernard A. "The Working Ladies of Lowell." *American Heritage* 12:2 (Feb. 1961). Accessed at www.americanheritage.com/articles/magazine/ah/1961/2, Apr. 17, 2007.

Wert, Jeffry D. *The Sword of Lincoln.* New York: Simon & Schuster, 2005.

Wheeler, Linda. "Music to Make War By." *Civil War Times*, Sept. 2007, pp. 64–67.

Wilburn, Robert C. "Gettysburg: Our Country's Common Ground." *Gettysburg Quarterly,* fall 2007, p. 2.

Wilkins, Martha Fifield. *Sunday River Sketches: A New England Chronicle,*   ed. Randall H. Bennett. Rumford, Me.: Androscoggin Publications, 1977.

Willis, Bob. "Exhibits at Virginia. Museum Reinvigorate Civil War Debate." *Providence (R.I.) Journal*, Mar. 4, 2007, p. A9.

"Women in the Civil War." Special issue of *Civil War Times Illustrated*, Aug. 1999.

Zeller, Bob. "Where the Earthworks Meet the Road." *Civil War Times*, Mar. 2002, pp. 62–65.

Source Notes by Chapter.

Notes: Andrew Jackson Bean (1828–1919)

1. William B. Lapham, *The History of Bethel, formerly Sudbury, Canada, Oxford County, Maine, 1768–1890* (Augusta, Me.: Press of the Maine Farmer, 1891), p. 482.

2. Marjorie Gibson and Lynn Bettlock, "Tuberculosis and Our Ancestors," *New England Ancestors* 6:3 (summer 2005), pp. 6–20.

3. Joseph S. Bean, *The Clan MacBean of North America, Inc.: A Genealogy and History.* 6th ed., revised from earlier edition in 3 vols. (Denver, Colo.: The Clan MacBean in North America, Inc., 1992), p. 208.

4. Stanley Russell Howe, "William Berry Lapham: Local Historian and Genealogist," *Bethel Courier* 27:4 (winter 2003), p. 1, p. 3.

5. Howe, "William Berry Lapham," p. 3.

6. Randall H. Bennett, "Dr. True As Historian," *Bethel Courier* 1:2 (June 1977); no pages; accessed at www.bethelhistorical.org/True_as_Historian.html

7. Donald Dale Jackson and the editors of Time-Life Books, *Twenty Million Yankees: The Northern Home Front* (Alexandria, Va.: Time-Life Books, 1985), p. 62.

8. Noah Andre Trudeau, *Out of the Storm: The End of the Civil War, April–June 1865* (Baton Rouge: Louisiana State Univ. Press, 1994), p. 391.

9. Gregory A. Coco, *The Civil War Infantryman: In Camp, on the March, and in Battle* (Gettysburg, Pa.: Thomas Publications, 1996), p. 124.

10. Email communication with Jeffrey Brown, archivist, Maine State Archives, Nov. 21, 2008.

11. Alyson Barrett, "Nursing the 'Dragon': Activist and Crusader Dorothea Dix. . . ," *Hallowed Ground*, fall 2008, p. 15.

12. Communication with Adele Floyd of Limerick Historical Society, Limerick, Me., Apr. 5, 2008.

13. Ann Stanford, "Images of Women in Early American Literature," in Marlene Springer, ed., *What Manner of Woman: Essays on English and American Life and Literature* (New York: New York Univ. Press, 1977), p. 200.

14. Joyce P. Jacobsen, *The Economics of Gender*, 3rd ed. (New York: Wiley-Blackwell, 2007), p. 141.

15. Marilyn Mayer Culpepper, *All Things Altered: Women in the Wake of Civil War and Reconstruction* (Jefferson, N.C.: McFarland, 2002), p. 225.

NOTES   Andrew Jackson Bean (1828–1919) *continued*

16. Federal Writers' Project, *Maine: A Guide "Down East,"* (Boston: Houghton Mifflin, 1937), p. 444.

17. *Maine: A Guide "Down East,"* p. 445.

18. Russell M. Lawson, *Passaconaway's Realm: Captain John Evans and the Exploration of Mount Washington,* (Hanover, N.H.: Univ. Press of New England, 2004), p. 108.

19. Rick Pusiak, "Sudbury USA! Strange But True 300 Years Ago," *Northern Life,* September 23, 2001, p. 3.

20. Randall H. Bennett, "Bethel Hill Village, Maine: A Walking Tour Presented by the Bethel Historical Society," Bethel Historical Society, 1999, p. 1.

21. Richard W. Judd, Edwin A. Churchill, and Joel W. Eastman, eds., *Maine: The Pine Tree State from Prehistory to the Present* (Orono: Univ. of Maine Press, 1995), pp. 218–29.

22. Judd et al., *Maine: The Pine Tree State,* p. 220.

23. Bean, *Clan MacBean of North America,* 6th ed., vol. 1, p. 188.

24. Burkhard Bilger, "Mystery on Pearl Street," *The New Yorker,* Jan. 7, 2008, p. 61.

25. Boston & Maine Railroad Historical Society archives, www.trainweb. org/bmrrhs/history, accessed Dec. 1, 2007.

26. Sybil Noyes, Charles Libby and Walter G. Davis, *Genealogical Dictionary of Maine and New Hampshire* (Baltimore, Md.: Genealogical Pub. Co., 2002.), p. 10.

27. Randall H. Bennett, *Bethel, Maine: An Illustrated History,* (Bethel, Maine: Bethel Historical Society, 1991), pp. 199–200.

28. "The Diary of Edgar Harvey Powers," *Bethel Courier* 31:2 (summer 2007), p. 4.

29. Lapham, *History of Bethel,* p. 110.

30. Lapham, *History of Bethel,* p. 409.

31. Lapham, *History of Bethel,* p. 410.

32. Stanley Russell Howe, "Life on the Home Front: Bethel [Maine] during the Civil War," a speech originally presented in 1983, revised and enlarged for publication in the *Bethel Courier* (winter 1983), accessed at www.bethelhistorical. org/Life_on_the_Home_Front_Bethel_During_the_Civil_War.

33. Jackson et al., *Twenty Million Yankees,* pp. 20–21.

34. Jack D. Coombe, *Thunder along the Mississippi: The River Battles That Split the Confederacy* (Edison, N.J.: Castle Books, 2005), p. 10.

35. Jackson et al., *Twenty Million Yankees,* p. 1.

36. Jackson et al., *Twenty Million Yankees,* p. 21.

37. Philip Sheridan, *Civil War Memoirs,* Introduction by Paul Andrew Hutton (Eyewitness to the Civil War series. New York: Bantam Books, 1991), ix.

38. William Loren Katz, *Eyewitness: The Negro in American History*, rev. ed. (New York: Pitman, 1971), pp. 92–93.

39. Geoffrey Perret, *Lincoln's War: The Untold Story of America's Greatest President As Commander in Chief* (New York: Random House, 2004), p. 18.

40. Donald W. Beattie, Rodney M. Cole, and Charles G. Waugh, eds., *A Distant War Comes Home: Maine in the Civil War Era* (Camden, Maine: Down East Books, 1996), p. 37.

41. Herbert Adams, "John Wilkes Booth Won Hearts in Portland," in Beattie et al., *A Distant War Comes Home*, p. 36.

42. Peter Cozzens, "General Grant's 'Living and Speaking Conscience,'" *Civil War Times*, October 2009, p. 29.

43. Jackson et al., *Twenty Million Yankees,* pp. 87, 89.

44. Jackson et al., *Twenty Million Yankees*, p. 115.

45. American Civil War Research Database, from Historical Data Systems, Duxbury, Mass. Accessed online at www.civilwardata.com, Nov. 4, 2007. Based on a report of the adjutant-general of the state of Maine.

46. Mike Crowe, "Confederate Ghost Ship," *Fishermen's Voice Monthly Newspaper*, Gouldsboro, Maine, Apr. 2005, p. 2.

47. Crowe, "Confederate Ghost Ship," p. 94.

48. John Davis Billings, *Hardtack and Coffee, or, The Unwritten Story of Army Life* (Lincoln: Univ. of Nebraska Press, 1993), p. 274.

49. Billings, *Hardtack and Coffee*, p. 118.

50. Billings, *Hardtack and Coffee*, p. 139.

51. Jackson et al., *Twenty Million Yankees*, p. 95.

52. Billings, *Hardtack and Coffee*, p. 277.

53. Bennett, *Bethel, Maine*, p. 75.

54. George W. Bicknell, *History of the Fifth Maine Regiment* (Portland, Maine: Hall L. Davis, 1871), p. 399.

55. "Regimental History," Fifth Maine Museum website, www.fifthmaine-museum.org, accessed Jan. 27, 2008.

56. Lapham, *The History of Bethel*), p. 273. Accessed at oxfordcounty.blogspot.com/2008/05/bethel-civil-war-soldiers.html, accessed Aug. 11, 2008.

57. "Dedication of Monument, October 3, 1889, Address of Colonel Clark S. Edwards," in Maine, Gettysburg Commission, *Maine at Gettysburg: Report of Maine Commissioners* (Portland, Me.: Lakeside Press, 1898; repr. Gettysburg, Pa.: Stan Clark Military Books, 1994), pp. 373, 385 ff.

58. Jay S. Hoar, *New England's Last Civil War Veterans* (Arlington, Tex.: Seacliff Press, 1976), p. 77.

59. www.nps.gov/gett/soldierlife, accessed Dec. 9, 2007.

60. www.historynet.com/magazines/civil_war_times, accessed Apr. 20, 2007.

61. Howe, "Life on the Home Front."

62. Bennett, "Bethel Hill Village, Maine," p. 4.

NOTES   Andrew Jackson Bean (1828–1919) *continued*

63. "Fifth Regiment Monument Dedication," in *Maine at Gettysburg*, p. 374.

64. Quoted in Jeffry D. Wert, *The Sword of Lincoln* (New York: Simon & Schuster, 2005), p. 27.

65. Excerpted from *The Road to Richmond: The Civil War Memoirs of Major Abner R. Small*, in Milton Meltzer, ed., *Voices from the Civil War: A Documentary History of the Great American Conflict* (New York: HarperTrophy, 1989). pp. 44–45

66. Gary (Butch) Fuller, *The Civil War Diary of H. G. Otis Perkins, Co. K, 5th Maine Infantry Regiment. A Soldier from Oxford, Maine*, privately printed; p. 35., p. 10.

67. Fuller, *The Civil War Diary of H. G. Otis Perkins*, p. 47.

68. E-mail communication with Kimberly A. MacIsaac, director, Fifth Maine Regiment Museum, March 12, 2008.

69. Howe, "Life on the Home Front."

70. Howe, "Life on the Home Front."

71. Fuller, *The Civil War Diary of H. G. Otis Perkins*, p. 35.

72. Ibid, p. 219.

73. Wert, *The Sword of Lincoln*, p. 333.

74. *Maine at Gettysburg*, p. 384.

75. Margaret E. Wagner, ed., *The American Civil War: 365 Days* (New York: Harry N. Abrams, 2006), s.v. August 10, [1863].

76. Wagner, ed., *American Civil War,* s.v. October 23, [1862].

77. Bennett, *Bethel, Maine*, p. 80.

78. Bennett, *Bethel, Maine*, p. 83, p. 88.

79. Beattie et al., *A Distant War Comes Home*, p. 180.

80. Probate Court certificate dated Oct. 2, 1867, but guardianship dated on it from September 3. Papers deposited at Bethel Historical Society by Roberta G. Pevear.

81. Bean, *Clan MacBean in North America*, p. 188.

82. Dick Chamberlain and Judy Chamberlain, *Civil War Letters of an Ohio Soldier: S.O. Chamberlain and the 49th Ohio Volunteer Infantry* (Flournoy, Calif.: privately printed, 1990), p. 65.

83. Pension history accessed at www1.va.gov/opa/feature/history, Jan. 28, 2008.

84. Trudeau, *Out of the Storm*, p. 392.

85. Robert C. Wilburn, "Gettysburg: Our Country's Common Ground," *Gettysburg* Quarterly, fall 2007, p. 2.

86. Margaret E. Wagner, ed., *The American Civil War: 365 Days* (New York: Harry N. Abrams, 2006), s.v. December 31, [1863].

87. E-mail communication with Kimberly A. MacIsaac, director, Fifth Maine Regiment Museum, Jan. 15, 2008.

88. "Regimental History," www.fifthmainemuseum.org.

89. Mary Elizabeth Massey, *Bonnet Brigades: American Women and the Civil War* (New York: Knopf, 1966), p. 130.

90. "Account of George A. Foster, Administrator of the Estate of Mary F. Beane." On file at Bethel Historical Society archives.

Notes: Eliza Howard Bean Foster (1835–1867)

91. Gail Collins, *America's Women: 400 Years of Dolls, Drudges, Helpmates, and Heroines* (New York: HarperCollins, 2003), p. 87.

92. Fuller, "On Woman in the Nineteenth Century" [1845], www.vcu.edu/engweb/transcendentalism/authors/fuller/sillahonfuller.html, accessed Oct. 2, 2007.

93. Eric Ecklison, "Samuel Slater: Father of the American Industrial Revolution," accessed at www.woonsocket.org/slater.htm, accessed Aug. 21, 2009.

94. Jackson et al., *Twenty Million Yankees*, p. 57.

95. Jackson et al., *Twenty Million Yankees*, p. 59.

96. www.legacy98.org/timeline.html, accessed Apr. 16, 2007.

97. Jill Lepore, "Vast Designs: How America Came of Age," *New Yorker*, Oct. 29, 2007, p. 92.

98. www.womenshistory.about.com/od/quotes/a/douglass, accessed Aug. 7, 2007.

99. Judd et al., *Maine: The Pine Tree State*, p. 333.

100. Paul E. Rivard, *A New Order of Things: How the Textile Industry Transformed New England* (Hanover, N.H.: : Univ. Press of New England), p. 102.

101. Thomas Dublin, ed., *Farm to Factory: Women's Letters, 1830–1860* (New York: Columbia Univ. Press, 1981), p. 21.

102. David Macaulay, *Mill* (Boston: Houghton Mifflin, 1983), p. 61.

103. Dublin, *Farm to Factory,* p. 22.

104. Rivard, *A New Order of Things* p. 31.

105. Judd et al., *Maine: The Pine Tree State*, p. 334.

106. Rivard, *A New Order of Things*, p. 103.

107. Rivard, *A New Order of Things* p. 105.

108. Rivard, *A New Order of Things* pp. 95, 98.

109. Macaulay, *Mill*, pp. 55, 69.

110. Laurence F. Gross, *The Course of Industrial Decline: The Boott Cotton Mills of Lowell, Mass., 1835–1955* (Baltimore, Md.: Johns Hopkins Univ. Press, 1993), p. 13.

111. Macaulay, *Mill*, p. 105.

112. "Lucy Larcom's Bethel," *Bethel Courier* 30:2 (summer 2006), p. 6.

113. Rosalind Miles, *Who Cooked the Last Supper? The Women's History of the World* (New York: Three Rivers Press, 2001), pp. 186–87.

114. Rosalind Miles, *Who Cooked the Last Supper,* p. 185.

Notes   Eliza Bean Foster (1835–1867) *continued*

115. Rev. Henry A. Miles, *Lowell, As It Was, and As It Is*, 2d ed. (Lowell, Mass.: N. L. Dayton, 1846), p. 34.

116. Rivard, *A New Order of Things*, pp. 50–51, 59–60.

117. Massey, *Bonnet Brigades*, p. 5.

118. Rivard, *A New Order of Things*, p. 66.

119. Shepley, Bulfinch, Richardson, and Abbott, *Lowell National Historical Park and Preservation District, Cultural Resources Inventory*, (n.p.: National Park Service, 1980), vol. 1, p. 1.

120. Shepley et al., *Lowell National Historical Park*, p. 2.

121. Shepley et al., *Lowell National Historical Park*, p. 9.

122. Shepley et al., *Lowell National Historical Park*, p. 4.

123. Shepley et al., *Lowell National Historical Park*, p. 7.

124. Stephen Mrozowski, Grace Ziesing, and Mary Beaudry. *Living on the Boott: Historical Archaeology at the Boott Mills Boardinghouses, Lowell, Massachusetts* (Amherst: Univ. of Massachusetts Press, 1996), xi.

125. Mrozowski et al., *Living on the Boott*, p. 4.

126. Gross, *Course of Industrial Decline*, p. 25.

127. Rivard, *A New Order of Things*, p. 116.

128. Rivard, *A New Order of Things*, p. 106.

129. Alice Kessler-Harris, *Women Have Always Worked: A Historical Overview* (New York: Feminist Press, 1981), p. 60.

130. www.fordham.edu/HALSALL/MOD/robinson-lowe..html, accessed Feb. 13, 2008.

131. Rivard, *A New Order of Things*, p. 64.

132. Eric Sloane, *Diary of an Early American Boy, Noah Blake, 1805* (New York: Ballantine, 1974), p. 90.

133. Lisa Stearns, *"The World of Barilla Taylor: Bringing History to Life through Primary Sources,"* *OAH Magazine of History* 12 (fall 1997); accessed at www.oah.org/pubs/magazine/womens/stearns.htm, Jan. 4. 2008.

134. Stearns, *"The World of Barilla Taylor."*

135. Bill of Mortality for the City, 1846, Lowell. Pollard Memorial Library.

136. Rosalind Miles, *Who Cooked the Last Supper?*, p. 187.

137. Henry A. Miles, *Lowell*, p. 102.

138. Jack Larkin, *The Reshaping of Everyday Life, 1790–1840* (New York: Perennial Library, 1989), p. 55.

139. Bernard A. Weisberger, "The Working Ladies of Lowell," *American Heritage*, 12:2 (Feb. 1961); accessed online at www.americanheritage.com/articles/magazine/ah/1961/62, accessed Mar. 29, 2008.

140. Harriet Robinson's autobiography, accessed at www.courses.wcupa.edu/johnson/robinson.html, Feb. 16, 2008.

141. Kessler-Harris, *Women Have Always Worked*, p. 57.

142. Kessler-Harris, *Women Have Always Worked*, p. 58.

143. Kessler-Harris, *Women Have Always Worked*, p. 20.

144. Gross, *Course of Industrial Decline*, p. 14.

145. Alice Ross, "Boarding Houses," *Journal of Antiques and Collectibles*, March 2003, accessed at www.journalofantiques.com/March03, accessed May 12, 2008.

146. Harriet Robinson's autobiography.

147. Mrozowski et al., *Living on the Boott*, pp. 47, 50, 65–66.

148. Ross, "Boarding Houses."

149. Alina Chrostek, "Occupational Health and Safety in Textile Mills," accessed at www.yale.edu/ynhti/curriculum/units/1996/2/96, accessed Mar. 28, 2008.

150. Marlene Springer, "Angels and Other Women in Victorian Literature," in Springer, ed., *What Manner of Woman*, p. 155.

151. Springer, "Angels and Other Women," p. 221.

152. Laurel Ulrich and Lois K. Stabler, "'Girling It' in Eighteenth-century New Hampshire," in Peter Benes, ed., *Families and Children*, annual proceedings of the Dublin Seminar for New England Folklife, 1985, pp. 24–31.

153. Dublin, *Farm to Factory*, pp. 31–32.

154. Dublin, *Farm to Factory*, p. 136.

155. Culpepper, *All Things Altered,* p. 219; Michael Haines, "Fertility and Mortality in the U.S.," 2008, www.eh.net/encyclopedia/article/haines.demography, accessed Sept. 12, 2009.

156. www.memory.loc.gov/ammem/cwphtml/tl1861.html, accessed Mar. 14, 2008.

157. www.civilwarhome.com/lincolntroops.htm, accessed Oct. 30, 2007.

158. www.enclopedia:jrank.org/Lob_Lip/LOWELL, accessed Nov. 2, 2007.

159. Jackson, *Twenty Million Yankees*, p. 8.

160. Wagner, ed., *American Civil War,* s.v. February 6, [1863].

161. Wert, *Sword of Lincoln,* p. 6.

162. Fuller, *The Civil War Diary of H. G. Otis Perkins,* p. 4.

163. "Fort Ward Museum and Historic Site," *Hallowed Ground*, fall 2008, back cover.

164. B. F. Cooling and Wally Owen, "Washington's Civil War Defenses and the Battle of Fort Stevens," *Hallowed Ground*, fall 2008, p. 24.

165. Cooling and Owen, "Washington's Civil War Defenses," p. 31.

166. Andrew S. Coopersmith, *Fighting Words: An Illustrated History of Newspaper Accounts of the Civil War* (New York and London: New Press, 2004), p. 78.

167. Records of Seattle Genealogical Society, Seattle, Wash.

168. Bruce Catton, *Terrible Swift Sword*, vol. 2 of *The Centennial History of the Civil War* (New York: Doubleday, 1963), p. 10.

NOTES   Eliza Bean Foster (1835–1867)   *continued*

169. Massey, *Bonnet Brigades*, p. 213.

170. Springer, "Angels and Other Women," p. 125.

171. Springer, "Angels and Other Women," p. 127.

172. Walter Geer, *Campaigns of the Civil War* (New York: Brentano's, 1926. Repr. Old Saybrook, Conn.: Konecky & Konecky, 2001), p. 409.

173. Sheridan, *Civil War Memoirs*, pp. 239–41.

174. Geer, *Campaigns of the Civil War*, p. 410.

175. Website of Civil War Preservation Trust, www.civilwar.org, accessed Jan. 25, 2009.

176. Henry Steele Commager, ed., *Living History: The Civil War, The History of the War between the States in Documents, Essays, Letters, Songs and Poems*; 1950; revised and expanded by Erik Bruun (New York: Tess Press, 2000), p. 268.

177. Commager, *Living History,* p. 269.

178. Ben McGrath, "Muscle Memory: The Next Generation of Bionic Prostheses," *New Yorker*, July 30, 2007, p. 41.

179. James M. McPherson, *Battle Cry of Freedom: The Civil War Era* (New York: Oxford Univ. Press, 1988), pp. 475–76.

180. Florence Cannon, "Our Honored Dead," *Quartermaster Review,* May–June 1952, www.qmmuseum.lee.army.mil/mortuary/Honored_Dead.htm, accessed Dec. 14, 2007.

181. John S. Bowman, ed., *The Civil War Almanac* (New York: Facts on File, 1983), p. 224.

182. "Collecting: U.S. Postage Stamps," *Country Living*, January 2008, p. 42.

183. Dirk Johnson, "Coffins, Hearses, and Other End-Time Curios," *New York Times,* Mar. 28, 2007, H-32.

184. Massey, *Bonnet Brigades*, pp. 218–19.

185. Hannah Geffert, "West Virginia Women and the Civil War Military Pension System," *The Journal of Women's Civil War History*, vol. 1, p. 112.

186. Jackson et al., *Twenty Million Yankees*, p. 135.

187. Culpepper, *All Things Altered,* p. 226.

188. Massey, *Bonnet Brigades*, pp. 198–19.

189. Emerson David Fite, *Social and Industrial Conditions in the North during the Civil War* (New York: Macmillan, 1910. Repr. Williamstown, Mass.: Corner House Publishers, 1976), p. 186.

190. Fite, *Social and Industrial Conditions,* p. 187.

191. William Schouler, *Massachusetts in the Civil War* (Boston: E. P. Dutton, 1868. Repr. Scituate, Mass.: Digital Scanning, 2007), pp. 296–300.

192. Gross, *Course of Industrial Decline,* pp. 15, 61, 94, 136.

193. Gross, *Course of Industrial Decline,* p. 63.

194. Gross, *Course of Industrial Decline,* p. 62.

195. Gross, *Course of Industrial Decline,* p. 64.

196. Henry A. Miles, *Lowell,* pp. 133–123.

197. Gross, *Course of Industrial Decline,* pp. 36–37.

198. Massey, *Bonnet Brigades,* pp. 143–44.

199. Schouler, *Massachusetts in the Civil War,* pp. 628–30.

200. Trudeau, *Out of the Storm,* p. 378.

201. Robin Young, *For Love and Liberty: The Untold Civil War Story of Major Sullivan Ballou and His Famous Love Letter* (New York: Thunder's Mouth Press, 2006), p. 110.

202. *Massachusetts Spy* (Worcester, Mass.), Jan. 3, 1838, page 4.

203. *Lowell* (Mass.) *Daily Courier,* Dec. 4, 1905, p. 5.

204. *Lowell* (Mass.) *Daily Courier,* Dec. 4, 1905, p. 5.

205. Chester G. Hearn, *When the Devil Came Down to Dixie: Ben Butler in New Orleans* (Baton Rouge: Louisiana State Univ. Press, 1997.), p. 239.

Notes: Henry Charles Foster (1834–1864)

206. Noyes et al., *Genealogical Dictionary of Maine and New Hampshire,* p. 242.

207. F. K. Hitching and S. Hitching, *References to English Surnames in 1601 and 1602* Baltimore, Md.: Genealogical Publishing Co., 1968,) xxvi.

208. Noyes et al., *Genealogical Dictionary of Maine and New Hampshire,* p. 242.

209. Margaret Chatelain, Karen Green, et al., "Chateauguay: A Study of Social and Historical Patterns in a Nineteenth Century Vermont Settlement," paper for Sociology 63, Human Communities, by students of the Vermont Off-Campus Study Program, 1970.

210. Blanche Brown Bryant and Gertrude Elaine Baker, eds, *The Diaries of Sally and Pamela Brown, 1832–1838; Hyde Leslie, 1887, Plymouth Notch, Vermont* (Springfield, Vt.: William L. Bryant Foundation, 1970).

211. www.eliwhitney.org, accessed Sept. 8, 2007.

212. Katz, *Eyewitness,* p. 93.

213. Katz, *Eyewitness,* p. 93.

214. McPherson, *Battle Cry of Freedom,* p. 497.

215. Commager, *Living History,* p. 573.

216. Ted Clarke, *Boston Curiosities: A History of Beantown Barons, Molasses Mayhem, Polemic Patriots, and the Fluff in Between* (Charleston, S.C.: History press, 2008), pp. 48–49.

217. Clarke, *Boston Curiosities,* p. 50.

218. Schouler, *Massachusetts in the Civil War,* pp. 344–45.

219. Catton, *Terrible Swift Sword,* pp. 13–14.

220. Schouler, *Massachusetts in the Civil War,* pp. 175–86.

Notes   Henry Charles Foster (1834–1864) *continued*

221. Katz, *Eyewitness,* p. 135.

222. Letter of John Dunban, Oct. 15, 1865, MS 150, Fondren Library, Rice University. Punctuation has been added for ease of reading.

223. Lawrence Lee Hewitt and Arthur W. Bergeron, Jr., eds., , *Louisianians in the Civil War* (Columbia: Univ. of Missouri Press, 2002), p. 73.

224. Hewitt and Bergeron, *Louisianians in the Civil War,* p. 101.

225. Hewitt and Bergeron, *Louisianians in the Civil War,* p. 30.

226. Hewitt and Bergeron, *Louisianians in the Civil War,* pp. 13–16.

227. Commager, *Living History,* p. 553.

228. Bell Irvin Wiley, *The Life of Billy Yank: The Common Soldier of the Union* (Baton Rouge: Louisiana State Univ. Press, 1971), p. 145.

229. Commager, *Living History,* p. 570.

230. Norman Bolotin, *Civil War A to Z: A Young Person's Guide to Over 100 People, Places, and Points of Importance* (New York: Dutton Juvenile, 2002), pp. 86–87.

231. Bolotin, *Civil War A to Z,* p. 22.

232. Chris Ballou Lillie, "Walt Whitman's Calling Card," *Civil War Times,* October 2008, p. 42.

233. Faye Lewellen, "Limbs Made and Unmade by War," *America's Civil War,* September 1995, pp. 38–39.

234. Lewellen, "Limbs Made and Unmade," p. 40.

235. Clark S. Edwards Papers, 1861–1903, Pearce Civil War Collection, Navarro College, letters of June 9, 1862, June 13, 1862, Aug. 24, 1862, Sept. 19, 1862, Oct. 5, 1862, May 2, 1863, June 2, 1863.

236. Clark S. Edwards Papers, letters of July 26, 1861, Apr. 6, 1862.

237. Edwards, Abail Hall, *"Dear Friend Anna": The Civil War Letters of a Common Soldier from Maine,* ed. Beverly Hayes Kallgren and James L. Crouthamel (Orono: Univ. of Maine Press, 1992), letters of October 1864, p. 106.; see p. 26 for another mention of how even dead officers were stripped.

238. "Dog Tags," www.armydogtags.com, accessed July 8, 2008.

239. "Old Court House/Civil War Museum," brochure from Winchester, Va., n.d.

240. "Dog Tags," www.armydogtags.com, accessed July 8, 2008.

241. Albert R. Fromberger, "Memorial Brass: Civil War I.D. Tags," www.memorialbrass.com/history.htm, accessed July 11, 2008.

242. Joseph Stahl, "Identification Disks," *America's Civil War,* September 2006, p. 48.

243. www.kenmore.org/foundation/arch_kenmore, accessed Aug. 2, 2008.

Notes: Andrew Jackson Bean Letters

244. See Bean Family Tree, wc.rootsweb.ancestry.com/cgi-bin/igm.cgi?op=DESC, accessed Oct. 9, 2007.

245. Massey, *Bonnet Brigades*, p. 213.

246. Theolphilus Perry, *Widows by the Thousand: The Civil War Letters of Theophilus and Harriet Perry, 1862–1864*, ed. M. Jane Johansson (Fayetteville: Univ. of Arkansas Press, 2000), p. 118.

247. Sloane, *Diary of an Early American Boy*, pp. 105–6.

248. See www.bkln-genealogy-info.com/Directory/1914_NYMedical.college.html, accessed Nov. 2, 2007.

249. Fite, *Social and Industrial Conditions*, p. 91.

250. Rivard, *A New Order of Things*, p. 26.

251. Bean, *Clan MacBean in North America*, p. 182.

252. Perry, *Widows by the Thousand,* p. 226.

253. David Blight, *Race and Reunion: The Civil War in American Memory* (Cambridge, Mass.: Belknap Press of Harvard University Press, 2001), p. 173.

254. Wiley, *Life of Billy Yank*, p. 183.

255. Stanley Russell Howe, executive director of the Bethel Historical Society, has discovered letters from only two others: William L. Grover of the 23rd Maine and Simeon Sanborn of the 5th (Howe, "Life on the Home Front).

256. Howe, "Life on the Home Front."

257. Union version of the first verse to "Dixie" (Linda Wheeler, "Music to Make War By," *Civil War Times*, September 2007, p. 64).

258. Wiley, *Life of Billy Yank*, p. 291.

259. Wiley, *Life of Billy Yank,* p. 292.

260. "'My Precious Loulie': Love Letters of the Civil War," Civil War Love Letters, accessed at www.spec.lib.vt.edu/cwlove/, Apr. 26, 2007.

261. "War Letters: Lost and Found," accessed at www.postalmuseum.si.edu/warletters/images/w1_02a.html, Apr. 24, 2007.

262. John R. Dunban, July 30, 1865, from Camp Jackson, La., MS 150, Fondren Library, Rice University.

263. Katcher, Philip, *The Civil War Source Book* (New York: Facts on File, 1992), p. 47.

264. Fuller, *Civil War Diary of H. G. Otis Perkins,* p. 106.

265. Commager, *Living History,* pp. 34–35.

266. Schouler, *Massachusetts in the Civil War*, pp. 285–86.

267. Schouler, *Massachusetts in the Civil War,* p. 341.

268. John R. Dunban, July 30, 1865, MS 150, Fondren Library, Rice University.

269. Hearn, *When the Devil Came Down to Dixie*, p. 44.

NOTES   Andrew Jackson Bean Letters *continued*

270. Chisholm, Daniel, *The Civil War Notebook of Daniel Chisholm: A Chronicle of Daily Life in the Union Army 1864–1865,* ed. W. Springer Menge and J. August Shimrak (New York: Orion Books, 1989), p. 20.

271. Hearn, *When the Devil Came Down to Dixie,* p. 47.

272. Edward T. Cotham, Jr., ed., *The Southern Journey of a Civil War Marine: The Illustrated Note-Book of Henry O. Gusley,* (Austin: Univ. of Texas Press, 2006), p. 192, n. 14.

273. Catton, *Terrible Swift Sword,* p. 246.

274. McPherson, *Battle Cry of Freedom,* p. 800.

275. Ari Hoogenboom, *Gustavus Vasa Fox of the Union Navy: A Biography* (Baltimore, Md.: Johns Hopkins Univ. Press, 2008), p. 224.

276. Hearn, *When the Devil Came Down to Dixie,* p. 35.

277. J. F. Loubat, *Narrative of the Mission to Russia, in 1866, of the Hon. Gustavus Vasa Fox, Assistant-Secretary of the Navy,* ed. John D. Champlin, Jr. (New York: D. Appleton, 1873), p. 20.

278. Wagner, ed., *American Civil War,* s.v. April 13, [1864].

279. Coombe, *Thunder along the Mississippi,* p. 102.

280. Coombe, *Thunder along the Mississippi,* p. 12.

312. Coombe, *Thunder along the Mississippi,* pp. 104–5.

313. Craig L. Symonds, "Damn the Torpedoes! The Battle of Mobile Bay," *Hallowed Ground,* winter 2008, p. 19.

314. Adolph A. Hoehling, *Damn the Torpedoes! Naval Incidents of the Civil War* (Winston-Salem, N.C.: John F. Blair, 1989), p. 106.

315. Symonds, "Damn the Torpedoes!," p. 24.

285. Wagner, ed., *American Civil War,* s.v. May 11, [1862].

286. Commager, *Living History,* p. 628.

287. John Broome, "My Own Account of the Fall of New Orleans," ed. Michael J. Miller, *Civil War Times Illustrated,* May 1987, pp. 39–40.

288. Rhodes, James Ford, *History of the Civil War, 1861–1865* (New York: Macmillan, 1917; repr. New York: Dover Publications, 1999), p. 123.

289. www.musicnet.org/robokopp, accessed Mar. 3, 2007.

290. Bowman, *Civil War Almanac,* p. 44.

291. Hewitt and Bergeron, *Louisianians in the Civil War,* pp. 92–93.

292. "The Battle of New Orleans," in *Harper's Brother's American History,* vol. 4, accessed at www.sonofthesouth.net/leefoundation/battle-new-orleans.htm, accessed Apr. 8, 2007.

293. Hewitt and Bergeron, *Louisianians in the Civil War,* p. 94.

294. Beattie et al., *A Distant War Comes Home,* p. 181.

295. Robert E. Denney, *Civil War Medicine: Care and Comfort of the Wounded* (New York: Sterling, 1995), pp. 8–9.

296. Katcher, *Civil War Source Book*, p. 121.

297. "Ailing Civil War Generals," *Civil War Times*, June 2007, p.8.

298. Denney, *Civil War Medicine,* p. 60.

299. www.americancivilwar.com/statepic/va/va, accessed Mar. 28, 2007.

300. Wagner, ed., *American Civil War,* s.v. November 5, [1864].

301. www.stphilipneri.org/teacher/ponchartrain, accessed Feb. 12, 2008.

302. www.nyhistory.org, accessed Feb. 12, 2008.

303. Denney, *Civil War Medicine,* pp. 8–9.

304. Beattie et al., *A Distant War Comes Home,* p. 196.

305. Clark S. Edwards Papers, unpaged.

306. Carmichael, review of *A Volunteer's Adventures,* p. 62.

307. Clark S. Edwards Papers, unpaged.

308. Wagner, ed., *American Civil War,* s.v. June 8 and September 7, [1862].

309. Coco, *The Civil War Infantryman*, p. 98.

310. Coco, *The Civil War Infantryman*, p. 98.

311. Smithsonian Institution site, www.historywired.si.edu/detail.cfm, accessed May 4, 2007.

312. Fuller, *Civil War Diary of H. G. Otis Perkins,* p. 106.

313. "Three of Josiah D. Pulsifer's Civil War Letters," *Androscoggin Historical Society Newsletter,* June 1995, accessed at http://www.rootsweb.com/~meandrhs/0695.html, accessed July 22, 2008.

314. Edward G. Longacre, *A Regiment of Slaves*: The 4th United States Colored Infantry, 1863–1866 (Mechanicsburg, Pa.: Stackpole Books, 2003), p. 41.

315. Chamberlain and Chamberlain, *Civil War Letters of An Ohio Soldier*, p. 16.

316. Chamberlain and Chamberlain, *Civil War Letters of An Ohio Soldier,,* p. 21.

317. Chamberlain and Chamberlain, *Civil War Letters of An Ohio Soldier*, p. 37.

318. Chamberlain and Chamberlain, *Civil War Letters of An Ohio Soldier*, p. 38.

319. Chamberlain and Chamberlain, *Civil War Letters of An Ohio Soldier*, p. 46.

320. Hearn, *When the Devil Came Down to Dixie*, p. 96.

321. McPherson, *Battle Cry of Freedom*, p. 623.

322. Hewitt and Bergeron, *Louisianians in the Civil War*, p. 35.

Notes: Eliza H. Foster's Notebook, 1863

323. Fite, *Social and Industrial Conditions*, p. 187.

324. Fite, *Social and Industrial Conditions*, p. 187.

325. Weisberger, "The Working Ladies of Lowell."

326. Massey, *Bonnet Brigades*, p. 145.

Notes   Eliza H. Foster's Notebook   *continued*

327. Harriet A. Engler, "Harriet's 2007 Catalog" (Danbury, Conn.: Harriet's TCS, 2006), p. 35.

328. Hearn, *When the Devil Came Down to Dixie*, p. 9.

329. www.bioguide.congress.gov/scripts/biodisplay.pl?index=B001174, accessed June 2, 2007.

330. Hearn, *When the Devil Came Down to Dixie*, p. 14.

331. Hearn, *When the Devil Came Down to Dixie*, p. 15.

332. Hearn, *When the Devil Came Down to Dixie*, pp. 226–28.

333. Jane Cunningham Croly, *Jennie June's American Cookery Book* (New York: American News Company, 1870), p. 313.

334. Chambers, Henry A., *The Civil War Diary of Captain Henry A. Chambers,* ed. T. H. Pearce (Wendell, N.C.: Broadfoot's Bookmark, 1983), p. 17.

335. Commager, *Living History*, p. 314.

336. Commager, *Living History*, p. 232.

337. Thomas Taber, ed., *Hard Breathing Days: The Civil War Letters of Cora Beach Benton, Albion, New York, 1862–1865* (New York: Almeron Press, 2003), pp. 403-4.

338. Fite, *Social and Industrial Conditions,* pp. 137–38.

339. Juanita Leisch, "Who Did What: Women's Roles in the Civil War," *The Journal of Women's Civil War History*, vol. 2, pp. 168–69.

340. Cotham, *Southern Journey of a Civil War Marine*, p. 135.

341. www.fordham.edu/HALSALL/MOD/robinson-lowell.html.

342. Engler, "Harriet's 2007 Catalog," pp. 19, 20–21.

343. Engler, "Harriet's 2007 Catalog," p. 18.

344. http://te.nytimes

345. "Richmond," National Park Service brochure, U.S. Department of the Interior, GPO.2003-496–196-40396.

346. Daniel P. Mason, letter from Camp Parapet near Carrollton, March 24, 1863.

347. Fite, *Social and Industrial Conditions,* p. 138.

348. Beattie et al., *A Distant War Comes Home, .* 182.

349. Beattie et al., *A Distant War Comes Home,* p. 230.

350. Jane Nylander, *Our Own Snug Fireside: Images of the New England Home, 1760–1860* (New Haven, Conn.: Yale Univ. Press, 1994) pp. 157–59, 161.

351. Bowman, *Civil War Almanac*, pp. 140, 144.

352. Hewitt and Bergeron, *Louisianians in the Civil War*, p. 133.

353. "Petersburg Region of Virginia Visitors Guide," Richmond: Virginia Tourism Corporation, n.d., p. 15.

354. Bowman, *Civil War Almanac*, p. 148.

355. Hewitt and Bergeron, *Louisianians in the Civil War*, p. 11.

356. Paul M. Angle, *A Pictorial History of the Civil War Years* (New York: Doubleday, 1967), p. 131.

357. See *The History of the Maine Fifteenth* (Holt's Unit) by Henry Shorey.

358. Meltzer, *Voices from the Civil War*, p. 98.

359. Bowman, *Civil War Almanac*, p. 160.

360. Beattie et al., *A Distant War Comes Home*, p. 6.

361. Bowman, *Civil War Almanac*, p. 161.

362. Kevin Morrow, "The Birth of Photojournalism: How Pioneering Civil War Cameramen Such As Mathew Brady and Alexander Gardner Forever Changed the Way the World Views Warfare," *Civil War Times*, Sept. 2007, p. 42.

363. Bowman, *Civil War Almanac*, p. 162.

364. Collins, *America's Women*, p. 265.

365. E-mail communication with Carole and Larry Meekers, Feb. 20, 2008.

366. www.pddoc.com/cw-chronicles, accessed Feb. 10, 2007.

367. Catton, *Terrible Swift Sword*, pp. 220–21.

368. "Battle of Sabine Pass," *The Handbook of Texas Online*, www.tsha.utexas.edu/handbook/online/articles/SS/qes2, accessed Mar. 1, 2008.

369. *The Handbook of Texas Online,* www.tsha.utexas.edu/handbook/online/articles/SS/qes2.html, accessed Feb. 6, 2007.

370. Johansson, *Widows by the Thousand*, p. 139.

371. Bicknell, quoted in Fuller, *Civil War Diary of H. G. Otis Perkins,* p. 85.

372. Hewitt and Bergeron, *Louisianians in the Civil War*, p. 67.

373. Stockwell, Elisha, *Private Elisha Stockwell, Jr. Sees the Civil War*, ed. Bryon R. Abernethy (Norman: Univ. of Oklahoma Press, 1958), p. 72.

374. Fremantle, Col. James. *The Fremantle Diary; being the journal of Lieutenant Colonel Arthur James Lyon Fremantle, Coldstream Guards, on his three months in the southern states, ed. Walter Lord* (New York: Capricorn Books, 1960), p. 224.

375. Bowman, *Civil War Almanac*, p. 167.

376. Katcher, *Civil War Source Book*, p. 50.

377. Jackson et al., *Twenty Million Yankees,* pp. 77–78.

378. Geer, *Campaigns of the Civil War*, p. 370, n. 7.

379. Katcher, *Civil War Source Book*, p. 96.

380. Wert, *The Sword of Lincoln*, p. 323.

381. Albert Balcom, Sherburne, N.Y., unpublished diary. Courtesy Charles Stewart, Attic Treasures Antiques & Collectibles, Madison, Georgia.

382. Bowman, *Civil War Almanac*, p. 179.

383. Bowman, *Civil War Almanac*, p. 179.

384. Johansson, *Widows by the Thousand*, p. 221.

385. www.civilwar.org/history/classroom/hc_redriverlist.htm, accessed Feb. 9, 2007.

386. Clark S. Edwards Papers, unpaged.

387. Clark S. Edwards Papers, unpaged.

NOTES   Eliza H. Foster's Notebook *continued*

388. "Three of Josiah D. Pulsifer's Civil War Letters," *Androscoggin Histori-cal Society Newsletter.*

389. "Richmond," National Park Service brochure.

390. McPherson, *Battle Cry of Freedom*, pp. 760–61.

391. Schouler, *Massachusetts in the Civil War*, p. 590.

392. MSS 1990.16, Louisiana State Museum, Baton Rouge, La.

393. Beattie et al., *A Distant War Comes Home*, pp. 78–79.

394. Clarke, *Boston Curiosities*, p. 50.

395. Albert Balcom, unpublished diary.

396. Warren Lee Goss, *Recollections of a Private: A Story of the Army of the Potomac* (New York: Thomas Y. Crowell, 1890; repr. Alexandra, Va.: Time-Life Books, 1981), p. 264.

397. Bob Zeller, "Where the Earthworks Meet the Road," *Civil War Times*, Mar. 2002, p. 62.

398. David Herbert Donald and Harold Holzer, *Lincoln in the Times: The Life of Abraham Lincoln, As Originally Reported in the New York Times* (New York: Macmillan, 2005), p. 211.

399. Angle, *Pictorial History,* pp. 180–81.

400. Joshua L. Chamberlain, from *The Passing of the Armies* (1915), quoted in Beattie et al., *A Distant War Comes Home*, p. 167.

401. Diary of Edward Heavey Davis, *Civil War Times Illustrated* Collec-tion, Handley Regional Library Archives, Winchester–Frederick County Histori-cal Society, Winchester, Va., accessed from U.S. Army Military History Institute Archives.

402. Henry L. Estabrooks, *Adrift in Dixie; or, A Yankee Officer among the Rebels* (New York: Carleton, 1866; repr. South Boston, Va.: South Boston–Hali-fax County Museum of Fine Arts and History, 2007), p. 42.

403. Estabrooks, *Adrift in Dixie,* p. 43.

404. Estabrooks, *Adrift in Dixie,* pp. 45–46.

405. E-mail communication from Jerry Holsworth of the Handley Regional Library, Winchester–Frederick County Historical Society, Winchester, Va., May 16, 2008.

406. "Houses of Healing," *Hallowed Ground*, fall 2008, p. 15.

407. Diary of Edward Heavey Davis, Civil War Times Illustrated Collection, accessed from U.S. Army Military History Institute Archives.

408. "Civil War Medicine," www.sonofthesouth.net/leefoundation/civil-war-medicine.htm, accessed Dec. 19, 2009.

409. Wert, *The Sword of Lincoln,* p. 390.

410. Drew Gilpin Faust, "'This is My Last Letter to You,'" *Civil War Times*, Feb. 2008, p. 32.

411. Bowman, *Civil War Almanac*, p. 224.

412. John Barry, "A Matter of Honor," *Newsweek*, Feb. 23, 2009, p. 32.

413. Jeanne Christie, "'No Place for a Woman,' City Point, Virginia, 1864–1865," *The Journal of Women's Civil War History*, vol. 1, pp. 31, 35.

414. Judith Geisburg, "Widows on the Battlefield: Platforms of Grief," excerpted from "Army at Home: Women and the Civil War on the Northern Home Front," in *Hallowed Ground* 10:4 (Winter 2009), pp. 28–30.

415. Geisburg, "Widows on the Battlefield," p. 32.

416. "Voices From the Civil War Online: War Widows," www.hstg.org/index/cgi/696, accessed Mar. 15, 2007.

417. www.oldandsold.com/articles02/glass-p, accessed Apr. 3, 2007.

418. Caleb Crain, "Brother, Can You Spare a Room?" *New York Times Book Review*, Mar. 29, 2009, p. 23.

Notes: Lewellyn Bean Diary

419. Bean, *Clan MacBean in North America*, p. 189.

420. Bean, *Clan MacBean in North America*, p. 875.

421. Bean, *Clan MacBean in North America*, p. 189.

422. Bean, *Clan MacBean in North America*, p. 190.

423. www.itd.nps.gov/cwss/

424. www.itd.nps.gov/cwss/

Notes: 5th Maine Volunteer Infantry, Activities, and Service

425. "Regimental History," www.fifthmainemuseum.org, accessed Apr. 20, 2008.

426. "Catalog No. 6," Salem, Mass.: Higginson Civil War Books, n.d., p. 13.

427. Janet Hewett, ed., *The Roster of Union Soldiers, 1861–1865*, Maine and New Hampshire volume (Wilmington, N.C.: Broadfoot, 1997), pp. 61–62.

428. L. W. Minnigh, *Gettysburg: What They Did Here,* (Gettysburg, Pa: N. A. Meligakes, 1924.), p. 7.

429. Minnigh, *Gettysburg*, p. 100.

430. Minnigh, *Gettysburg*, p. 78.

431. "Dedication of Monument, October 3, 1889," in *Maine at Gettysburg*," in *Maine at Gettysburg*, pp. 378–79.

432. "Dedication of Monument, October 3, 1889," in *Maine at Gettysburg*, pp. 366, 367, 368, 372.

433. "Regimental History," www.fifthmainemuseum.org, accessed Apr. 29, 2008.

434. "Dedication of Monument, October 3, 1889," in *Maine at Gettysburg*, p. 378.

Notes 5th Maine Volunteer Infantry, Activities, & Service *continued*

435. "Dedication of Monument, October 3, 1889," in *Maine at Gettysburg*, p. 378.

436. Bicknell, *History of the Fifth Maine Regiment*, p. 33.

437. Elisha Hunt Rhodes, *All for the Union A History of the 2nd Rhode Island Volunteer Infantry in the War of the Great Rebellion. . .* , ed. Robert Hunt Rhodes (Lincoln, R.I.,: A. Mowbray, 1985), p. 53.

Notes: 5th Maine Volunteer Infantry, Roster

438. Beattie et al., *A Distant War Comes Home*, p. 39.

439. George W. Bicknell, *History of the Fifth Maine Regiment: A History of Its Part and Place in the War for the Union*, p. 401.

440. "Regimental History," www.fifthmainemuseum.org, accessed April 30, 2008.

Notes: 26th Massachusetts, Activities and Service

441. Hearn, *When the Devil Came Down to Dixie*, p. 64.

442. Hearn, *When the Devil Came Down to Dixie,* p. 65.

443. Hearn, *When the Devil Came Down to Dixie,* pp. 223–24.

Notes: Bibliography

444. Kathryn Skelton, "Jay Hoar and the Civil War*,"* *Sun Journal* (Lewiston, Me.), May 24, 2009, A-5.

445. Beattie et al., *A Distant War Comes Home*, p. 3, Note 1.

446. "Civil War Bibliograpny," www.civilwarbibliography.com/bookCatDetail, Dec. 14, 2007.

ACKNOWLEDGMENTS.

THE ORIGINAL LETTERS OF Henry Foster, Andrew Jackson Bean, and Eliza Bean Foster are held by the Bethel Historical Society, Bethel, Maine. This extensive correspondence and Eliza Foster's 1863 diary as well as various other documents, personal possessions, and photographs were presented to the society's archive by Roberta C. "Bobbi" Pevear in November 2005.

Bobbi dedicated years of grunt work to the original letters forming the basis of this book. She deciphered and transcribed them on the typewriter, maps and magnifying glass close at hand.

On November 8, 2007, Randall H. Bennett, curator of collections and assistant director of the Bethel Historical Society, acting on behalf of the society's officers and trustees, gave written permission to Bobbi Pevear and Ann Chandonnet to edit, annotate and publish the letters and diary.

I would like to thank John M. Jackson, Special Collections, University Libraries, Virginia Tech; John Heiser, ranger and historian with the Gettysburg National Military Park; Frances S. Pollard of the Virginia Historical Society; and Greg Lambousy, director of collections, Louisiana State Museum. Thanks go also to Lawrence Matthew, and to Amanda York Focke, assistant head of special collections at the Fondren Library, Rice University.

Thanks go to Sandra Oliver for encouragement.

Jade L. Oxton, head clerk at the Edson Westlawn Cemetery, helped get Eliza and Henry's marker shifted from the horizontal to the vertical.

Thanks go to Anita B. Loscalzo, curator of the New England Quilt Museum (Lowell, Massachusetts); Melanie Davis; Dani Fazio of the Maine Historical Society; and Adele Floyd and Margueritte Ilsley Hayes of the Limerick (Maine) Historical Society. (Margueritte lives on the 1810 Limerick homestead settled by Benjamin Hayes, older brother of John, father of Sylvanus.) Thanks go also to V. Dabney and Rebecca Tucker of Plymouth, Vermont.

The generosity of many has benefited this project. In particular I wish to thank Charles Stewart of Attic Treasures Antiques in Madison, Georgia.

Many thanks go to Pam Juengling, Reference Department, and Melinda McIntosh, genealogy specialist, both with the University of Massachusetts Lowell; and Kim MacIsaac, curator/director of the Fifth Maine Museum; Nancy A. Pope, historian, Smithsonian National Postal Museum; Joseph W. McKinney; Beth Burns, director of tourism for Culpeper, Virginia; Barbara Dickinson; Maricarol Miller, manager of the Old Court House Civil War Museum (Winchester, Virginia); and Jerry Holsworth of the Handley Regional Library (Winchester).

Virginia Eastman of Danville, New Hampshire, aided me in identifying Daniel Eastman—a Lowell house painter (and her great-great-grandfather). Thanks go to Jeffrey and Lara Hooper of Londonderry, New Hampshire, and Jeffrey Brown of the Maine State Archives.

Gratitude flows to Sally Reeves, president of the Louisiana Historical Society. In that neck of the woods, I would also like to thank Dr. Wilbur Meneray and Lynn D. Abbott of Tulane University; Kathryn Page, curator of maps, manuscripts and special projects at the Louisiana State Museum; Camilla Fulton of the University of Illinois at Urbana-Champaign; Tony Lewis, Beth Sherwood, and Tom Lanham, all of the Louisiana State Museum; as well as Daniel Hammer of the Williams Research Center (New Orleans, Louisiana).

Thanks go to my brother Jan Russell Fox for giving me Thomas Dublin's *Farm to Factory: Women's Letters, 1830–1860.* You planted the seed, kiddo.

Donald Ouellette shared original issues of *Harper's Weekly.*

Historian Michael C. Hardy and Wayne McLaughlin of the National Park Service helped nail down the identity of Charles Henry Richardson. Curtis Mildner shared twenty letters written by George L. Berry of

Company D, 5th Maine. Luther Hanson of the Quartermaster Museum helped with burial details.

Thanks to the Clan MacBean, Inc., for trusting me with the original diaries of Lewellyn Bean.

Thanks go to Dracut genealogist Arthur "Bud" Paquin.

And, last but hardly least, thanks to Barbara Brannon of Winoca Press, who expertly helped us tell Eliza's story.

The role mills have played in my family must be acknowledged: my great-grandfather, Joseph Damase King (Roi/Roy; 1871–1949), a French-speaking immigrant from Quebec, collected rents from mill houses in Salmon Falls, New Hampshire.

During World War II, my great aunt Dena King Colburn supervised the "secret" stitching of parachutes in a Lowell mill.

My aunt Louise Fox Atkinson was one of the first female graduates majoring in textile engineering at Lowell Tech (class of 1940).

My aunt Nancy Cloutman Banaian checked the tensile strength of wool thread being spun in a mill.

My late, loving mother-in-law, Blanche Duchesne Chandonnet, worked in a Lowell mill where she contracted tuberculosis. As a toddler, my husband, Fernand Chandonnet, was confined with his older sister Lucille to an orphanage for seven years while their mother recovered on the cold, open-air sleeping porches of a tuberculosis sanitarium. As a teen, Fern was employed in a wool mill in Lowell. He found dead sheep in bales of raw wool and sweated in a hot, humid atmosphere where filaments of fleece circulated lazily in the air like schools of infinitesimal fish "so that you felt as if you were working underwater." More recently, Fern drove thousands of miles to museums, archives, battlefields, and sites such as Andersonville, doing the laundry while I scribbled notes, and rendering thoughtful support—as he has during so many "projects." Kiss. Kiss.

In the late 1800s, Zotique Pierre Chandonnet (1847–1917), a dredger captain with experience on the Saint Lawrence River, emigrated to

Lowell to dredge canals. Zotique's son Arthur designed canal locks.

Finally, heartfelt thanks go to the Ludwig Vogelstein Foundation for a grant that funded visits to Gettysburg, Antietam, and Winchester.

Ann Chandonnet.

INDEX.

Names followed by* are from the roster of the Fifth Maine Volunteer Infantry Regiment; names followed by** are from the roster of the 26th Massachusetts. Page numbers in italics denote illustrations.

INDEX *continued*

INDEX *continued*

INDEX *continued*

INDEX *continued*

INDEX *continued*

THIS VOLUME

was composed in the

Times New Roman and Warnock Italic fonts

in Adobe InDesign CS4 for the Macintosh computer.

Winchester cemetery, with markers for
Civil War veteran Capt. Benjamin D.
Parks of Iowa and Staff Sgt. Craig W.
Cherry, who served in Afghanistan. Photo
by Fernand L. Chandonnet.

LaVergne, TN USA
27 May 2010
184190LV00003B/6/P